THE CHRONICLE OF THE DISCOVERY AND CONQUEST OF GUINEA VOL. II

By Gomes Eannes de Azurara

Translated by Charles Raymond Beazley and Edgar Prestage

This Volume continues and ends the present Edition of the *Chronicle of Guinea*, the first part of which was published in 1896 (vol. XCV of the Hakluyt Society's publications). Here we have again to acknowledge the kind advice and help of various friends, particularly of Senhor Batalhaā Reis and Mr. William Foster. As to the Maps which accompany this volume: the sections of Andrea Bianco, 1448, and of Fra Mauro, 1457-9, here given, offer some of the best examples of the cartography of Prince Henry's later years in relation to West Africa. These ancient examples are supplemented by a new sketch-map of the discoveries made by the Portuguese seamen during the Infant's lifetime along the coast of the Dark Continent. The excellent photograph of Prince Henry's statue from the great gateway at Belem is the work of Senhor Camacho. As to the Introduction and Notes, it is hoped that attention has been given to everything really important for the understanding of Azurara's text; but the Editors have avoided such treatment as belongs properly to a detailed history of geographical advance during this period.

C.   R.   B.
E. P.

April 1899.
[Pg i]

INTRODUCTION.

n this it may be well to summarise briefly, for the better illustration of the *Chronicle* here translated, not only the life of Prince Henry of Portugal, surnamed the Navigator, but also various questions suggested by Prince Henry's work, *e.g.*—The history of the Voyages along the West African coast and among the Atlantic islands, encouraged by him and recorded by Azurara; The History of the other voyages of Prince Henry's captains, not recorded by Azurara; The attempts of navigators before Prince Henry, especially in the fourteenth century, to find a way along West Africa to the Indies; The parallel enterprises by land from the Barbary States to the Sudan, across the Sahara; The comparative strength of Islam and Christianity in the Africa of Prince Henry's time; The State of Cartographical Knowledge in the fourteenth and fifteenth centuries, and its relation to the new [Pg ii]Portuguese discoveries; The question of the "School of Sagres," said to have been instituted by the Navigator for the better training of mariners and map-makers.

I.—THE LIFE OF PRINCE HENRY.

Henry, Duke of Viseu, third[1] son of King John I of Portugal, surnamed the Great, founder of the House of Aviz, and of Philippa of Lancaster, daughter of John of Gaunt and niece of King Edward III of England, was born on March 4th, 1394.

We are told by Diego Gomez,[2] who in 1458 sailed to the West Coast of Africa in the service of Prince Henry, and made a discovery of the Cape Verde islands, that in 1415 John de Trasto was sent by the Prince on a voyage of exploration, and reached "Telli," the "fruitful" district of Grand Canary. Gomez here gives us the earliest date assigned by any authority of the fifteenth century for an expedition of the Infant's; but in later times other statements were put forward, assigning 1412 or even 1410 as the commencement of his exploring activity. This would take us back to a time when the Prince was but sixteen or eighteen years old; and though it is probable enough that [Pg iii]Portuguese vessels may have sailed out at this time (as in 1341) to the Canaries or along the West African coast, it is not probable that Henry took any great share in such enterprise before the Ceuta expedition of 1415. In any case, it is practically certain that before 1434, no Portuguese ship had passed beyond Cape Bojador. Gil Eannes' achievement of that year is marked by Azurara and all our best authorities as a decided advance on any previous voyage, at least of Portuguese mariners. We shall consider presently how far this advance was anticipated by other nations, and more particularly by the French. Cape Non, now claimed by some as the southernmost point of Marocco, had been certainly passed by Catalan and other ships[3] before Prince Henry's day; but it had not been forgotten how rhyme and legend had long consecrated this point as a fated end of the world. Probably it was still (c. 1415) believed by many in Portugal—

"Quem passar o Cabo de NãoOu tornará, ou não."

and the Venetian explorer, Cadamosto, preserves a mention of its popular derivation in Southern Europe from the Latin "Non," "as beyond it was believed there was no return possible." The real form was probably the Arabic Nun or "Fish."[4]

[Pg iv]Prince Henry's active share in the work of exploration is usually dated only from the Conquest of Ceuta. Here we are told in one of our earliest authorities (Diego Gomez) he gained information, from Moorish prisoners, merchants, and other acquaintance "of the passage of traders from the coasts of Tunis to Timbuktu and to Cantor on the Gambia, which led him to seek those lands by the way of the sea;" and, to come to details, he was among other things, "told of certain tall palms growing at the mouth of the Senegal [or Western Nile], by which he was able to guide the caravels he sent out to find that river." It will be important hereafter to examine the evidence which had been accumulated for such belief up to the fifteenth century: now it will be enough to say: 1. That Prince Henry was probably of the same opinion as the ordinary cartographer of his time about the peninsular shape of Africa. 2. That the "shape" in question was usually satisfied with what we should now call the Northern half of the Continent, making the Southern coast of "Guinea" continue directly to the Eastern, Abyssinian, or Indian Ocean. 3. That trade had now (c. 1415) been long maintained between this "Guinea coast" and the Mediterranean seaboard—chiefly by Moorish caravans across the Sahara. 4. That something, though little, was known in Western Christendom about the Christian faith and king of Abyssinia; for "Prester John's" story in the fifteenth century had really become a blend of rumours from [Pg v]Central (Nestorian) Asia and Eastern (Abyssinian) Africa.

In Prince Henry's work we may distinguish three main objects—scientific, patriotic, and religious. First of all he was a discoverer, for the sake of the new knowledge then beginning. He was interested in the exploration of the world in general, and of the sea-route round Africa to India in particular. Dinis Diaz, returning from his discovery of Cape Verde (Az., ch. xxxi.), brought home a "booty not so great as had arrived in the past," but "the Infant thought it very great indeed, since it came from that land", and he proportioned his rewards to exploration rather than to trade profits. Nuno Tristam in 1441 (Az., ch. xiii.) reminds Antam Gonçalvez that "for 15 years" the Infant has "striven ... to arrive at ... certainty as to the people of this land, under what law or lordship they do live."

Azurara, though always more prone to emphasize the emotional than the scientific, himself assigns as the first reason for the Infant's discoveries, his "wish to know the land that lay beyond the isles of Canary and that cape called Bojador, for that up to his time, neither by writings nor by the memory of man, was known with any certainty the nature of the land" (Az., ch. vii.).

Again, Henry was founding upon his work of exploration an over-sea dominion, a "commercial and colonial" empire for his country. He desired to see her rich and prosperous, and there cannot be any reasonable doubt that his ideas agreed with [Pg vi]those of Italian land and sea travellers in the thirteenth and fourteenth centuries. He and they were agreed in thinking it possible and very important to secure a large share of Asiatic, especially of Indian, trade for their respective countries. By exploring and making practicable the maritime route around Africa to the Indies, he would probably raise Portugal into the wealthiest of European nations. Azurara's "second reason" for the "search after Guinea" is that "many kinds of merchandise might be brought to this realm ... and also the products of this realm might be taken there, which traffic would bring great profit to our countrymen."

Thirdly, Prince Henry had the temperament of a Crusader and a missionary. Of him, fully as much as of Columbus, it may be said that if he aimed at empire, it was for the extension of Christendom. Azurara's three final reasons for Henry's explorations all turn upon this. The Prince desired to find out the full strength of the Moors in Africa, "said to be very much greater than commonly supposed," "because every wise man" desires "a knowledge of the power of his enemy." He also "sought to know if there were in those parts any Christian princes" who would aid him against the enemies of the faith. And, lastly, he desired to "make increase in the faith of Jesus Christ, and to bring to Him all the souls that should be saved."

It has often been pointed out how the Infant was aided in his work by the tendencies of his time and country; how in him the spirit of mediæval [Pg vii]faith and the spirit of material, even of commercial, ambition, were united; how he was the central representative of a general expansive and exploring movement; and how he took up and carried on the labours of various predecessors. At the same time it must be recognised that his work forms an epoch in the history of geographical, commercial, and colonial advance; that he gave a permanence and a vitality to the cause of maritime discovery which it had never possessed before; that even his rediscoveries of islands and mainland frequently had all the meaning and importance of fresh achievements; that he made his nation the pioneer of Europe in its conquest of the outer world; and that without him the results of the great forty years (1480-1520) of Diaz, Columbus, Da Gama, and Magellan must have been long, might have been indefinitely, postponed.

Barros (*Decade I*, i, 2) tells us a story, probable enough, about the inception of the Infant's plans of discovery. He relates how one night, after much meditation, he lay sleepless upon his bed, thinking over his schemes, till at last, as if seized with a sudden access of fury, he leapt up, called his servants, and ordered some of his *barcas* to be immediately made ready for a voyage to the south along the coast of Marocco. His court was astonished, and attributed this outburst to a divine revelation. It was natural enough—the resolution of a man, weary with profound and anxious thought, to take some sort of decisive action, to embark without [Pg viii]further delay on the realisation of long-cherished schemes.

To summarise the course of the Prince's life, from 1415, before entering on any discussion of special points: After the Conquest of Ceuta he returned to Portugal; was created Duke of Viseu and Lord of Covilham (1415), having already received his knighthood at "Septa"; and began to send out regular exploring ventures down the West Coast of Africa—"two or three ships" every year beyond Cape Non, Nun, or Nam. In 1418 he successfully went to the help of the Governor of Ceuta against the Moors of Marocco and Granada.[5] On this second return from Africa, when in 1419 he was created Governor of the Algarve or southmost province of Portugal, he is supposed by some to have taken up his residence at Sagres,[6] near Cape St. Vincent, and to have begun the establishment of a school of cartography and navigation there. All this, however, is disputed by others, as is the [Pg ix]tradition of his having established Chairs of Mathematics and Theology at Lisbon.[7]

In 1418-20, however, his captains, João Gonçalvez Zarco and Tristam Vaz Teixeira, certainly re-discovered Porto Santo and Madeira.[8] In 1427, King John and Prince Henry seem to have sent the royal pilot, Diego de Sevill, to make new discoveries in the Azores; and, in 1431-2, Gonçalo Velho Cabral made further explorations among the same; but the completer opening up and settlement of the Archipelago was the work of later years, especially of 1439-66. We shall return to this matter in a special discussion of Prince Henry's work among the Atlantic islands. To the same [Pg x]we must refer the traditional purchase of the Canaries in 1424-5 and the settlement of Madeira in the same year,[9]confirmed by charters of 1430 and 1433. King John, on his death-bed, is said to have exhorted Henry to persevere in his schemes, which he was at this very time pursuing by means of a fresh expedition to round Cape Bojador, under Gil Eannes (1433). Azurara from this point becomes our chief authority down to the year 1448, and this and the subsequent voyages are fully described in his pages. Gil Eannes, unsuccessful in 1433,[10] under the stimulus of the Infant's reproaches and appeals passed Cape Bojador in 1434;[11] and next summer (1435) the Portuguese reached the Angra dos Ruyvos (Gurnet Bay), 150 miles beyond Bojador, and the Rio do Ouro, 240 miles to the south. Early in 1436 the "Port of Gallee," a little North of C. Branco (Blanco), was discovered by Baldaya, but as yet no natives were found; no captives, gold dust, or other products brought home. Exploration along the African mainland languished from this year till 1441;[12] but in 1437 the Prince took part in [Pg xi]the fatal attack on Tangier, and in 1438 the death of King Edward caused a dispute over the question of the Regency during the minority of his young son Affonso. Throughout these internal troubles Henry played an important part, successfully supporting the claims of his brother Pedro against the Queen-mother, Leonor of Aragon. All this caused a break of three or four years in the progress of his discoveries; but the colonisation of the Azores went forward, as is shown by the license of July 2, 1439, from Affonso V, to people "the seven islands" of the group, then known.

In 1441[13] exploration began again in earnest with the voyage of Antam Gonçalvez, who brought to Portugal the first native "specimens"—captives and gold dust—from the coasts beyond Bojador; while Nuno Tristam in the same year pushed on to Cape Blanco. These decisive successes greatly strengthened the cause of discovery in Portugal, especially by offering fresh hopes of mercantile profit. In 1442 Nuno Tristam reached the Bight or Bay of Arguim,[14] where the Infant erected a fort in 1448, and where for some years the Portuguese made their most vigorous and successful slave-raids. [Pg xii]Private venturers now began to come forward, supplementing Prince Henry's efforts by volunteer aid, for which his permission[15] was readily granted. Especially the merchants and seamen of Lisbon and of Lagos, close to Sagres, showed interest in this direction. Whatever doubts exist as to the earlier alleged settlement of the Infant at Cape St. Vincent, it is certain that after his return from Tangier (1437) he erected various buildings[16] at Sagres, and resided there during a considerable part of his later life. This fact is to be connected with the new African developments at Lagos.[17]

In 1444 and 1445 a number of ships sailed with Henry's license to "Guinea," and several of their commanders achieved notable successes. Thus Dinis Diaz, Nuno Tristam, and others reached the Senegal. Diaz rounded Cape Verde in 1445,[18] and in 1446 Alvaro Fernandez sailed on as far as the River Gambia (?) and the Cape of Masts (Cabo dos Mastos). In 1445, also, João Fernandez spent seven months among the natives of the Arguim coast, and brought back the first trustworthy account of a part of the interior. Gonçalo de Sintra and Gonçalo Pacheco, in 1445, and Nuno Tristam in 1446,[19] fell victims to the hostility of the Moors [Pg xiii]and Negroes, who, perhaps, felt some natural resentment against their new visitors. For, in Azurara's estimate, the Portuguese up to the year 1446 had carried off 927 captives from these parts; and the disposition and conversion of these prisoners occupied a good portion of the Infant's time. He probably relied on finding efficient material among these slaves for the further exploration and Christianization of the Coast, and even of the Upland. We know that he used some of them as guides and interpreters.[20]

One of the latest voyages recorded by Azurara is that of "Vallarte the Dane" (1448), which ended in utter destruction near the Gambia, after passing Cape Verde. The chronicler, though writing in 1453, does not continue his record beyond this year, 1448; his promise to give us the remainder of the Infant's achievements in a second chronicle seems never to have been fulfilled; and his descriptions of Madeira and the Canaries, in the latter part of the *Chronicle of Guinea*, are unfortunately of only slight value for the history of discovery. Yet, before the Prince's death in 1460[21] and in the last six years of his life, several voyages of some importance prove that Azurara's silence is merely accidental. Cadamosto's two journeys of [Pg xiv]1455-6, and Diego Gomez' ventures of 1458-60, advanced West African discovery almost to Sierra Leone. The former, a Venetian seaman in the service of Prince Henry, also explored part of the courses of the Senegal and the Gambia and gained much information about the native tribes. One of his chief exploits, an alleged discovery of the Cape Verde islands, has been disputed in the name of Diego Gomez, who in 1458-60 twice sailed to Guinea, and on the second voyage "sighted islands in the Ocean, to which no man had come before." We postpone this point for further examination, only adding that we believe Cadamosto's prior claim to be sound, although the islands in question do not appear in any document before 1460.

Meanwhile the Prince, when his explorations (from 1441) first began to promise important results, obtained from Pope Eugenius IV a plenary indulgence to those who shared in the war against the Moors consequent on the new discoveries,[22] and from the Regent D. Pedro he also gained a donation of the Royal Fifth on the profits accruing from the new lands, as well as the sole right of permitting voyages to these parts. The Infant's work, was moreover, recognised in bulls of Nicholas V (1455) and of Calixtus III (March 13th, 1456). In earlier life—apparently soon after the capture [Pg xv]of Ceuta and the embassy of Manuel Palæologus asking for help against the Turks—he had been invited, Azurara tells us, by a predecessor[23] of the Pontiffs above-named to take command of the

"Apostolic armies," and similar invitations reached him from the Emperor of Germany,[24] the King of England (Henry V or VI)[25] and the King of Castile.[26] We may also briefly notice in this place, referring to a later page for a more detailed treatment of the subject, that the Infant, in 1445 and 1446, repeated his earlier attempts (in 1424 and 1425) to secure the Canaries for Portugal, both by means of purchase and of armed force; and that, from 1444-5 especially, he colonised, as well as discovered, and traded with increased energy in the Madeira Group, the Azores, and (if his experiment at Arguim in 1448 may stand as an example) even on the mainland coast of Africa.

The Infant's share in home politics was considerable, but this is not the place to discuss it at any length. It is probably a correct surmise that his ultimate ambition on this side was to detach Portugal as far as possible from Spain and Peninsular interests, and by making her a world-power at and over sea, to give her that importance she could never of herself acquire in strictly European politics. We have already noticed that after the victory of Ceuta he seems to have been made Governor for [Pg xvi]life of the Algarve province[27] of Portugal, by his father King John (1419); that he was a leading promoter of the scheme for the Tangier campaign of 1437;[28] and that after the death of his brother King Edward (Duarte), the successor of King John (September, 1438), he supported the claims of his eldest surviving brother, Pedro, as regent and guardian of the young Affonso V, and by his wise counsels effected a reconciliation with Affonso's mother Leonor, acting for a time as partner in a Council of Regency with Pedro and the Queen. Further, it must be said that, in 1447, when a long succession of differences between D. Pedro and his royal ward ended in an armed rising of the former against "evil Counsellors," Henry stood by the Sovereign, and took, if not an active, at least a passive part in overthrowing the insurrection, which was ended by the battle of Alfarrobeira (May 21st, 1449). Finally, it is recorded that "the Navigator" somewhat recovered the military honour he had compromised at Tangier, by his successes in the [Pg xvii]African expeditions of Affonso V, especially at the capture of Alcacer the Little in 1458; in this last year he received his Sovereign in due form at or near Sagres, before sailing for "Barbary." His traditional but on the whole credible work as Protector of the Studies of Portugal has been alluded to already, in connection with his alleged foundation of professorships of mathematics and theology in the University of Lisbon, and of a school of nautical instruction and of cosmography at Sagres. This point, however, will be reconsidered in a following section.[29]

It is perhaps in his connection with the fall of D. Pedro that the severest criticism has been passed upon Henry the Navigator. "Genius is pitiless" it has been said; and the action of the younger brother has been blamed as a piece of ruthlessness and ingratitude, though extolled by Azurara as a proof of loyalty under temptation. It may have seemed to him impossible to support any rebellion, however justified, against royal authority, or even to take the position of a neutral, when the central government of his country was on its trial. Our sympathies are usually with Pedro, as the most wise, liberal, and learned of his people—with one exception—and as the victim of the intrigues of courtiers, especially of King John's bastard son, the Count of Barcellos and Duke of Braganza; but the Governor of Algarve parted for ever from his favourite brother [Pg xviii]when he took up arms to right himself; and perhaps he was not more wrong than the people of England in refusing to allow the nobles of the Tudor time to dictate to even the most despotic of our more modern English sovereigns.[30]

The Infant was, among his other dignities, Master of the Order of Christ, which, as the direct successor of the Templars in Portugal, held a very high rank, and was, by its "artificial ancestry," as Hobbes would have said, one of the most ancient Orders in Christendom. Henry's father, King John, had been also at one time Head of an Order of Chivalry, the Knights of Aviz; but on coming to the throne he had obtained a dispensation from his vow of celibacy as Master, a dispensation which his son never required. The banner of this Order seems to have floated over most if not all of Prince Henry's African expeditions; in its name he required the aid of Pope Eugenius IV; its special duty—military order as it was in origin—should have been to spread the Christian faith in Moslem and heathen Africa: perhaps its work was considered to extend only to the slaying of Moslems, or Moormen, and the bringing back [Pg xix]to Europe of heathen Africans who could be reared as Christians in Portugal. No mission to preach the faith seems to have been undertaken by the Fraternity. Upon this Order the Prince bestowed the tithes of the Island of St. Michael in the Azores, and one half of its sugar revenues; also the tithe (afterwards reduced to the twentieth) of all merchandise from Guinea, as well as the ecclesiastical dues of Porto Santo, Madeira, and the Desertas. The Prince's nephew, D. Fernando, succeeded him (in 1460) in the Mastership of the Order of Christ.[31]

It has sometimes been said that the Infant Henry was also titular King of Cyprus. This assertion is derived from Fr. Luiz de Souza (*Historia de S. Domingos*, Bk. VI., fol. 331) and José Suares de Silva (*Memoirs of King João I.*), who tell us that the Prince was elected King of Cyprus. But this "Kingdom" remained in the posterity of Guy de Lusignan till 1487; and the mistake has probably arisen from a confusion of Henry, Prince of Galilee, son of James I., King of Cyprus, with Prince Henry of Portugal.[32]

In prosecuting his explorations, Prince Henry incurred heavy expenses. His own revenues were not sufficient, and he was obliged to borrow largely. Thus, in 1448, he owed his bastard half-brother, [Pg xx]the Duke of Braganza, 19394½ crowns of gold, to pay which he had pledged his lands and goods; and this debt was afterwards increased by 16084 crowns, as stated in the declaration of the Duke of Braganza, November 8, 1449, and in the will of the same nobleman. These debts were partly paid by his nephew and adopted son, D. Fernando, and partly by Fernando's son, D. Manuel.

[1] Fifth, counting two children who died in infancy.

[2] As repeated by Martin Behaim (see Major, *Henry Navigator*, pp. 64, 65). Gomez was Almoxarife, or superintendent, of the Palace of Cintra.

[3] Some of which had reached at least as far as Cape Bojador, as depicted on the Catalan Map of 1375.

[4] So Zul-nun, Lord of the Fish, is a term for the prophet Jonah (see Burton, *Camoëns*, iii, p. 246).

[5] On this occasion he planned, but did not attempt, the seizure of Gibraltar.

[6] Sagres, from "Sacrum Promontorium," the ordinary name of Cape St. Vincent in the later classical Geography; "à 91 Kilom. Ouest de Faro,... sur un cap, à 4,500 metres E.S.E. du Cap St. Vincent" (Viv. St. Martin). The harbour is sandy, protected from the N.-W. winds. A Druid temple stood there, and the Iberians of the Roman time assembled there at night. It was a barren cape, its only natural vegetation a few junipers. O. Martins (*Filhos de D. João I*, p. 77), suggests that the name of *Sagres* did not come into ordinary use till after the Prince's death, 1460.

[7] In 1431 he is said to have purchased house-room for the University of Lisbon; on March 25th, 1448, to have established there a professorship of theology; and on September 22, 1460, to have confirmed this by a charter dated from his Town at Sagres. The Professor was to have twelve marks in silver every Christmas from the tithes of the Island of Madeira (see Azurara, *Guinea*, c. v). As to the Chair of Mathematics, we only know that it existed in 1435; that the Infant was interested in this study; and that tradition connected him with a somewhat similar foundation at Sagres. The houses purchased in Lisbon for the University were bought of João Annes, the King's Armourer, for 400 crowns. Hence, according to some, came the Prince's title of "Protector of Portuguese Studies."

[8] O. Martins thinks these island discoveries were a surprise to Henry, who at first only contemplated discovery along the mainland coast South and East towards India. We do not believe in this limitation of view (see Barros, *Dec. I*, Lib. I, c. 2, 3).

The previous voyage of the Englishman Macham to the "Isle of Wood" ("Legname" on the fourteenth-century Portolani) is another controversial matter which must be taken separately.

[9] Zarco and Vaz became Captains Donatory or Feudal Under-lords of Madeira, as Bartholemew Perestrello (whose daughter Columbus married) of Porto Santo.

[10] It has been shewn, *e.g.*, by the British Admiralty Surveys, that the old stories of dangerous reefs and currents at Bojador, "such as might well have frightened the boldest mariner of that time," are unfounded, like the old belief in strong Satanic influence at this point.

[11] 1432, according to Galvano (see Barros, *I*, i, 4).

[12] Till 1440, according to the opposition chronology of O. Martins.

[13] O. Martins dates *Porto do Cavalleiro*, 1440; *C. Branco*, 1442.

[14] *Aliter*, 1443 (Barros, *I*, i, 7) or 1444 (Galvano, who apparently dates the discovery of the Rio do Ouro 1443). See, in this connection, Affonso V's Charters of October 22, 1433, and February 3, 1446, granted to Prince Henry. In 1442 the Infant was created a Knight of the Garter of England. He was the 153rd Knight of the Order; and his collar descended, through many holders, to the late Earl of Clarendon.

[15] Necessary by decree of the Regent Pedro, for any "Guinea" or African voyage (Azurara, *Guinea*, ch. xv).

[16] Especially a palace, a church or chapel, and an observatory.

[17] Which seems to have shown the way, in this respect, to its greater sister, Lisbon.

[18] 1454 in O. Martins.

[19] 1447, according to Barros (*I*, i, 14) and Galvano.

[20] Cf. Azurara, *Guinea*, chs. xiii, xvi.

[21] *Aliter* 1462 or 1463 (Galvano and Barros, who also date the discovery of C. Verde and the Senegal by "Dinis Fernandez," 1446: Barros, *I* i, 9, 13); but this date is certainly incorrect.

[22] Barros and Galvano make Prince Henry obtain Indulgences from Pope Martin [V, who reigned 1417-31] in 1441-2, by the embassy of Fernam Lopez d'Azevedo (see p. xv).

[23] Martin V?

[24] Sigismund?

[25] Henry VI made the Infant a Knight of the Garter, and is more likely than the conquering Henry V to have asked a foreign Prince to aid him against the French.

[26] John II.

[27] Technically "kingdom."

[28] The "Marocco Campaigns" of 1418, 1437, 1458, etc., were apparently considered by Prince Henry as only another side of his coasting explorations and projected conquests. Having then no idea of the enormous southerly projection of Africa, he probably aspired to a Portuguese North African dominion, which should control the Continent. For Guinea, in the ideas of the time, was commonly supposed to be quite close to Marocco on the south-west and west. Apparently, soon after 1437, Henry was just starting on another Moorish expedition, when the King and Council "hindered the voyage" (see Az., ch. v, p. 20 of our version).

[29] "School of Sagres," etc.

[30] It has been suggested, *e.g.*, by Sir C. Markham, that the portrait of the Infant in mourning dress prefixed to the Paris MS. of Azurara represents him immediately after the death of D. Pedro. It is perhaps more likely a mark of sorrow for D. Fernand, the Constant Prince, who died in his Moorish captivity, June 5th, 1443, and whose heart was conveyed to Portugal, June 1st, 1451, and buried at Batalha, Prince Henry joining the funeral procession at Thomar.

[31] Already, in 1451, Henry had designated him as his heir.

[32] Santarem corrects this; see note in Major's *Henry Navigator*, p. 306. So Azurara's allusion, "No other *uncrowned* prince in Europe had so noble a household,"—*Guinea*, ch. iv.

VOYAGES OF PRINCE HENRY'S SEAMEN ALONG THE WEST AFRICAN COAST.
(*Not recorded by Azurara.*)

Prince Henry's work was, above all, justified by its permanence. Unlike earlier ancient and mediæval attempts at West African exploration, his movement issued in complete success. Azurara gives us, no doubt, a fairly complete account of the earlier stages of that movement, but it is probable that even his record omits some of the ventures undertaken from Portugal along the West African mainland; while it is certain that we must look elsewhere for a completer picture of the Infant's activity among the Atlantic Islands and in the Great Ocean. These additional sources of information must be examined in turn. First of all, it will be advisable to finish the chronicle of West African coasting down to the Navigator's death. After that, the triumphant prosecution of this line of advance to the Cape of Good Hope will call for a brief notice. And, thirdly, something must be said about the progress of [Pg xxi] discovery and colonisation in the archipelagos of Madeira, the Canaries, the Azores, and the Cape Verdes, especially considered in relation to that Westward route to India which Columbus advocated and commenced.

It has already been stated that although Azurara's Chronicle officially ends in 1453, and appears to record nothing later than the events of 1448, yet very important expeditions were sent forth in the last years of the Prince's life, especially those of Cadamosto[33] and Diego Gomez. An attempt has been made to prove that the second voyage of Cadamosto, on which he claimed to have discovered the Cape Verde Islands, is untruly reported and may be dismissed as fabulous. But there seems no sufficient ground for this. "In an account of travels, printed long after its author's death, some contradictory statements, possibly arising through copyists' errors, do not justify such a conclusion." And the mistakes contained in the assailed narrative are not serious or unexplainable enough for rejecting it as a whole.[34] Luigi, Alvise, or Aloysius, da Ca da[Pg xxii]Mosto[35] was a young Venetian (a noble, according to some) who had embarked on August 8, 1454, with Marco Zeno on a commercial venture,[36]and was delayed by storm near Cape St. Vincent while on his voyage from Venice to Flanders. He now heard of the "glorious and boundless conquests" of Prince Henry, "whence accrued such gain that from no traffic in the world could the like be had. The which," continues the candid trader, "did exceedingly stir my soul, eager as it was for profit above all other things, and so I made suit to be brought before the Infant"—who was then at the village of Reposeira, near Sagres. Cadamosto was easily persuaded to sail in the service of Portugal,[37] and set out, with Vicente Diaz, on March 22, 1455. He visited Porto Santo and Madeira, and at Cape Branco began a "peaceful exploration" of the interior, for the study of its natural conditions, inhabitants, trade, and so forth. Proceeding to the Senegal, he continued his investigations; which were extended to the Canaries as well as to Madeira. He notices the fort built by the Prince's [Pg xxiii]orders in the Bight of Arguim (1448), and the new start lately made by Portuguese trade with the natives. This trade at Arguim had included nearly a thousand slaves a year, so that the Europeans, who used to plunder all this coast as far as the Senegal, now found it more profitable to trade. Slave-raiding among the Azanegue tribes north of the Senegal had ceased, "for the Prince will not allow any wrong-doing, being only eager that they should submit themselves to the law of Christ."[38] Before passing Cape Verde, Cadamosto met with two ships, one commanded by a Genoese, Antonio, or Antoniotto, surnamed Ususmaris or Uso di Mare,[39] the other by an unnamed Portuguese in Henry's service. The expeditions united and sailed on together to the Gambia, where they were unable to open intercourse with the natives, and so returned to Portugal. Cadamosto gives very full descriptions of the life, habits, government, trade, etc., of both the "Moors" (Azanegues) and Negroes (Jaloffs) of Guinea, which have been often noticed,[40] and sometimes paraphrased; and which show a great development [Pg xxiv]of commercial interest and statesmanlike inquiry on anything recorded in Azurara. At his furthest point the explorer noticed that the North Star was so low that it appeared almost to touch the sea, and here he seems to have seen the Southern Cross.

In the next year, 1456, Cadamosto sailed out again with Antoniotto Uso di Mare, made straight for Cape Branco, and found, three days' sail from this point, "certain islands" off Cape Verde "where no one had been before."[41] The explorer then, in his own as well as in the official, "Ramusian," or Venetian, account, proceeded to the Gambia, opened trade successfully with the natives, and explored the coast "about 25 leagues" beyond this river as far as the Bissagos Islands, or some point of the mainland not far distant.

Cadamosto's account of his two voyages is rightly praised[42] as "detailed and vivid." He certainly compiled a map of his journeys, for in noticing the river Barbasini beyond Cape Verde, he says: "I have named it so on the Chart which I have made." The interesting suggestion, that some of Benincasa's portolanos (especially that of 1471) [Pg xxv]were based on Cadamosto's descriptions and plans of the West African shore-land, is hardly susceptible of proof, but it is not without some corroborative evidence, as may be seen elsewhere.[43] Also, "the journeys of this Marco Polo of West Africa were undertaken in a more scientific spirit, and were more free from chivalrous outrages," than most of those who preceded him along this coast.[44] This is not merely due to himself. It appears from his express statements that the Infant now discouraged slave-raiding, and urged his captains to something of higher value than seal and sea-calf hunting. The value of Cadamosto's work was mainly in his observations and descriptions. He advanced only a little way beyond some of the Prince's earlier explorers (*e.g.*, Alvaro Fernandez), except for his discovery of the Cape Verde islands, but he seems to have named[45] and mapped out more carefully than before a good many points of the littoral beyond Cape Verde, and his writings surpass in geographical value anything to be found in Azurara. His notes are also of high value for ethnology and anthropology, and give a better account of the trade-routes, etc. of North-west [Pg xxvi]Africa than any Christian writing of the time. Finally, he is more reliable than many subsequent and more pretentious travellers, and his narrative is as picturesque and effective as it is reliable. For "one inquisitive person shall bring home a better account of countries than twenty who come after him."

A little subsequent to what we may suppose was the second return of the Venetian adventurer from Africa, in 1456, the Infant sent out Diego Gomez with orders to "go as far as he could." The explorer passed a "great river beyond the Rio Grande," when strong currents in the sea alarmed him and caused him to put back. Like Cadamosto, however, he trafficked and conversed with the natives, especially of the Gambia, and gained some useful information about their trade, politics, and geography. Some of the facts he related about wars among the negro states of the interior were confirmed by a "merchant in Oran," who corresponded with the Prince.[46] As a result of Gomez' first voyage, the Infant seems to have sent out, in 1458, a mission to convert the negroes of the Gambia "with a priest, the Abbot of Soto de Cassa, and a young man of his household named John Delgado." Two years after this (*i.e.*, in 1460) Gomez went out again. Near the Gambia he fell in with two ships—one under Gonçalo Ferreira, of Oporto, who was trading in horses with the negroes for [Pg xxvii]native produce; the other was under Antonio Noli, of Genoa. Soon after, Gomez and Ferreira seized an interloper, one De Prado, who had come to Cape Verde without permission to dispose of a rich cargo, as Gomez was informed by a "caravel from Gambia." It is noticeable how the West African trade had now increased, and how many expeditions are incidentally mentioned in this one record of Gomez.

He concludes by stating that he and Noli left the mainland coast, and after sailing two days and one night towards Portugal, "sighted islands in the Ocean," which are described in terms very similar to Cadamosto's. These were certainly the Cape Verde Islands of modern geography, which are first mentioned in documentary history in a Portuguese Decree of December 3rd, 1460. Gomez makes no reference to any previous visit or claim of a prior discovery of these islands, but that is natural enough.

Was such a previous visit made? Around this point, and the consequent prior claim of the Venetian, a long controversy has been waged, which is briefly discussed in the section of this Introduction on the "Atlantic Islands" (especially pp. xcii-xcvi).

The second voyage of Diego Gomez was probably among the last ventures of which the Prince received any account. He must have died soon after the second return of the explorer, who seems to have attended him in his last illness (13th November, 1460). But it is probable that before his end he had prepared for the expedition which Pedro de [Pg xxviii]Sintra carried out in 1461, and which is described by Cadamosto, apparently before the close of 1463.

[33] 1507 (Vicenza) Edition, is the earliest text of Cadomosto's Voyages, printed in "Paesi novamente retrovati et novo mondo da Alberico Vesputio Florentino intitulato." This was republished at Milan in 1508; and in this year two versions appeared: 1. In Latin, by Madrignano, "Itinerarium Portugallensium ...," Milan. 2. In German, by Jobst Ruchamer, "Neue unbekanthe landte," Nürnberg. In 1516 appeared in Paris a French version by Mathurin du Redouer: "Sensuyt le nouveau monde ..." A good many discrepancies occur in these various editions and translations.

[34] See pp. xcii-xcvi of this Introduction.

[35] House or Family (Casa) of Mosto.

[36] In 1454 the Venetian Senate ordered three galleys to be equipped for the voyage to Flanders and England; and ordered Marco Zeno, as commander, to enquire about the goods of Venetian subjects landed in England.

[37] The Prince was said especially to wish for Venetians to enter his service, as they knew more about the spice trade than anyone; and he was convinced that his expeditions

would ultimately find spices (*i.e.*, in India). As to Vicente Diaz, cf. Azurara's *Guinea*, chs. lx, lviii, etc.

[38] Cf. Azurara, *Guinea*, end of ch. xcvi.

[39] This seems one of the earliest notices of non-Portuguese craft in these waters. But Uso di Mare was almost certainly in the Prince's service, like "Vallarte the Dane," and "Balthasar the German," noticed in Azurara, *Guinea*, chs. xvi. and xciv. Uso di Mare's letter to his creditors of December 12, 1455, seems to show that the expedition had returned before Christmas.

[40] As in the collections of Ramusio, Temporal, Astley, and Stanier Clarke; in Major,*Henry Navigator*, chs. xv.-xvi.; and in "Heroes of Nations" life of Prince Henry, ch. xvi.

[41] Of these two were "very large," and on these they landed, finding no inhabitants but plenty of animal life. Five more isles were sighted in the distance, but not visited. They called the first discovered "Boa Vista," and the largest of the group "St. James," from the day of the discovery. This is, of course, the Santiago which forms the centre of the Cape Verde archipelago.

[42] See Nordenskjöld, *Periplus*, 120, and Map section of this Introduction; also pp. xcii-xcvi of the same.

[43] See p. cxxxii of this Introduction.

[44] The same change is observable in the narrative of Diego Gomez. Cf. his treatment of the Chief Bezeghichi, whom he freely releases when in his power, in order to make him less "bitter against the Christians."

[45] *E.g.*, the rivers Barbasini, Casamansa, Santa Anna, St. Domingo, and Cape Roxo.

[46] An allusion of high importance. See the section of this Introduction, "Preliminary African Exploration," especially pp. xlv, etc.

VOYAGES OF THE PORTUGUESE COMPLETING PRINCE HENRY'S WORK.

A word must be added on the completion of Prince Henry's work after his death, and by agents whom in many cases he had trained. King Affonso V, though rather more of a tournament king than a true successor of the great Infant, such as John II, had yet caught enough of his uncle's spirit to push on steadily, though slowly, the advance round Africa. In 1461 he repaired the fort in the Bight of Arguim and sent out Pedro de Sintra[47] to survey the coast beyond Cadamosto's furthest point. De Sintra proceeded 600 miles [Pg xxix]along the "southern coast of Guinea," passed a mountain which was called Sierra Leone (according to one account) from the lion-like growl of the thunder on its summits, and turned back at the point afterwards known as St. George La Mina.[48] Soon after (probably in 1462), Sueiro da Costa followed De Sintra,[49] but without any new results, and it was not till 1470 that a fresh advance was made.[50] In 1469 King Affonso leased the West African trade to Fernam Gomez, a citizen of Lisbon, for five years, Gomez paying 1,000 ducats a year. To this lease was annexed the condition that Gomez should make annual explorations along the unknown West coast of Africa for 300 *miglia*, counted from Sierra Leone, "where Pedro de Sintra and Sueiro da Costa turned back."[51]

Accordingly, in 1470, Gomez sent out João de Santarem and Pedro de Escobar, accompanied by the two leading Portuguese pilots, Martin Fernandez and Alvaro Esteves, as "directors of the navigation." On the 29th December, they discovered St. Thomas island, and on 17th January, 1471, the [Pg xxx]Isle of St. Anne, afterwards Ilha do Principe, both close to the Equator on the open side of the Bight of Biafra.

Another voyage seems to have been made, under Gomez' auspices, in 1471. Fernando Po now reached the island in the angle of the Central African coast which is still called after him; and men began to find that the Eastern bend of the continent, which had been followed since 1445-6 with some hope of a direct approach to Asia, now took a sharp turn to the South.

In spite of this disappointment, Fernandez and Esteves in 1472-3 passed beyond the furthest of earlier travellers, and crossed the Equator[52] into that Southern Hemisphere on the edge of which the caravels had long been hovering, as mariners like Cadamosto saw ever more clearly stars unknown in the Northern Hemisphere, and ever more nearly lost sight of the Arctic pole. In 1474-5 Cape Catherine, two degrees South of the Line, was reached, and here the advance of exploration stopped for a time till the accession of John II in 1481.

[Pg xxxi]Now, in six years, the slow advance of the past sixty was exceeded.[53] Less than four months after his father's death, John, who as heir apparent had drawn part of his income from the African trade and its fisheries, sent out Diego de Azambuga, who in 1482 built under the King's orders the celebrated fort at St. George La Mina. He trafficked with success, but made no great advance along unknown Africa, even if he commenced a new era in the permanent colonisation of the Continent. King John was not disposed to be satisfied with this. In 1484, Diego Cão was ordered to go as far to the South as he could, and not to "wait anywhere for other matters." He penetrated to the mouth of the Zaire or Congo, where he erected (at Cape Padron?) a stone pillar in sign of possession,[54] and brought back four natives to Portugal. These he took out with him in his second voyage [Pg xxxii](1485); on this expedition Martin Behaim was (wrongly) said to have accompanied him. Cão claimed in this year to have reached 22° S. lat., half way between the Congo and the Cape of Good Hope; but this is probably an exaggeration;—18° S. lat.[55] perhaps marks his furthest point, rather than Walvisch Bay, as in the old tradition.

After Cão's return, King John renewed his efforts with fresh energy. Already, in 1484, a negro embassy to Portugal had brought such an account of an inland prince, one "Ogane, a Christian at heart," that all the Court of Lisbon thought he must be the long lost Prester John, and men were sent out to seek this "great Catholic Lord" by sea and land.

Bartholemew Diaz sailed in August 1486, with two ships, to try his fortune by the sea-route, and even if he could not reach the Prester's country, to discover as far as possible on the "way round Africa." Two other envoys, Covilham and Payva, were sent out by way of "Jerusalem, Arabia, and Egypt," to find the Priest-King and the Indies; [Pg xxxiii]yet another expedition was to ascend the Negro Nile, or Senegal, to its supposed junction with the Nile of Egypt; a fourth party started to explore a road to Cathay by the North-East Passage.

Bartholemew Diaz, accompanied by João Iffante, rounded the southernmost point of Africa, and passed some way beyond the site of the modern Port Elizabeth. The picturesque story of his voyage is well known. He sailed with two vessels of 50 tons apiece, in the belief that "ships which sailed down the coast of Guinea might be sure to reach the end of the land by persisting to the South." His first pillar was set up at Angra dos Ilheos,[56] at the south side of Angra Pequena. He made another stay at Angra das Voltas, in 29° S. lat., immediately after passing the Orange River. Then, putting well out to sea, Diaz ran thirteen days due south before the wind, hoping by this wide sweep to round the furthest point of the Continent, which many traditions agreed in fixing not very far from his last halting-place. Finding the sea and air at last becoming cold, he changed his course to east, and as no land appeared after five days, to north. In this last course the Portuguese reached a bay where cattle were feeding, named by the Portuguese Angra dos Vaqueiros, now Flesh Bay.[57]After putting ashore two natives [Pg xxxiv](probably some of those lately carried from Congo to Portugal, and sent out again to act as scouts for the European explorers), Diaz continued east to a small island still called "Santa Cruz," W. of our Port Elizabeth, and even further to a river called, after his partner, Rio do Iffante, now the Great Fish River, in 32° 23' S. lat., and midway between the present Port Elizabeth and East London, where the coast begins gradually but steadily to trend north-east. Here the expedition put back, sighting on its homeward way the Land's End, or "Cape of Storms," re-named by John II "Cape of Good Hope" on their return. Almost at the same time as Diaz' reappearance in Lisbon (Dec. 1487), Covilham, who had reached Malabar by way of Egypt, wrote home from Cairo more than confirming the hopes already drawn from the success of the last maritime ventures. "If you keep southward, the continent must come to an end. And when ships reach the Eastern Ocean, let your men ask for Sofala and the Island of the Moon (Madagascar), and they will find pilots to take them to India."

Yet another chapter of discoveries was opened by King John's expeditions for the ascent of the Western Nile, and for the exploration of the North-East Passage to Cathay. Neither of these achieved complete success, but some more light was gained upon the interior of Africa (where the Portuguese made such notable advances in the sixteenth century); it has even been claimed, but apparently without foundation, for the explorers of John II, that [Pg xxxv]a Portuguese discovery of Novaia Zemlya rewarded their enterprise.

The great voyage of Vasco da Gama (1497-9) connected and completed the various aims of Portuguese enterprise, to which Prince Henry had given a permanent and organised form.

Though he was not able to see in his own lifetime the fulfilment of his plans, both the method of a South-East Passage, and the men who finally discovered it, were, in a true sense, his—were inseparably associated with his work. The lines of Portuguese advance, a generation after his death, continued to follow his initiative so closely, that, when a different route to the Indies was suggested by Columbus, the government of John II refused to treat it seriously. And yet it was to the Infant's movement—in part, at least—that Columbus owed his conception. "It was in Portugal," says Ferdinand Columbus, "that the Admiral began to surmise that if men could sail so far south, one might also sail west and find lands in that direction." In another place[58] it will be questioned how far a Portuguese movement America-wards can be credited to the mariners of Prince Henry's own time. It is plain that, whether he or his captains ever thought favourably of the chances of the Western route, he and they alike devoted their main energies to its rival, the Eastern or African coasting way. It is equally [Pg xxxvi]plain, on the other hand, that the Infant's work produced a new interest in the world-science of geography throughout Christendom, and so was indirectly responsible for quite as much as it directly aimed at accomplishing.

[47] This voyage is described by Cadamosto as an appendix to his own voyages. A young Portuguese who accompanied De Sintra described to Cadamosto the stretch of coast now discovered beyond the Rio Grande, the anchorages of the fleet, and the names given to points on the shore. "This account, without any rhetorical embellishment, is of special interest as a specimen of a Portuguese sailing-direction from a sailor of Henry the Navigator's School" (Nordenskjöld, *Periplus*, 121). De Sintra reached 5° further South than any before him. His nomenclature still survives at many points: *e.g.*, Cape Verga, Sierra Leone, Cape Santa Anna, Cape del Monte, Cape Mesurado. Cape Sagres, "the highest promontory they had ever seen," between Cape Verga and Cape Ledo, has been re-named. De Sintra also noticed especially a "great green forest"—"Bosque de St. Maria," in 5° 30' N. lat. (?)—and near his furthest point (at Rio dos Fumos) an immense quantity of smoke from native fires. Cf. Hanno's language in his *Periplus*, on the fiery rivers running down into the sea; and see J. N. Bellin's *Petit Atlas Maritime*, Paris, 1764; Part iii, Map 105.

[48] Elmina.

[49] According to some, he accompanied De Sintra in the voyage of 1461.

[50] Cadamosto explicitly says that when he left Portugal on February 1, 1463, no voyages had been made in continuation of De Sintra's venture, recorded by him.

[51] According to Cadamosto's account, De Sintra had gone a good deal further.

[52] It is not very clearly recorded who first crossed the line among the Portuguese sailors of this time. Some conclude as stated in text, but Nordenskjöld believes it was "perhaps Lopo Gonçalvez, after whom a promontory directly south of the Equator is named"; he also thinks this great event was accomplished on Gomez' first expedition, under Santarem, Escobar, Fernandez and Esteves, in 1470-1. As to progress eastwards, towards India, it was much exaggerated by many. While his caravels were still off the Guinea coast, King Affonso V believed the meridian of "Tunis, and even of Alexandria," had been already passed.

[53] It is probably right to ascribe great importance to the work of Fernam Gomez, during his five years' lease. His wealth gave a new character to the equipment of the African Expeditions of Portugal. Formerly there had been too much waste of energy through indefiniteness of object; too much discretion had been left to mariners themselves; now the definite contract for geographical discovery with the Crown caused a more rapid and continuous advance, and long stretches of coast were explored and mapped.

[54] According to King John's orders. Wooden crosses (often of Madeira wood?) had hitherto been erected by Portuguese discoverers in new lands. Now stone pillars 6 ft. high were to be used, and on them was to be inscribed, in Portuguese and Latin, the date, with the name of the reigning monarch, and those of the discoverers.

[55] Near C. Frio. So it is placed (at *Arenarum Aestuarium* or *Manga das Arenas*) on Pl. X in Livio Sanuto's *Geographia* of 1588. We have mentioned that Martin Behaim, of

Nüremberg, claimed to have accompanied Cão to West Africa; but his globe, so famous afterwards, executed in 1492 at the order of the Nüremberg Town Council, shows very little evidence of this. Behaim's West Africa is often obstinately Ptolemaic, at the end of the century which had revolutionised the knowledge of this part of the world. He inserts all the legendary Atlantic islands, and puts the Cape Verdes far out of their proper place.

[56] ? Diaz Point, at the *Serra Parda* or "Dark Hills" of Barros.

[57] Some way beyond Cape Agulhas, and immediately to the east of the River Gauritz.

[58] See the section of this Introduction on the "Atlantic Islands," especially pp. ciii-cvi.

AFRICAN EXPLORATION PRELIMINARY TO PRINCE HENRY'S WORK.

The first recorded African expedition along the Atlantic coast of Africa was, if we accept the account of Herodotus, that of the Phœnicians sent out by Pharaoh Necho (*c.* 600 B.C.), who started from the Red Sea and returned by the Pillars of Hercules and the Mediterranean.[59] Almost at the same time (*c.* 570 B.C., according to Vivien de St. Martin's estimate) the great Phœnician settlement of Carthage attempted in reverse order a voyage of colonisation and discovery along the West of the Continent outside the Straits. Eratosthenes refers to Phœnician (or Carthaginian) settlements already existing on what is now the coast of Marocco, both inside and outside the "Pillars;" this new expedition under Hanno was intended to strengthen the old, as well as to found new plantations. It is often compared with a similar venture, "to explore the [Pg xxxvii]outer coasts of Europe," undertaken by Himilco, probably about the same time.[60]

Hanno[61] sailed from Carthage, according to our authority, with sixty pentecontors, carrying 30,000(?) people, colonists and others, first to Cerne,[62]which was as far distant from the Pillars of Hercules as the Pillars were from Carthage. Then he ascended the river Chretes[63] to a lake. Twelve days' voyage south of Cerne he passed a promontory with lofty wooded [Pg xxxviii]hills,[64] and a little beyond this, a great estuary.[65] Five days more to the south brought him to the Western Horn,[66] and on the other side of this he coasted along a "fragrant shore," with "streams of fire running down into the sea," and "fiery mountains, the loftiest of which seemed to touch the clouds," and which he named[67]"Chariot of the Gods."[68] Three days' sail beyond this was his furthest point, the Southern Horn,[69] whence he returned directly to Carthage.

It is very difficult to identify Hanno's positions, and this is not the place to attempt a fresh investigation.[70] But the tradition of this *Periplus* having[Pg xxxix]reached far beyond the Straits of Gibraltar—farther than any venture of the earlier Middle Ages, or of the classical period—may be regarded as reliable, and some position on the Sierra Leone coast may provisionally be taken as its ultimate point of advance.

The African voyages of Sataspes under Xerxes, and of Eudoxus of Cyzicus under Ptolemy Euergetes II, cannot be regarded as of much importance. Neither probably reached Cape Verde (even if we are to attach any belief to their narratives). Sataspes[71] declared that his ship was stopped by obstructions in the sea at a point where lived on the ocean shore a people of small stature, clad in garments made of the palm-tree.[72] This was "many months'" sail south of Cape Soloeis or Cantin, and may stand for the neighbourhood of the Senegal, if it be not a mere traveller's tale invented by Sataspes, as Herodotus seems to have thought, to excuse his failure to the Great King. Eudoxus[73] claimed to have[Pg xl]sailed so far, first along the eastern and then, along the western, coasts of Africa, that he practically circumnavigated the Continent; but all the details with which we are favoured go to disprove his claim. For instance, he implies that the Ethiopians reached by him on his farthest point S.W. "adjoined Mauretania." On the eastern coast he picked up a ship's prow from a vessel which he was told had been wrecked coming from the westward, and which mariners of Alexandria identified as a ship of Gades—a very unlikely story in the face of the currents on the East African coast.

According to Pliny,[74] Polybius the historian also made a reconnaissance down the West coast of Africa, in the lifetime and under the order of Scipio Æmilianus. He seems to have passed the termination of the Atlas chain, but Pliny's language does not warrant us in going any further.[75] He interweaves [Pg xli]in his narrative the voyage of Polybius with the great measurement of the Roman world under Augustus by Agrippa, which is perhaps in part commemorated by the Peutinger Table, and which evidently took into its view the Hesperian Promontory,[76] and the Chariot of the Gods. Some have claimed for Polybius a voyage as far as the latter point, but this, if understood in the sense of Sierra Leone, is highly improbable.

We must not here delay over classical attempts at African continental exploration; but it will be right to notice briefly: That in the age of Pliny, as shown by the *Periplus of the Erythraean Sea* (*c.* 70 A.D.), and in the age of Ptolemy, as shown in his *Geography* (*c.* 139-162 A.D.), the knowledge of the Græco-Roman world was extended down the East coast of Africa at least as far as Zanzibar and its neighbourhood, and down the Western coast to Cape Soloeis, or Cape Cantin: That beyond these points only vague ideas obtained, though occasional travellers had ventured further: That in the interior of Africa only the North coast region, viz., Egypt and the "Barbary States," were thoroughly well known, though expeditions had at times crossed the Sahara, reached the Sudan, and ascended the Nile to the [Pg xlii]marshes situate in 9° N. lat.: That, even if never seen or visited, at least something had been heard of the African Alps in the neighbourhood of the Great Lakes, as well as of those lakes themselves: That Ptolemy's work marks the highest point of ancient knowledge in Africa, which began to decline from the age of the Antonines: That it is not probable even Ptolemy had any definite notions about the Niger, though his text names such a stream in West Africa, and his Map lays it down in a position not very distant from our Joliba: That it is clear he was conscious of the vast size of the Continent in a way that none of his predecessors had grasped, while utterly ignorant of its shape towards the South, so that he even denied the primary fact of its practically insular form.

Leaving to another section any notice of ancient exploration among the African islands, it would also appear that Statius Sebosus, Juba, and Marinus of Tyre all made contributions to the knowledge of West Africa. These contributions are now only preserved in the allusions or paraphrases of other authors; but it is clear that Sebosus, perhaps identical with a Sebosus who was a friend of Catulus and a contemporary of Sallust and Cæsar, had made independent inquiries concerning the West or Ocean coast of the Continent;[77] that Juba,[78]who made the [Pg xliii]Nile rise in Western Mauretania, did similar work in the time of Augustus; and that Marinus preserved some original records of Roman expeditions which crossed the Great Desert,[79] apparently from Tripoli and Fezzan to the neighbourhood of the Central Sudan States.

As the Roman Empire broke up, geographical knowledge naturally suffered, and Africa shared in this loss. But a considerable recovery was effected through the work of the Arabs, to whom the Infant Henry owed much.

Confining our attention to Continental exploration, we may remark among other particulars: (1) That the Arab migration[80] to the East coast beyond Guardafui in the eighth century began the extension [Pg xliv]of Moslem trade-colonies, which at last reached Sofala. (2) That the coast near Madagascar, as well as that island itself, seems to have been known to the great Arab traveller and geographer Masudi ("Massoudy") in the tenth century. (3) That the same writer considered the Atlantic or Western Ocean unnavigable, but that even he preserves a record of one Arab voyage thereon.[81] (4) That Edrisi, in the twelfth century, records another voyage which touched the African mainland a good distance beyond the Straits of Gibraltar.[82] (5) That Ibn Said, in the thirteenth century, relates a discovery of Cape Blanco.[83] (6) That overland communication between the Barbary States and the negroes of the Sudan was originated by the Arabs, as a regular line of commerce, probably from the eleventh century at least.

This last point is one which requires special [Pg xlv]consideration. By sea the Arabs did scarcely anything to prepare the way for the Christian discoveries of the fifteenth century in Africa (except along the Eastern coast), but by land they were the most important helpers and informants of Prince Henry.[84] Islam effected the conquest of the Barbary States, politically in the seventh century, dogmatically in the course of about 200 years after the days of Tarik and Musa. By the end of the eleventh century the faith of Mohammed had begun to spread and take deep root in the Sudan,[85] having [Pg xlvi]already made its way into many parts of the Sahara. With the Moslem faith came the Moslem civilisation. The caravan trade across the desert now commenced [Pg xlvii]between Negroland and the Mediterranean; "Timbuktu" was founded by Moslems, probably drawn in large measure from the Tuareg, in about 1077-1100; and the Central Sudan States, from Sokoto to Darfur and Kordofan, passed under Mohammedan influence between A.D. 1000 and 1250. With the fresh migration of Nomad Arabs which seems to have taken place about A.D. 1050, from Upper Egypt to West Africa, a distinct advance of Islam in Central Africa is to be noticed by way of Kanem, Bornu, Sokoto, and the Niger Valley; this new wave reached Jenné, Ghiné, or "Guinea", on the Upper Valley of the Niger.

Even earlier than this a movement seems to have been in progress from the opposite direction—first south along the west coast, and then east up the valley of the Senegal and similar inlets. The tradition preserved by John Pory[86] is approved by the most recent research—at least in its general conclusions. The Moslems "pierced into" the [Pg xlviii]Sahara in, or a little after, 710, and "overthrew the Azanegue, and the people of Walata;" in "the year 973 (others say about 950) they infected the negroes and first those of Melli." During the ninth century, Islam made progress among the Sahara tribes, and the influence of this faith promoted intercourse between the desert tribes and the great commercial centres of the North African coast—a movement which was furthered by the Almoravide revival of the eleventh, and the Almohade of the twelfth, century. The former started from a reformed Moslem "community," settled on an island at the mouth of the Senegal—in other words, it shows Islam already finding centres for recovery and expansion in Negroland, exploring the Sudan from the north and west, creeping along the Atlantic Ocean, and spreading from the neighbourhood of Cape Verde into the interior of the populous land to the south of the Great Desert.

Here we may notice that Edrisi takes a point called Ulil as his starting-place in reckoning measurements, and especially longitudes, in the Sudan. This Ulil is fixed by all our authorities as close to the sea, in the centre of a salt-producing district; and it may be supposed to have been in the neighbourhood of the Senegal estuary.[87] To the east, Ulil bordered on Gana, Ghanah, Guinoa, Geneoa, or "Guinea," which, at least in name, was the first [Pg xlix]objective of Prince Henry's expeditions, and was famous for its slave export, and its money of "uncoined gold."[88] The name of the country was probably derived from its chief city of Jenné, variously described by Leo Africanus, in the sixteenth century, as a large village; by the earlier geographers—especially Edrisi in the twelfth century, and Ibn-Batuta in the fourteenth—as a spacious and well-built city on an island in the Niger, lying west from Timbuktu.

Between Ghanah or Jenné, and Ulil, according to some writers, lay the kingdom of Tokrur, while Andagost was on the northern boundary of Ghanah close to the Sahara. All these were Moslem states like Melli or Malli (W.S.W. from Timbuktu), and carried on trade with Barbary across the desert long before the days of Prince Henry. One of the earliest important converts to Islam in the Sudan was Sa-Ka-ssi, of the dynasty of Sa in the Songhay [Pg l]country on the Middle Niger (*c.* A.D. 1009-1010). From this time the states on the Middle Niger became a centre of Mohammedan influence, especially after the foundation of Timbuktu about 1077. When Ibn-Batuta visited these parts in 1330, he found the negroes of the Niger full of Moslem devotion, enjoying a commerce with Mediterranean Africa, and mostly acknowledging the lead of Melli, which kingdom, according to him, had been founded in the early thirteenth century by the Mandingo.[89]

Among the Lake Chad States progress was also made in the eleventh century. The first Moslem Sultan of Bornu (Hami ibnu-l-Jalil) is recorded about 1050;[90] and a similar conversion happened in Kanem about the same time. This latter kingdom was then much more important than now, and dominated much even of the Egyptian Sudan. Hence in the fourteenth century Islam obtained a strong footing in Darfur, as it had already in Baghirmi and Wadai.[91] Already in the twelfth century, Kordofan and the extreme east of the Sudan had been partially Moslemised by Arabs from Egypt, who had come south after the fall of the Fatimite Caliphs.

Along the eastern coast, in spite of the early [Pg li]spread of Moslem settlements from Magadoxo southward, Islam was very slow in penetrating the interior. Here the Arabs chiefly devoted themselves to maritime commerce, and for a long time their intercourse with the inland tribes was not of a kind to open up the country. Caravans with slaves and natural products came down to the coast towns, but the merchants of the latter seem to have been content with waiting and receiving. But on this side of Africa was a Christian kingdom, which was now—in Prince Henry's days—becoming more familiar to Europe: Abyssinia, the kingdom of Prester John, as the Portuguese of later time identified it. The original seat of the Priest-King, as described (chiefly from Nestorian information) by Carpini, Rubruquis, Marco Polo, and other Asiatic travellers of the thirteenth century, was in Central Asia, but the Abyssinian state offered so close a parallel, that it was naturally recognised by many as the true realm of Prester John, when the first clear accounts of it came into Mediæval Europe. The Asiatic prototype, moreover, was only temporary; it had apparently ceased to exist in the time of Polo himself, who spread its fame so widely; whereas its Abyssinian rival was both permanent and ancient enough to be noticed in pre-Crusading and even in pre-Mediæval literature. As the Renaissance movement progressed in Europe, learned men of the West gained from their reading an ever clearer realisation of this isolated Christianity of the East; and, as the trade of the [Pg lii]later Middle Ages spread itself more widely, the Venetians seem to have made their way to the Court of the Negus, even before John II of Portugal sent Covilham and Payva (1486) to find the Prester. Probably the beginnings of this Italian intercourse with Abyssinia may be placed as far back as the lifetime of Prince Henry (c. 1450).

The Christianity of Nubia, which dated from the fourth century like that of Abyssinia itself, was still vigorous in the twelfth,[92] but from that time it began to fail before the incessant and determined pressure of Islam. Ibn-Batuta,[93]about 1330-40, found that the King of Dongola had just become a Moslem. Father Alvarez, in 1520-7, considered that the Nubian Christianity which had once extended up the Nile from the first Cataract to Sennaar had become extinct; though he would not allow that the mass of the Nubians had adopted any other religion in its place;[94] and himself, he tells us, had met a Christian who, in travelling through Nubia, had seen 150 churches.[95] But, in the course of the sixteenth and seventeenth centuries, all Nubia embraced Islam; and even in 1534, Ahmad Gragne, King of Adel, in one of his attacks upon Abyssinia, is said to have had 15,000 Nubian allies, apparently all Mohammedans.[96]

[Pg liii]In Prince Henry's day, then, we may fairly assume that the old Christianity of East Africa was practically limited to Abyssinia; but when Azurara tells us of the Infant's desire "to know if there were in those parts[97] any Christian Princes,"[98] and again more explicitly, "to have knowledge of the land of Prester John,"[99] it is possible that some dim acquaintance with the old tradition of an isolated African (as well as of an isolated Asiatic) Church, was at the root of his endeavour.

At the end of the twelfth century, Islam had already begun to encroach upon the coast of what is now Italian "Erythraea;" and about 1300 A.D. a Musulman army attacked the ruler of Amhara. At this time the realm of the Negus seems to have been completely cut off from the Red Sea;[100] but it was not till the early sixteenth century that Abyssinia was in serious danger of becoming a province of Islam, from the attacks of Ahmad Gragne (1528-1543), which, however, ended in complete failure.

To return to the North coast of Africa. Here, by the capture of Ceuta, Prince Henry gained a starting-point for his work; here he is said (probably with truth) to have gained his earliest knowledge of the interior of Africa; here especially he was brought in contact with those Sudan and Saharan [Pg liv]caravans which, coming down to the Mediterranean coast, brought news, to those who sought it, of the Senegal and Niger, of the Negro kingdoms beyond the desert, and particularly of the Gold land of "Guinea." Here also, from a knowledge thus acquired, he was able to form a more correct judgment of the course needed for the rounding or circumnavigation of Africa, of the time, expense, and toil necessary for that task, and of the probable support or hindrance his mariners were to look for on their route.

We must, however, qualify in passing the statements of Azurara, in ch. vii, which would imply that Christianity had for ages been utterly extinct in North Africa. "As it was said that the power of the Moors in ... Africa was ... greater than commonly supposed, and that there were no Christians among them." "During the one-and-thirty years that he had warred against the Moors, he had never found a Christian King nor a lord outside this land,[101] who for the love of ... Christ would aid him."[102] The old North African Church, though constantly declining, survived the Musulman Conquest of the seventh and eighth centuries for nearly 800 [Pg lv]years. True, its episcopate, which could still muster 30 members in the tenth century, was practically extinct by the time of Hildebrand[103] (Pope Gregory VII), and in 1246 the Franciscan missionary bishop of Fez and Marocco was the only Christian prelate in "Barbary"; but a number of native Christians still lingered on, though without Apostolic succession. In 1159, the Almohade conqueror, Abdu-'l Mu'min ben Ali, on subduing Tunis, compelled many of these to change their faith; but all through the next centuries, down to 1535, a certain number of Tunisians preserved their ancient religion so far that, when Charles V gained possession of the city in the above-named year (1535), he congratulated these perseverants on their steadfastness. The same fact is evidenced by the tolerant behaviour, as a rule, of the Mediæval Barbary States towards Christians, both native and European.

Thus they employ Christian soldiers, among others; grant freedom of worship to Christian [Pg lvi]merchants and settlers; and exchange letters with various Popes, especially Gregory VII, Gregory IX, Innocent III, and Innocent IV, on the subject of the due protection of native Christians.[104] Traces of Christianity were to be found among the Kabyles of Algeria down to the time of the capture of Granada (1492), when a fresh influx of Andalusian Moors from Spain completed the conversion of these tribes,[105]—a conversion which, as Leo Africanus notices, was not inconsistent with some survivals of Christian custom. Similar survivals have been alleged among the Tuâreg of the Sahara, the "Christians of the Desert" at the present day.

Two practical questions arise for our special purpose from this summary of the mediæval progress and fifteenth-century status of Islam in Africa. These questions have been partly answered already, but we may here re-state them to generalise our conclusions. 1. What information was the Infant able to gain from the "Moors" for his own plans? and 2. [Pg lvii]Was this "Moorish" information so valuable as to account, in any great degree, for the Prince's perseverance and success in his task?

To the former query it may be replied: 1. That the "Arabs and Moors" of the early fifteenth century could give the Infant detailed and correct information, not only about the Barbary states and the trade-routes of the Sahara, but also about many of the Western and Central Sudan countries, and about the general course and direction of the "Guinea coast" both to the west and south of the great African hump. Especially could they describe the kingdom of Guinea, centreing round the town of Jenné on the Upper Niger, which was the chief market of their Negro trade in slaves, gold, and ivory. This kingdom, then, reached almost to the Atlantic on the lower valley of the Senegal, where in earlier times a place called Ulil had been marked by Edrisi and other Arab geographers, as independent of Ghanah but important for traffic. Also, the Moors were acquainted with the country of Tokrur,[106] which may be supposed to occupy the upper valley of the Senegal, becoming perhaps, in Prince Henry's time, merely a province of Guinea. Further, they could give much information about the States of Timbuktu and Melli, to the east of Guinea, on the Middle Niger, about the gold land [Pg lviii]of Wangara, in the great bend to the south of that river, and about the Songhay, afterwards so powerful, whose capital was at Gao, at the extreme N.E. angle of the Negro Nile, or Joliba. The Arab travellers and writers seem generally to have made but one river out of the Senegal, the Niger, Joliba, or Quorra, and the Benué or "river of Haussa."

De Barros explicitly states that the Moors told Prince Henry how on the other side of the Great Desert lived the Azanegues, who bordered on the Jaloff negroes, where began the kingdom of Guinea, or Guinanha. From other sources we know, as already stated, that the Infant obtained from the same informants[107] definite descriptions of the Senegal estuary, its "tall palms," and other landmarks. For here, rather than at any point more to the south, was the Guinea coast proper of the fifteenth century; though in the Bull of Pope Nicholas V, granting to Portugal (1454) all the lands that should be discovered "from the Cape of Bojador and of Nun throughout the whole of Guinea, as far as its *Southern shore*, or even to the Antarctic Pole and the Indies," our modern extension of the term is virtually admitted.

17

2. And, in the second place, granting what has just been said, it is obvious that the Moorish [Pg lix]information was important enough to have very considerable influence on the Infant's plans, and especially to furnish him with hopes of success, and reasons for perseverance in the face of opposition and repeated failure.

Our materials for the Prince's life are so inadequate that we can hardly decide, from the silence of our authorities, that he was entirely ignorant, even at second hand, of all that the Arab geographers or travellers had written about Africa. Especially is this the case with Edrisi (1099-1154), whose work was composed in the Christian kingdom of Sicily, and owed much to Christian writers. And perhaps the same hope applies to Ibn-Batuta (*fl.* 1330), who, living at a time so near to the epoch of the Prince's voyages, had revealed the Western Sudan to the Moslem world—and so to any Christians conversant with Moslem trade and enterprise—far more thoroughly than ever before. These are only two examples among those Moslem geographers, whose work may have been brought to the Infant's notice during his visits to Ceuta.

* * * * *

We have now to see what progress had been made by Christian nations in the exploration of Africa immediately before Prince Henry's time. The Crusades were not merely expeditions to recover the Holy Sepulchre: they were the outward sign of the great mediæval awakening of Europe and Christendom, which, beginning in the eleventh century, has never slumbered since, and which, in [Pg lx]the Infant's days, was passing through that great transition we call the Renaissance. On the geographical side this movement took first of all the direction of land travel, and achieved such great discoveries in Asia that a new desire for wealth and commercial expansion was kindled in Europe, with the special object of controlling the Asiatic treasures which Marco Polo and others had described. Islam, however, interposed a troublesome barrier between Central Asia, India and China on the one side, and European trade or dominion on the other. Hence, from the thirteenth century, we find a new series of attempts to reach the Far East by sea from the Atlantic and Mediterranean coasts. It was not till the last years of Prince Henry's life that any serious attempts were made to explore the interior of Africa, but expeditions along its shores were sent out long before his time to reconnoitre for a sea-route to India.[108] We have already remarked that the Infant represents in his own life-work the leading transition in this movement, from a tentative, impermanent, and unorganised series of efforts, to a continuous, properly directed, and successful plan; but some notice must be taken of those ventures [Pg lxi]which immediately prepared his way. Leaving out of sight, for another section as far as possible, the voyages which are concerned only with the Atlantic islands, or aim in a rudimentary way at finding a Western route to Asia, it is possible to mention several genuine attempts to anticipate the Portuguese along the Eastern or African mainland course.

The first of these, as far as known, is the voyage of Lancelot Malocello, of Genoa, in 1270. There is no proof that he started, like the adventurers of 1291, to find the ports of India: it is probable his ambitions were more modest; but we do not know how far he reached along the African mainland—only that he touched the Canaries, and staying there some time built a castle in Lancarote[109] island.

The next venture in this direction is also Genoese. In May, 1291,[110] Tedisio Doria and Ugolino de Vivaldo, with the latter's brother and certain other citizens of Genoa, equipped two galleys "that they might go by sea to[wards] the ports of India and bring back useful things for trade." But "after they had passed a place called Gozora,[111] nothing more [Pg lxii]certain has been heard of them." This is confirmed by Pietro d'Abano, writing in 1312; but in the fifteenth century one of Prince Henry's captains, the Genoese colleague of Cadamosto, Antoniotto Ususmaris or Uso di Mare, professed to give some more details. On December 12th, 1455, he wrote his creditors a letter, in which he stated[112] that the two galleys of "Vadinus and Guido Vivaldi," leaving Genoa in 1281 "for the Indies," reached the "Sea of Ghinoia," where one ship was stranded, but the other sailed on to a city of Ethiopia called Menam, where lived Christian subjects of Prester John, who held them captive. None ever returned, but Uso di Mare himself spoke with the last surviving descendant of those Genoese.[113]Menam, he concludes, was on the sea coast, near the river Gihon.[114]

It is difficult to attach great weight to Uso [Pg lxiii]di Mare's letter, which looks like an attempt to amuse his creditors with interesting adventures; but the voyage of 1291, with or without the survival of 1455, is sufficiently remarkable. It is the first direct attempt of Europeans in the Middle Ages to find a sea-route to India around Africa; its far-reaching design contrasts forcibly with the more modest projects of nearly all similar attempts before Prince Henry's time, and it is not improbable that some of its work survived, though officially unrecognised.[115]

The Hispano-Italian voyage of 1341 appears to have been solely occupied with the exploration of the Canaries, which were now becoming pretty well known, and we leave over any further notice of this for the present; but the Catalan expedition of 1346 was to some extent similar, both in object and method, to the Genoese expedition of 1291. "The ship of Jayme Ferrer," according to the Catalan Mappemonde of 1375, "started for the River of Gold[116] on St. Lawrence's Day, 1346."[117] To the same effect the Genoese archives[118] assert "On [Pg lxiv]the Feast of St. Lawrence there went forth from the city of the Majorcans one galley of John Ferne the Catalan, with intent to go to Rujaura.[119] Of the same nothing has since been heard."[120] And on the Map of 1375 already noticed, upon the third sheet, is depicted off Cape Bojador the picture[121] of the ship in question adjoining the legend above-quoted. We may notice, however, that Guinea, the gold land of Africa, and not India, was the objective of this voyage—although Guinea was the first step on the African route to India—and that the venture, as Major says, was apparently designed only for the discovery of the supposed Negro river in which gold was collected: a guess of Mediterranean merchants[122] from the information of Moorish middlemen.

Beginning with the year 1364, the French also claimed to have made important advances along the African coast route. The men of Dieppe, it is said, repeatedly sailed beyond Cape Verde, and even Sierra Leone, and founded settlements on what was afterwards called the La Mina coast.[123] [Pg lxv]These stations, called Petit Paris, Petit Dieppe, etc., lasted till 1410, when home troubles caused their abandonment,[124] like the temporary evacuation of the French Ivory Coast Settlements after 1870; but during the forty or fifty years of their existence, they carried on a regular trade with the Norman ports.

This tradition admits that it has lost its proofs in the destruction of the Admiralty Registers at Dieppe in 1694, but it is possible that some articles[125]may be discovered dating from this early commerce, which can supply fresh evidence. In itself, the Dieppese story is not impossible, and we shall see in another section, from the witness of the Map of 1351 and other portolanos, how plausible it appears, together with still greater ventures. But as things at present stand, it must be considered as a "thing not proven."[126]

[Pg lxvi]Reliable evidence of French voyages to the Gold Coast of Guinea can only be quoted for the sixteenth century. Thus Braun in 1617, and Dapper [Pg lxvii]some time shortly before 1668, inspected buildings and collected traditions from the natives on that shore which alone would prove these later expeditions, if they were not confirmed by several documents in Ramusio, Temporal, and Hakluyt.[127] Equally [Pg lxviii]reliable is the tradition of Béthencourt's *Conquest of the Canaries* in 1402, etc.; yet the authors of this history, Béthencourt's chaplains, give no hint of any knowledge possessed by their countrymen about the mainland coast beyond Cape Bojador, but rather imply the reverse. Finally, though so many of the best sixteenth-century maps are Dieppese, none of these show the fourteenth-century settlements, which are also wanting in all charts of the earlier time. The controverted names are first found on a map of 1631, by Jean Guérand; and this is probably not unconnected with the fact that in 1626 Rouen and Dieppe united for trade with the Guinea coast.

It is of course possible, as M. d'Avezac long ago argued from the evidence of the great Portolani of the fourteenth century, especially the Laurentian or Medicean[128] of 1351, the Pizzigani[129] of 1367, and the Catalan of 1375, that some unrecorded advance was accomplished along the African mainland coast during the middle years of this century; the imperfection of our records must never be forgotten; and we shall return to this question in another section. But nothing definite and certain can be gathered about the coast beyond Cape Bojador, except in a few small points.[130] With the Atlantic islands the case was very different.

19

[Pg lxix]The expedition[131] (1402-12) of the Sieur de Béthencourt, Lord of Granville la Teinturière, of the Pays de Caux in Normandy, was chiefly concerned with the Canaries[132]—like the voyages of the Spaniards Francisco Lopez (1382), and Alvaro Becarra (? 1390, etc.) But, after achieving fair success in the islands, De Béthencourt attempted (apparently in 1404) an exploration of the mainland coast "from Cape Cantin, half way between the Canaries and Spain," to Cape "Bugeder" or Bojador,[133] the famous promontory to the right or east of the Canaries. But this was left unfinished; and De Béthencourt's chaplains, in describing their Seigneur's intentions beyond the "Bulging Cape," can only fall back on a certain Book of a Spanish Friar,[134] which [Pg lxx]professed to give a description of Guinea, and the River of Gold. This last was said by the Friar to be 150 leagues from "the Cape Bugeder," and the French priests declare that "if things were such as described," their lord hoped sometime to reach the said river, "whereby access would be gained to the land of Prester John, whence come so many riches."

Thus the French colonists in the early fifteenth century, in Prince Henry's boyhood, know nothing first-hand, nothing save half-legendary rumours, about the African coast beyond Cape Bojador. They are anxious to reach the River of Gold, and traffic there, but they do not know the way. Of Petit Paris, Petit Dieppe, La Mine, and other Norman settlements or factories beyond Cape Verde, they give no sign.

The late and doubtful[135] tradition of Macham's discovery of Madeira (*c.* 1350-1370) does not concern the exploration of the African mainland, except that after the death of the "discoverer" in [Pg lxxi]his island, some of his sailors were said to have escaped in the ship's boat (according to the story) to the Continent, to have been made prisoners by the Berbers, and to have been held in slavery till some of the survivors were ransomed in 1416. But all this, if true, belongs to the well-known coast within Cape Non, and in no manner furthered exploration, except as regarded the island group of Madeira and Porto Santo.[136]

Fra Mauro preserves a tradition[137] of two voyages from India or the East coast of Africa round the Southern Cape—one in 1420, the other at an unfixed date. These, he says, had been accomplished by a person with whom he actually spoke, who claimed to have passed from Sofala to "Garbin," in the middle of the West coast, as it is marked on Fra Mauro's planisphere. If genuine, they would be the last anticipations of Prince Henry's enterprises left to chronicle; but few have placed much confidence in these statements, which seem indeed incredible in the form they are related by the Venetian draughtsman.

[59] Herod. ii, 158-9; iv, 42. These mariners took three years on their voyage: landed, sowed crops, and lived on the harvest during seasons unfavourable to navigation (especially autumn); during part of their journey they were astonished to find the sun on their right hand.

[60] This is first noticed by Aristotle, "On Marvellous Narratives," § 37; by Mela, *De Situ Orbis*, iii, 9; and by Pliny, *Natural History*, ii, 67, § 167-170, and elsewhere. The *Periplus* of Himilco seems to have been worked up by Avienus (*c.* 400 A.D.) in the first 400 lines of his poem, "*De Ora Maritima.*"

[61] One account of Hanno's voyage was preserved on a Punic inscription in the temple of "Kronos," "Saturn," or Moloch, at Carthage; the inscription was translated into Greek by an unknown hand, probably about 300 B.C.; and this version of the *Periplus* still remains to us. See Pliny, *Hist. Nat.*, ii, 67; v, 1, 36; vi, 31; *Solinus*, 56; *Pomponius Mela*, iii, 9. The first edition of the Greek text is by Gelenius, Basel 1534; the best by C. Müller, in *Geographi Graeci Minores.* Cf. also an edition by Falconer, London, 1797; an edition by Kluge, Leipsic, 1829; Rennell, *Geography of Herodotus*, 719-745, 4to ed.; Bunbury, *Ancient Geography*, i, 318-335; Walckenaer, *Recherches sur la Géographie de l'Afrique*, p. 362, etc.; Vivien de St. Martin, *Le Nord de l'Afrique dans l Antiquité*, pp. 330-400; Major, *Henry Navigator*, 90, etc., 1868; Charton, *Voyageurs Anciens*, i, 1-5, Ed. of 1882; Gossellin, *Recherches sur la Géographie des Anciens*, i, pp. 70-106; A. Mer, *Mémoire sur le Périple d'Hannon*, 1885; Campomanés, *El Periplo de Hannone illustrado*, appended to his *Antiquedad maritima de Cartago* (1756); Bougainville, *Acad. des Inscr. et Belles Lettres*, xxvi, xxvii, and especially xxviii, p. 287.

[62] Near Cape Non.

[63] This can hardly be the Senegal and Lake Nguier, as suggested by V. de St. Martin.

[64] Cape Verde?

[65] The Gambia?

[66] Cabo dos Mastos?

[67] Burton, with characteristic recklessness, insists on the Camaroons Mt. as the Chariot of the Gods ("Abeokuta and Camaroons Mt."); Fernando Po being another of the "lofty fiery mountains" seen by Hanno at this point.

[68] In the Sierra Leone range?

[69] Near Sherboro' island?

[70] Some (*e.g.*, Gossellin) would refer the whole group of localities here named to the extreme N.W. or Maroccan coast of Africa. But the "lofty green headland," the Western and Southern Horns, the Chariot of the Gods, the gorillas captured by the seamen, hardly seem to allow of this restriction. Ancient enterprise was far more satisfactory than ancient observation, and the inaccuracies of the latter should not make us deny the former. Here the initial measurement, of the distance from Cerne to the Pillars as being equal to the distance from the Pillars to Carthage, because the time occupied in sailing was equal, seems not only too vague a reckoning, but inaccurate as ignoring one great difference. Inside the straits, Hanno's duty was simply to sail forward; outside, he had to plant colonists at suitable spots,—along a coast, moreover, not so well known as that of North Africa to the Carthaginians.

[71] *Herodotus*, iv, 43. Similar excuses were given, *e.g.* (1) by Pytheas in the North Sea; (2) by Arab and Christian mediæval voyagers off Cape Non and Cape Bojador; (3) by Arabs off Cape Corrientes (on the E. Coast of Africa).

[72] They lived in towns, he adds, possessed cattle, were of harmless and timid disposition, and fled to mountains on the approach of the strangers.

[73] *Posidonius*, in *Strabo*, ii, 3, § 4. Eudoxus made three voyages (see also Pliny, *Hist. Nat.*, ii, 67, who bases his statement, like Mela, iii, 9, on Cornelius Nepos); in the first two he sailed to India and was driven to points on the East African coast; on the third he attempted to sail round Africa to India by the West, but evidently did not reach any distance beyond S.W. Mauretania (near C. Non). His first voyage must have been before B.C. 117 (d. of Ptolemy Euergetes II, Physcon), his other two subsequent to that year. The narrative of Eudoxus was exaggerated by Pliny and Pomponius Mela into the story that the navigator had actually accomplished, in his own person, the voyage round Africa from the Red Sea to Gades; but his achievements may be limited thus: Two voyages from Egypt to India; a short distance of African coasting beyond Guardafui, probably not as far as Zanzibar; a short distance on the west coast beyond the S.W. coast of our Morocco, probably not beyond Cape Non, or at furthest Cape Bojador.

[74] *Hist. Nat.*, v, i.

[75] The text here is very confused and difficult, but the best editors give the following text for Pliny's words: "He (Polybius) relates that beyond Atlas proceeding west there are forests.... Agrippa says that Lixus is distant from Gades 112 miles. From the Chariot of the Gods to the Western Horn is 10 days' voyage, and midway in this space *he* (*i.e.*, Agr., not Pol.) has placed Mt. Atlas."

[76] Or Western Horn.

[77] He was also the alleged author of a *Periplus*, and a treatise on the *Wonders of India*, but he is only known by Pliny's quotations.

[78] The younger, "King of Numidia."

[79] Such as those of Julius Maternus and Septimius Flaccus, which perhaps reached Lake Chad, probably in the time of Trajan (98-117 A.D.), and of Cornelius Balbus under Augustus (19 B.C.), which conquered the Garamantes of Fezzan.

[80] This migration led to the foundation of Magadoxo, 909-951, and of Kilwa, 960-1000; later on of Malindi, Mombasa, and Sofala. See Krapf, *Travels and Missionary Labours*, etc., p. 522; G. P. Badger, *Imams ... of Oman*, p. xiii; El-Belâdzory, *Futûh-el-Buldân* (Ed. Kosegarten), pp. 132-135. The immigrants came from the Red Sea and Syria, according to Dr. Krapf, from Oman and the Persian Gulf according to Badger (though Krapf admits a later Persian element as well). This was the migration of the "Emosaids" ('Ammu-Sa'îd, or People of Sa'îd?). They, in one tradition, claimed to be the clan of Said, grandson of Ali; "a mythical personage," according to Badger, who substitutes "Sa'îd, grandson of Julánda" the

Azdite; the latter, in this 'Omâni migration, was accompanied by his brother Suleimân. The traditional date is A.D. 740, and onwards.

[81] Masudi, ch. 12 of the *Meadows of Gold*. The adventurer was Khosh-Khash, the "young man of Cordova," who returned with great riches, from Guinea (?).

[82] See the section of this Introduction upon the Atlantic Islands, pp. lxxv-lxxvii. Edrisi's Maghrurin or Wanderers probably sailed from and returned to Lisbon before 1147, the date of the final Christian capture of that city, and touched the African mainland at a point over against Madeira.

[83] By one Ibn Fatimah, who was wrecked at Wad-Nun, a little North of Cape Non, put off in a sloop with some sailors, and at last came to a glittering white headland, from which they were warned off by some Berbers. They learned afterwards that it was one mass of deadly serpents. Thence turning North they landed and went inland to the salt market of Tagazza, and finally returned home.

[84] Cf. what is said about Prince Henry's correspondent, the merchant at Oran, p. xxvi of this Introduction.

[85] Various early Arab MSS., lately found by the French in Tombuttu ("Timbuktu"), especially the *Tarik-es-Sudan* of "Abderrahman ben Amr-Sadi-Tombukkti," according to Félix Dubois (*Tombouctou la Mystérieuse*), supply important rectifications of the standard accounts here; *e.g.* (1) Islam is found in the Western Sudan from the close of the ninth century. (2) The Songhay were converted in 1010; were for a time subject to the Kings of Melli; but gained freedom in 1355. (3) The Songhay took Timbuktu in 1469; and from this date, for more than a century, dominated all the West and Central Sudan from their capital at Gao. (4) Jenné, on the Upper Niger, was the furthest point westward of the original Songhay migration from Nubia. It was founded in 765; was converted to Islam in 1050, but "Pagan idols" were not completely rooted out till 1475. (5) Jenné was, in the Middle Ages, the greatest emporium of the Western Sudan, far outshining Timbuktu, which owed its foundation in part to Jenné. (6) Jenné was also a chief centre of Sudanese Islam. Its great Mosque, built in the eleventh century, partially destroyed in 1830, was the finest in all Negroland. (7) Its control of the salt and gold trade, as well as of most other branches of Sudanese merchandise, was such that it gave the name of Guinea to a vast region of West Africa, especially along the coast. (8) But Timbuktu, geographically, stood between Jenné and Barbary, and so between Jenné and Europe, and prevented Jenné from becoming famous in Christendom. (9) Jenné was connected primarily with a migration from East to West; Timbuktu, with a migration from North to South. (10) Timbuktu was founded [α] by the Tuareg, who owed their new energy in part to Moslem migrations from Spain, *c*. 1100 (1077 according to some authorities); [β], by merchants from Jenné, who made it an emporium in the twelfth century. (11) In the twelfth century, Walata, or Gana, in the great bend of the Niger [? dominated by Jenné] was the most prosperous commercial district of West Soudan; but in the thirteenth century the conquests of the Kings of Melli [placed by these authorities west-south-west of Timbuktu, to the north of the Upper Niger] disturbed the old trade-routes, and diverted commerce to Timbuktu; which, however, was never itself very populous, and served chiefly as a place of passage and commercial rendezvous. (12) From 1330 to 1434 the Kings of Melli were usually masters of Timbuktu, where they built a pyramid minaret for the chief mosque; but at least during some years of the fourteenth century, Timbuktu was conquered by an invasion from Mossi. (13) From 1434 to 1469, the Tuareg regained possession of Timbuktu, and drove out the Melinki; but in 1469 the Songhay took the town, and held it for more than 100 years. (14) In the fourteenth century the Kings of Melli built a great palace in Timbuktu, which did not disappear till the sixteenth century. (15) From the fourteenth century Timbuktu was the intellectual capital of the Sudan. This was due to the Spanish-Moorish influence. (16) The patron saint and doctor of Timbuktu, Sidi Yahia, was practically contemporary (1373-1462) with Prince Henry the Navigator. (17) The town of Kuku, Kuka or Kokia, in the W. Sudan, mentioned by mediæval Moslem travellers, was probably either a city on or near the Niger, immediately south of Gao, the Songhay capital; or else Gao itself, which is sometimes called Kuku or Gogo. Even this place was conquered by Melli, in the fourteenth century, which thus dominated part of the Central Sudan. The ruins of the great mosque at Gao still

commemorate Kunkur Musa, King of Melli, who built this house of prayer on his return from the Mecca pilgrimage, about 1325. See *Tarik-es-Sudan*, composed about 1656, and giving a history of the Sudan down to that year: the fragments remaining of the *Fatassi* of Mahmadu-Koti (1460-1554); *Nil-el-Ibtihaj bitatriz el-dibaj*, or Supplement to the Biographical Dictionary of Ibn-Ferhun by Ahmed Baba, 1556-1627.

[86] In his "Summary Discourse of the Manifold Religions in Africa," printed at the end of the Hakluyt Society's Edition of Pory's (1600) Translation of *Leo Africanus*, vol. iii, especially pp. 1018-1021.

[87] See Edrisi, Climate I, § i; Wappaüs, *Heinrich der Seefahrer*, pp. 65, etc.

[88] Similar language is used by Abulfeda, who calls it the seat of the King of Gana (whither come the western merchants of Segelmesa), situate on a Nile, twin-brother of the Egyptian, which flows into the Ocean; also by Ibn-al-Wardi, who calls Ghanah city one of the greatest in the land of the Blacks, placed on both sides of the Negro Nile, and resorted to for gold by merchants, twelve days' journey from Segelmesa. Edrisi (Climate I, section ii; ed. Jaubert, i, 16-18; also see i, 11, 13, 15, 19-20, 23, 106, 109, 173-4, 206, 272) is the most specific of all. "Ghanah the Great, made up of two towns on the banks of a sweet-water river ... the most populous and commercial city in Negroland. Merchants come there from all surrounding countries, and from the extremities of the West ... it was built in A.H. 510" (= A.D. 1116) (see also Leo Africanus, Hakluyt Soc. ed., pp. 124, 128, 822, 840).

[89] See Ibn-Batuta (Defrémery and Sanguinetti), iv, 395, 421-2; also Oppel, *Die religiöse Verhältnisse von Afrika*, Zeitschrift of Berlin Geog. Soc., xxii, 1887.

[90] See Otto Blau, *Chronik von Bornu*, p. 322, Z. D. M. G., vi, 1852.

[91] The more complete Islamising of Wadai, Darfur, and Baghirmi did not take place till the sixteenth and seventeenth centuries. See Slatin Pasha, *Fire and Sword in Soudan*, pp. 38-42; T. W. Arnold, *Preaching of Islam*, chs. iv, xi.

[92] Edrisi, Climate I, section iv; vol. i, p. 35 (Jaubert). See Duchesne, *Eglises Séparées*.

[93] *Ibn-Batuta*, iv, 396. (Defrémery and Sanguinetti).

[94] See *Alvarez*, Hakl. Soc. Edition, p. 352.

[95] Ruins?

[96] See Nerazzini, *Musulman Conquest of Ethiopia*, Rome 1891. (Ital. Transl. from Arab MS.).

[97] Africa.

[98] *Azurara*, c. vii.

[99] *Ibid.*, c. xvii.

[100] See Maqrīzī, *Histoire des Sultans Mamlouks de l'Egypte*, Quatremère, 1837-45, t. ii, Pt. 11, p. 183.

[101] Portugal.

[102] To find such a "Christian Lord" in the person of Prester John was said to have been one of the chief objects of D. Pedro's travels. This object Pedro avowed in Cairo; and with this, among other aims, he visited not only Egypt but Sinai and the Red Sea (see Martins, *Os Filhos*, pp. 83, 97, 121-2, etc., and pp. xvii-xviii of this volume).

[103] In 1076, the Church of Barbary could not provide three bishops to consecrate a new member of the Episcopate, and Gregory VII named two bishops to co-operate with the Archbishop of Carthage (See Migne, *Pat. Lat.*, cxlviii, p. 449; Mas Latrie, *Rélations de l'Afrique septentrionale avec les Nations chrétiennes au Moyen Age*, p. 226). In 1053, Leo IX declared that only five bishops could be found in North Africa (Migne, *P. L.*, cxliii, p. 728). On the thirty bishops of the tenth century, see Mas Latrie, *Ibid.* pp. 27-8. It is curious to find Gregory II, in *c.* 730, forbidding St. Boniface of Mainz to admit emigrants from North Africa to Holy Orders without inquiry (Migne, *P. L.*, lxxxix, p. 502)—a remarkable proof of mediæval emigration.

[104] See Mas Latrie, *Afrique Septentrionale, passim*, and especially pp. 61-2, 192, 266-7, 273.

[105] See C. Trumelet, *Les Saints de l'Islam* (1881), pp. xxviii-xxxvi. In this connection we may notice one or two other traces of intercourse between the Moslems of Granada and those of Africa, *e.g.* (1) Ibn-Batuta's mention of the tomb of the poet Abu Ishak es Sahili,

born in Granada, died and buried in Timbuktu, 1346. (2) Leo Africanus' notice of the stone mosque and palace in Timbuktu, the work of an architect from Granada in the fifteenth century. On Timbuktu, see Ibn Batuta (Def. and San.), iv, 395, 426, 430-2; Leo Afr. (Hakluyt Soc.), 4, 124, 128, 133-4, 146, 173, 255, 306, 798, 820, 822-4, 842.

[106] But in one view Tokrur is merely a generic name for the Sudan and Sudanese, and is only by mistake converted into a definite kingdom by Arab writers of second-rate authority.

[107] From the same he may have heard the tradition of Bakui's voyage in 1403, from the Maroccan coast to about the latitude of the Bight of Arguim, a parallel adventure to Ibn Fatimah's. See above, p. xliv.

[108] Raymond Lulli ["of Lull"] is thought by some to have made the first definite suggestion of this route in the central mediæval period. This "doctor illuminatus" was born at Palma in Majorca, 1235, became a Franciscan Tertiary in 1266, and died 1315. We may perhaps connect him with the very early school of portolano-draughtsmanship in the Balearics. See Map section of this Introduction.

[109] = Lancelote? See pp. lxxviii-lxxix.

[110] According to some authorities, 1281. See Giustiniani, *Castigatissimi Annali di Genova*, 1537, fol. cxi, verso. Giustiniani refers to Francesco Stabili, otherwise Cecco d'Ascoli, in his Commentary on the *De Sphaera Mundi* of Sacrobosco (John of Holywood, in Yorks, *c.* A.D. 1225). The year 1291 corresponds with the fall of Acre, and the consequent embarrassment of the Syrian overland routes to Inner Asia.

[111] At or near Cape Non, which, on the Pizzigani Map of 1367, is marked "Caput Finis Gozole."

[112] This statement, it has been conjectured, was intended for use in a "forthcoming globe or map." Uso di Mare's statement was first noticed by Gräberg af Hemsö. See Peschel, *Erdkunde*, p. 179 (Ed. of 1865); Major, *Henry Navigator*, 99-106 (Ed. of 1868), P. Amat di S. Filippo, *Studi biografici*, etc. (Ed. of 1882), i, p. 77, for recent studies on the general question of the Genoese Voyage of 1291, and Uso di Mare's letter. The earliest modern notice of the account of this voyage in the Public Annals of Genoa was by G. H. Pertz, in his memoir, "Der älteste Versuch zur Entdeckung des Seewegs nach Ostindien", offered to the Royal Academy of Sciences at Munich, March 28th, 1859 (*Festschrift*, Berlin, 1859). The Genoese Annals referred to are a continuation of the Chronicles of Caffaro. Muratori has printed an abstract of the narrative. See also Nordenskjöld, *Periplus* (1897), pp. 114, 116; *Nouvelles Annales des Voyages*(d'Avezac), vol. cviii, p. 47.

[113] In 1455?

[114] Nile.

[115] Thus it has been pointed out that two of Tedisio Doria's galleys were registered in a legal document of 1291, under the names of St. Antonio and Allegrancia, and that the name Allegranza, applied for some time to one of the Canaries, was perhaps derived from this ship. Either from this or from Malocello's venture of 1270, the islands of Lançarote and Maloxelo in the same group probably took their names. Lançarote was marked with the red cross of Genoa on most Portolani down to a late period of the sixteenth century.

[116] *I.e.*, Guinea.

[117] 10th August.

[118] See Papers presented to Archives of Genoa by Federico Federici, 1660. Reference discovered by Gräberg af Hemsö.

[119] The River of Gold.

[120] Yet, proceeds this record, the "river [of gold] is a league wide and deep enough for the largest ship. This is the Cape of the end ... of W. Africa."

[121] Nordenskjöld, *Periplus*, p. 114 (1897), gives a confirmation from experience. "There is hardly any doubt that the ship-drawing on the Atlas Catalan is in the main correct.... Even in my time, Norwegians went out fishing on Spitzbergen in large undecked boats, somewhat like that of Ferrer."

[122] Such as dealt in Guinea products, especially malaguette pepper, at Nismes, Marseilles, and Montpellier.

[123] "The Mine" of Hakluyt and early English geographers.

[124] See the MS. edited by Margry, and given in Major's Introduction to his *Life of Henry the Navigator*; the *Short History of the Navigation of Jean Prunaut of Rouen*; also *La Relation des Costes d'Afrique appelées Guinées*, by Sieur Villaut de Bellefond, Paris, 1669; L. Estancelin, *Recherches sur les voyages des navigateurs normands*, 1832; Père Labat, *Nouvelle rélation de l'Afrique Occidentale*, 1728; Pierre Margry, *Les Navigations Françaises du XIVme au XVIme siècle*, 1867. The French claim is fully admitted by Nordenskjöld, *Periplus*, 115-6 (1847), but of course vigorously denied by the Portuguese, whom Major supports.—*Henry Navigator*, Introduction, pp. xxiv-li, and text, pp. 117-133.

[125] Especially some of the ivory carvings said to have been made from spoils of this fourteenth-century trade.

[126] The "short history" of Prunaut's navigation assigns September, 1364, for the start of the first voyage; makes the sailors reach "Ovideg" at Christmas ("Ovidech" in Barros,*Decade I*, occurs as a native name for the Senegal); and tells us the anchorage was at C. "Bugiador," in "Guinoye." The blacks, called Jaloffs or Giloffs, had never seen white men before. Small presents were exchanged for "morphi" or ivory, skins, etc. Next year (?) Prunaut (called "Messire Jean of Rouen" throughout), returned with four ships and acquired land from the natives. Here he built houses for wares and habitation, and proposed to his men to settle there permanently. They agreed, but quarrels prevented the foundation of the colony. In September, 1379, Prunaut sailed again to Guinea with a very fine ship, *Notre Dame de bon Voyage*, but lost many men from sickness; he himself returned after Easter, 1380, with much gold. After this Prunaut was made a captain in the French navy. Next year (1381) the *Notre Dame* again went out with the *St. Nicholas* and*L'Espérance*, of Dieppe and Rouen. The first-named cast anchor at La Mine, where Prunaut built a chapel, a castle, a fortalice, and a square house, on a hill called the "Land of the Prunauts." Near this were Petit Dieppe, Petit Rouen, Petit Paris, Petit Germentrouville; French forts were also built at Cormentin and Acra. But from 1410 all this prosperity decayed; in eleven years only two ships went to the gold coast, and one to the Grande Siest; and soon after the wars in France destroyed this commerce altogether.

Villaut de Bellesfond, Estancelin, and Labat, narrate the same incidents as follows: Charles V encouraged commerce, so in November, 1364, the Dieppese fitted out two ships, of 100 tons each, for the Canaries. About Christmas they reached C. Verde, and anchored before Rio Fresco, which in 1669 was still called "Baie de France." Afterwards they went on to a place they called "Petit Dieppe," and the Portuguese "Rio Sestos," beyond Sierra Leone; for objects of small value they gained gold, ivory, and pepper; returning in 1365 they realised great wealth; and in September of the same year the merchants of Rouen joined with those of Dieppe to fit out four ships, two for trade between Cape Verde and Petit Dieppe, the other two for exploration of the coast beyond. One of these last stopped at Grand Sestere, on the Malaguette coast, and loaded pepper; the other ship traded on the Ivory Coast, and went on as far as the Gold Coast, and depôts were fixed at Petit Dieppe and Grand Sestere, which was re-named Petit Paris. Factories or "Loges" were established to prepare cargoes for the ships. The native languages long retained French words, as was found in 1660. In 1380 the Company sent out *Notre Dame de bon Voyage*, of 150 tons, from Rouen to the Gold Coast (September). At end of December they reached the same landing where the French had traded fifteen years before. In the summer of 1381 the *Notre Dame* returned to Dieppe richly laden; in 1382 three ships set sail together, September 28th, viz, *La Vierge, Le Saint Nicholas*,*L'Espérance*. *La Vierge* stopped at La Mine, the first place discovered on the Gold Coast. The *St. Nicholas* traded at Cape Corse and at Mouré below La Mine, and*L'Espérance* went as far as Akara, trading at Fanting, Sabon and Cormentin. Ten months after, the expedition returned with rich cargoes. Three more ships were sent out in 1383, one to go to Akara, the others to build an outpost at La Mine; there they left ten or twelve men, and returned after ten months. A church was afterwards built for the new colony, and in 1660 this still preserved the arms of France. After the accession of Charles VI, the African trade was soon ruined. Before 1410 La Mine was abandoned, and until after 1450 the Normans, it is believed, abandoned maritime explorations.

[127] See De Bry's *Collection des petits Voyages*, Frankfort, 1625; Oliver Dapper's*Description of Africa* (in Dutch), Amsterdam, 1668; Ramusio's *Collection*, Ed. of 1565,

iii. p. 417 *verso*, in the *Discorso sopra la Nuova Francia*; Dr. David Lewis' *Letter to Burleigh*, March 9, 1577. Santarem's *Priority of Portuguese Discoveries, etc.* (1842), is mainly directed against the French claims.

[128] Genoese.

[129] Venetian.

[130] Unless the contour of the Laurentian Map of 1351 is held to prove a circumnavigation of Africa shortly before 1351. The comparative accuracy of this outline, so incredibly good as mere guesswork, must remain one of the chief *cruces* of Mediæval geography.

[131] See the *Book of the Conquest and Conversion of the Canarians by Jean de Béthencourt*, written by Pierre Bontier, monk, and Jean le Verrier, priest. Edited for the Hakluyt Society by R. H. Major, 1872.

[132] See section of this Introduction on the African Islands, pp. lxxxii-lxxxiv.

[133] Buyetder on the Catalan Atlas of 1375.

[134] This is identified by Nordenskjöld, *Periplus* 79, following Espada, with the recently rediscovered *Libro del Conosçimiento de todos los reynos & tierras & señorios que son por el mundo & de las señales & armas que han cada tierra & señorio por sy & de los reyes & Señores que los proueen*. This was lost sight of till 1870, when it was found by Marcos Jimenez de la Espada, who published it in the *Boletin de la Sociedad Geographica de Madrid* 1877. "It is certainly not a record of actual travel, but probably the description of an imaginary journey, compiled with the help of a richly illustrated typical portolano, reports by far-famed and travelled men, and such geographical works as were accessible to the author. Many names here occurring are, however, not to be found on the portolanos of the fourteenth century.... Every city or country spoken of in the book has a chapter to itself, followed by a representation of the flag or arms of the State. These also seem ... taken from some portolano." See the *Conquest of the Canaries*(Hakluyt Soc. ed., ch. 55). The *Conosçimiento* cannot well be of later date than 1330-1340. In many places it copies Edrisi.

[135] Admitted by Nordenskjöld with singular facility: *Periplus*, pp. 115-6. As to the Portuguese sailor named Machico, and the possibility that the Machico district of Madeira was named after him or one of his descendants, see below, pp. lxxxiv-lxxxv.

[136] See Atlantic Islands.

[137] See Map section.

THE ATLANTIC ISLANDS.
I. BEFORE PRINCE HENRY.

The history of the exploration of the Azores, the Canaries, and the Madeira group, before Prince Henry's time, seems to deserve a special notice in this place.

[Pg lxxii]It is pretty certain that the Fortunate Islands of ancient geography were our Canaries. Eudoxus of Cyzicus was said to have discovered off the West African coast an uninhabited island, so well provided with wood and water, that he intended to return there and settle for the winter. According to Plutarch, Sertorius (B.C. 80-72) is said to have been told by some sailors whom he met at the mouth of the Baetis[138] of two islands[139] in the ocean, from which they had just arrived. These they called the "Atlantic Islands," and described as distant from the shore of Africa 10,000 stadia (1,000 miles), and enjoying a perpetual summer. Sertorius wished to fly from his war with the Romans in Spain, and take refuge in these islands, but his followers would not agree to this.[140]

Leaving out of serious consideration the Atlantis story in Plato's *Timaeus*(which may possibly owe something to early Phœnician and Carthaginian discoveries among the Atlantic islands), it is noticeable that no such Western Ocean lands occur in Strabo (B.C. 30). On the other hand the Canaries are described by Statius Sebosus, as reported in Pliny[141] (B.C. 30-A.D. 70), and by King Juba the younger of Mauretania (*fl.* B.C. 1); are laid down under the name of Fortunate Islands by Ptolemy; and are adopted in his reckonings as the Western limit [Pg lxxiii]of the world. Sebosus mentions Junonia, 750 miles from Gades; near this, Pluvialia and Capraria; and 1,000 miles from Gades, off the South-west coast of Mauretania or Marocco, the Fortunatae, Convallis or Invallis, and Planaria.

Juba[142] again makes five Fortunate Isles: Ombrios, Nivaria, Capraria, Junonia, and Canaria, all fertile but uninhabited. Large dogs were found, however, in the last-named, and two of these had been brought to Juba himself, who called the island after them. Date-palms also abounded. Juba also, according to Pliny, discovered the Purple islands (Purpurariae) off the coast of Mauretania, which have been carelessly identified by some with the Madeira group, though wanting the two essential conditions of Juba's description: (1) producing Orchil; (2) lying very close to the shore of Mauretania. Lançarote and Fuerteventura agree with Juba's conditions on these points,[143] but then why are they made a separate group from Nivaria, etc., which are undoubtedly [Pg lxxiv]the main body of the Canaries? Juba's account is the most clear and valuable we have from ancient geography, dealing with the Canaries, and is far better than that[144] of the Alexandrian geographer. Ptolemy lays down the Fortunate Islands—assuming the Canaries to be meant—incorrectly both in latitude and longitude, in a position really corresponding better to that of the Cape Verdes. Hence it has been supposed that he confounded the two groups in one; whereas the Cape Verdes, lying out to sea 300 miles from the Continent, are not likely to have been known, even in his day. An error in position is so common with Ptolemy that it is quite unnecessary to be disturbed by it. But he clearly had some definite knowledge that islands existed in the ocean to the west of Africa, and in his map he probably reproduces the statements of others, without first-hand information of his own, assigning such a position as suited best with his theories. For he not merely brings the southernmost of the Fortunate Isles down to 11° N. lat., but scatters the group through 5° of latitude, placing the northernmost in latitude, 16° N. His names vary much from Juba's, for he gives us six: Canaria, the Isle of Juno, Pluïtala,[145] Aprositus (the Inaccessible), Caspiria, and Pinturia or Centuria; at the [Pg lxxv]western extremity of these, after the example of Marinus, he drew the first meridian of longitude.[146]

The Arabs seem to have lost all definite knowledge of the Atlantic islands, an impossible possession to a race with such a deep horror of the Green Sea of Darkness. Masudi, indeed, tells us a story, already noticed, of one Khoshkhash, the young man of Cordova, who some years before the writer's time[147] had sailed off upon the Ocean, and after a long interval returned with a rich cargo; but nothing more definite is said about this venture.

Some tradition of the Canaries or the Madeira group seems to have been preserved among Moslem geographers, under the name of Isles of Khaledat, or Khaledad, but we have only one narrative from the collections of these authors which suggests a Musulman visit to the same. This is found in Edrisi, in its earlier form, and must refer to some time before 1147, when Lisbon finally became a Christian city. It probably belongs to a year of the eleventh century, and has perhaps left its impression in the Brandan legend as put forth in the oldest MS., of about 1070.

The Lisbon Wanderers, or Maghrurin, from Moslem Spain, commemorated by Edrisi and by Ibn-al-Wardi, [Pg lxxvi]did not apparently venture to the South of Cape Non, but they seem to have reached the Madeira group as well as the Canaries. The adventurers were eight in number, all related to one another. After eleven days' sail, apparently from Lisbon, they found themselves in a sea due[148] West of Spain, where the waters were thick, of bad smell, and moved by strong currents.[149] Here the weather became as black as pitch. Fearing for their lives they now turned South, and after twelve days sighted an island which they called El Ghanam, the Isle of Cattle,[150] from the sheep they saw there without any shepherd. The flesh of these cattle was too bitter for eating, but they found a stream of running water and some wild figs. Twelve more days to the South brought them to an island[151] with houses and cultivated fields. Here they were seized, and carried prisoners to a city on the sea-shore. After three days the King's interpreter, who spoke Arabic, came to them, and asked them who they were and what they wanted. They replied, they were seeking the wonders of the Ocean and its limits. At this the King laughed, and said: "My father once ordered some of his slaves to venture upon that sea, and after sailing it for a month, they found themselves deprived of sun-light and returned without any result." The [Pg lxxvii]Wanderers were kept in prison till a west wind arose, when they were blindfolded and turned off in a boat. After three days they reached Africa. They were put ashore, their hands tied, and left. They were released by the Berbers,[152] and returned to Spain, when a "street at the foot of the hot bath in Lisbon took the name of 'Street of the Wanderers.'"

El Ghanam has been identified by Avezac and others with Legname, the old Italian name for Madeira, and their description of the "bitter mutton" of that island has suggested to some the "coquerel" plant of the Canaries, which in more recent times gave a similar flavour to the meat of the animals who browsed upon it.[153]

Some have conjectured that the "White Man's Land" and "Great Ireland," which the Norsemen of Iceland professed to have seen in 983-4, 999, and 1029, was a name for the Canaries, rather than for any point of America, but this appears entirely conjectural—though it is probable enough that some of the Vikings in their wanderings may have visited these islands. In 1108-9, King Sigurd of Norway meets a Viking fleet in the Straits of Gibraltar [Pg lxxviii]("Norva Sound");[154]and in the course of their many attacks on the "Bluemen" or Moors of "Serkland" (Saracen-land) the Northern rovers who reached the New World, Greenland, and the White Sea, may well have sighted and ravaged the Fortunate Islands of the Atlantic, beyond Cape Non.

No further reference, even conjectural, to the Atlantic Islands is known until the later thirteenth century, when the Mediæval revival in Christian lands, finding its expression in the Crusades and in the Asiatic land-travels of John de Plano Carpini, Simon de St. Quentin, Rubruquis, and the Polos, among others, led to attempts in search of a maritime route to India from the Mediterranean ports. The earliest of these followed immediately on the return of the elder Polos from Central Asia (1269).

In 1270 the voyage of the Genoese, Lancelot Malocello, already referred to as a possible reconnaissance on the African coast route to the Far East, resulted in a re-discovery of some of the Canaries. At any rate, he stayed[155] long enough to build himself a "castle" there; and the recognition of this island, as well as of the adjoining "Maloxelo," as Genoese on maps of the fourteenth, fifteenth, and sixteenth centuries,[156] was probably due to this. [Pg lxxix]During Béthencourt's "Conquest," some of the followers of his colleague, Gadifer de la Salle, stored barley, we are told, in an old castle which had been built by Lancelot Maloisel. It has been supposed that Petrarch, writing c. 1335 A.D., and referring to the armed Genoese fleet which had penetrated to the Canaries a generation before (*a Patrum memoria*), was thinking of Malocello's venture, but the expression is better suited to the Expedition of 1291, led by Tedisio Doria and the Vivaldi.

It is possible that the Portuguese followed up Malocello's visit by voyages of their own (besides the well-known venture of 1341) before the year 1344,[157]when Don Luis of Spain obtained a grant of the Canaries from the Pope[158] at Avignon (November 15, 1344). This grant conferred on Luis de la Cerda, Count of Talmond, the title of Prince of Fortune, with the lordship of the [Pg lxxx]Fortunate Islands, in fief to the Apostolic See, and under a tribute of 400 gold florins, to be paid yearly to the Chair of St. Peter. The Pontiff also wrote to various sovereigns, among others to the King of Portugal, Affonso IV, recommending the plans of Don Luis to their support. To this Affonso replied (February 12, 1345), reminding the Pope that he had already sent expeditions to the Canaries, and would even now be despatching a greater Armada if it were not for his wars with Castille and with the Saracens.

As early as 1317, King Denis of Portugal secured the Genoese, Emmanuele Pezagno (Pessanha), as hereditary admiral of his fleet. Pezagno and his successors were to keep the Portuguese navy supplied with twenty Genoese captains experienced in navigation and the earliest Portuguese ventures were almost certainly connected with this arrangement.

This was shown in the expedition of 1341, which left Portugal for the Canaries under Genoese pilotage, and quite independently of Don Luis, as far as we know. It was composed of two vessels furnished by the King of Portugal, and a smaller ship, all well-armed, and manned by Florentines, Genoese, Castilians, Portuguese, and "other Spaniards."[159] [Pg lxxxi]They set out from Lisbon on July 1, 1341; on the fifth(?) day they discovered land; and in November they returned. They brought home with them four natives, many goat and seal skins, dye-wood, bark for staining, red earth, etc. Nicoloso de Recco, a Genoese, pilot of the expedition, considered these islands nearly 900 miles distant from Seville. The first[160] discovered was supposed to be about 150 miles round; it was barren and stony, inhabited by goats and other animals, as well as by naked people, absolutely savage. The next[161] visited was larger than the former, and contained many natives, most of them nearly naked, but some covered with goats' skins. The people had a chief, built houses, planted palms and fig trees, and cultivated little gardens with vegetables. Four men swam out to the ships, and were carried off. The Europeans found on the island a sort of temple, with a stone idol, which was brought back to Lisbon.

From this island several others were visible—one remarkable for its lofty trees,[162] another containing excellent wood and water, wild pigeons, falcons, and birds of prey.[163] In the fifth visited were immense rocky mountains reaching into the clouds.[164] Eight other islands were sighted. In all, five of the new-found [Pg lxxxii]lands were peopled, the rest not. None of the natives had any boats, and there was no good store of harbours. On one island was a mountain, which they reckoned as 30,000 feet high, and on its summit a fortress-like rock, with a mast atop of it rigged with a yard and lateen sail—a manifest proof of enchantment. No wealth was found in any of the islands, and hence perhaps the venture of 1341 was not followed up by Portugal for many years; but it is probable that the results of this year are commemorated in the delineation of the Fortunate Isles upon the Laurentian Portolano of 1351.[165]

Nothing, so far as we know, was done for the further exploration of the Canaries (after 1341) till 1382, when one Captain Francisco Lopez, while on his way from Seville to Galicia, was driven south by storms, and took refuge (June 5th) at the mouth of the Guiniguada, in Grand Canary. Here he landed with twelve of his comrades; the strangers were kindly treated, and passed seven years among the natives, instructing many in the doctrines of Christianity. Suddenly Lopez and his men were accused of sending into Christian countries a "bad account" of the islands, and were all massacred. Before dying, they seem to have given one of their converts a written "testament," and this was found by the men of Jean de Béthencourt in 1402.

Apparently, very shortly before the invasion of [Pg lxxxiii]the latter (? in 1390-5), another Spaniard, Alvaro Becarra, visited the islands,[166] and it was (according to one authority) from information directly supplied by him and two French adventurers who accompanied him, that De Béthencourt was induced to undertake his expedition.

The Lord of Grainville set out with a body of followers, among whom the knight Gadifer de la Salle was chief, from Rochelle, on May 1st, 1402. Eight days' sail from Cadiz, he reached Graciosa. Thence he went to Lançarote, where he built a fort called Rubicon. Going on to Fuerteventura, he was hampered by a mutiny among his men, and by lack of supplies. He returned to Spain, procured from Henry III of Castille what he needed, and reappeared at Lançarote. During his absence, Gadifer, left in command, accomplished a partial exploration of Fuerteventura, Grand Canary, Ferro, Gomera and Palma. The "King" of Lançarote was baptised on February 20th, 1404; but after this, Gadifer quarrelled with his leader and returned to France. All attempts to conquer the Pagans of Grand Canary were fruitless, and De Béthencourt finally quitted the islands, appointing his nephew Maciot[167] to be governor in his place of the four [Pg lxxxiv]Christian colonies in Palma and Ferro, Lançarote and Fuerteventura.

The Madeira group are laid down[168] in the *Conosçimiento de todos los Reynos* of the early fourteenth century, as well as in the Laurentian Portolano of 1351; in the Soleri Portolani of 1380 and 1385; and in the Combitis Portolan of about 1410. But in 1555,[169] A. Galvano, in his *Discoveries of the World*, claimed that an Englishman in the reign of Edward III(?) was the discoverer. He was copied by Hakluyt in 1589, and English patriotism has been loath to surrender the tradition.

"About this time," says Galvano [viz., between 1344 and 1395, the two dates named immediately before and after this entry], the "island of Madeira was discovered by ... [Robert] Macham,[170] who sailing from England, having run away with a [Pg lxxxv]woman,[171] was driven by a tempest ... to that island, and cast ashore in that haven, which is now called Machico, after ... Macham." Here the ship was driven from its moorings; and, according to one account[172] both lovers died; according to the older version, Macham escaped to the African mainland, and was finally saved and brought to the King of Castile. His old pilot, Morales, was supposed to have guided J. G. Zarco in Prince Henry's rediscovery of Madeira (1420). Azurara, however, says nothing about Macham; and it has been conjectured, from a document rediscovered in 1894, that the Machico district of Madeira—whose title, given by the Portuguese in 1420, has often been quoted as an acknowledgement of Macham's claim—

derived its name from a Portuguese seaman of that name, who was living in 1379, or from one of his relations.[173]

The Azores, or Western Islands, are also (in part) laid down in the *Conosçimiento* above quoted (of about A.D. 1330), and in the Medicean Portolano of [Pg lxxxvi]1351;[174] and when the Infant sent out Gonçalo Cabral[175] in this direction he was aided, it is said, by an Italian portolano, on which the aforesaid islands were depicted.[176] But no record of any voyage thereto earlier than that of Diego de Sevill[177] (1427) has been preserved; nor did any one before the Prince's time attempt, as far as is known, the colonisation or complete exploration of the Azores. To these, however, like the other Atlantic [Pg lxxxvii]islands, Nordenskjöld's emphatic words[178] apply, as the cartographical evidence requires. To some extent at least all these groups "were known ... to skippers long before organised ... expeditions were sent to them by great feudal lords." Absolute novelty in geographical discovery is one of the most difficult things to prove, and in no field of historical inquiry does the saying more often occur to the inquirer: "Vixere fortes ante Agamemnona, multi."

The Cape Verdes is the only group of Atlantic Islands as to which we may be reasonably sure that the mediæval discovery at least was not made before Prince Henry's lifetime. Here the Infant's claim of priority is probably most in danger from Phœnician and Carthaginian sailors;[179] but even here the challenge is not very serious, unless we insist on considering as proven a number of pretensions which are almost impossible to substantiate.

[138] Guadalquivir.
[139] Madeira and Porto Santo(?)
[140] Plutarch, *Sertorius*, c. 8.
[141] Pliny, *Hist. Nat.*, vi, 32.
[142] Copied by Solinus and many mediæval writers (see Pliny, *Hist. Nat.*, vi, 31). Juba's work was dedicated to Caius Cæsar, B.C. 1, when just about to start on an expedition to the East. Ombrios, from its mountain lake, has been identified with Palma; Nivaria more easily with Teneriffe and Canaria with Grand Canary; Junonia is difficult to fix, as we have the statement that a second and smaller island of the same name is in its neighbourhood; Capraria is supposed to be Ferro. The remaining two of our modern archipelago, Lancarote and Fuerteventura, are supposed by some to be the "Purpurariae" of Juba.
[143] And are therefore accepted as the Purpurariae by D'Anville Gossellin, Major, and, with some hesitation, by Bunbury.
[144] "A mere confused jumble of different reports." Bunbury, *Anc. Geog.* ii, 202.
[145] Perhaps a corruption of Sebosus' Pluvialia. "The Inaccessible" is possibly Teneriffe. Canaria and the Isle of Juno are of course identical with Juba's nomenclature.
[146] Cerne, so important a mark in Hanno's *Periplus*, he places in the Ocean 3° from the mainland, in clear opposition to the Carthaginian authorities whom some have thought he possessed and used. Cerne is in latitude 25° 40', and east longitude 5° on Ptolemy's map.
[147] *C.* A.D. 950.
[148] They started with a full east wind.
[149] Sargasso Sea?
[150] Madeira?
[151] One of the Canaries?
[152] At a point named Asafi or Safi (at the extreme south-west of our Marocco), said to have been named after the Wanderers' exclamation of dismay: Wa Asafi—"Alas! my sorrow." Cf. Edrisi, Climate III, section i (ed. Jaubert, i, 201); Climate IV, section i (J., ii, 26-9). Safi is in 32° 20' N. Lat.
[153] See Berthelot, *Histoire Naturelle des Iles Canariens*.
[154] "Saga of King Sigurd" (in *Heimskringla*), ch. vi.
[155] In Lançarote island?
[156] Cf. especially the *Conosçimiento* of early fourteenth century; the Laurentian Portolano of 1351; the Soleri Portolani of 1380 and 1385; the Combitis Portolan of early fifteenth century; the so-called Bianco of 1436. On a Genoese map of 1455, executed by Bartholomew Pareto, is a more explicit legend over against Lançarote Island: "Lansaroto Maroxello Januensis." See also the *Conquest of ... Canaries*, by De Béthencourt's chaplains, ch. xxxii; and Major's note, pp. 55-6 of the Hakluyt Society's edition of this Chronicle.

[157] Ships from Portugal (according to Sántarem, *Cosmographie*, i, 275, copied by Oliveira Martins, *Filhos de D. João*, i, 68), visited the Canaries under Affonso IV, between *1331* and 1344. Perhaps this is only a loose reference to the expedition of 1341.

[158] Clement VI. Major, *Prince Henry*, 140, and *Conquest of Canaries* (Hakluyt Soc.), xi, has apparently confused matters, giving the date of 1334 (in the Pontificate of Benedict XII), and implying a grant by Clement VI.

[159] The account that has come down to us is by Boccaccio(?) (discovered in 1827 by Sebastiano Ciampi, who identified the handwriting), and was professedly compiled from letters written to Florence by certain Florentine merchants residing in Seville. Among these, "Angelino del Tegghia dei Corbizzi, a cousin of the sons of Gherardino Gianni," is especially mentioned.

[160] Major conjectures Fuerteventura.

[161] Grand Canary?

[162] Major here suggests the pines of Ferro.

[163] Gomera?

[164] Probably Teneriffe. Palma has also been suggested, with less likelihood.

[165] See the section of this Introduction on "Maps and Scientific Geography;" also Wappäus, *Heinrich der Seefahrer*, pp. 174-5.

[166] Ayala, *Chronicle of Henry III of Castille*, asserts that in 1393, mariners of Biscay, Guipuzcoa, and Seville, visited the Canaries, and brought back spoils. Teneriffe they called the Isle of Hell (Inferno), from its volcano. They also landed on other islands of the group which they called Lencastre, Graciosa, Forteventura, Palma, and Ferro. See also Martins, *Os Filhos de D. João I*, p. 68.

[167] See Azurara, *Guinea*, c. xcv, lxxix, etc.

[168] Under the names of Lecmane, Lolegname, Legnami [Madeira, the "Isle of Wood"]; Puerto or Porto Santo; and I. desierta, deserte, or deserta. The last alone is wanting in the Combitis Portolan.

[169] Still earlier in 1508, Valentin Fernandez, a printer of Munich, issued the story in a MS., re-discovered in this century. Later, in 1660, Francisco Manoel de Mello published it in his *Epanaphoras de Varia Historia Portuguesa (III)*, Lisbon, 1660. Mello's account was professedly derived from an original narrative by Francisco Alcaforado, a squire of Prince Henry, now lost. Fernandez, Galvano, (copied by Hakluyt) and Mello, all tell practically the same story, but with varying details.

[170] Or Machin, or O'Machin, or as Nordenskjöld, *Periplus*, 115, also reads: Mac Kean. N. accepts the whole of the Macham story with extraordinary readiness.

[171] Anne d'Arfet, or Dorset.

[172] Mello's.

[173] See J. I. de Brito Rebello, in Supplement to *Diario de Noticias* of Lisbon, published in connection with the fifth centenary of Prince Henry's birth, 1894. The document referring to Machico is dated April 12th, 1379, and by this, King Ferdinand, "the handsome," of Portugal, gives to one Machico, "mestre de sua barcha," a house in the Rua Nova of Lisbon. This was discovered by Rebello in the Torre do Tombo, acting on a hint given by Ernesto do Canton. Before this, the Macham story was attacked by Rodriguez d'Azevedo, in 1873. See the *Saudades da terra* of Dr. G. Fructuoso, pp. 348-429.

[174] It is not at all certain, as Major assumes (*Prince Henry*, 1868, p. 235), that this group was first discovered by "*Portuguese*" vessels under Genoese pilotage."

[175] In 1431, etc.

[176] See Nordenskjöld, *Periplus*, 118 A; also P. Amat di S. Filippo, *I veri Scopritori delle isole Azore*, Ital. Geog. Soc. Bolletino, 1892.

[177] We learn about the voyage of Sevill from the Catalan Map of Gabriel Valsecca, executed between 1434 and 1439, which (1) gives a very fair representation of several of the Azores, under the names: Ylla de Oesels (St. Mary), Ylla de Fruydols (St. Michael), Ylla de Inferno (Terceira), Ylla de Guatrilla (St. George), Ylla de Sperto (Pico), and another of which the name has been effaced: (2) Bears the inscription: These islands were found by Diego de Sevill, pilot of the King of Portugal, in 1427. [Some have tried to read the MS. date as 1432 (xxxii for xxvii) but the text is against them]. In the Mediceum, or Laurentian Portolano, of

1351, St. Mary and St. Michael are laid down as Insule de Cabrera; St. George, Fayal, and Pico, as Insule de Ventura sive de Columbis; Terceira (?) as Insula de Brazi[l]. On the Catalan Map of 1375, we have San Zorzo (= St. George, "Jorge"); I. de la Ventura (= Fayal); Li Columbi (= Pico); I. di Corvi Marini (= Corvo); Li Conigi (= Flores). On the so-called Andrea Bianco of 1436 (probably a re-edition of a much earlier map), St. Michael appears as Cabrera. Corvo and Flores first appear on the Catalan Atlas of 1375, as far as present knowledge goes.

[178] *Periplus*, 116 A.

[179] It is probable that the "Gorgades" of the Greeks were derived from Phœnician accounts; but it is very doubtful whether these represent the Cape Verdes. Ptolemy, as we have seen, places the southern extremity of his Fortunate Isles much in the true position of Santiago, though extending them north through 5 degrees of latitude.

2.—THE ATLANTIC ISLANDS
IN PRINCE HENRY'S LIFETIME.

Azurara also requires some words of supplement as to the progress of discovery and colonisation [Pg lxxxviii]among the Atlantic Islands in Prince Henry's lifetime.[180] And, first, in the Azores. After the first voyages of Diego de Sevill and Gonçalo Cabral, the latter (according to Cordeiro) sought unsuccessfully for an island which had been sighted by a runaway slave from the highest mountain in St. Mary; at last, corrected by the Prince's map-studies, he found the object of his search on the 8th May, 1444, and named it St. Michael, being the festival of the Apparition of the Archangel.[181] The colonisation of this (even more than of other islands in the group) was impeded by earthquakes, but was nevertheless commenced on September 29, 1445. From the number of hawks or kites[182]found in St. Michael and St. Mary, the present name now began to supersede all others[183] for the Archipelago. The island now called Terceira,[184] but originally "The Isle of Jesus Christ," was apparently discovered before A.D.1450, either by Prince Henry's sailors, or by an expedition of [Pg lxxxix]Flemish mariners or colonists under one Josua van der Berge, a citizen of Bruges, who claimed the exclusive, honour of this achievement under date of 1445. Hence, in some Netherland maps and atlases, of later date, the Azores are called The Flemish Islands.[185] On the other hand, Cordeiro has printed the Infant's charter of March 2, 1450, to Jacques de Bruges,[186] his servant, giving him the Captaincy of the Isle of Jesu Christ, because the said Jacques had asked permission of the Prince to colonise this uninhabited spot. Jacques de Bruges bore all the expenses of this colonisation, and may have been specially recommended to Henry by his sister, the Duchess of Burgundy. He had married into a noble Portuguese family, and had previously rendered some services to the Infant.

Graciosa was colonised by Vasco Gil Sodré, a Portuguese, who had been under Prince Henry's orders to Africa, and at first intended to join in the settlement of Terceira, but afterwards passed over to Graciosa. The captaincy of this island he divided for some time with his brother-in-law, Duarte Barreto.

San Jorge received its first inhabitants through a venture of Willem van der Haagen,[187] one of Jacques [Pg xc]de Bruges' companions: Van der Haagen brought two shiploads of people and plant from Flanders, but afterwards abandoned the city he had founded there, and transferred himself to the more fertile island of Fayal. The last name brings us to one of the controversial points in the early history of the Azores.

According to the received account, Fayal was first settled by a Fleming noble, Jobst Van Heurter,[188] Lord of Moerkerke, father-in-law of Martin Behaim, who commemorated this event in a legend on his globe of 1492. The famous Nuremberger declares that the Azores were colonised in 1466, after they had been *granted by the King of Portugal to his sister, Isabel, Duchess of Burgundy*; that in 1490 Job de Huerter came out to settle with "some thousands of souls," the Duchess "*having granted these islands to him and his descendants*," that in 1431, *when Prince Pedro was Regent,* Prince Henry sent out two vessels for two years' sail beyond Finisterre, and sailing west 500 leagues, they found these *ten* uninhabited islands; that they called them Azores from the tame birds they found there; and that the King began to settle the islands with "domestic animals" in 1432. This account is full of inaccuracies, and from the documents,[189] [Pg xci]noticed by Father Cordeiro, by Barros, and by the*Archivo dos Açores*, it appears probable that the grant of Fayal to Jobst van Heurter as first Captain

Donatory was made after Prince Henry's death, perhaps in 1466, by Henry's successor, D. Ferdinand, at the request of the Duchess of Burgundy, and that this grant was confirmed by the Crown of Portugal; which, however, retained its sovereign rights over all the Azores, and did not part with them to the Duchess or anyone else.

Jobst van Heurter, some time after he had obtained the grant or sub-lease of Fayal, appears also to have become Captain Donatory of Pico, with a commission to colonise this island.

Flores and Corvo were first granted, as far as our records go, to a lady of Lisbon, Maria de Vilhena, [Pg xcii]likewise after the death of Prince Henry. It is said that Van der Haagen,[190] when he moved from S. Jorge to Fayal, did so at the invitation of Jobst van Heurter, who had been there four years, and now promised him a part of the island. The two quarrelled, however, and "Silveira" left Fayal and went to Terceira. Some time after this he visited Flanders, and returning to the Azores by way of Lisbon, became the guest of D. Vilhena, who had received a grant of Flores and Corvo. She now proposed to Van der Haagen that he should colonise and govern these islands for her, which he did for seven years.

* * * * *

Next, as to the Cape Verde islands. There is no positive ground for supposing that any Europeans discovered or colonised these before Prince Henry. The ancient Gorgades, Hesperides, and so forth have been identified with them by some, but all this remains in the state of guess-work—guess-work which has no great probability behind it.

But as to the discovery of the Cape Verdes in the Infant's lifetime, a controversy exists between the claims of Cadamosto and Diego Gomez, which must be shortly noticed. It is happily beyond controversy that five at least of the Archipelago were discovered within the Prince's own "period," as their names occur in a document of December 3, 1460, hereafter noticed.

[Pg xciii]Cadamosto's claim to the discovery of the Cape Verde islands has been denied[191] on the following grounds:

1. A mariner sailing from Lagos in early May could not anchor at Santiago on SS. Philip and James' day (May 1st), as stated by Cadamosto.

2. Cadamosto drove three days before the wind from Cape Blanco W.N.W. to Bonavista. But this lies 100 miles S.W. of Cape Blanco.

3. Cadamosto claims to have seen Santiago from Bonavista, which is impossible.

4. Cadamosto is wrong in speaking of any river in Santiago as a "bow-shot wide," or of salt and turtles as found in the island.

To this it has been replied:

1. The first point is probably founded on a misprint. As a correction, d'Avezac[192] has suggested that Santiago was so called because the expedition *set out* on May 1st. It has also been noticed that the German and French versions of Cadamosto's Italian text (which contains this mistake) give March and not May as the month of sailing, while the translation in Temporal's *Histoire de l'Afrique* has July. Once more the festival of St. James (July 25th) has been suggested,[193] in exchange for that of [Pg xciv]SS. Philip and James. In support of this, the most likely alternative to a simple blunder, caused by haste, carelessness, and lapse of time, it is pointed out that Cadamosto seems to have arrived at the islands during the rainy season; that this season prevails from mid-June to November; and that the festival of St. James would agree with the time required for a voyage from Lagos, even if commencing not in March or May, but as late as the beginning of July.

This date is apparently confirmed by the earliest known official document which relates to the Cape Verde Islands, viz., a decree, dated December 3rd, 1460, issued just after the death of Prince Henry.[194] In this is given a list of seventeen islands discovered by the Infant's explorers, beginning with the Madeiras and Azores, and ending with five of the Cape Verdes, S. Jacobe (Santiago), S. Filippe (Fogo), De las Mayaes (Maio), Ilha Lana (Sal?), and S. Christovão (probably Bonavista). The only festival of St. Christopher in the Calendar falls on the day of St. James, or July 25th. We may notice that in the earliest map containing these islands,[195] Cadamosto's name of Bonavista prevails, as now, over "St. Christopher."

2. This charge seems founded on a mistranslation. In the original text of 1507, after a description of the process of putting out to sea from Cape Blanco, [Pg xcv]we have these words:[196] "and the following night there arose a strong wind from the south-west, and in order not to turn back we steered west and north-west ... so as to weather and hug the wind for two days and three nights." That is, the contrary wind met with after leaving Cape Blanco did not turn the ships back, as they managed to sail close to it.[197]

It is probable, however, that the text is corrupt, and it is only too common in records of this time to have mistakes as to points of the compass creeping into the record of voyages performed some time before. In any case, it is surely not enough to upset the whole of Cadamosto's narrative.

3. Here Cadamosto seems to have made no mistake, in his first printed text of 1507. The islands have never been properly surveyed, but Prof. C. Doelter, in his work *Ueber die Kapverden nach dem Rio Grande* (1884), speaks of seeing Bonavista from the Pico d'Antonio on Santiago, together with all the rest of the group, even the more distant Sal and St. Vincent. It is therefore quite probable that Cadamosto's [Pg xcvi]sailors did see Santiago from Bonavista, and this feat was certainly possible.

4. In this once more Cadamosto is clearly right, and the attempt to discredit him ridiculous. Salt is so abundant in the Cape Verdes, especially in the western group, that these were at one time called the "Salt islands." Turtles are also common enough in the rainy season, and are mentioned by plenty of visitors and residents.[198] Lastly, the river in Santiago, "a bow-shot across," does not correspond to any fresh-water stream found there, but by this expression may be intended an inlet of the sea, like the Rio d'Ouro of Prince Henry's sailors, north of Arguim. Curiously enough, this very expression—"a bow-shot wide"—is employed by Dapper of the Estuary at Ribeira Grande in Santiago; while Blaeuw's *Atlas* (Amsterdam, 1663) speaks of the same point in exactly similar terms: "à son embouchure large d'environ un trait d'arc."

* * * * *

Thirdly, the attempts of Prince Henry to acquire possession of the Canaries for Portugal may be noticed. In 1414, Maciot de Béthencourt, nephew and heir of the famous John, "Jean le Conquérant," having, under threat of war from Castille, ceded the islands to Pedro Barba de Campos, Lord of Castro Forte, sailed away to Madeira; and in 1418, according to some authorities, he made a sale of the "Fortunatae" to Henry of Portugal. This was [Pg xcvii]not enough for him, as afterwards he made a third bargain with the Count of Niebla; while meantime Jean de Béthencourt himself left his conquests by will to his brother Reynaud. Pedro Barba de Campos soon parted with his new rights, which passed successively to Fernando Perez of Seville, and the Count of Niebla. But the latter, though now uniting in himself all Spanish claims to the islands, did not cling to them, but made over everything to Guillem de las Casas, who passed on his rights to Fernam Peraza, his son-in-law. While this transference was going on in Castille and in France, Henry, in the name of Portugal, attempted in 1424 to settle the question by sending out a fleet under Fernando de Castro, with 2,500 foot and 120 horse. With this force he would probably have conquered the Archipelago, in spite of the costliness and trouble of the undertaking, if the protests of Castille had not led King John I to discourage the scheme and persuade his son to defer its execution.

In 1445,[199] seven of the Prince's caravels visited the islands, received the submission of the chiefs Bruco and Piste in Gomera (who had already experienced the Infant's hospitality and become his "grateful servitors"), and made slave-raids upon the islanders of Palma. Alvaro Gonçalvez de Atayde, João de Castilha, Alvaro Dornellas, Affonso Marta, and the page Diego Gonçalvez, with many others, [Pg xcviii]took part in this descent, which did not altogether spare the friendly Gomerans, and brought on the perpetrators the severe rebuke of Prince Henry.

In 1446, however, he followed up the reconnaissance of 1445 by another attempt at complete conquest, which also seems to have ended in failure, though the account that remains is very inadequate; perhaps in the future it may be supplemented from the disinterred treasures of Spanish documentary collections. We only know that Henry obtained, in 1446, from the Regent D. Pedro a charter, giving him the exclusive right to sanction or forbid all Portuguese voyages to the Canaries; that in 1447 he conferred the captaincy of Lançarote on Antam Gonçalvez,[200] and that Gonçalvez sailed to establish himself there. So far, according to Azurara; Barros and the Spanish historians would antedate all these measures of 1446-7 by several years. In 1455 Cadamosto, sailing in the Portuguese service, visited and described the islands, and in 1466 Henry's heir, D. Fernando, made one more attempt to reclaim the Canaries for Portugal. It failed, and in 1479 the islands were finally adjudged to Spain, or the now united monarchy of Castille and Aragon.

* * * * *

Fourthly, in the Madeira group, colonisation made progress during the Infant's lifetime. After the discoveries of 1418-20,[201] Madeira itself was divided up[Pg xcix]under the feudal lordship of John Gonçalvez Zarco and Tristam Vaz Teixeira; the former receiving the captaincy of the northern half with Machico for his chief settlement; the latter obtaining the southern portion, with Funchal as capital, and the Desertas as an annexe. From the language of the Infant's Charter[202] of September 18th, 1460, this settlement appears to have taken place in 1425, when the Prince was 35 years old.

According to Gaspar Fructuoso, Zarco, in clearing a path through the forests of Madeira, set the woodland on fire, and seven years elapsed before the last traces of the conflagration were extinguished. The seven years is, no doubt, an extra touch; but a fire of tremendous severity must have taken place, from Cadamosto's account.[203] The whole island, he declares, had once been in flames; the colonists only saved their lives by plunging into the torrents; and Zarco himself had to stand in a river-bed for two whole days and nights, with all his family. Yet, according [Pg c]to Azurara, so much wood was soon exported from the island to Portugal, that a change was produced in the housebuilding of Spain: loftier dwellings were built; and the Roman or Arab style was superseded by one originating in the new discoveries among the Atlantic Islands. Almost all Portugal, Cadamosto tells us in 1455, was now adorned with tables[204] and other furniture made from the wood of Madeira.

In the settlement of Porto Santo, Bartholemew Perestrello, a gentleman of the household of Prince Henry's brother, the Infant John, took part[205] with Zarco and Vaz. Perestrello imported rabbits, which destroyed all the colonists' experiments in crops and vegetable planting; but receiving the captaincy of the island, he made some profit from breeding goats and exporting dragon's blood. His grant of Porto Santo, originally for his lifetime only, was extended by decree of November 1st, 1446, to a donation in perpetuity for himself and his descendants. On the death of Bartholemew, Prince Henry bestowed the captaincy on his son-in-law, Pedro Correa da Cunha, in trust for the first Governor's son Bartholemew, who was still a minor. Da Cunha later contracted with young Bartholemew's mother and uncle—the widow and brother of the first grantee—for a sum of money in return for a cession of his interim rights; and [Pg ci]Prince Henry authorised this contract by a decree from Lagos (May 17th, 1458), confirmed by King Affonso V at Cintra (August 17th, 1459).

Young Bartholemew entered into his governorship in 1473, and it was formally confirmed to him (15th March, 1473) by Affonso V. It was his sister, a daughter of the elder Bartholemew, named Felipa Moñiz de Perestrello, whom Christopher Columbus married in Lisbon; after which he lived for some time in Porto Santo, enjoying the use of Perestrello's papers, maps, and instruments.

Before many years had passed, Madeira became famous for its corn and honey, its sugar cane,[206] and, above all, its wine. The Malvoisie[207] grape, introduced from Crete, throve excellently, and at last produced the Madeira of commerce. When Cadamosto visited the island, in 1455, he found vine culture already advanced, and become the staple industry of the colonists, who exported red and white wine annually to Europe, and found a market for the vine staves as bows.

As early as 1430[208] the Infant issued a charter, regulating the settlement of Madeira; herein Ayres Ferreira (whose children, "Adam and Eve," were the first Europeans born in the island) is mentioned as a companion of Zarco. An early tradition, which has not yet been substantiated, also maintained that [Pg cii]Prince Henry instituted family registers for his colonists in this group.[209] In 1433 (September 26th), King Duarte, in a charter from Cintra, granted the islands of Madeira, Porto Santo, and the Desertas to the Infant Henry; and in

1434 (October 26th), the spiritualities of the same were bestowed on the Order of Christ.[210] In December, 1452, a contract was made at Albufeira between the Infant D. Henry and Diego de Teive, one of his "esquires," for the construction of a water-mill to aid in the manufacture of cane-sugar,[211] the third part of the produce to go to the Prince. Finally, in 1455, on Cadamosto's visit, the island possessed four settlements and 800 inhabitants, and this prosperity seems to have steadily continued. The charter of 1460[212] has been already noticed.

From the work of the Portuguese among the Atlantic Islands arises one question of special [Pg ciii]interest. Did this westward enterprise of Prince Henry's seamen, which undoubtedly carried them in the Azores and Cape Verdes a great distance (from 20 to 22 degrees) westward of Portugal, lead them on further to a discovery of any part of the American mainland?

On the strength of an enigmatical inscription in the 1448 Map of Andrea Bianco, such a discovery of the north-east corner of Brazil in or before this year has been suggested;[213] but this, it must be admitted, [Pg civ]is quite lacking in demonstrative evidence, however possible in itself. Yet once more, the "accidental" discovery of this same Land of the Holy Cross by Cabral in 1500 has been urged to much the same effect. For, if really accidental, a similar event might well have happened in earlier years—especially from the time of the Azores settlement of 1432, etc.; or if not accidental, it was based on information obtained from older navigators, who reached the same country.[214] Such older navigators towards the west were said to have been Diego de Teive and Pedro Velasco, who in 1452 claimed to have sailed more than 150 leagues west of Fayal; Gonçalo Fernandez de Tavira, who in 1462 sailed (in one tradition) W.N.W. of Madeira and the Canaries; Ruy Gonçalvez de Camara, who in 1473 tried to discover land west of the Cape Verdes; with a certain number of later instances. Some weight has also been attached to a statement [Pg cv]of Las Casas, that on his third voyage, in 1498, Columbus planned a southern journey from the Cape Verde Islands in search of lands—especially because, proceeds Las Casas, "he wished to see what was the meaning of King John of Portugal, when he said there was *terra firma* to the South. Some of the ... inhabitants of ... Santiago came to ... him,[215] and said that to the South-West of the Isle of Fogo[216] an island was seen, and that King John wished to make discoveries towards the South-West, and that canoes had been known to go from the Guinea coast to the West with merchandise."

Further, Antonio Galvano, after speaking of a voyage which took place in 1447, goes on to mention another (undated, but probably conceived by the author as falling within a year or two of the last) in these terms. "It is moreover told that in the meantime a Portuguese ship, coming out of the Straits of Gibraltar, was carried westwards by a storm much further than was intended, and arrived at an island where there were seven cities, and people who spoke our language." This, however, is too much like an echo of the old Spanish tale of the Seven Bishops and their cities in the Island of "Antillia."

In the same connection a number of still looser and more doubtful assertions exist in Portuguese archives and chronicles. Thus, in 1457, the Infant D. Fernando, as heir of Prince Henry, planned [Pg cvi]Atlantic explorations; in 1484 and 1486 similar designs were entertained—possibly on the strength of Columbus' recent suggestions, which are known to have directly occasioned one unsuccessful venture at this time; and in 1473 João Vaz da Costa Cortereal was reported, by a now-exploded legend, to have actually discovered Newfoundland.

[180] See Major, *Prince Henry*, pp. 238-245 (Ed. of 1868), mainly based upon Father Cordeiro's *Historia Insulana*, 1717.

[181] Azurara (*Chronicle of Guinea*, c. lxxxiii.) says that the Regent, D. Pedro, having a special devotion to this saint, and being much interested in the re-discovery of the Azores, caused this name to be given. Prince Henry afterwards granted the Order of Christ the tithes of St. Michael, and one-half of the sugar revenues.

[182] "Azores" in Portuguese.

[183] "Western Islands," etc.

[184] "The Third," apparently in order after—1. St. Mary (reckoned with the Formigas); 2. St. Michael. Its arms were the Saviour on the Cross, and it was probably sighted by the Portuguese on some festival of the Redeemer.

[185] "De Vlaemsche Eylanden." So on Amsterdam maps of 1612 (Waghenaer); 1627 (Blaeuw's *Zeespiegel*) and others, such as the Atlas Major Blaviana, ix, Amsterdam, 1662, p. 104.

[186] *I.e.*, Josua van der Berge. In 1449, according to Galvano and Barros (1, ii, 1), King Affonso V formally sanctioned the colonisation of the Azores.

[187] "Da Silveira" in Portuguese.

[188] "Joz de Utra" in Portuguese.

[189] Several documents exist relating to the Government, etc., of the Azores during Prince Henry's life; for instance:—(1) A royal charter of July 2, 1439, dealing with colonisation. (2) A similar charter of April 5, 1443, exempting the colonists from tithe and customs. (3) A similar charter of April 20, 1447, establishing the same exemption for the island of St. Michael, granted to the Infant D. Pedro. (4) A similar charter of March, 1449, to the Infant D. Henry, licensing him to people the Seven Islands of the Azores. (5) A similar charter of January 20, 1453, granting the Island of Corvo to the Duke of Braganza. (6) A donation of September 2, 1460, from the Infant D. Henry to his adopted son, the Infant Dom Fernando, of the Isles of Jesus Christ and Graciosa. [To which may be added: A royal charter of December 3, 1460, transferring to the Infant D. Fernando, Duke of Viseu, the grant of the Archipelagos of Madeira and the Azores, vacant by the death of D. Henry.] See *Archivo dos Açores*, i, 3, 5, 6, 7, 9, 11; Martins,*Os Filhos do D. João*, pp. 261-2 (where the date of Gonçalo Velho Cabral's discovery of the Formigas is given as 1435); *Documents* in Torre do Tombo, Gaveta 15, Maço 16, No. 5, of September 16, 1571.

[190] "Da Silveira." See above, p. lxxxix.

[191] *E.g.* By Major, *Prince Henry*, 1868, p. 286-8, based on Lopes de Lima's *Ensaios sobre a Statistica das Possessoẽs portuguezas*, Lisbon, 1844; see Zurla's *Dissertazione* of 1815.

[192] "Iles d'Afrique"....

[193] On the strength of Temporal's text in the *Histoire de l'Afrique*,... Lyons, 1556, by H. Y. Oldham, *Discovery of Cape Verde Islands* (paper of 15 pages; see especially 9-12).

[194] See *Indice cronologico das Navigacoẽs ... dos Portuguezes*, Lisbon, 1841; Oldham, *op. cit.*, pp. 12-13.

[195] The Benincasa of 1463.

[196] "E la nocte sequente ne a fazo un temporal de garbin cum vento fortevole, diche per non tornar in driedo tegnessemo la volta di ponente e maistro salvo el vero per riparar e costizar el tempo doe nocte e III zorni." Oldham, *loc. cit.* 11.

[197] Oldham adds: "If *nocte sequente* means, as it would seem, the night of the day following that on which Cape Blanco was passed, the ships would have had time to reach a point from which a West or West-south-west course would lead to Bonavista. Moreover, the Latin text gives the wind as South."

[198] See Astley's *Voyages and Travels*, vol. i, Book iv, ch. 6.

[199] *Al.* 1443. See Azurara, *Guinea*, chs. lxviii-lxix.

[200] Presumably the same man who "brought home the first captives from Guinea" in 1441. Cf. Azurara, *Guinea*, ch. xcv.

[201] Cadamosto's statement that Porto Santo had been found 27 years before his first voyage, has caused some to date this journey 1445, instead of 1455, reckoning from Zarco's discovery of 1418, and has led others to post-date Zarco's discovery by ten years; but the number XXV is no doubt a slip for XXXV. This is a very common form of error at this period. Thus, in the "Cabot" Map of 1544, the year of the original Cabotian discovery of North America is given as MCCCCXCIIII, instead of MCCCCXCVII, by a (probable) malformation of the V, or simple inattention of the draughtsman. Also, in Grynaeus we have MCCCCCIV for MCCCCLIV.

[202] Endowing the Order of Christ with the Spiritualities of these islands.

[203] On his visit in 1455.

[204] It has been also suggested, that the wooden crosses set up by Henry's orders in new-discovered lands were from the material thus provided.

[205] He accompanied Zarco in the second voyage of 1420.

[206] Introduced from Sicily.

[207] "Malmsey," or "Malvasie," from Monemvasia or Malvasia in the Morea, the original seat of its culture.

[208] See Cordeiro, *Historia Insulana*, Bk. III, ch. XV.

[209] The late Count de Rilvas communicated this fact to Mr. R. H. Major.

[210] *Documentos ... do Torre do Tombo*, p. 2.

[211] See Gaspar Fructuoso, *Saudades da terra*, ed. Azevedo (1873), pp. 65, 113, 665; Martins, *Os Filhos de D. João*, pp. 80 and *n.* 1, 258 and *n.* 2.

[212] This was issued on September 18th, 1460, bestowing the ecclesiastical revenues of Porto Santo and Madeira on the Order of Christ, the temporalities on King Affonso V. and his successors. It must be taken in connection with the Charters of June 7th, 1454, December 28th, 1458, and September 15th, 1448, all relating to the trade of Guinea, and the first two conferring special privileges on the Order of Christ, or revising such privileges already granted; see the *Collection* of Pedro Alvarez, Part III, fols. 17-18; Major, *Prince Henry*, 303.

[213] The inscription apparently runs "Isola Otinticha xe longa a ponente 1500 mia;" which has been translated—(1) "Genuine island distant 1,500 miles to the west." (2) "Genuine island, 1,500 miles long to the west." (3) "Genuine island extends 1,500 miles to the west." Also, reading ... a [= e] la sola otinticha. (4) "Is the only genuine ..." (The first line being altogether separate in sense from what follows—"xe longa," etc.) Once more, supplying "questa carta," (5) "This map is the only genuine one," leaving the second line unintelligible. (6) "Genuine island, stretching 1,500 miles westwards, ten miles broad." And lastly, reading Antillia for Otinticha, (7) "Island of Antillia," etc. (This would explain the difficulty of the Antillia Isle being otherwise absent from the 1448 Bianco.) See Desimoni, in *Atti della Società ligure di Storia patria*, 1864, vol. iii, p. cxiv; Canale, in *Storia del Commercio degl'Italiani*, 1866, p. 455; Fischer, *Sammlung ... Welt- und See-Karten italienischen Ursprungs*, Venice, 1886, p. 209; *Proceedings R. G. S.*, London, March 1895, pp. 221-240. Whatever the explanation, it must be remembered that this Map and Inscription were never produced by Portugal as evidence of a Pre-Columbian discovery, either in 1492-3, or later, in formal negotiations with Spain—as at Badajoz in 1524. It is possible that the delineation and legend in question were added by a later hand; and it is probable that, if really inserted by Bianco himself, the reference is to one of the legendary Atlantic Islands under a new form. It cannot well be identified with that stated by Galvano to have been discovered about 1447, for the latter was reached by a course of 1,500 miles due west from the Straits of Gibraltar, which would bring us to the Azores. The coast line of the "Genuine Island" is, moreover, quite inconsistent with the north-east shore-land of South America.

[214] The most singular point in this controversy is that the pilots of Cabral's fleet professed to recognise the new land as the same they had seen marked on an old map existing in Portugal. This is stated by one John, "Bachelor in Arts and Medicine, and Physician and Cosmographer to King Emanuel." He accompanied the expedition of 1500, and declared that the country where Cabral landed was identical with a tract marked upon a Mappemonde belonging to Pero Vaz Bisagudo, a Portuguese.

[215] Columbus.

[216] In the Cape Verdes.

THE "SCHOOL OF SAGRES," ETC.

Few things in connection with the life of Henry the Navigator are more interesting than the tradition of his educational and intellectual work, especially for the furtherance of geography, in the alleged School of Sagres and other supposed foundations or benefactions. Unfortunately, this tradition is not as clearly established as it might be, and it has been made more difficult by constant exaggeration. Not content with asserting that the Infant aimed at drawing the commerce of Cadiz and Ceuta—without reckoning other ports—to his town at Sagres, some have indulged in pictures of a geographical university established by the Prince upon this headland—pictures which are quite beyond any known means of verification.

These flourishes, however, need not cause one to run into another extreme, and deny that Sagres became, during the latter part of Henry's life, especially from 1438 to his death, the centre of the exploring movement and the scientific study which the Infant inspired. At Sagres,[217] according to [Pg cvii]what may be called the older view—which, resting mainly upon Barros, is adopted by Major, de Veer, Wauwermans, and even Martins—Prince Henry usually resided, not merely during the last years of his life, or after his return from the Tangier expedition of 1437, but from the time of his reappearance in Portugal after the relief of Ceuta in 1418. At first, however (1418-1438) it was called Tercena[218] Nabal, or Naval Arsenal, after it emerged from the stage of a little harbour of refuge for passing ships; and only afterwards did it become (from 1438 onwards) the Villa do Iffante, "my town," from which some of Prince Henry's charters are dated. Shortly before the completion of Azurara's chronicle, according to this view, the town was fortified with strong walls and enlarged by the building of new houses.[219] In this settlement (within the narrow space of some 100 acres), there were said to have been, besides the Infant's own Court or palace, a church, a chapel,[220] [Pg cviii]a study, and an observatory (the earliest in Portugal), together with an arsenal, a dockyard, and a fort. Here cartography and astronomical geography were diligently studied, and practical mariners were equipped for their work.

Two original statements of Portuguese authors have been often quoted to support this tradition. The first comes from John de Barros, the Livy of Portugal (A.D. 1496-1570). "In his wish to gain a prosperous result from his efforts, the Prince devoted great industry and thought to the matter, and at great expense procured the aid of one Master Jacome[221] from Majorca, a man skilled in the art of navigation and in the making of maps and instruments, who was sent for, with certain of the Arab and Jewish mathematicians, to instruct the Portuguese officers in that science." Secondly, we have the statement of the mathematician Pedro Nuñes, that the Infant's mariners were "well taught and provided with instruments and rules of astrology and geometry which all map-makers should know."[222] On the other [Pg cix]hand, it has been contended that there is no satisfactory evidence of the Infant's town having ever been finished, or of the Prince ever having lived there continuously, except during the last years of his life; and that our best authorities do not warrant us in believing that the settlement was even begun before the Tangier expedition. Henry's earlier charters are, with one exception, dated from other places, and his residence before 1438 seems to have been usually at Lisbon, Lagos, or Reposeira. Further, we have no right to speak of the "School," or "University," or "Academy" of Sagres; there may have been both teachers and learners, but there was nothing of an "institution for instruction" in the Prince's establishment.

Such is the minimising view; and most, in face of this sharp divergence, will agree with Baron Nordenskjöld that a really critical study of the subject, especially from a local antiquarian, is desirable. Very plausibly does Nordenskjöld himself sum up the probabilities of the case when he concludes that "a small school of navigation, important for the period in question, has probably received from laudatory biographers the name of an 'Academy.'"[223]The Swedish geographer, however, adds from his own [Pg cx]special researches some important observations. He believes that in the La Cosa map of 1500[224] we have work which was based upon the observations of the Infant's captains, who, as shown in these results, were evidently able to keep reliable reckoning and take fairly correct altitudes. "Further, the extension of the normal or typical portolano along the West coast of Africa, as on the portolanos of Benincasa and others of the latter part of the fifteenth century, is shown by the legends of the same to have been based on observations made during the marine expeditions of Prince Henry."

No charts or other productions of the "Sagres School," in any definite sense of this term, no geographical or astronomical works emanating from the "Court" of the Infant, are now extant. But it may reasonably be inferred from passages in Azurara's *Chronicle of Guinea* that such charts were not only draughted under the Prince's orders, but used by his sailors;[225] Cadamosto tells us of the chart he kept on his voyage of 1455, probably by direction of the Infant; while it is probably true that the "extension of the portolanos beyond Cape Bojador, in Benincasa,[226] for instance, as well as in Fra Mauro's work of 1457-9, [Pg cxi]depended on information given by native and foreign skippers" sent out by Henry. Of course, it is obvious, in the light of present knowledge, that neither he nor his school in any sense invented the portolano type; although the mention of Master Jacome of Majorca reminds us of one of the earliest centres of the new scientific cartography[227] (which was probably first made effective by Catalan skippers and draughtsmen), and suggests that the Infant was in touch with the best map-science of the time. "Neither is it correct to say that he introduced hydrographic plane charts or map graduation in accordance with geographical co-ordinates."

But his life was almost certainly not without direct influence in the improvement of cartography, and the extension of the scientific type of map beyond its fourteenth-century limits—an improvement which we see in the great map of Fra Mauro executed shortly before the Infant's death. Also, he made his nation take a real interest in geographical discovery, broke down their superstitious fear of ocean sailing, and made a beginning in the circumnavigation of Africa. He altered the conditions of maritime exploration by giving permanence, organisation, and governmental support to a movement which had up to this time proved disappointing for lack of these very means. And he certainly improved the art of shipbuilding, which [Pg cxii]Cadamosto remarks upon as having rendered the caravels of Portugal the best sailing ships afloat.

As to the build of these caravels we are fortunately not without data. Cadamosto, indeed, though he describes them as the best sailing ships at sea in his time, does not give any details; but from other sources[228] it is possible to form some idea of their peculiar features. They were usually 20-30 metres long, 6-8 metres in breadth; were equipped with three masts, without rigging-tops, or yards; and had lateen sails stretched upon long oblique poles, hanging suspended from the masthead. These "winged arms," when their triangular sails were once spread, grazed the gunwale of the caravel, the points bending in the air according to the direction of the wind. They usually ran with all their sail, turning by means of it, and sailing straight upon a bow-line, driving before the wind. [Pg cxiii]When they wished to change their course, it was enough to trim the sails.

It was with this type of vessel that the Madeira and Canary groups were "gained from the secrets of the Ocean;" that the Azores, at a distance of twenty-two degrees west of Portugal, and in the heart of the Atlantic, were discovered and colonised; and that open sea navigation of almost equal boldness was successfully employed in the finding and settlement of the Cape Verdes. Before the end of the year 1446, according to Azurara's estimate, the Infant had sent out fifty-one of these ships along the mainland coast of Africa, and they had passed 450 leagues[229] beyond Cape Bojador, which before the Prince's time was the furthest point "clearly known on the coast of the Great Sea." Also, the work of the "School of Sagres" may perhaps be recognised in Azurara's further claim that "what had before been laid down on the Mappemonde was not certain, but only by guesswork," whereas now it was "all from the survey by the eyes of our seamen," and that "all this coast towards the South with many points our prince commanded to add to the sailing chart."

It has been noticed that D. Pedro, according to the Portuguese tradition, presented Henry with a copy of Marco Polo's travels, and a map of the same, either drawn by the explorer himself or by one who knew his works, and belonged to his own [Pg cxiv]city. Thereby, we are told, the work of the Infant was much furthered, and Galvano suggests that the same was extant in 1528, and that it contained many wonderful anticipations of later discoveries.[230]

It has also been surmised, without any certain evidence,[231] that D. Pedro presented his brother with various maps of Gabriel Valsecca,[232] and with the writings of Georg Purbach, the instructor of Regiomontanus. Much more certain and interesting is the allusion to the Infant's collection of old maps in the history of the discovery of St. Michael (1443-4) in the Azores. A runaway slave, having escaped to the highest peak in the Isle of St. Maria, [Pg cxv]sighted a distant land, and returned to his master to gain pardon with this news. Prince Henry was informed of this, consulted his ancient charts, and found them confirm the slave's discovery. So he sent out Gonçalo Velho Cabral to seek for the same. Cabral failed; but on his returning to the Prince, the latter showed him from the ancient maps how he had only missed it by a slight error of direction. On his second trial the explorer was successful, and reached St. Michael on May 8, 1444.

* * * * *

Prince Henry's connection with the Coimbra-Lisbon University (founded by King Dinis in 1300) opens another side of the same question. We have already mentioned the tradition that in 1431 the Infant provided new quarters in the parish of St. Thomas, in Lisbon, for the teachers and students, and afterwards established Chairs of Theology and Mathematics. This has been called by some a "Reform of Ancient Schools" under his influence and direction;[233] and recent enquiry[234] has endeavoured to prove that the Protector of Portuguese Studies was also the founder (in 1431) of a Chair of Medicine, and the donor of a room or lecture-hall in which was painted by his order a picture of Galen. In 1448 the Infant subsidised the Chair of Theology by a grant of twelve marks of [Pg cxvi]silver annually from the revenues of Madeira.[235] It is perhaps noteworthy that the Prince does not appear to have founded any lectureship, or made any benefaction to promote directly the study of geography, though ancient texts bearing on this subject were now beginning to attract considerable attention. It may be open to question how far a university would then have welcomed an instructor in practical navigation or draughtsmanship; but students would have probably listened to lectures upon Ptolemy, or Strabo, or other classical geographers, and thereby a great impetus might have been given to the new exploring spirit. Thus in general we may fairly conclude that, so far as the Portuguese seamen of the next generation, Bartholemew Diaz, Da Gama, Cão, and others, "received their training from the Infant's School," it was usually through a rougher and more practical tradition than that of a class-room—by means of older mariners who had served in the Prince's ships rather than by university lecturers whom he had appointed.

[217] See Azurara, *Guinea*, iv; Barros, *Asia*, Decade I, i, 16.

[218] From the Venetian *Darcena*; see Goes, *Chron. do pr. D. João IV*; O. Martins,*Filhos de D. João I*, p. 75.

[219] It retained its importance till the Prince's death, when it gradually declined; it was sacked by Drake in 1597; and ruined by earthquakes. Finally it became again as deserted as before the Infant's time. Ferdinand Denis believed that before the Lisbon earthquake of 1755 there were traces of a much earlier habitation of the Sagres Promontory, including buildings (Moorish?) at least as old as the XIth century. The headland measures only one kilometre in circuit, half a kilometre in its extreme length.

[220] Prince Henry's will refers to the Church of St. Catherine, and the Chapel of St. Mary; see the *MS. Collection* of Pedro Alvarez, iii; Martins, *Os Filhos de D. João*, p. 74. The observatory was not on Sagres Cape proper, but "un peu en avant quand on vient de l'Ouest" (V. St. Martin).

[221] Jacob or James, who, according to one tradition, came to the Infant's "Court" shortly after the disaster of Tangier, in or about 1438. To this name the Viscount de Juromenha in his notes to Rackzynski, *Les Arts en Portugal*, 205, adds that of Master Peter, the cartographic artist of the Infant, who illuminated his maps in colours and adorned them with legends and pictures. The existence of this Peter rests upon a document at Batalha discovered by Juromenha. See also O. Martins, *Filhos de D. João I*, p. 73.

[222] Wauwermans, *Henri le Navigateur et l'Academie Portugaise de Sagres*, gives little or no help towards the controverted question which he assumes as settled in his title. It is a general essay on the course of fifteenth-century exploration; its most useful portions are devoted to tracing the connections between geographical study in Portugal and the Netherlands.

[223] Nordenskjöld, *Periplus*, 121 A.

[224] Plates xliii and xliv of Nordenskjöld's *Periplus*.

[225] See Azurara, *Guinea*, ch. lxxviii; Nordenskjöld, *Periplus*, 121; Santarem, *Essai sur Cosmographie*, vol. iii, p. lix. Affonso Cerveira, Azurara's predecessor, was probably not a "pupil" of the "Sagres School," as some have supposed.

[226] Especially in his works of 1467-8 and 1471.

[227] In the Balearic isles. See pp. cxvii-cxix of this Introduction.

[228] See Osorio, *Vida e feitos d'el rei D. Manoel*, i, p. 193; O. Martins, *Os Filhos de D. João I*, p. 75; Candido Correa, *Official Catalogue of the Naval Exposition of 1888 in Portugal*, where was exhibited a facsimile of an old caravel; see also the plans in D. Pacheco Pereira's *Esmeraldo*, and the article in the *Revista Portuguesa Colonial*, May 20th, 1898, pp. 32-52.

In the last-named study, which is specially worthy of notice, we have a detailed account of (1) the *Barca*, (2) the *Barinel*, (3) the *Caravel*, (4) the *Nau*, which are classed as *navios dos descobrimentos*, followed by the *navios dos conquistas*, viz., (5) the *Fusta*, (6) the *Catur*, (7) the *Almadia de Cathuri*, (8) the *Galé*, (9) the *Galiota*, (10) the *Brigantim*, (11) the *Galeaça*, (12) the *Taforea*, (13) the *Galeão*, (14) the *Carraca*. Illustrations of Nos. 1, 3, 4, 5, 6, 8, 10, and 13 are added.

[229] Azurara, *Guinea*, ch. lxxviii.

[230] "... Venice ... whence he [Pedro] brought a map which had all the circuit of the world described. The Strait of Magellan was called the Dragon's Tail; and there were also the Cape of Good Hope and the coast of Africa.... Francisco de Sousa Tavarez told me that in the year 1528, the Infant D. Fernando showed him a map which had been found in the Cartorio of Alcobaça, which had been made more than 120 years before, the which contained all the navigation of India with the Cape of Good Hope."—Galvano,*Discovery of World, sub ann.* 1428.

[231] But see Gaspar Fructuoso, *Saudades da terra* (ed. Azevedo, 1873), bk. ii, p. 9; Cordeiro, *Historia Insulana*, ii, p. 2; Santos, *Memoria sobre dois antigos mappas, etc.*, in *Mem. de Litt. da Academia*, viii, pp. 275-301; O. Martins, *Os Filhos de D. João I*, p. 72.

[232] One of which (A.D. 1434-1439) is our authority for the earliest known Portuguese voyage to any part of the Azores; viz., that of Diego de Sevill in 1427 (a date hypothetically converted by Major into 1432). This map of Valsecca's only gives St. Mary and the Formigas as known in 1439; see pp. cxxxi, cxxxiv of this Introduction.

[233] See O. Martins, *Filhos de D. João I*, pp. 63-4.

[234] Cf. Max. Lemos, *A medicina em Portugal*, 1881.

[235] J. S. Ribeiro, *Historia dos estabel. scientific, litt. e art. de Portugal*, i, p. 31.

[Pg cxvii]MAPS AND SCIENTIFIC GEOGRAPHY UP TO AND DURING PRINCE HENRY'S LIFE.

Ancient maps were not without high merits in certain cases, and a little after Prince Henry's time the Renaissance editions of Ptolemy played a very important part in geographical history. But in the first part of the fifteenth century neither the work of the Alexandrian astronomer and cartographer, nor the ancient road maps of the Roman Empire and surrounding lands[236] seem to have been sufficiently known for the exercise of much influence in the progress of discovery or of geographical knowledge. The same result follows, for different reasons, in the case of almost all the earlier mediæval maps and charts,[237] which are quite unscientific in character, and often rather picture books of natural history legends than delineations of the world.

Strictly scientific map-making begins with the Mediterranean portolani. The earliest existing specimen of these is of about 1300, but the type then formed[238] must have been for some time in process of elaboration; and it is even probable [Pg cxviii]that a fully-developed example from the middle of the thirteenth century may yet be discovered.

"A sea-chart—probably a portolano—is mentioned as early as the account of the Crusade of St. Louis, in 1270."[239] So in Raymond Lulli's *Arbor Scientiæ*, written about 1300, we have reference to compass, chart and needle, as necessary for sailors.[240] Once again, it is probable that Andrea Bianco's planisphere of 1436[241] is only a re-edition of a thirteenth-century work, when the "Normal Portolano" was just in process of making, but had not reached even the comparative perfection of the Carte Pisane, Carignano, or Vesconte examples.

The earliest dated portolan is that of 1311, by Petrus Vesconte; and from this time the maps of this class, whose central feature is an accurate Mediterranean coast-line, increase rapidly, being indeed all reproductions of one type,[242]occasionally [Pg cxix]introducing additions or corrections, especially in outlying parts, but not often varying much from one another in the central portions. The type is reasonably believed by some[243] to have originated among the Catalans, either of Spain, France, or the Balearic Isles, well within the thirteenth century.[244] In connection with this, we may recall the point mentioned by Barros, that Prince Henry the Navigator obtained the services of Master Jacome, or James, from Majorca to instruct the Portuguese captains in navigation, map-making, and the proper handling of nautical instruments.

These plans of practical seamen are a striking contrast, in their often modern accuracy, to the results of the literary or theological geography portrayed in such works as those of the "Beatus School," or of Robert of Haldingham.[245]Map surveys of [Pg cxx]this kind were apparently unknown to the ancient world. The old *Peripli* were sailing directions, not drawn but written; and the only Arabic portolan known to exist was copied from an Italian example. Long after the Italian leadership in exploration and commerce had begun to pass away, Italian science kept control of cartographical work; thus, among the early portolani, not only the majority—413 out of 498—but the most valuable, were executed by the countrymen of Carignano and Vesconte.

This department of geographical history is only just beginning to be appreciated at its full value—as marking the vital transition from ancient to modern, from empirical to scientific—but this need not surprise us much. The portolani, as has been well said, never had for their object to provide a popular or fashionable amusement; they were not drawn to illustrate the works of classical authors or learned prelates; still less did they illustrate the legends and dreams of chivalry and historical romance; they were seldom drawn by learned men; and small enough in return was the acknowledgment which the learned but too often made them, when the great geographical compilers of the Renaissance and Reformation times incorporated the earlier coast-charts in grander and more ambitious works.

Unquestionably, however, it is in maps of the portolano type that we must look for Prince Henry's primary geographical teachers, though the influence of books—and even of the older theoretical designs in cartography—must not be forgotten. Therefore, [Pg cxxi]to understand his position—to realise what he had to draw from—we must briefly describe the chief designs which it was possible for him to consult for his scientific purposes, for his Ptolemaic ambition, διοθῶσαι τὸν ἀρχαῖον πίνακα.

(1) The "Carte Pisane" of the latest thirteenth or earliest fourteenth century is probably only a copy of an earlier work, though now itself our earliest example of the portolano type. The Mediterranean on this example (as well as the Black Sea, where it has survived injury) shows the new scientific or surveying method, but the Atlantic coasts of Spain and France, and still more the shore-lines of Britain, are of a different and inferior character. This alone points to an earlier date than, *e.g.*, the works of Vesconte and Dulcert. In West Africa only a part of the Maroccan coast now remains.

(2) The Map of Giovanni di Carignano,[246] of *c*. 1300?-1310, though much damaged, shows the Black Sea and Britain with contours differing somewhat from the ordinary portolan; and the same is noticeable in the Baltic. The West African coast does not extend to Cape Non. Another work by Carignano, of *c*.1306, "specially referring to Central Asia," is said to exist, but its present position is unknown.

(3) A portolan of the early fourteenth(?) century, belonging to Professor Tammar Luxoro, of Genoa, [Pg cxxii]in 1882, and usually called after him, is believed by Nordenskjöld to be a "slightly altered copy of the normal portolano in its original form." In N.W. Africa it only gives us the shore-line as far as Sallé, with a series of names, beginning at Arzilla.[247]

(4) Marino Sanudo the Elder, to his work, *Liber Secretorum fidelium Crucis*, written between 1306 and 1321, added an atlas of ten maps. Among these, I-V form an ordinary portolano, corresponding especially with Vesconte's work,[248]but giving us no special information upon Africa; while No. VI is the famous map of the world often reproduced. Here a thoroughly conventional Africa is laid down, of the "Strabonian" or "Macrobian" type: its length, from east to west, traversed by the Negro Nile from near the Mountains of the Moon to the Atlantic, is equal to fully twice the breadth from north to south. The deep inlet in the West African coast penetrating east to a "Regio VII Montium" immediately south of the Negro Nile, is a prototype of the similar feature in Fra Mauro, and is perhaps only an exaggeration of the Sinus Hesperius of Ptolemy. This map was probably known to Prince Henry, like the book it accompanied, which contained many important particulars of fourteenth-century trade and navigation. The Mappemonde is a compromise between, or combination of, the portolano and [Pg cxxiii]the Mediæval theoretical map, and is quite a landmark in the history of cartography.

(5) Pietro Vesconte of Genoa has left three or four works executed between 1311 and 1321, and still extant, viz.: (α) Of 1311, which lacks the Western Mediterranean and West Africa, what remains giving us a "normal portolano" of the Levant and Black Sea. (β) Of 1318, depicting the entire Mediterranean, etc., with the Atlantic, North Sea coasts of Europe (in ten plates), and West Africa as far as "Mogador." (γ) Of 1318 (in six maps), which for our purposes need not be discriminated from (β); and lastly (δ) Of 1320, a map of the world, with plans of cities, a special chart of Palestine, etc. The Mappemonde, which principally concerns us here, is extremely like Sanudo's, and is perhaps the work of the same artist—Vesconte himself. Another work, of 1321, by Vesconte, is mentioned in Santarem,[249] but its whereabouts is now unknown.

Once more a work of 1327, signed "Perrinus Vesconte fecit ... MCCCXXVII in Veneciis" is conjectured to be only another "normal-portolan" by *Pietro*Vesconte.

(6) Angelino Dulcert, a Catalan, composed in August 1339, in Majorca ("in civitate Majoricarum") a portolan of great merit. Dulcert's Baltic somewhat resembles Carignano's, but with more numerous legends. A star ("the Star in the East") placed by this draughtsman south of the [Pg cxxiv]Caspian is copied, or at least paralleled, in the Atlas Catalan of 1375 (No. 9, p. cxxvi), in the Andrea Bianco of 1436, and in the Borgian map of 1430-50, as well as in the Anonymous Catalan planisphere hereafter noticed (No. 14, p. cxxviii). Dulcert's Africa probably served in some respects as a prototype for the Catalan Atlas of 1375, and Prince Henry may have studied the Continent in one or other of these delineations, which are among the most complete pictures of the Sahara coasts and Sudan interior coming down from any period before that of his voyages. Some of the Canaries are marked in about their right position, with Lançarote showing the Cross of Genoa, and Fuerteventura to the south, while almost in the latitude of Ceuta appear "Canaria," St. Brandan's Isle, etc. On the mainland a long stretch of shore-line is given beyond Cape Non or Nun, but it is drawn very conventionally in a S.S.E. direction, with seven names,[250] or titles, and an inscription of two lines, the whole seeming to show pretty clearly that the draughtsman knew nothing at first hand of the coast between Non and Boyador, but was led to conjecture a continuation of the Desert Littoral. In the Interior, the Atlas range, the large seated figure of a king with sceptre, and most of the towns depicted on eminences, reappear with slight alterations in the Atlas Catalan; which, however, adds many details.

[Pg cxxv](7) Next comes the most famous, and perhaps in some respects the most advanced, specimen of the early portolani: that usually quoted as the Medicean or Laurentian Portolan of 1351 ("Atlante Mediceo," or "Portolano Laurenziano-Gaddiano"). The author was anonymous, but almost certainly a Genoese, and his work consists of eight plates, or tables. The second of these is the Mappemonde, which is the only one that need be noticed here. The Africa of this map, taken as a whole, is drawn with a nearer approach to general correctness than on any chart anterior to the voyage of B. Diaz in 1486;[251] both the Guinea coast to the Camaroons, and the southern projection of the Continent, are extraordinarily well conceived for the time. No details or names are inserted on the W. African mainland shore beyond Cape Bojador and the River of Gold—"Palolus."[252] In this it is similar to the Pizigani map of 1367.[253]

(8) Francisco Pizigano, of Venice, 1367-1373, aided by his brother Marco, executed two famous works still extant: (α) In 1367, a large chart comprising a good deal beyond the normal portolano's Mediterranean and Black Sea;—*e.g.*, part of the Scandinavian Peninsula, the Baltic, the Caspian, etc. [Pg cxxvi]It is signed, "MCCCLXVII, Hoc opus compoxuid Franciscus Pizigano Veneciar et domnus In Venexia meffecit Marcus die xii Decembris." (β) In 1373, a normal portolano, signed "MCCCLXXIII a die viii de zugno Francischo Pisigany Venician in Venexia me fecit." The N.W. Africa of these two maps shows no advance on the Laurentian Portolano.

(9) The Atlas Catalan of 1375 is said to have been executed for Charles V of France, in whose library it was entered with the title, "Une quarte de mer en tableaux faicte par manière de unes tables, painte et historiée, figurée et escripte, et fermant a quatre fermoners de cuivre." It is in six plates, the last four of which compose a mappemonde—"the most comprehensive cartographic work of the fourteenth century," especially rich in legends, and

showing us the normal portolan, for shore-lines, blended with the theoretical map, for the interiors of countries, all designed on the most elaborate scale. The West African coast on this example is brought down to, and a little beyond, Cape Bojador, southwest of which appear the Catalan explorers of 1346[254] in their boat, with an inscription.[255] Beginning with Arzilla, and continuing south, we have besides the recognisable Sallé, Cantin, Mogador, and No[n], 35 other names before we reach Cavo de Buyet(e)der, after which we have only the[Pg cxxvii]legend "Danom," and the conclusion, "Cap de Finister(r)a occidental de Affricha."[256] More attention is given to the interior of North Africa in this design than in any other map of the fourteenth century.

(10) Guglielmo Soleri, of Majorca, between c. 1380 and 1385, executed two designs of some value, both "normal-portolans:" (α) is undated, probably executed about 1380, and signed "Guill'mo Soleri civis Majoricarum me ficit." (β) is inscribed "Guillmus Solerii civis Majoricarum me fecit anno MCCCLXXXV."

In (β) West Africa has a fairly good extension, a little beyond the latitude of the Canaries, where the rough and torn southern edge of the map cuts across all.[257]

(11) Next in order comes an anonymous Atlas of 1384 (?) in six sheets, usually called, after two of its possessors, the Pinelli-Walckenaer Portolano. It is probably a Genoese work. Its West Africa extends about as far as (or a little beyond) the Soleri of 1385, to what is apparently Cape Bojador, slightly south of the Canaries. Ten names occur beyond C. Non, among them Cavo de Sablon and Enbucder.[258] The little harbour existing to the south of Bojador seems indicated here.

[Pg cxxviii](12) And now, coming to the fifteenth century, we have first the "Combitis" Portolan of c. 1410—an anonymous work, but inscribed "Haec tabula ex testamento domini Nicolai de Combitis devenit in Monasterio Cartusiae florentinae." This is, in some respects, closely similar to the Vesconte of 1318.

(13) Another cartographer of the early fifteenth century is Cristoforo Buondelmonte—otherwise Ensenius—whose "Description of the Cyclades" is accompanied by maps; who was the author of an important graduated chart of the North of Europe; and who also left a roughly-sketched mappemonde—perhaps a copy of a much older work—which may conceivably have been known to Prince Henry and have encouraged his explorations. This shows an Africa somewhat similar in contour to Fra Mauro's of 1457-9, but almost without names.[259]

(14) Last among these works of the "Preparatory Time," we may take an anonymous Catalan planisphere of the early fifteenth century (in the National Library of Florence) closely resembling the great Atlas of 1375.

This completes the list of important maps for the period immediately preceding the new Portuguese discoveries, and shows us the most likely [Pg cxxix]examples of cartography for Prince Henry's study. Some of these he may have owned; many of them he probably inspected in person or by deputy.

It is probable enough that he was acquainted with some of the pre-scientific or "theoretical" designs, such as those of the "Beatus" type from the eighth and subsequent centuries; those which are to be found illustrating manuscripts of Sallust, Higden, Matthew Paris, St. Jerome, or Macrobius' Commentary on the "Dream of Scipio;" and those of Arabic geographers like Edrisi[260]—to name only a few examples—but he can hardly have derived much assistance from them. The great thirteenth century wheel-map pictures—as, for instance, those we know as the Hereford or Ebstorf Mappemondes—expressed the very antithesis of his spirit; and the same must be said of the greater part of the Mediæval cartography before the appearance of the portolani.

From certain books of travel, such as those of Carpini, Rubruquis, Odoric, Pegolotti, or Marco Polo, he may, however, have received great assistance. The merchants and missionaries who opened so much of Asia to the knowledge of Europe during the Crusading period, furnished the most direct stimulus for the discovery of a direct ocean route to the treasures of the East. And to find such a route by the circumnavigation of Africa was, as we have [Pg cxxx]suggested before, one of the primary objects of the Infant's life and work.

But, in addition to the Maps of his predecessors, the Infant was almost certainly acquainted with some of the chief cartographical works of his own time, falling within the period of his exploring activity, and we must finish this brief survey with some notice of these. Continuing the catalogue, we have

(15) A map by Mecia de Viladestes of 1413. This is a Catalan portolano, signed "Mecia de Viladestes me fecit in ano 1413," and is noticeable as containing a reference to the voyage of Jayme Ferrer in 1346, similar to that on the great Catalan atlas of 1375.[261]

(16) Four, or possibly five, specimens of Jacobus Giroldis' draughtsmanship belonging to the years 1422-1446, viz., (α) a Mediterranean portolan of 1422, signed "MCCCCXXII mense Junii die primo Jachobus de Giroldis Veneciis me fecit;" (β) a Portolan atlas in six sheets, of A.D. 1426, thought by some to resemble the work of Andrea Bianco in river-markings, legends, etc. This work possesses a distance-scale, but no graduation for latitude. It is inscribed, "Jachobus de Ziraldis [Ziroldis?] de Veneciis me fecit ... MCCCCXXVI." The West Africa of this work ends at Bojador ("Buider"), and gives us thirty-nine names between Arzilla and [Pg cxxxi]this point. Its nomenclature here is very similar to, though somewhat less full than, that of the Catalan atlas (1375).[262] Besides these two works, Giroldis has left others of less importance, viz., (γ), a Portolan atlas of 1443, consisting of six maps; (δ), a Portolan atlas, also of six maps, dated 1446; (ε?), a Portolano, unsigned, in the Bibliotheca Ambrosiana at Florence, which is perhaps his work.

Passing by the (for our purposes) less important Portolans of Battista Becharius, or Beccario, of Genoa, executed in 1426 and 1435; of Francisco de Cesani of Venice (1421), of Claudius Clavus[263] (1427), of Cholla de Briaticho (1430), there are only about ten maps or atlases belonging to this period which have still to be noticed, and which with some probability may be connected with the work of Prince Henry.

These are—not counting the lost map brought back by D. Pedro from Venice in 1428,—

(17) The Atlas of 1435-1445, by Gratiosus Benincasa, of Ancona.

(18) The so-called Andrea Bianco of 1436.

(19) The Andrea Bianco of 1448.

(20) The Portolano of 1434-39 by Gabriele de Valsecca, of Majorca, together with one of 1447 by the same draughtsman.

[Pg cxxxii]

(21) The anonymous planisphere of 1447.

(22) The planispheres of 1448 and 1452, by Giovanni Leardo (Leardus), of Venice.

(23) The planisphere of 1455, by Bartolommeo Pareto, of Genoa; and

(24) The planisphere of 1457-9, by Fra Mauro of the Camaldolese Convent of Murano, in Venice.

As to these, we need only remark:

No. (17) is the earliest known work of Gracioso Benincasa, consists of sixty-two maps, and belongs to a MS. giving sailing directions, etc. Its West Africa does not call for special remark, though the later discoveries of Prince Henry's lifetime are admirably illustrated in the same draughtsman's work of 1468, 1471, etc.

No. (18) consists of ten maps, including a graduated Ptolemaic mappemonde, and a circular world-map, somewhat resembling Vesconte, probably copied and re-edited from a very early portolan, with a certain theoretical extension.[264]The original of this is supposed by some to have been a late thirteenth-century work; its West African names and detailed charting end at Cape Non—an incredibly backward point for the time of revision, viz., A.D. 1436. A ship is, however, depicted in full sail far down the west coast[265] of a Continent whose general shape is [Pg cxxxiii]conceived as "Strabonian" or "Macrobian," with its length from east to west, and consequently possessing a long southern shore. The Negro Nile flows straight from Babylon or Cairo, into the Atlantic, near (but north of) the picture labelled Rex de Maroco. The western Mediterranean, Adriatic and Ægaean, as well as the Black Sea and Caspian, are poorly drawn, and suggest an early and crude type of portolan.

No. (19), signed "Andrea Biancho venician comito di galia mi fexe a LONDRA MCCCCXXXXVIII," was probably executed with a special view of illustrating the discoveries of the Portuguese along West Africa, and contains the enigmatical inscription in the S.W., which some have construed into a Portuguese discovery of South America about this time.[266] Besides the interest of this controversy, and of the fact that it was one of the first scientific maps drawn in England, this chart gives us in West Africa some of the earliest indications of the new Portuguese discoveries. Thus, beyond Cape Bojador, or Buyedor, we have on the mainland shore-line twenty-seven names reaching to Cape Roxo or Rosso, and including Rio d'Oro, Porto [Pg cxxxiv]do Cavalleiro ("Pro Chavalero"), the Port of Galé ("Pedra de Gala"), Cape Branco, Cape St. Anne, and Cape Verde.

This example has often been spoken of as the earliest map-register of Prince Henry's discoveries, but herein it must yield to

No. (20), the Valsecca (Vallesecha) of 1434-9, which mentions the discoveries of Diego de Sevill in the Azores in 1427,[267] and maps the north-west coast of Africa scientifically to Cape Bojador (Bujeteder) and "theoretically" for some way beyond.

No. (21), of 1447, inscribed, "... Vera cosmographorum cum marino accordata terra, quorundam frivolis narrationibus rejectis MCCCCXLVII," denotes, as Nordenskjöld points out, not any connection with Marinus of Tyre (by means of a since lost MS., or otherwise), but merely the author's purpose, viz., "to present here a picture of the world, according to the conception of learned cosmographers, adapted to or grouped round a skipper-chart or portolan of the Inner Sea."

West Africa, in this chart, does not present anything specially noteworthy.

No. (22). Similar in purpose to No. (8) are both the Leardo Maps of 1448 and 1452, which in detail are somewhat similar to the Bianco of 1436.

The West African coast of these Designs does not call for special notice.

No. (23), of 1455, signed "Presbiter Bartolomeus [Pg cxxxv]de Pareto civis Janue ... composuit ... MCCCCLV. in Janua," is not of high value for its date, and shows no evidence of correspondence with Prince Henry's work. The West Africa of this design need not be specially noticed here.

No. (24), the most famous of the whole series, is more fully noticed on pp. cxl-cxliv. Fra Mauro was, perhaps, helped by Cadamosto among others. It is noteworthy that the Doge Foscarini, in the letter quoted below, pp. cxl-cxli, couples the success of Cadamosto and the work of Fra Mauro, as two things which should induce Prince Henry to persevere.[268]

A new mappemonde,[269] discovered by Kretschmer in the Vatican Library, and noticed in his monograph of 1891, is of 1448; while under date of 1444, Santarem refers to a "Portolan portugais inédit," which is not further known.

These were the works[270] which in cartography bore [Pg cxxxvi]most closely upon the Infant's explorations; and we may here summarise the evidence of the same as to the advance of knowledge along the West African coast and among the Atlantic Islands.

At the beginning of the fourteenth century, as we have seen, there is no cartographical evidence of knowledge extending far beyond the Straits of Gibraltar—either down the mainland shore or [Pg cxxxvii]among the Islands in the Ocean. But on Dulcert's Portolan of 1339, and on other productions of the same epoch, such as the *Conosçimiento* of about 1330, we meet with some of the Islands, and with the Continental coast as far as Bojador. Thus, in the *Conosçimiento* and the Laurentian Portolano of 1351, "the most important of the Azores, the Madeira group, and the Canary Islands, are denoted by the names they still bear," or by the prototypes of these names.[271] The same Medicean or Laurentian map of 1351, the Pizzigani of 1367-1373, the Catalan[272] of 1375, and others, "bear inscriptions even beyond C. Bojador"—inscriptions, however, which do not in their scattered and half-fabulous character give any decisive evidence of actual exploration to the south of this point before Henry's time.[273]Moreover, the shape of Africa in the "Atlante Mediceo" of 1351,[274] suggests—though it can hardly be said to prove—actual observations far beyond Cape Bojador made by the crews of storm-driven or India-seeking ships. But, after all, the map knowledge shown of Africa to the south of latitude 26° N. was so incomplete and so vague—perhaps even in the Laurentian Portolan the engrafting of a great

47

theory on a tiny plant of fact—that the claim of first discovery in [Pg cxxxviii]more southern regions cannot well be refused to Gil Eannes, Dinis Diaz, Cadamosto, and the other explorers of the Infant's school.

On the other hand, all the Atlantic groups, except the Cape Verdes and some of the Azores, were evidently known in whole or part to some of the fourteenth-century navigators and draughtsmen.

A good deal of hearsay knowledge about the interior of Africa is also indicated, as we have seen, in some of these maps, especially the Dulcert of 1339, and the Catalan of 1375; and in this connection we must refer to what has been said upon the trade-routes of North Africa; but these elaborate pictures of mountain ranges, Moslem kings, traders with their camels, and towns on eminences, have little more pretence to scientific accuracy than the Negro Nile of so many old geographers, which is probably a mistaken combination of the real but separate courses of the Benue, the Niger, and the Senegal.

Once more we have seen that the first two portolani plainly influenced by Prince Henry's discoveries are the Valsecca[275] of 1434-9 and the 1448 map of Andrea Bianco, drawn in London; and that the 1436 Bianco is probably a copy[Pg cxxxix]of a thirteenth-century work, showing no clear evidence of the new explorations. As to the Bianco of 1448, we may here add a word to what has been already said. On this example we find the west coast of Africa end suddenly with Cape Rosso, or Roxo, immediately south of Cape Verde, and "from this point the coast is drawn straight eastward in a style which indicates that the country beyond is unknown;" the "outline of this southern shore of Africa being delineated according to the maps of the Macrobius type." The work of 1448 is frequently copied in following years; as, for example, on several designs of Gratiosus Benincasa (1435 to 1482), wherein the west coast of Africa, from Ceuta to Cape Verde, "has the same contours and the same names."[276] All of these charts are believed by Nordenskjöld to be copies of the same Portuguese original. On the other hand, "Benincasa's Atlas of 1471 is widely divergent as regards the legends, and extends much further south.[277] It reproduces the discoveries along the coast down to Pedro de Sintra's voyage of 1462-3, and seems in part to be based on direct information from Cadamosto."[278]

[Pg cxl]
Lastly, a more special notice must be taken of the great map of Fra Mauro, 1457-9.

In this undertaking[279] Andrea Bianco is said to have assisted, and the work was (either originally or in copy) executed for the Portuguese Government, and assisted by the same. King Affonso V supplied the draughtsmen with charts on which the recent discoveries of Prince Henry's seamen were laid down. Payment was liberal (12 to 15 sous a day to every one of the common artisans and copyists); and the Doge Francesco Foscarini, "when he witnessed the plan and the beginning of Mauro's work," trusted that Prince Henry would find therein fresh reasons for pressing on his explorations. The completed mappemonde was sent to Portugal, in charge of Stefano Trevigiano, on April 24th, 1459. This was based, perhaps, in part on the map, or maps, illustrating the voyages of Marco Polo, in the Doges' Palace in Venice, apparently on one of the walls of the Sala della Scudo. The "Polo" portions of the New Design were, however, chiefly in the Far [Pg cxli]East. In N.W. Africa, Cape Verde and Cape Rosso are marked, and near the S.W. coast of the Continent is a long inscription about the Portuguese voyages, stating that the latter "here gave new names to rivers, bays, harbours, etc., and that they made new charts, of which he (Fra Mauro) had had many in his possession." At the extreme south point of Africa is the name "Diab," with a legend telling how an Indian junk was said to have been storm-driven to this point in about 1420, and (without reaching land) to have sailed further westward for 2,000 miles during forty days. After this the Indians turned back, and after seventy days' sail, returned to Cavo di Diab, where they found on shore a huge bird's egg, as large as a barrel.[280] Fra Mauro had also himself spoken with a trustworthy person, who said that he had sailed from India past Sofala to "Garbin," a place located in the middle of the west coast of Africa close to "Dafur." "Fundan," again, a little south of Cape Rosso, may represent some Portuguese coast-name which has not elsewhere survived.

Yet, apart from these references, there is but little evidence of the new discoveries forthcoming, and, from a critical point of view, Fra Mauro's planisphere is somewhat disappointing. True it is in certain regions (its Mediterranean and Black Sea, for instance), of the portolano type, but in the more outlying parts of the world, and even in much [Pg cxlii]of Africa, it is far more similar to one of the old Macrobius type of wheel-maps (continued in such fifteenth-century specimens[281] as the "Borgian" design of *c.* 1430), than to a specimen of enlightened cartography like the "Laurentian" example of 1351. The traditional centre at Jerusalem is not taken, but a point slightly north of Babylon serves instead. In Africa numerous tribes and cities are marked even beyond the Equator, in regions inscribed as "Inhabitabiles propter calorem;" but the general shape of the west coast is hardly satisfactory. Fra Mauro knows nothing of the great bend of the Guinea coast; N.W. Africa appears not as a great projection, but only as a gently-sloping shoulder of land; Cape Verde is not the westernmost point of the Continent. This position is given to the traditional "Promontory of Seven Mountains" (north of the Western Nile), which we have met with in earlier examples. To the south of the Green Cape appears a long and narrow inlet of sea,[282] which can hardly be supposed to represent in any way the South coast of "Guinea" from Sierra Leone to Benin, but perhaps is a combination and exaggeration of the great estuaries so recently visited by Henry's seamen—the Gambia, the Casamansa, the Rio Grande or Geba, [Pg cxliii]and others. The Western or Negro Nile is drawn as flowing straight from Meroe in Nubia to the Atlantic, passing through a great swamp (Lake Chad?), an elongated piece of open water in the country of Melli (the Middle Niger in flood?), and the course of the Senegal. South of Cape Roxo, the coast, trending gradually south-east, exhibits a very broken contour and is fringed with many islands—evidence only too certain that the draughtsman is working by the light of imagination. Finally, although Africa is rightly conceived as on the whole projecting into the Southern Ocean, and having its length or greatest dimension from south to north rather than from east to west, it is greatly twisted out of shape by the inclination S.E., which bends round its southmost point almost to the longitude of Guzerat.[283] The general size of the Continent, however, is more accurately guessed[284] than on most maps of this or earlier time. Here Fra Mauro is nearer the truth even than the Laurentian Portolano of 1351, so far superior to the work of 1457-9 in many respects. Parallels of latitude and meridians of longitude are not indicated in the Camaldolese mappemonde, which has been sometimes referred to as "an immeasurable advance on all earlier cartography;" and the importance of this [Pg cxliv]famous design, as an index to current geographical ideas, and as a world-picture of great size and magnificence, possessing in its time considerable official importance, must not lead us to take it as an example of cartographical perfection.

* * * * *

The use of the magnetic needle is essentially connected with the portolan type of map; this instrument was well known to Prince Henry's sailors, and is referred to by the Infant himself as being, like the sailing chart, a necessity for navigators.[285] But it could hardly come into general employment till men reached beyond the mediæval stage of a magnetic needle enclosed in a tube so as to float on water.

In the Discovery of the Compass four stages may be distinguished:

(1) The discovery of a species of stone with polar-magnetic qualities, *i.e.*, with the power of attracting iron.

(2) The discovery that steel or hardened iron could be made polar-magnetic by rubbing it with a lode-stone.

(3) The discovery that the magnet (or magnetised iron) possessed the quality of definite direction, one of its poles always indicating the north, if it were so supported or suspended that it could move freely.

(4) The discovery of using the magnetised iron needle as a compass.

[Pg cxlv]The first dates from a high antiquity, and is noticed by Plato, Theophrastus, Pliny, Ptolemy, Claudian, and many writers of the Mediæval as well as of the Classical period. The subsequent advances we cannot date, for Europe, earlier than the twelfth century; when Alexander Neckam and Guyot de Provins (*c.*1190-1200) show us that some investigators had advanced as far as the third of the stages above recounted.

It is now generally understood that magnetic cars, "based on the same principle as the compass," were used in China much earlier than this. The Helleno-Roman world of antiquity, in describing the magnet, only dwelt on its attraction for iron, and did not notice its power of indicating the poles; whereas the Celestials were aware in the first place of the communication of magnetic fluid to iron, and in the second place of the mysterious power of iron so magnetized, as early as about A.D. 120. The earliest use of the water-compass in China is fixed by Klaproth at A.D. 1111-17; and as to the magnetic figures or magnetic cars with which in earlier times Chinese junks sailed to the south of Asia, and Chinese travellers made their way across the plains and mountains to the west of their country, it must not be assumed that their use was universal. Thus, in the fifth century A.D., when Wu-Ti, afterwards Emperor, stormed Singanfu (417A.D.), he seized upon one of these as a great curiosity.

It is uncertain, as already remarked, when the complete compass, or even the polarity of the [Pg cxlvi]magnet, was first discovered in Europe. We may, however, note the following evidence:

(1) Alexander Neckam, an English monk of St. Albans (born 1157, died 1217), who had studied for some time in the University of Paris, refers more than once to what we may suppose was a compass needle, placed on a metal point.[286]This, he implies, was then in common use among sailors, and was not merely a secret of the learned. For, "when the mariners cannot see the sun clearly in murky weather or at night, and cannot tell which way their prow is tending, they put a needle above a magnet, which revolves until its point looks North and then stands still." These words were probably written between 1190-1200.

(2) Guyot de Provins, a satirist of Languedoc, in his poem, *La Bible*, written about 1200, wishes the Pope would more nearly resemble the Pole-star,[287]which always stands immovable in the firmament and guides the sailor. Even in darkness and mist [Pg cxlvii]can the Pole-star make itself felt. For the mariner has only to place in a vessel of water a straw pierced by a needle which has been rubbed with a black and ugly stone, that will draw iron to itself; and the point of the needle unfailingly turns towards the Pole-star.

(3) Jacques de Vitry, the French historian-bishop, writing about 1218, in his*Historia Orientalis*, speaks of "the iron needle which always turns to the North Star after it has touched the magnet" or "adamant."[288]

(4) "An unknown singer of the same period" speaks of sailors to Friesland, Venice, Greece or Acre, finding in the Pole-star a sign-post in heaven. Even in darkness and mist the star can still help them, for it has the same power as the magnet of attracting iron. So mariners attach an iron needle to a piece of cork and rub it with a black lodestone. The cork and needle are then put into water, and never fail to point to the north.

(5) Brunetto Latini, writing about 1260, tells how Roger Bacon showed him[289]a magnet, a stone black and ugly, and explained its use. If one rubbed a needle with it, and then put the needle, fixed to a straw, in water, the point of the needle always turned towards "the Star." By this the sailor [Pg cxlviii]could hold a straight course, whether the stars were visible or no.

(6) In the *Landnamabok*, or Icelandic Book of Settlement, the main text of which was finished before 1148, there occurs a passage, probably added about 1300,[290] which describes a voyage of the ninth century (*c.* 868) to Iceland, and explains the use of ravens to direct this early course—"for at that time the sailors of the northern countries had not yet any lodestone."

(7) The Arabic author of the *Baïlak el Kibjaki*, or "Handbook for Merchants in the Science of Stones," relates how, in 1242, on a voyage from Tripoli to Alexandria, he himself witnessed the use of the polarized needle. He adds that Moslem merchants sailing to India, instead of the magnet-needle attached to a straw, tube or cork, used a hollow iron fish which, thrown into water, pointed north and south.

"Subsequently the instrument was improved by degrees, till it assumed the shape of a box, containing a needle moving freely on a metal point, and covered by a compass-rose." It is here probably that the share of Amalfi is to be found,[291] and it may have been Flavio Gioja, or some other [Pg cxlix]citizen of the oldest commercial republic of Italy, who first fitted the magnet into the box, and connected it with the compass-card, thus making it generally and easily available.[292]

This it certainly was not in Latini's time. "No mariner could use it (the polarized magnet), nor would sailors venture themselves to sea ... with an instrument so like one of infernal make." In the latter part of the thirteenth century, and not before, its use seems to have crept in among Mediterranean pilots and captains, and in the course of the fourteenth century it was almost universally accepted.

A mistake has been made on one point. The first scientific (or portolano) type of map is generally associated with the first scientific use of the magnet; but portolani began while men had not advanced beyond the use of the primitive water-compass above described; and "accurate determination by means of this" must have been very difficult on a tossing sea. "A comparison of the contours of the Mediterranean, according to various portolanos, with a modern chart, shows that the normal portolano contained no mistake due to the misdirection of the compass."[293] Nor do the earliest portolani contain any compass-roses or wind-roses. Gradually these were introduced into the new [Pg cl]charts, *e.g.*, they are found in the Catalan Atlas of 1375, in the Pinelli of 1384, and in many fifteenth-century portolani; but not till the sixteenth century do we have a number of these roses drawn on the same mapsheet.

The use of the quadrant by Prince Henry and his sailors is expressly mentioned by Diego Gomez; but neither in this case, nor in that of the compass, are we warranted in assuming (as some authorities have done) that to the Infant is due the first use of astronomical instruments at sea.

C. RAYMOND BEAZLEY.
13, THE   PARAGON,   BLACKHEATH.
March 27th, 1899.

FACSIMILE OF PRINCE HENRY'S INITIAL SIGNATURE.
[I. D. A. = Iffante Dom Anrique.

[236] *E.g.*, the Peutinger Table.

[237] Viz., before the end of the thirteenth century; see *Dawn of Modern Geography*, ch. vi, on "Geographical Theory in the Earlier Middle Ages," and especially pp. 273-284, 327-340, 375-391.

[238] *E.g.*, in the Carte Pisane and the work of Giovann de Carignano.

[239] See d'Avezac, *Bolletino d. Soc. Geog. Ital.*, 1874, p. 408; Nordenskjöld, *Periplus*, 16 A.

[240] See d'Avezac, *Coup d'œil historique sur la projection des Cartes de Geographie*(1863), p. 38.

[241] Reproduced in part at the end of this edition of *Azurara*, vol. i, Plate 4.

[242] Thus Nordenskjöld sums up after an exhaustive review of all the chief early portolans: "Not only are the coast-legends the same, even the ... names in red ink of places considered of special importance to navigators were not essentially different in the three centuries from Vesconte to Voltius. Moreover: (1) The Mediterranean and Black Sea have exactly the same shape on all these maps; (2) a distance-scale, with the same unit of length, such as otherwise is used only on the Spanish and French Mediterranean coasts, occurs on all these maps, independently of the land of their origin; (3) the distances across the Mediterranean and Black Sea, measured with this scale, agree perfectly on the different maps; (4) the conventional shape given to many islands and capes remain almost unaltered on portolanos from the fourteenth to the sixteenth century. So that it may be thought proved that all these portolanos are only amended codices of the same original" (*Periplus*, 45 A).

[243] *E.g.*, Nordenskjöld, in his last work (*Periplus*, 46, 47).

[244] Nordenskjöld conjectures probably between 1266 and 1300.

[245] Cf. (1) the Beatus maps of "St. Sever," "Ashburnham," "Turin," "London," of 1109, "Valladolid," "Madrid," etc., of the tenth, eleventh, and twelfth centuries; (2) the Hereford *Mappemonde* of the late thirteenth century, with which may be compared the Ebstorf world-map of c. 1300; see Konrad Miller, *Die ältesten Weltkarten*, Heft v, 1896.

[246] Signed "Johannes presbyter, rector Sancti Marci de Porta Janue me fecit." A priest answering to this description flourished in Genoa, 1306-1344; this may have been a younger relative.

[247] No Atlantic islands exist on the Tammar Luxoro portolan.

[248] Konrad Kretschmer believes Sanudo's maps to have been draughted entirely or principally by Vesconte.

[249] *Essai sur l'Histoire de la Cosmographie*, i, 272, ed. of 1849.

[250] One being merely "Plagae Arenae."

[251] See *Azurara*, Hakluyt Soc. ed., vol. i, Reproduction at end, No. 1

[252] For Pactolus (?).

[253] A considerable knowledge of the Atlantic Islands is also shown, sixteen names being given. This number, however, is less than we have in the *Conoscimiento* of slightly earlier date, *c.* 1330 (?).

[254] Jayme Ferrer, etc.

[255] Quoted and discussed above, pp. lxiii-lxiv.

[256] Names are given to twenty-seven islands in the Atlantic, among them St. Brandan's isle, most of the Canaries, the whole Madeira group and several of the Azores.

[257] The Soleri of 1380 gives twenty Atlantic islands; nineteen appear in the Soleri of 1385 (some legendary). In neither is any addition made to earlier lists.

[258] Bojador?

[259] Reproduced in Nordenskjöld, *Periplus*, 111, and labelled only "before 1481." The only name on the West African mainland is well down S.W., "India [portus?] pbīs fons." The deep indent on the middle of the W. African coast, noticed in several other maps and even in Fra Mauro, appears here on a great scale.

[260] Twelfth century.

[261] A work by the same author, of 1457, is said to be at the Carthusian Monastery of Segorbe, near Valencia, but it is not yet fully identified, and is supposed by some to be the same as that just noticed.

[262] The same is the case with the Atlantic Islands; but though giving us fewer actual isles, it supplies more names to points therein—thirty-two in all.

[263] An important chart for N. European cartography, and for the fact that it is one of the earliest graduated non-Ptolemaic maps.

[264] See *Azurara*, Hakluyt Soc. ed., vol. i, Map No. 4 at end of volume.

[265] Is this an addition of the Editor to bring it up to date? The reviser must, however, have added very largely to this map; *e. g.*, both Russia and Turkey (?), as here depicted, do not correspond at all to the *late* thirteenth century, but agree better with the fifteenth; though for 1436 Russia seems unduly magnified. *Imperium Tartarorum* appears immediately north of the Sea of Azov. The Moslem prince near the Bosphorus is probably meant for the Ottoman Sultan.

[266] See pp. ciii-cvi.

[267] See p. cxiv of this Introduction.

[268] See Major, *Henry Navigator*, p. 312.

[269] The "Walsperger," *Eine neue mittelälterliche Weltkarte.*

[270] On all these maps, see especially G. Uzielli and P. Amat di S. Filippo, *Studi biographici e bibliographici sulla storia della Geografia in Italia*, ii, Mappemonde, etc., dei secoli xiii-xvii, Roma, 1882—especially pp. 49, 52, 54, 55, 57-8, 60, 62, 64, 66, 72-3, 230-1; Theobald Fischer, *Sammlung Mittelälterlicher Welt und See-karten*, Venice, 1886, pp. 111, 117-9, 127, 150-5, 207-213, 220; Santarem, *Atlas*, 1849; Santarem, *Essai sur l'histoire de la Cosmographie*, etc., 1849-52; Santarem, *Notices sur plusieurs monuments géographiques du moyen âge*, etc. (Bull. Soc. Géog., 3ᵉ série, vii, Paris, 1847), especially pp. 289, 295; Santarem, *Recherches sur la priorité des découvertes portugaises*, 1842; C. Desimoni and L. T. Belgrano, "*Atlante ... posseduto dal Prof. Tammar Luxoro ...*" in *Atti della societa ligure di storia patria*, v, Genoa, 1867; K. Kretschmer, *Marino Sanudo der Altere*, in *Zeitschrift d. Ges. f. Erdkunde*, Berlin, xxvi, 1891; H. Simonsfeld, in *Neues Archiv für altere deutsche Geschichtskunde*, vii, especially pp. 43, etc., Hannover, 1881; E. T. Hamy, *La mappemonde d'Angelino Dulcert* (Bull. Géog. Hist, et Descr., 1886-7); ibid., *Les origines de la Cartographie de l'Europe Septentrionale*, 1888; ibid., *Cresques lo Juheu, note sur un géographe juif Catalan de la fin du xive siècle*, 1891; Jomard, *Atlas ("Monuments de la Géographe"), 1862; Choix de Documents Géographiques conservés a la Bibl^que Nat^le*, especially p. 4, Paris, 1883; Buchon and Tastu, *Notices et Extraits des MSS. de la Bibliothèque du Roi*, xiv, 2nd

partie, Paris, 1841, especially p. 67; G. Marcel, *Recueil des Portolans*, Paris, 1886; Hommaire de Hell, in *Bulletin de la Soc. de Géog.*, 3ᵉ série, vii, Paris, 1847, p. 302; M. A. P. d'Avezac (-Maçaya) "... *Notice sur un Atlas de la Bibl*ᵗʰᵉᵘᵉ *Walckenaer*" (Bull. Soc. Géog., 3ᵉ série, viii, Paris, 1847), especially p. 142, etc.; P. Matkovic, in*Mittheilungen der K. K. Geog. Gesellsch.*, vi, p. 83, etc., Vienna, 1862; Cortambert,*Introduction à l'Atlas ... par feu M. Jomard* (Bull. Soc. Géog., 6ᵉ série, xviii, Paris, 1879) p. 74; R. H. Major, *Henry the Navigator*, London, 1868; *Notice des objets exposés dans la section de Géographie*, Paris, 1889 (Exposition), especially p. 14; Lelewel,*Géographie de Moyen Age*, especially *Epilogue*, pp. 167-184, Brussels, 1857; Placido Zurla, *Il Mappemonde di Fra Mauro Camaldolese*, Venice, 1806; A. E. Nordenskjöld,*Facsimile Atlas*, Stockholm, 1886; *Periplus*, Stockholm, 1897.

[271] *E.g.*, Legname for Madeira, "The Isle of Wood."

[272] We must note that the ship of the Catalan explorers, with the accompanying legend commemorative of the expedition of 1346, is depicted in this map *as well to the south of Bojador.*

[273] Though Nordenskjöld seems to think otherwise.

[274] See *Azurara*, vol. i, Plate 1, at end of volume.

[275] The Valsecca Map delineates the West African coast to Cape Bojador (C. de Bujeteder). Beyond this the outline of the coast is "suggested" for a distance about as great as from the Straits to Bojador, but with no names or legends except "Plagens arenosas," "Tarafal," "Bujeteder," and at the extreme south, "Tisilgame."

[276] This is especially true of the Benincasa of 1467. Nordenskjöld gives twenty-eight parallel names from this and the Bianco of 1448 between Bojador and Capes Verde and Rosso.

[277] To Rio de Palmeri, immediately beyond Cape St. Anne.

[278] This may be seen, as Nordenskjöld suggests (*Periplus*, p. 127), by comparing the names on the lower part of Benincasa's West Africa with the following names occurring in Cadamosto's account of De Sintra's voyage: Rio di Besegue, Capo di Verga, Capo di Sagres, Rio di San Vicenzo, Rio Verde, Cape Liedo, Fiume rosso. Capo rosso, Isola rossa, Rio di Santa Maria della nave, Isola di Scanni, Capo di Santa Anna, Fiume della palme, Rio de Fiume, Capo di monte, Capo Cortesi, Bosco di Santa Maria. Benincasa, however, appears to have access to other sources besides Cadamosto, as many of his names are not found in the latter.

[279] See Zurla, *Il Mappemonde di Fra Mauro*, Venezia, 1806, p. 62; Humboldt's*Kritische Untersuchungen*, i, p. 274; Ongania and Santarem's Reproductions of the Map itself; Nordenskjöld's *Periplus*, 127-8.

[280] Egg of the Rukh, or Roc?

[281] Cp. also the elliptical Florentine example of 1447 (Nordenskjöld, *Facsimile Atlas*, 116), or Leardus' Mappemondes of 1448 and 1452 (*ibid.* 61).

[282] "Sinus Ethiopicus:" very similar to that depicted on the Leardus of 1448. On the southern side of this is "Fundan."

[283] Perhaps a Ptolemaic concession.

[284] Still more is this the case with Asia, where Fra Mauro is in some ways more satisfactory than anywhere else, and contrasts well even with the "Harleian" or Dieppe Map of *c.* 1536, and many other similar works.

[285] *Azurara*, ch. ix.

[286] Cf. Neckam's references. (α) In his work, *De Utensilibus*: "Qui ergo munitam vult habere navem . . . habeat etiam acum jaculo superpositam: rotabitur enim et circumvolvetur, donec cuspis acus respiciat Septentrionem, sicque comprehendent quo tendere debeant nautae, cum Cynosura latet in aeris turbatione, quamvis ea occasum nunquam teneat propter circuli brevitatem." (β) In his *De Naturis Rerum*, c. 98: "Nautae ... mare legentes, cum beneficio claritatis solis in tempore nubilo non sentiunt, aut ... cum caligine ... tenebrarum mundus obvolvitur, acum super magnetem ponunt, quae circulariter circumvolvitur usque dum ejus motu cessante, cuspis ipsius Septentrionalem Plagam respiciat."

[287] "La tresmontaine."

[288] "Acus ferrea, postquam adamantem contigerit, ad stellam septentrionalem ... semper convertitur; unde valde necessarium est navigantibus in mari."
[289] In Oxford, A.D. 1258. This is not a very certain tradition.
[290] See Nordenskjöld, *Periplus*, 50. "The *Landnamabok* was written by Are Torgillson Frode, who died in 1148;" but "the passage here in question first occurs in a copy or revision by Hauk Erlandsson, who lived at the end of the thirteenth century and the beginning of the fourteenth."
[291] "Prima dedit nautis usum magnetis Amalphis."
[292] Such a compass-box is figured on the margins of some MSS. of Dati's *Sphera* of the early fifteenth century. See Nordenskjöld *Periplus*, p. 45.
[293] *Periplus*, p. 47.

HAKLUYT. S. I. V. C

[Pg 129]

AZURARA'S CHRONICLE OF THE DISCOVERY AND CONQUEST OF GUINEA.

CHAPTER XLI.
How they took the ten Moors.

or that night there was no other agreement, save that each one took all the rest he could; but on the next day they all joined together to advise what they ought to do, for it was not a suitable place in which to take prolonged repose. And the captains, falling to talk about the matter, agreed among themselves that they should enter into their boats with certain of their people, and Luis Affonso Cayado as captain (who was to go along the shore), and that he should land with some of his men, leaving with the boats another in his place. Then he was to make his way by land with those men whom he took with him, and the boats were to follow after him a short way from the beach, while the caravels came two leagues behind, so as not to be discovered. And as they marched in this order they fell in with the track of Moors who were going into the Upland, and they went in doubt whether they should [Pg 130]follow that track and go after them, holding that it might be a perilous matter to enter so far into the country where they had been now discovered, as they did not know the people that might be in the land. But their will, which was now burning to accomplish the affair, left no place to bare reason; and without more fear they went forward till they arrived at a place about three leagues further on where there were some few Moors, the which not only lacked courage to defend themselves, but even the heart to fly. And these were in all ten, counting men, women, and children.

CHAPTER XLII.
How Alvaro Vasquez took the thirty-five Moors.

When those ten Moors had been brought off to the caravels, Alvaro Vasquez, like a man of noble birth, being desirous to show to all the others that he loved the service of his lord, spake with Dinis Eannes, to whom appertained the charge of the government for that day, saying that it appeared to him a good thing to order the people to go forth, since their coming from their own country was principally for that end. "How can you ask," said Dinis Eannes, "that we should again sally forth where we have been so often, insomuch that all this land has had warning of our presence? And of two things me seemeth that one would happen; either we should not light upon any Moors to take away, or we should encounter so many that it would be to our great danger to make an attack upon them; and so much the more as I am ill disposed for a fight by reason of weariness. Wherefore me thinketh it would not be well for us to sally forth again, as far as this land lieth, but that we should go onwards till we come to a place where we know well they could not be advised of us." And as they were going in accordance [Pg 131]with that resolve, one part of the night being already passed, Alvaro Vasquez, still constant to his first design, came again to Dinis Eannes, and begged him to let him go on shore and entrust him with the charge of his captaincy, for that he knew many would go with him of right good will. "Inasmuch as this sally pleaseth you so greatly," said Dinis Eannes, "I only ask you that in your going you take good advisement that you bring no harm on yourselves nor sorrow on the rest of us." Then Alvaro Vasquez called Diego Gil, that other esquire of whom we spoke before, for he knew him for a brave man and one of his own upbringing; and they went through the other caravels in such wise that they gathered together those persons whom they thought sufficient for their safety. And all together they went on shore—there being yet some part of the night left for their march—but ere they had pressed on any farther, Alvaro Vasquez, wishful to admonish them, spake unto them thus. "Friends and Gentlemen, although I am not one of those three principal captains whom we brought with us from our kingdom, let it suffice that I am committed to you as captain by him who had the charge to command you. And because want of order is often a greater obstacle[A] than the multitude of the enemy, I desire first to know of you if it please you to have me for captain in this affair, that I may command you as men well pleased to receive governance; for much better were it that you should tell me now at this present, where we cannot well receive any harm, than when we are away from here, in some place where your disobedience might do hurt, not only to me, but also to every one of us in this company."

"We are all well content," said the others with one voice, "that you should be our captain, and well it pleaseth [Pg 132]us to obey you as fully as any one of the other captains, and even better, if we can more perfectly do it."[B]

"Now," said he, "it seemeth well to me that we should go forward according to the same ordinance as on the other day, to wit, that I should go with some of you others along the land, and that the remainder should keep in the boats within call of us." And so, setting out and following the coast a good way, they fell in with a cape, to which they gave the name of St. Anne;[113] and immediately after that they lighted upon an arm of the sea which ran up into the land about four leagues, and appeared to them as though it were a river. And on reaching the entrance of the same, Alvaro Vasquez waited for the others in the boats, and when they had come up he bade them wait for him there, whilst he went along that water, for he conceived that if any people lived in that land it would be there. The others said that such an expedition would be very perilous, if only because the sun was already very high, and the heat of it was great, and they were very weary for the great lack they had had of sleep, and the toil of some in rowing, and of others in going on foot; and all the more because even if there were in that place a number of inhabitants, yet they could not make any good booty among them, because of necessity they would discern them from afar; and that if the natives perceived themselves strong enough to fight with them, they would await them, but if not, they could put themselves in safety quite easily. Alvaro Vasquez nevertheless pursued his journey as one who had determined to accomplish some great matter if his fortune were not contrary; and so, going forward about a league and a half, one of the company said to the Captain, "Methinks I see along this stream some rising objects like houses." The Captain looked attentively, and right well [Pg 133]perceived that it was a village, and so it appeared to all the others who were there. "Now," said Alvaro Vasquez, "our booty is before our eyes, but it is so clearly discovered that of necessity we shall be seen before we can arrive at it; and because it doth not appear to me to be so great a settlement as that it can hold a people with whom we cannot cope, still, in order that we may achieve some sort of success, let each one run as fast as he can, and so let us stoutly fall upon them, and if we are not able to make captives of the young men, yet let us seize upon the old men, the women, and the little children, and let us take such advisement that whosoever putteth himself on his defence shall be slain without pity; and as to the others, let us seize them as best we can." And before he had quite finished these reasons, many of them began to increase their pace, while others were running as fast as they could; and the Moors,[114] like unwary people, little recking of such a danger, when their enemies came upon them, were all thrown into that confusion which the fortune of the case required. And when they saw men coming upon them so suddenly and so boldly, and armed with weapons quite strange to them, they were altogether amazed. Whereat our men took so much the greater boldness, seeing their timorous disorder, and at once began to seize upon as many of them as they could, and seeing that some sought to put themselves on their defence, they slew them without mercy. But the affair lasted not long at that time, for that the enemy soon began to fly. And there were many amongst them who then looked on their wives and children for the last time, and in a short space the booty would have been much larger if that arm of the sea had not been so near that many of them escaped into it, inasmuch as for the most part, not only the men but also the women and the children, all knew how to swim. And others who were bold and light-footed, trusting in their fleetness, [Pg 134]escaped through all; though some were deceived in it, for they found others of our men who followed and captured them in spite of their lightness of foot, so that in all there were taken captive thirty-five, besides some that perished. Of a surety that Esquire who, as we have said, was their captain, found no little praise for that deed of his, since for a great space they discoursed of his energy and diligence, giving him thanks for the great toil he had undergone, as well for the service of the Infant as for the profit of them all in that journey. And, moreover, those who had stayed in the caravels were not a little glad at the coming of their partners with so good a profit, and this joy of theirs was much increased when they had heard in full measure the particulars of the adventure which the others had had.

[A] To victory.
[B] Our intended action.

CHAPTER XLIII.
How they returned on shore, and of the Moor that they took.

Now the others who had remained in the caravels, seeing the toil of their partners, conceived that it would be to their great loss if they did not dispose themselves to some other matter as great, so that in future they should not receive dishonour. And so some of them joined together on the following night, and entering into their boats, they travelled two days and two nights and landed, but with all their great toil they were not able to capture more than one Moor; and with his guidance they set out to search for some three villages, which were a good way in the Upland. But they did not find in them anything that they could carry off, for they were already emptied of people, since the Moors who had fled had warned the whole country as far as their news could reach. And so they turned back to their ships, ill satisfied with the toil they had taken.

[Pg 135]CHAPTER XLIV.
How they sailed to the Land of the Negroes.

And now, perceiving that they could win no further profit in that land by reason of the advisement that the Moors had already received, the captains began to consult with the chief men of their ships concerning the manner of the action they should take.

"We," said some, "are not able, nor ought we to wait longer in this land, since we know that our stay brings no profit with it, but rather manifest loss, for we are wasting our provisions and wearying our bodies without hope of success. Wherefore it would be a counsel profitable for us, since God hath given us enough, that we should turn back to our country, contenting ourselves with the booty we have taken, the which is not so small that it will not be of value sufficient to compensate for our toils, and to save us from shame in the presence of our neighbours."

"Of a surety," replied others, "such a return would be shameful for such men as we are, for if we were to turn back in this wise it would be indeed an abatement of our honour; but let us go to the land of the negroes, where Dinis Diaz with one only ship went last year to make his capture; and even if we do nothing more than see the land, and afterwards give a relation thereof to the lord Infant, this would be to our honour.[C] Let us reach it, then, since we are so near, and though we accomplish but little, a great profit will be ours." All agreed that it was very well that they should go to that land, for it might be that God would then give them a greater success than they expected.

[Pg 136]And so they hoisted their sails forthwith and pursued their voyage, and sailing on their course a space of 80 leagues they came near to the coast of Guinea,[115]where they made them ready with their boats to land, but when the black men caught sight of them they ran down to the shore with their shields and assegais, as men who sought to make themselves ready for battle; but although they showed so fierce a countenance, yet our men would have gone on shore if the roughness of the sea had consented thereto; and, far as they were from the shore, our men did yet perceive that it was a land very green, peopled by human folk and tame cattle, which the inhabitants of the land had with them for their use. And they would have gone further on still, but the storm increased upon them with much distemperature of the weather, so that they were forced to turn back without remedy.

[C] Lit., "would be a part of," etc.

CHAPTER XLV.
How they forced their way upon shore.

Now that tempest lasted for the space of three days, and they were kept continually running backwards before a contrary wind, but after those three days were ended, that great tempest abated, and the weather became serene, when they had now come to the point where[116] they had previously captured the seven Moors; and on that day the captaincy happened to be with Mafaldo, and he waited for the other caravels to come up. And when they were all assembled in full day light, he came upon the deck of his ship and spake thus to the other captains: "You see right well that we are near to the place where we took the seven Moors, and you know that according to the track of those men which we lighted on, and the nets of their fishery, the land ought in reason to be peopled. Wherefore, if you [Pg 137]think it well, I desire to go on shore and see if I can obtain any booty." And as you see that among many men there are always divers purposes, some began at first to say that such a sally appeared to them useless, since they had got enough wherewith to make their return to their own land, as they had already said before they set out for the land of the Negroes. Others again said that, forasmuch as the expedition was perilous, they ought to go by night and not by day.

"Now," said Mafaldo, "I am your captain to-day, and you are one and all bound to obey me as fully as you would obey the Infant our lord if he were present, and you may suppose that I do not love my life less than each one of you loveth his. Wherefore, my purpose is, notwithstanding your reasonings, to sally forth, for even supposing that the land be peopled it is not to be presumed that the Moors will be even now on the shore waiting for us. And if we go by day we shall have reason to see the country better, and know in what direction we have to go."

The others replied that it sufficed he was captain, for though the contrary opinion might be in favour with some of the company, it was necessary they should obey him; but they begged him to consider well the affair, for they would not turn back, no, not for any mishap that might befall them. The boats were at once lowered, and those who were to go forth were accoutred ready for starting, and, in fact, set out at once. They were in all about thirty-five men-at-arms, and as they went on their way towards the land, one of the men in the boats said to the captain, "I know not if you see what I do?" "And what do you see," said the captain, "that we do not?" "I see," said he, "as me thinketh, that those black things that are upon those banks of sand are the heads of men, and the more closely I look at them, the more it seemeth to me that I am right, and if you look narrowly you will see that [Pg 138]they are moving." And the captain ordered the boats to stop still a little, whereat the Moors concluded that they were discovered, and forthwith they discovered themselves to the number of fifty men, apparelled for fighting, though with no other arms than lances. And when all had thus come forth, Mafaldo made his boats approach near to the shore, at which the Moors showed great pleasure, some wading into the water as high as their necks, and others lower, all of them desirous to get at the Christians. And when Mafaldo saw them thus on the beach, displaying a countenance of such hardihood, he signed to the other boats to draw near to him; and when they were all together he made them stop rowing, and began to speak to them in this wise: "Friends, you know the end for which we came forth from our country; how it was for the service of God, and of the Infant our lord, and for the honour and profit of ourselves, wherein by the grace of that great Lord who created all things, we have had a good enough profit of our booty without any danger to ourselves; yet all our honour is in being 500 leagues from our country in unknown lands, increasing our past victories with new adventures. And since God knoweth our good wills, He hath appointed us a place and time in the which we may gain an honourable victory; for you see before you those Moors with such pride, as if they held us in siege with great advantage to themselves and without hope of succour, provoking us, like men secure of victory over things already vanquished. And although they are more in number than we by a third, yet they are but

Moors, and we are Christians, one of whom ought to suffice for two of them. For God is He in whose power lieth victory, and He knoweth our good wills in His holy service. But if we do not join battle with them it would be to our great dishonour, and we should make them full of courage against any others of our Law. Wherefore my counsel is, that the boats should all three [Pg 139]together row straight among them, and then that each one should do the best he can."

"Your purpose," said the others, "is good enough and full of profit, but what are we to do if many more of their people are lying hidden? For just as these were lying in wait, so there may now be ambushed a much greater number of them unknown to us, and if there is a snare laid and we land, our perdition is assured." Others did not seek to correct these matters, but began to complain, saying that if they were always to reason thus, they would never do a single brave deed. "Is it right," said they, "to see our honour before our eyes, and to leave the matter thus through fear of a hap so doubtful? All the men opposed to us are not sufficient to withstand ten of ours in a fight. For they are but a handful of Moorish knaves, who have never learnt to fight except like beasts, and the first man to be wounded among them will frighten all the others, so that they will not know how to face our arms any longer. Bold indeed would be the men that have their armed ships in the Strait of Ceuta, and through all the Levant Sea, if they were to dread such a hostile gathering as this." These last reasons were well in accord with the will of the captain, and those that spake them were much praised of him.

Wherefore he commanded that in each boat three men should place themselves in the prow with lances and shields to protect themselves and those that rowed, if perchance they should be shot at by the Moors; and as soon as they should have rowed the boats ashore, these men were to leap out at once with their weapons. And he commanded the cross-bow men to keep their cross-bows charged, ordering their shots in such wise that their bolts should be employed to the best advantage. And after this he had the boats rowed as vigorously as possible, telling them to go bow forward among the Moors as had been before determined; the which matter was straightway put in action; and all [Pg 140]shouting with a loud voice, "St. George," "St. James," "Portugal," leapt out upon them as men who feared little the valour of their enemies. And as if in a matter which God Himself willed to ordain, the Moors at the first onset at once discharged their arms, from which no Christian received any dangerous hurt; but, on the contrary, they proved of use later on, for our men possessed themselves of these arms and used them as if they had been their own.

CHAPTER XLVI.
Of the battle that they had, and of the Moors that they took.

When the Moors had lost their arms the Christians considered the victory as won, and began to strike their enemies very briskly like men burning with the first wrath,[D] and when some had fallen dead upon the ground, the others began to fly. And you can imagine what haste they would be in; but although the swiftness of the two parties was unequal by reason of the arms that our men carried, and although they were not so used to running, yet the will, that often increaseth the power,[E] made them equal to their enemy, so that four or five of those Moors became utterly weary, and when our men came up with them they sought the last remedy for their safety, and they threw themselves on the ground as though they besought mercy. And this they obtained, more especially because if our men had killed them the profit would not have been so great. And those in front awaiting the others, who were coming on behind, spake with them, saying that it would be well nevertheless to follow up those Moors; for it could not be but that they had wives and children thereabouts; and that [Pg 141]their journey should not be towards any other part except where they had left them; for though they were wearied they could not be so weary but that if they could catch sight of those women and children they would take a great part of them. And so, leaving some to guard those captives, they went forward, quickening their forces as much as possible. And the Moors, before they arrived at their habitation, began to give tongue, though they were wearied, as men who called or warned other people whom they perceived to be near them, and this made the Christians perceive that their lodgment could not be far off.

For that cry of theirs was nothing else but their warning of their wives and sons, that they might be able to place themselves in safety before they reached them. And at their cries the women came out of the settlement, and because the land is very flat they saw how swiftly their husbands were hastening along, followed by our men. For which reason all of them began to take up their children on their necks, and others in their arms, and others before them, guiding them so as best to escape; and so flying, each their own way, through that plain, the Christians caught sight of them and their children, which was the principal part of their satisfaction. And they waxed bold in hope that their strength would not diminish or prevent their following up the pursuit; and though they were already weary enough, they now quickened their pace like men who desired to come where their wills led them. But since the distance was great and they were already very much weakened, the Moorish women also having but freshly started, they were not able to follow very far; so that after taking a few they could not go forward any more; nay, it was needful for them to await the others who were coming behind, and tell them of their weakness, which had reached such a point that they felt without the strength so much as to return. Wherefore they [Pg 142]decided to turn back, seeing that they could do no more; but first of all they took some repose there, the which was very necessary to them, seeing the greatness of their toil. And so the booty on that day amounted to twelve captives, what of men and women; but above all their gain, the valour with which they assailed their enemies was worthy of high honour, and I believe that up to this point no Moors had been taken with so honourable a victory as these were. Oh how some of those others who had stayed in the ships dispraised themselves, and blamed their captains because they had not helped them to a share in that honour. Nor were they able to listen gladly to the others in all the recital of their victory, for it appeared to them that they had done nothing in comparison with the toil of the others. There they began to take counsel what should be their course after that achievement; and leaving out the long debate they had about this, it was finally determined to enter into certain bays which were between Cape Branco and Cape Tira;[117] for they considered that in those islands they could not fail to make some gain. And in this all agreed, since the hope of profit was of equal strength in the purposes of all.

[D] Of battle.
[E] Of combatants.

CHAPTER XLVII.
How they found the turtles in the Island.

The next day they took their course as they had determined, and when they got within the shoals they saw an island which was further out than all the others, but small and very sandy. Here they put out their boats to see if they could find anything that they looked for; and well it appeared that the Moors had been there but a little time before, from the nets and other fishing tackle that [Pg 143]they found, and especially a great multitude of turtles,[118] which were about one hundred and fifty in number. And since all those who read[F] this history may not have a knowledge of this animal, let them know that turtles are nothing but sea-tortoises, whose shells are as large as shields; and I have seen some like them in this our Kingdom in the lake of Obidos, which is between Atouguya and Pederneira. And although in these islands there is an abundance of good things caught in the sea, the Moors deem this creature of especial value. Now our men, considering that those people had passed to the other islands—for it seems they had caught sight of them—agreed not to take anything of what they found there, for the Moors would surely return to the island, and this would be a part of their security, by means of which, when they themselves returned thither, they could get a victory over them.

[F] Lit., will read.

CHAPTER XLVIII.
How they returned again to the Island, and of the Christians that perished.

Fortune would be false to its nature were it always to turn in one direction; so now, playing its accustomed part, it would not permit our ships to return altogether joyful with their share of victory; for, as it is written in the *Commentaries* of Cæsar, enemies cannot endure a continued distress, nor friends a constant pleasure. Therefore we will narrate this event, sad though it be, in this place, that our history may keep its right order. And it was so, that on the next day very early, the boats returned to the Island according to the agreement they had made before, but they [Pg 144]did not find there the nets nor the other tackle of fishery, but only the turtles which were tied with ropes; but they supposed that the Moors, although they had snatched away their tackling, could not be very far distant; and so, standing there and looking out on every side, they saw another Island, which was separated by an arm of the sea that ran between the two, to wit, that in which they were, and the other they saw there. And being anxious to meet with those Moors, and thinking that fortune would not be less gracious to them in that encounter than in all the others they had had in that voyage, they determined to go to the said Island, to see if they could light upon what they so desired to meet, not knowing the hidden secret that contrary fortune had in store for them. So with haste they put themselves into their boats, in the which they passed over to the said Island, and like men of small advisement, not seeking to consider the hurt that might befall them, they began to spread themselves over the Island as boldly as if they were going through their own property in time of great security. And as Bernard said in the Rule which he gave to Richard, Lord of Castello Ambrosio, upon the government of his household, that he who doth not consider that his enemy may meditate that which he himself meditateth, exposeth himself to danger; so the Moors having the same thought that our men had had, and standing on their guard more carefully, had arranged three ambushes as well as they could, behind some mounds of sand that were there, where they waited until they perceived that our men were near them. Then, seeing their great advantage, they discovered their treachery, and came out stoutly upon our men, like those who sought to avenge the captivity of their relations and friends. And although their multitude was great in comparison of the fewness of our people, yet the latter did not turn back, but faced them like men in whom fear had not got the upper hand of valour: contending with [Pg 145]their enemies a very great space, during which the Moors received great hurt, for the blows of the Christians were not dealt in vain; but at last our people, seeing the greatness of the danger and how they needs must retire, began to retreat, not like men who fled, but with all the caution and valour that such a case required. And, of a surety, the battle was very great, and fought as by men who did so with right good will; but the greater part of the hurt, till they arrived at the boats, fell ever upon the Moors, for of them many died in that retreat, whereas of the Christians, though some were wounded, not one had yet fallen. And when they had now arrived near the boats, since that of Alvaro Gil was the nearest or easiest to enter, there were gathered into that one, and also into Mafaldo's, the greater part of our Christians; but the remainder, seeking to regain the ship's boat of Gonçallo Pacheco, fell into the extremest peril, for the boat was large, and though it had the lightest load, yet they were not able to launch it like the other boats, which were smaller, so that it stuck fast upon the shore: for it seemeth that the tide was in the last quarter of its ebb. And some of those men who knew how to swim, seeing their danger so near at hand, threw themselves into the water, in which they saved their lives by swimming; but the others, who did not know that art, were forced to frame their wills to patience in the receiving of a troublous death, defending themselves, however, as long as strength gave them aid. And so there was an end made of seven, whose souls may God, in His mercy, receive in the habitation of the Saints.

And as the Holy Scripture saith, that he who prayeth for another prayeth for himself, may it please you who read this history to present your prayer to God, that by your intercession their souls may receive some increase in glory. The others in the two boats, seeing the death of those men happen in this manner, betook themselves with [Pg 146]great sadness to the caravels; and in this sadness they departed to Arguim[119] to take in water, of which they were much in need. And the Moors took the[G] boat to the river of Tider, where they broke up the greater part of her, for they tore out the planks with the nails, but I wot not to what end, for their wit did not suffice to make good use of these. And some said afterwards that they had heard it said by some of those Moors who chanced to fall into our hands, that their countrymen ate those dead men; and although, on the other hand, other of our captives denied this, seeking to excuse their countrymen of a matter so monstrous, at any rate it is certain that their custom is to eat the liver of their captives and to drink their blood: not as a general thing, but only, as was said, in the case of those who had killed their fathers, or sons, or brothers, counting this as a very great vengeance. And this seemeth to me a matter of no doubt, as 'tis said in the book of Marco Polo[120] that many nations in those Eastern parts were generally accustomed to those cannibal actions; and I see, too, that it is even now a common mode of speech among us, when we reason of some man who beareth hatred against another, that he hath such ill-will to his adversary that, if he could, he would eat his liver and drink his blood.

But now let us leave these matters, and return to our history.

[G] Captured.

CHAPTER XLIX.

How Lançarote and the others of Lagos asked of the Infant permission to go to Guinea.

Meseemeth the memory of the death of Gonçallo de Sintra should have profited those of whose hurt I have [Pg 147]spoken in the last chapter, for by it they might have taken some warnings and very easily escaped the destruction that befell them; and it would have profited them, I say, if they had left their boats afloat, considering the custom[1] of the sea, since they could not fix the time of their return for certain; but the good fortune of their other enterprises gave them an hope that was not sure, for they thought that it would assist them in this affair even as in others.

But now, leaving these matters on one side, let us collect our strength and go out again and avenge these men. So you must know that Lançarote, that knight of whom we have spoken, being as he was Collector of the Royal Taxes[121] in Lagos, came to the Infant, together with the judges and the alcayde and the officers of the corporation of that town, in the name of all the chief men of the place, and spake to him in this wise:—

"It is well known to your Highness how the dwellers in this our town, from the time that Ceuta was taken even unto this present, have always rendered service, and do still render service, with their bodies and ships, in the war against the Moors, for the service of God and of the King our lord. And so in the time of the other kings, when the coast of this kingdom was harassed by the Moors, our ships were the first to arm against them, as it is found in writings and remembered in the memories of men of great age. Therefore, my lord, since your Grace gave order to seek for this land of Guinea, you know well how in this place you have fitted out the more part of your armaments, wherein you received all the service that lay in our power. And since, my lord, after the due obedience we must render to the King, your nephew, our lord, we are most chiefly bound to love and serve you, we have been considering some manner in which our service to you may [Pg 148]be of special moment, in such wise that by the desert of our great toil, our honour may be exalted in the memories of the men of future ages. And even if we were to receive no more guerdon for our toil than that, we should hold it as sufficient; but we are certain that over and above this we shall gain great profit, especially in the hope we have of receiving from your lordship great rewards on our return from this service of ours. And in truth, my Lord," said they, "the deed will be of such a sort that the dwellers in this place, even after your time, so long as there is an inhabited region amongst us, will be bound to pray God for you.

"And if some in their malice should seek to be so ingrate as to strive to deny this, in presence of your benefits, which they will have daily before their eyes, they would themselves be their own chief accusers, for they will see before their eyes great lineages of servants, both men and women, which they have obtained for their service, and their houses abounding in bread, which hath come to them from the isles which were peopled through your means; yea, and there are ancient writings which will perpetually speak of the great privileges and liberties which they obtained from you. Wherefore, my Lord, we having considered about all this; and seeing that you toil every day more and more in the war against the Moors; and learning that, in the expedition that Lançarote made with his caravels, a great multitude of Moors was found at the isle of Tider, wherein Gonçallo de Sintra was afterwards slain; and perceiving that[1] the Moors of the said island are now able to cause great hindrance to your ships—therefore we desire, with the approval of your Grace, to take arms against them, and either by death or capture to break their strength and power in such wise that your ships may sail [Pg 149]along all that coast without fear of any. And if God shall crown our deed with a victorious issue, we shall be able, besides effecting the destruction of our enemies, to make booty of great worth, through which you will receive for your fifth a great profit, and in this we also shall not be without our share. And to this, my Lord, may it please you to make your answer, that we may speedily pursue our voyage, while the summer time giveth us favourable weather therefor."

[H] Of ebb and flow.
[I] Almoxarife.
[J] Lit., inasmuch as.

CHAPTER L.
How the Infant replied to the men of Lagos, and of the armament that was made ready against the said island.

"Great matters," replied the Infant, "be often disprized where things of small moment are much commended; for better is the mean man who liberally offereth his whole self than the grandee who in niggardly wise tendereth his share. And, moreover, the offering of your good wills is of greater price than the great services of more powerful men, which were not granted me with so good a grace. And, for my certitude of this, I need not a surer testimony than your past deeds, by the which I am constrained to honour and advance you, with that love and good will which I show to the chief men of each one of my towns or villages, in the which, by the grace of the King my Lord, I hold, after him, full and entire jurisdiction. And as for the permission you require of me to go against the Moors of the Isle of Tider, it is much to my pleasure to grant it you, and to grant you also for this my grace and aid: yea, such a request as yours is much to be commended, for one should not so much prize the hope of a share in profit as discern and praise the good will which has moved you to this.

[Pg 150]

"And now, forthwith," said he, "you can put your matters in train for starting, and you may ask of me anything which you require to aid you in your preparations, for I will not be less liberal to you in this than I would be to any of my Household who by my own especial command were making themselves ready for the said voyage."

And at these words of his all made great obeisance, kissing his hands in the name of all those others for whom they had come. Now, when all the others in the place had heard the message, they began at once to make ready to arm their caravels and pursue their voyage as speedily as they could; and the news of this armament went out through all parts of the Kingdom, which news stirred up others to join themselves to the said company. But I believe that this was not without the especial order of the Infant, since, as I have said before, no one could go to Guinea without the allowance of that lord.

CHAPTER LI.
How the caravels quitted Lagos, and what captains were in them.

On this occasion it happened that the Infant Dom Henry was summoned on the part of his brother Dom Pedro, who was Regent of the kingdom in the name of the King, as we have said already, to go to Coimbra and knight Dom Pedro of Portugal, eldest son of the said Regent, who was then Constable of these realms; and who was ordered to go to Castille, as in fact he did. Forasmuch as the King Don John the Second, who was then King of that realm, was in trouble with his cousins, the King of Navarre and the Infant Don Henry, who was master of the Order of Santiago, and other grandees of that kingdom who were with them, because of the great enmities which had sprung [Pg 151]up between the said King and those lords, owing to the Constable Don Alvaro de Luna. For he, being a man of common origin and manners, by superabundance of fortune or some other hidden secret, came to such a pitch of power that he did whatever he pleased in the kingdom, so that for his sake were slain and destroyed the principal men of Castille, as you will learn more at length in the General Chronicle of the kingdom, since of necessity the said actions must be touched on there. Right well did the Infant Dom Pedro give the world to understand the great dignity that he recognised in his brother, for he held it as a greater honour that his son should receive knighthood at the hand of his uncle than at that of any other Prince of Spain.

And among the things which I have heard say the Infant spake to that son of his, when he left him, was this: that he charged him to remember the order of chivalry which he had received, and especially from whose hand he had received it, the which matter was no small charge for him. But before the Infant Dom Henry had thus set out from Lagos, he left in the chief command of all those ships, Lançarote, the same knight of whom we have already spoken; and this was done with the consent of all the other captains: for though there were then a sufficiency of notable persons worthy of great honour, yet, knowing the judgment and discretion of that man, it was their pleasure that he should have this charge. For there was there Sueiro da Costa, Alcayde of that city of Lagos, who was a nobleman and a fidalgo, brought up from boyhood in the court of the King, Dom Edward; and who happened to have been in many notable actions. For he was in the battle of Monvedro[122] with the King, Don Fernando of Aragon, against the men of Valencia,[K] and he was at the [Pg 152]leaguer of[123]Balaguer,[L] in which were performed very great matters; and he was with the King Ladislaus[M] when he assailed the city of Rome; and he was with the King Louis of Provence in all his war; and he was at the battle of Agincourt, which was a very great and mighty battle, between the Kings of France and England; and he was in the battle of Vallamont[N] with the Constable of France against the Duke of Ossestre; and in the battle of Montsécur, in which were the Count of Foix[O] and the Count of Armagnac; and he was at the taking of Soissons[P]and at the raising of the sieges of Arrasa[Q] and Ceuta,[R] in which matters he always approved himself a very valiant man of arms. And this Sueiro da Costa was father-in-law of Lançarote.[124] And there were also in that captaincy Alvaro de Freitas, Commander of Aljazur, which belongeth to the order of Santiago, a nobleman, and one who had made very great prizes among the Moors of Granada, and of Bellamarim; and Gomez Pirez, commander of the King's galley, of whom we have already spoken in another chapter; and Rodriguez Eannes of Travaços, a servant of the Regent, who was a very zealous squire, and toiled to the utmost of his power to increase his honour. And there was also Pallenço, a man who had often fought against the Moors, and who spent his whole life in the service of God and of the kingdom, undertaking and accomplishing by himself very great actions (as we have said in the General Chronicle of the Kingdom) after Ceuta was taken. Other good and honourable persons chanced to be in the said company, whom we omit to mention, so as not to be too lengthy: such as Gil Eannes, a knight and dweller in that town, and Stevam Affonso, and others. And to speak briefly there were armed in that place and year[125] [Pg 153]fourteen caravels, besides some others that were armed in Lisbon and in the Madeira Islands, to wit, those of Dinis Diaz,[126] who was the first to reach the land of the Negroes, and of Tristam,[S][127] one of the captains of the island,[T] who went there in person with his caravel; besides the vessel of Alvaro Gonçalvez d'Atayde, who was then preceptor to the King, and afterwards Count of Atouguya; moreover, John Gonçalvez Zarco, who had the other captaincy in Madeira,[U] sent there two caravels; and other ships were there, of whose masters we do not care to make express mention in this place. Only it were well you should know that in this year there were armed to go to that land of the Negroes twenty-six caravels, not counting the Fusta of Pallenço; and among these the thirteen ships of Lagos started first, and after them the others, each one as it best could; but they did not all together take part in the affair of Tider.

And as the history cannot be recounted as well as might be, for that the voyage was not made by all the caravels in company, we will only say what we can, in the best manner that we can speak.

[K] Vallença.
[L] Vallaquer.
[M] Lançaraao.
[N] Cabo de Caaes.
[O] Fooes.
[P] Sansoões.
[Q] Ras.
[R] Cepta.

CHAPTER LII.

Of how the caravels met at Cape Branco, and how Laurence Diaz fell in with the caravels of Lisbon.

It was on the tenth day of August when the fourteen caravels set out from Lagos; and forasmuch as they were not able to follow one route in company, and many times tempests overtook them which separated one from the other, they made agreement as usual to await one another at Cape Branco. And starting all together with a favourable tide and wind for their journey, when they were [Pg 154]only a little way distant from the coast, some of the ships began to show that they sailed better than the others, and among them all that of Laurence Diaz began to take the lead. But now, leaving this vessel and the others to pursue their voyage, we will return a little to speak of the three caravels of Lisbon, which were left in grievous case by reason of the loss of their seven men who were slain, and we will see if we can give them any consolation. And it was so, that after that event of ill fortune, while they were wholly desperate of obtaining vengeance on that occasion, they made sail towards the isle of Arguim, where they arrived with the intention of watering, and thence proceeding to the kingdom.[IV] And when they were just ready to set out, they began, as it chanced, to speak about their voyage: to wit, how many leagues they should follow in one course and how many in another, when the sail of the ship of Laurence Diaz began to appear. And when they saw this, all were so much the more joyful, especially as they knew that it was a ship of Christian folk, and what was more, of Christians from this Kingdom of Portugal, because no vessel of that kind, or like unto it, was to be seen in that part save what came from our land. Suffice it that this caravel joined the others, whereat the minds both of the one and of the other party were very joyful, and especially the minds of those who were there before, when Laurence Diaz told them of the coming of the other caravels, and of the purpose for which they came. "You others," said Laurence Diaz, "should take great delight in our arrival, as it seemeth to me; and since you desire revenge for the hurt you have sustained, you have now an opportunity to take such vengeance. And since the being avenged by other hands could not be so much to your contentment, you should now put off your [Pg 155]departure, that you may be with us in the conquest of this island, by the which you will have manifold gain. First you will obtain honour and profit; and secondly you will witness the injury of your enemies, along with the vengeance taken for your hurt; while in the third place you will be the first to take the news of this to the lord Infant, and may it please God that the news I speak of be such as we hope, for thereby your reception shall be so much the better, and with a greater increase of reward."

"You may well believe, Laurence Diaz," answered those captains, "that no other words were needed to move us to such a deed, but only our own good wills; but on account of certain difficulties amongst ourselves, it is necessary that we first take counsel about what you say."

"That should be done at once," said Laurence Diaz, "for my stay here must not be long, inasmuch as I fear that the other caravels will be already at the island, and I should have a great displeasure if they were to accomplish anything without me."

The others said they would speak about the matter that very night, and very early they would give him an answer. And to leave out their prolixities, I will say in a word that their councils were divided. On the one side some said that despite all contrary reasons they ought to make their way straight home, since they already had booty with which they could reasonably make their voyage, and this was all the more necessary as provisions were failing them, which all could see right well. Moreover, the accomplishment of that deed (to which Laurence Diaz urged them) was not certain; for it might be that the caravels would encounter some contrary fortune, by which occasion they would be stayed, to no purpose wasting their victuals, in which rested the sustenance of their life. Others, however, said that it would be a great disgrace to them if they were so near and did not join themselves to [Pg 156]the company which essayed that action. "Were we already" said they, "half way on our voyage, and chanced upon such an encounter, we should turn back;[V] how much the more therefore, when we are now, as it were, on the shores of the said island, and when we are invited to it for the service of God and the lord Infant. Of a surety we should be ill-accounted of were we to leave such an emprise for any consideration at all."

All fell in with this accord, for the greater part of the company agreed with this second resolution. Thereupon they arranged to order their provision in such wise that the victuals might last them a longer time; and so much were their wills disposed to this venture that some said that, in good sooth, it would be better to throw a moiety of those Moors[VI] into the sea, rather than relinquish a matter so honourable for their sakes, and one in which they might get vengeance for the death of their companions. The agreement was thus concluded, and on the next day they gave their answer to Laurence Diaz, in whose company they started at once for the Ilha das Garças, where for three days they waited the coming of the other caravels, refreshing themselves with the birds of that island, of which there was there a great multitude. More especially may we speak of some birds there, that are not in our land, which are called hornbills, and are all white, of a size greater than swans, and with beaks of a cubit's length or more, and three fingers in breadth; and they look like the engraved sheaths of swords, so wrought and with such ornamentation as if they had been made artificially with the aid of fire to give them beauty; and the mouth and maw is so great that the leg of a man, however large it were, would go into it as far as the knee.[128] Now when those three days were passed the other caravels began to come, [Pg 157]arriving at Cape Branco two by two and three by three, as they chanced to meet. But there did not meet there more than nine ships, to wit, those of Lançarote and of Sueiro da Costa, and of Alvaro de Freitas, and of Gil Eannes, and of Gomez Pirez, and certain others of the town of Lagos.

[S] Vaz.
[T] Madeira.
[U] Besides Tristam Vaz.
[V] Of Portugal.
[W] And join the enterprise.
[X] Their prisoners.

CHAPTER LIII.
Of how Lançarote held a council at Cape Branco.

Those nine caravels being thus met together, for they had yet no news of that of Laurence Diaz, Lançarote bade all the other captains go on shore that he might speak with them about the course that might seem good for them to take; and these captains were very quickly ready. And when they were all together joined in council, Lançarote said: "My noble friends, although it pleased the lord Infant my lord, to give me charge of your captaincies, you being of such honourable estate as you are, yet I fail not to know, as is right, how to treat you with the honour that I ought, and in this wise give you that authority which your honourable persons merit; and putting aside Sueiro da Costa, whom I regard as a father by reason of his daughter who is my wife, I hold nearly all of you[Y] as brothers, some by our having been brought up together, and some by ancient friendship, and others by long acquaintance. Therefore I hope that you will counsel and aid me as a friend and brother, beyond what you are bound in reason to do, in such wise that I may be a worthy captain of such honourable personages as you, for I do not purpose to do anything, either great or small, without your counsel. And for God's sake, let each one imagine that the charge[Z] [Pg 158]is principally his own, and so, as if it were a private matter, let him labour to discover proper remedies for our case. And in truth I am right glad when I consider that I am consulting such discreet personages, who have seen and experienced such great and honourable matters, and whose experience will be a very great help in our undertaking, since the government and direction of the matters which are to come depend chiefly upon the good understanding of things past." "Now," said he, "we here assembled are nine caravels, as you see, and you know that in all we set out fourteen from Portugal. I desire therefore to know of you what it seemeth to you that we should do. Whether perchance we ought to start at once as we are, or whether it would be better to await the others who have to come."

"We thank you for your good purpose," said Alvaro de Freitas (speaking for himself and the others, for being a knight as he was, and moreover of high and noble rank, as we have said already, it pleased all the other captains to give him that authority). "We thank you," said he, "and you may be sure that there is not any one here who will not aid and counsel you, not only as captain and friend, but as if you were his own self; and the reasons for this are many, and therefore I now forbear to touch upon them. Let it suffice that all of us know you for a brave and valiant man, so much so that not only are you deserving of the captaincy of these few men and ships, but of many more besides. And as to the counsel that you ask, it seemeth to me that although all the fourteen caravels must meet together for the invasion of the Island of Tider, as was agreed at our outcoming, yet I think it would be well if we who have arrived here already were to go at once to the Ilha das Garças,[129] and there wait two or three days, according to the arrangement that we have. For that is a place where we cannot be seen by the other [Pg 159]side, but if we remain near this Cape we shall readily be discovered, in which case we shall not escape one of two things: either the Moors will leave that Island, or so many will enter it that when we wish to attack it we shall be in very great danger. And if peradventure those other five caravels do not arrive at the Ilha das Garças within a few days, my determination would be not to wait any longer for them, but simply to carry out what we have[130] been ordered. And if it be the will of God to aid us, as I hope in Him, since it is in His service before all else that we are come here, that aid which will be ours when we are all met together will likewise be the portion of those of us who are here, or peradventure in greater measure, since just as we feel our necessity to be the greater, so we shall have recourse to His aid with greater devotion; and whereas when we were all joined together, we should place our hope in the strength of men, now, seeing ourselves to be few in number, we shall rest our chief succour on His aid. And now, from henceforth, said he, you will be able to ordain that which seemeth to you to have the advantage over my counsel." "In good sooth," replied they all, "your counsel is so good and so profitable that anything we should say over and above would be superfluous, or perchance even mischievous, as distracting us from the true path in which your good words have set us."

[Y] Lit., you others.
[Z] Of this expedition.

CHAPTER LIV.
Of how they found the other caravels at the Isle of Herons, and of the counsel that they took.

Great pleasure was theirs when they came within sight of the Ilha das Garças and saw the four caravels which were lying at rest, in whatsoever guise they were there; for it mattered not whether they formed part of their company, [Pg 160]since they knew them to be from the kingdom of Portugal, wherefore they hoped that their assistance would supply the want of the others which they expected before. The news of this sight ran through all the caravels, as they came up one after another, and in this all received great pleasure, and especially the common people, in that they saw the captains had taken their determination to attempt the enterprise, and would not now be hindered by the non-arrival of the others, as hath been written above. And as people who did not know how to conceal their gladness, they made their instruments to sound, and raised chants, and so fell to eating and drinking as men full of good confidence of victory. And arriving at the ships that lay anchored there, they charged their bombards and culverins, and made therewith a salute in signal of the pleasure of their hearts, in the which pleasure the others who were already lying there at rest were not without their share. But all this increased twofold the sorrow of the Moors who lay, as they had been put, under the decks of the vessels, for though they could not understand the language, yet the sound of the voices right well assured them of the opposite of what they desired. I will not occupy myself in describing the embracings of our men when they all met together, forasmuch as reason itself will tell you what they must have been at such a place and time; only let us imagine that we see them leap from ship to ship, and that those who had set out from Portugal more recently, now offered to their comrades who had gone before the food of which they knew they stood in need. And so, in doing this and in taking repose at night, they spent their time until the next day, when by the order of Lançarote they went on shore, in order that all might take counsel together. And when they were assembled, he said how all could right well perceive the delay of the other caravels, and how God willed that they should meet [Pg 161]there those three ships which some time ago had set out from the kingdom, together with one of the five,[AA] which before they hoped to meet. And he showed them that now there lacked but one of their complement of fourteen. So that while they had already resolved to attack their enemies with nine ships, they could the more readily do so with thirteen, but that they should consider if it were well to depart straightway, or to wait some little time longer.

All said that the delay would be harmful, and they saw no profit in it, and that they ought to start at once with good fortune, and the earlier they could begin that action the better it would be; and in this all agreed, for in such a time and place there was no fear of contrary suggestions, nor of companions betraying their secrets to the enemy. "Now, then, that you have resolved," said Lançarote, "to set out upon this enterprise in any case, it were well that you, who have already seen many dispositions appertaining to such an enterprise as this, should remind yourselves of them, and aid me in arranging our expedition, that we may go on in good order." And omitting all the various opinions which were mooted in their debate, it was finally determined that they should proceed on this wise. From the whole company that was in the caravels they were to choose two hundred and twenty-eight men, because it appeareth that they needed so many in the partition that had been ordered of their forces, and of these the footmen and lancers were to go in the battle of which Alvaro de Freitas was captain. Behind him followed Lançarote with all the crossbowmen and archers, and in the rear guard were Sueiro da Costa and Dinis Eannes de Graã with all the men-at-arms. And they determined to start very early, so that before dawn they might attack the [Pg 162]settlement of Tider Island; and three boats with pilots in them went before the caravels, the pilots being men who had already been in that land, and who knew the way.

[AA] *I.e.*, the ship of Laurence Diaz.

CHAPTER LV.
How those people landed on the Island of Tider.

I am wroth with those pilots in that they so far wandered from the course they should have taken, for of a surety if fortune had not intermeddled in the mistake of that voyage, the victory would have been much more perfect. But the blame for this was not so much with the pilots as with the darkness of the night, for although they had been there before, the previous occasions were not so many that these men could fairly be blamed very much for their mistakes at this time. Perhaps, too, the true cause of the misadventure was the water, which was at the neap, so that our men found it in many places so shallow that they could not float[AB]; so that finding themselves on dry ground they were compelled to wait for the aid of the flood tide, which they did not get till it was high noon. Oh, what complaints were to be heard among our men at seeing themselves thus hindered of their purpose by something in which their strength could avail nothing. "Ah, God," said they, "Thou willest to be less favourable to this our enterprise than Thou hast been many times to others, who had not so fervent a purpose to serve Thee This day, on which Thy Holy Name might have cause to be so much glorified and our honour so much exalted, Thou givest place to the feeble power of one element of Thy creation, which is of force to hinder us. Have mercy on us by Thy sacred pity, and aid us, for we are Thy [Pg 163]servants, sinners though we be, for the greatness of Thy benignity is more than the multitude of our sins. And if Thou didst exert Thy power to open a way for the Children of Israel through the midst of the waters, and madest the sun to turn back at the request of Joshua against the course of Nature, why wilt Thou not show as great a favour to this Thy people, so that Thy miracle may appear before our eyes, and that these waters may rise before their time, and that our voyage may be directed to gain a perfect victory."

So toiled those seamen during that night as best they could, but for the two reasons that I have already given, they did not reach the island till the sun was high. And before they arrived at the harbour where they had to disembark, they arranged that all the caravels should join together, and they sailed in so close together that the men jumped from one into another. And then there arose among them a new opinion, for some said that it was not in reason that they should land, inasmuch as it was well known that many Moors were collected there, and they would certainly be more in number than they were before, on account of the caravels from Lisbon, which had visited the place some days ago and had lost in that island, not fifteen days before, the seven men of whom we spoke. At least, they said, they ought not to land that day, inasmuch as they supposed that the Moors were numerous, and were lying hid in ambushes, since none appeared. And this surmise was not confined to a few, but prevailed throughout the greater part of the rank and file. "Friends," said the captains, "it is for war, and for war alone, that we are come to this land; and this being so, we must not be timid, for if we fight our battle by day it will be much more to our honour than if we fight by night—attacking the Moors of this island, and expelling them, by sheer force of arms rather than by any cunning or stratagem. Better the [Pg 164]former way of battle, even if we fail to kill or take a single man, than the latter with a night capture of a thousand prisoners. And so in God's name," said they, "let us set forth at once, and let us take land in our predetermined order". And with these words they began forthwith to disembark, and as soon as they were all on shore, they put their ranks in order; and Lançarote, by agreement with all the other captains, took the Banner of the Crusade, which the Infant Dom Henry had given him (and you already know how those who died under the said banner were absolved from sin and punishment, according to the grant of the Holy Father, whose mandate you have seen and the tenor thereof). And this banner was entrusted to Gil Eannes,[131] Knight of the Infant's Household, a native of Lagos, about whom we have spoken to you before. And although Lançarote understood the value and virtues of this man, yet he made him swear forthwith and took fealty of him, that not for fear nor for danger would he leave the said banner till death; and the others also swore to him that in consequence they would toil to guard and defend him even to the last moment of their life. And when these things were done, our men, so arrayed, began to move forward in the predetermined order, and went a space of three leagues over sand, the day being very hot, till they arrived at the place of Tider,[AC] which is in the interior of the said island, close to which they saw a multitude of Moors drawn up as if to fight. Now this sight was a very joyful one to the Christians, and so they bade "sound the trumpets," and went at them with right good will; but the Moors, losing their first courage, began to fly, casting themselves into the water and swimming across a creek which maketh that land an island, to the which[AD] their women and children had passed over already with all their poor goods; [Pg 165]but they were not able with all their haste to prevent our men from killing eight of them and taking four. And there one of the men of Lagos was wounded, for he sought to outstrip the others to show his valour, so that almost of his own free will he received the said wounds of the which he afterwards died when at sea, and may the Lord God receive his soul into the company of the saints. And so the Moors having been routed, the Christians, perceiving that a longer stay there would not profit them, betook themselves to that place where the enemy had had their habitations before, and there they found a supply of water, which after the heat and toil they had suffered gave them great pleasure, for many would have perished with thirst if they had not found it. Also they discovered there cotton trees, although there were not many of them.

Now the weariness of some of our men was so great that they could not by any means return on foot; but they found a great succour for their need in some asses, of which there were many in the island, and riding on these they returned to their ships. But before they entered into their boats, there were some that asked that noble man, Sueiro da Costa, that he would consent to be knighted; and to this he agreed, either at the pressing demands of his friends, or because he desired it for his own greater honour: saying that it pleased him so long as he received it from the hand of Alvaro de Freitas,[132] since he knew him to be such a knight that his own knighthood would be beyond reproach. And at this all the company were very glad, and especially those chief men who knew him.[AE]And so that noble man was made a knight, and I marvel at his so long toiling in the profession of arms and being so distinguished in the same, without ever having been willing to [Pg 166]receive that honour of knighthood until this occasion. Of a surety, saith our Author, I well believe that though Alvaro de Freitas was such a noble knight, and it had happened to him to create others like him,[AF] yet never had his sword touched the head of so noble and so eminent a man; nor was the said Alvaro de Freitas a little honoured by the circumstance that Sueiro da Costa sought to be knighted at his hand, when he could have obtained the same from very honourable kings and great princes, who would have been very content to show him that grace for the knowledge they had of his great valour.

That night they went back to their caravels to rest, and on the next day they went on shore, to perform the knighting of Dinis Eannes de Graã, the which was likewise done by the hand of Alvaro de Freitas. And there the caravels of Lisbon took leave of the others, because they perceived that their stay there was no longer necessary, and provisions failed them, so that if their voyage were delayed by any contrary hap they would of necessity be placed in great suffering. But it may well be believed that if they had known that so many Moors were yet to be slain and taken in that island, they would not have departed so quickly,[AG] if only for the fulfilment of a greater vengeance. Of the other Moors who were taken at Tider, Lançarote and the other captains sent one to Cape St. Vincent; and to Sta. Maria da Augua da Lupe, a hermitage which is in that district of Lagos, they sent another to be sold, that with the price of him ornaments might be bought for that church.

[AB] Their boats.

[AC] Tidre.
[AD] Viz., island.
[AE] Sueiro da Costa.
[AF] Sueiro da Costa.
[AG] But would have waited.

[Pg 167]CHAPTER LVI.

How they returned again to Tider, and of the Moors that they took.

Me seemeth it is not necessary that we should speak of the arrival of the caravels at Lisbon, nor that we should fill up this writing of ours with a recital of the sale of the Moors, as we found it in the account of Affonso Cerveira, from whom we have borrowed this record; for already the men of that city[AH]were accustomed to the coming of Moors from that land: for, as saith Fra Gil de Roma, in the first part of his first book,[133] *De Regimine Principum*, "the property of temporal goods, as regards the desires of men is of such a kind that before a man possesseth them, they appear to him much more valuable than in truth they are; but after he hath acquired them, the contrary happeneth, for however vast and good they may be, he holdeth them not in so great account." And returning to our history: as soon as those three caravels had set out, there arrived other three out of those four which had failed to come before, and among these there was no small complaining that they had not been with their companions at the invasion of the island; for although the fighting was not greater than we have related, it appeared to them that whatever they might do they could not hope to win any honour;[AI] and so like men who felt jealous at it, they called upon the others forthwith to order a sortie upon the land: and upon this matter they took counsel, and after some debate they determined that the three smallest caravels should go to the ford of the creek of Tider, and that the people of the other caravels should go likewise in the boats. For it might be that the natives would return [Pg 168]to the island, in which case they could take some of them in that spot.

And beginning to put their plan in action, they set out in the night; yet they were not able to reach the passage till day. And arriving there, they saw the Moors on the other side; and the Christians being in front of the ford—which was a broad sheet of water, though shallow, except for the distance of a stone's cast that could not be crossed without swimming—the Moors stood still on the other side of it looking at them.[AJ] But of them they seemed to have small fear indeed; and their countenances showed that it was so, for they were dancing and rejoicing like men who are secure from their enemies, to whom they made those signs, as if to enrage them by scoffing at their approach. But it would have been well for them if they had been better advised, and especially if they had remained further in the creek, where the water was deep, for so they would have been in greater security in regard to what chanced to them afterwards. The Christians, besides the desire they had to get at them, when they saw their behaviour, which was that of enemies who despised them, felt doubly eager to fight, although the Moors were many more in number.

So, although they suffered great hindrance from the water, which was between ebb and flow, the ardent desire they had forced them to pursue their purpose. And so they began to enter into the water till they came to that deep place which could not be passed without swimming, and arriving there they halted, as they held the crossing to be dangerous. And while they stood there battling as it were with themselves, for courage urged them on, and fear replied to courage with the threat of death, there happened to be among them a youth of the Infant's chamber, whom [Pg 169]I afterwards knew as a noble esquire, and who was now going as purser in one of these caravels—for it was the custom of the Infant not to give the position of an esquire to any youth of his court till he had exercised himself in some feat of arms; and according to their merit he granted them in the future such dignity as he thought they deserved. Now this youth, who was named Diego Gonçalvez, mastered by the ardour of his courage, spake to a man of Lagos who was near him, called Pero Allemam[134] (I do not know if it was because he was a native of that country of Germany, or if it was a nickname that had been given him), and asked him if he would join him in swimming across. "By my faith," replied the other, "you could not ask me a matter I would grant you with greater willingness;" and before he had finished his answer he plunged into the water and began to swim, and the youth with him; and after him an esquire of the

Infant's Household, named Gil Gonçalvez, who had been at the taking of the first Moorish prisoners, under the captaincy of Antam Gonçalvez, and also in the war waged against those other Moors who border upon our Spain, and he had the reputation of being a valiant man. And immediately after them went another youth of the Prince's Household, who was named Lionel Gil, and a son of that knight to whom the banner of the crusade had been entrusted, and many others followed after these. But the enemy, though they saw them, judged this movement of their toil to be but play, boldly trusting in their multitude, and thinking that victory would hasten to them as it had come the other day, when they slew the seven men from the other caravels. But our men, as soon as they gained a foothold, stood erect and pressed on as far as they could until the enemy fell on them. So the Christians, in order to gain the land, and the Moors in order to prevent them, began their fight, plying their lances, by the which there could well be seen [Pg 170]the hatred there was between them. But the fight on the part of the Moors was not so much from enmity as in defence of their women and children, and still more for the salvation of their own lives. Our men wondered greatly at the courage they perceived in their enemies; and though the comparison was unequal in the number of the two parties, for the Moorish company was very much greater, yet, God being willing to aid His own, they slew out of hand sixteen, and the others were routed in a very short space. And although the love of their women and children was of surpassing strength before all other passions of theirs, as is natural in all men, yet, seeing themselves routed, all their care was to provide for their own safety; for, however terrible other matters may be, death doth put an end to all. And so, being conquered, they began to fly, and there perished many of them. But because the heat was very great, and our men were sore wearied, they were not able to pursue them far; but they took fifty-seven of them, and with them returned to the caravels.

[AH] Lisbon.
[AI] After what had already been accomplished.
[AJ] The Christians.

CHAPTER LVII.
How they went to Tira.

Though all had toiled in that action, and though all deserve a meed of praise and honour for the same, yet principally the aforesaid Diego Gonçalvez and that man of Lagos who passed over with him are to be praised, for the reason that I have already mentioned: for to the beginnings of an enterprise the greater praises are due. And, in fact, it was so regarded by the Infant, for he bestowed a rich reward upon them afterwards, as he was ever accustomed to do upon those who served him well. So, when those captured Moors had been brought on board the ships, our men began at once to ask of [Pg 171]some of them, separately, where they thought they would find the others that had escaped from the company; and our prisoners made reply that their opinion was that the rest would be at a settlement called Tira, which was on the mainland by the sea-shore, about eight leagues distant. And considering that the earlier they went after them the more profitable their going would be, for they imagined that such a short time having elapsed they would find the Moors quite off their guard—for this reason, then, they set off at once that very night with three caravels, the smallest and lightest in their fleet, and all the other people went in the boats, taking with them two Moorish women to show them the way. And in the first quarter of the night they arrived at a point where they left their ships and landed; and because they did not conceive it yet to be a fit time to start, they rested there till the dawn began to break, and by the aid of its brightness they began to make their way. And coming to a crossing of a little arm of the sea, they fell in with a multitude of canoes, among which was the boat which the Moors had taken from the caravels of Lisbon, but it was now almost broken up. However, they took it with them to carry back to the caravels. And passing on, they fell in with a Moor, whom they killed—as I believe because he himself sought the way to it. And so they arrived over against Tira and two other villages, but they did not find in these anything that they sought, since the Moors had all fled. And so they had to turn back to the caravels, and thence they passed over to Tider, where they rested by reason of the water that was there. While they were staying there, the captains bade some of them go for asses, that the weak ones might return on them to the ships; and while these were carrying out what had been commanded them, they met with five Moors, whom they took with but little trouble. And so being returned, [Pg 172]Lançarote said that as it was now late they should rest for that night, and that on the next day he wished to discuss certain matters with them, which they would know then.

CHAPTER LVIII.
Of the words that Lançarote spake.

On the next day, when all the principal men were met together by order of the chief captain, as you have heard already, as well as all the others who wished to come, Lançarote said:—"Friends and gentlemen,—In that it was the grace of the Infant, our lord, to make me your captain, and your pleasure and will consented that it should be so, and because I here represent his person, I now in his name thank you all for your great toil and good will, which I have found in one and all of you in this action, whereto you came in his service: the which I will myself recount to him when it please God that we stand again before him, in such wise that for the deserts of your toil you may obtain that guerdon which you so justly merit.

"Now you know how we set out from our town with the main object of coming to the conquest of this island, and as God hath willed to despatch and guide us to it, we owe Him for this much thanks; for even though we did not take so many Moors as formerly, yet our victory was adequate, since in half a day we surrounded and attacked them as you have seen, and great as was their number, they left the field to our triumph, and we entered into their country and took their property without any hindrance; thus securing for ourselves honour and praise among all those who shall have a true understanding of the matter. And as for our coming here, according to the plan we brought with us, the matter has been performed, so that I cease to be your captain: for, according to the directions [Pg 173]that I have from the lord Infant,[1135] after the capture of this island each one of you may do what he pleaseth, so as to go wherever he may perceive his advantage or profit to lie. And so it seemeth good to me that these few prisoners we have taken should be divided in such wise that each one may have his own rightful share and go wherever he thinks best. And for my part, I assure you that I am ready for whatever toil or peril may come to me in the service of God and of the Infant, my lord, for with so small a booty I do not intend to go back to his presence." All the rest replied that what Lançarote had said was very well considered, and they began forthwith to divide the booty[AK] into equal parts, according to which each one received what his lot gave him. And after that, Lançarote required of all the other captains what they were wishful to do. Sueiro da Costa and Vicente Diaz, the owner of a ship, and Gil Eannes and Martin Vicente, pilot, and John Diaz, also owner of a ship, replied that forasmuch as their caravels were small and winter was very near, they held it as perilous to remain and proceed any further, wherefore they intended to return home to Portugal. But of the manner of their return we will speak fully later on in this history.

[AK] Of captives.

CHAPTER LIX.
Of the words which Gomez Pirez spoke, and how they went to the land of Guinea.

Gomez Pirez, who was there in that caravel of the King as chief captain, being a man of valour and authority, began to speak of his purpose before them all on this wise: "Me seemeth," said he, "that the determination of the captains of these little caravels is to turn back to the kingdom, in [Pg 174]fear of the danger that may come upon them if the winter finds them further than we are now. But as for you others, honorable sirs and friends, you know right well the will of the lord Infant: how much store he setteth on knowing somewhat of the land of the Negroes, and especially of the river of Nile,[1136] for which reason I am resolved to make my voyage to that land, toiling as much as I can to get at it; and I purpose also to gain the most perfect knowledge that I can of other matters, and on this I place all my hope of the greatest guerdon that I can gain on this voyage: a guerdon that will not be small for me, for I know how the lord Infant will show me grace and honour for it, whereby I may obtain a greater profit; and since I have a ship good enough, I should do wrong in taking any other course than this,[AL] and if any one of the rest of you desire to keep me company I will hold fast to all your ordinance so long as it be not outside this plan of mine."

"Of a truth I tell you," replied Lançarote, "that this purpose of yours was also mine above all else, before you had said anything concerning it; and it pleaseth me to fall in with your proposal, inasmuch as it was so commanded me of the Infant, my lord." "And I," said Alvaro de Freitas, "am not a man to hold aloof from such a company; but I say, let us press on by all means whither soever you desire to go, be it even to the terrestrial Paradise."[1137] With these men three others agreed, to wit, Rodrigue Annes de Travaços, a knight of the Regent's household, and Laurence Diaz of the same standing in the household of the Infant Dom Henry, and Vicente Diaz, a trader. And all these, being settled in this purpose, began at once to pursue their voyage. And after these there set out other two caravels, to wit, one of Tavilla, and another belonging to a man of Lagos called Bicanço, but concerning [Pg 175]the voyage of these latter we will defer our account to another place, forasmuch as they did not arrive at the land of the Negroes.

And so those six caravels having set out, pursued their way along the coast, and pressed on so far that they passed the land of Sahara, belonging to those Moors which are called Azanegues, the which land is very easy to distinguish from the other[AM] by reason of the extensive sands that are there, and after it by the verdure which is not to be seen in it[AN] on account of the great dearth of water there, which causeth an exceeding dryness of the soil. And to this land resort usually all the swallows, and also all the birds that appear at certain times in this our kingdom, to wit, storks, quails, turtle-doves, wry-necks, nightingales and linnets, and other birds of various species. And many are there, by reason of the cold of the winter, that go from this land[AO] and journey to that one[AP] for the sake of its warmth. But other kinds of birds leave it in the winter, such as falcons, herons, ring-doves, thrushes, and other birds that breed in that land, and afterwards they come and take refuge in this because of the food they find here suitable to their nature. And of these birds the men of the caravels found many upon the sea, and others on land at their breeding-places. And since I have begun to speak of this matter, I will not omit to say a little more about the divers other kinds of birds and fishes that I hear are to be found in that land: among which we may speak first of all of some birds called flamingoes, which are of the same size as herons, with necks as long, but with short feathers; also their heads are small in comparison with their bodies, but their beaks are huge, though short, and so heavy that their necks are not well able to support the weight of them, in [Pg 176]such wise that for the aid of these same necks they always have their beaks against their legs and rested upon them, or else upon their feathers for the residue of the time.[1138] And there also are other birds larger than swans, called hornbills, of which I have already spoken. And as for the fishes of these parts, there are some that have mouths three or four palms long, some smaller and others larger, in which mouths there are teeth both on the one side and on the other, so close together that a finger could not be put between one and another, and all are of fine bone, a little larger than those of a saw and farther apart; and these fish are some as large as and others greater than sharks, and the jaw-bones of these are in size not greater than those of other fish. And there is another kind of fish there, as small as mullet, that have, as it were, crowns on their heads, like gills, through which they breathe; and if they are turned over and put with these crowns below in a basin, they lay hold so firmly that on attempting to withdraw them they lift the basin with them, even as the lampreys do with their mouths while they are quite[1139] alive. And there are also many other birds and animals and fish in that land whose appearance we do not care to describe at length, as it would be an occasion of wandering too far from our history.

[AL] Viz., pushing forward.
[AM] Which they had now come to.
[AN] The Sahara.
[AO] Portugal.
[AP] The Sahara.

CHAPTER LX.

How those caravels arrived at the river of Nile, and of the Guineas that they took.

Now these caravels having passed by the land of Sahara, as hath been said, came in sight of the two palm trees[1140] that Dinis Diaz had met with before, by which they understood that they were at the beginning of the land of the Negroes. And at this sight they were glad indeed, and would have [Pg 177]landed at once, but they found the sea so rough upon that coast that by no manner of means could they accomplish their purpose. And some of those who were present said afterwards that it was clear from the smell that came off the land how good must be the fruits of that country, for it was so delicious that from the point they reached, though they were on the sea, it seemed to them that they stood in some gracious fruit garden ordained for the sole end of their delight. And if our men showed on their side a great desire of gaining the land, no less did the natives of it show their eagerness to receive them into it; but of the reception they offered I do not care to speak, for according to the signs they made to our men from the first, they did not intend to abandon the beach without very great loss to one side or the other. Now the people of this green land[141] are wholly black, and hence this is called Land of the Negroes, or Land of Guinea. Wherefore also the men and women thereof are called "Guineas," as if one were to say "Black Men." And when the men in the caravels saw the first palms and lofty trees as we have related, they understood right well that they were close to the river of Nile, at the point where it floweth into the western sea, the which river is there called the Senegal.[AQ] For the Infant had told them that in little more than 20 leagues after the sighting of those trees they should look out for the same river, for so he had learnt from several of his Azanegue prisoners.[142] And so, as they were going along scanning the coast to see if they could discern the river, they perceived before them, as it might be about two leagues of land measure, a certain colour in the water of the sea which was different from the rest, for this was of the colour of mud. And they thought that this might arise from shoals, so they took their soundings for the safety of [Pg 178]their ships, but they found no difference in this place from the others in which there was no such movement, and at this they were all amazed, especially by the difference in colour. And it happened that one of those who were throwing in the sounding lead, by chance and without any certain knowledge, put his hand to his mouth and found the water sweet. "Here we have another marvel," cried he to the others, "for this water is sweet;" and at this they threw a bucket forthwith into the sea and put the water to the test, all drinking of it as a thing in which nothing was wanting to make it as good as possible. "Of a surety," said they, "we are near the river of Nile, for it seemeth that this water belongeth to the same, and by its great might the stream doth cut through the sea and so entereth into it."[143] Thereat they made signs to the other caravels, and all of them began to coast in and look for the river, and they were not very long in arriving at the estuary.

And when they were close to its mouth, they let down their anchors on the seaward side, and the crew of the caravel of Vicente Diaz launched their boat, and into it jumped as many as eight men, and among them was that Esquire of Lagos called Stevam Affonso, of whom we have already spoken, and who afterwards died in [AR]Canary; he had undertaken a part of the armament of that caravel.

And as all the eight were going in the boat, one of them, looking out towards the mouth of the river, espied the door of a hut, and said to his companions: "I know not how the huts of this land are built, but judging by the fashion of those I have seen before, that should be a hut that I see before me, and I presume it belongs to fishing folk who have come to fish in this stream. And if you think[Pg 179]well, it seemeth to me that we ought to go and land beyond that point, in such wise that we may not be discovered from the door of the hut; and let some land, and approach from behind those sandbanks, and if any natives are lying in the hut, it may be that they will take them before they are perceived." Now it appeared to the others that this was good advice, and so they began to put it into execution. And as soon as they reached the land, Stevam Affonso leapt out, and five others with him, and they proceeded in the manner that the other had suggested. And while they were going thus concealed even until they neared the hut, they saw come out of it a negro boy, stark naked, with a spear in his hand. Him they seized at once, and coming up close to the hut, they lighted upon a girl, his sister, who was[AS] about eight years old. This boy the Infant afterwards caused to be taught to read and write, with all other knowledge that a Christian should have; and many Christians there be who have not this knowledge as perfectly as he had, for he was taught the prayer of Pater Noster, and the Ave Maria, and the Articles of Faith, and the precepts of the Law,[AT] and the various works of mercy, and many other things; so that some said of this youth that the Infant had bidden train him for a priest, with the purpose of sending him back to his native land, there to preach the faith of Jesus Christ.

73

But I believe that afterwards he died without ever reaching man's estate. So those men entered into the hut, where they found a black shield made of hide, quite round in shape, a little larger than those used in that country, the which had in the middle of it a boss of the same hide as the shield itself, to wit, of an elephant's ear, as was afterwards learnt from certain Guineas who saw it; for they said that they made all their shields of the hide of that animal, and that they[Pg 180]found it so much thicker than was necessary[AU] that they cut off from it more than half, lessening it with devices they had made for this purpose. And the same men said, moreover, that the size of the elephants was so great that the flesh of one would make a good meal for 2,500 men, and that this meat they reckoned among themselves to be very good, and that they made no use of the tusks, but threw them away; and I learnt that in the East of this part of the Mediterranean Sea[144] the tusks of one of those elephants were well worth 1,000 doubloons. And when they had captured those young prisoners and articles of plunder, they took them forthwith to their boat. "Well were it," said Stevam Affonso to the others, "if we were to go through this country near here, to see if we can find the father and mother of these children, for, judging by their age and disposition, it cannot be that the parents would leave them and go far off." The others said that he should go, with good luck, wherever he pleased, for there was nothing to prevent them following him. And after they had journeyed a short way, Stevam Affonso began to hear the blows of an axe, or of some other iron instrument, with which some one was carpentering upon a piece of timber, and he stopped a little to assure himself of what he had heard, and put the others into the same attention. And then they all recognised that they were near what they sought. "Now," said he, "do you come behind and allow me to go in front, because, if we all move forward in company, however softly we walk, we shall be discovered without fail, so that ere we come at him, whosoever he be, if alone, he must needs fly and put himself in safety; but if I go softly and crouching down, I shall be able to capture him by a sudden surprise without his perceiving me; but do not be so slow of pace that you will come late to my [Pg 181]aid, where perhaps I may be in such danger as to need you."

And they agreeing to this, Stevam Affonso began to move forward; and what with the careful guard that he kept in stepping quietly, and the intentness with which the Guinea laboured at his work, he never perceived the approach of his enemy till the latter leapt upon him. And I say leapt, since Stevam Affonso was of small frame and slender, while the Guinea was of quite different build; and so he[AV] seized him lustily by the hair, so that when the Guinea raised himself erect, Stevam Affonso remained hanging in the air with his feet off the ground. The Guinea was a brave and powerful man, and he thought it a reproach that he should thus be subjected by so small a thing. Also he wondered within himself what this thing could be; but though he struggled very hard, he was never able to free himself, and so strongly had his enemy entwined himself in his hair, that the efforts of those two men could be compared to nothing else than a rash and fearless hound who has fixed on the ear of some mighty bull. And, to speak truth, the help that the rest of the company were to render to Stevam Affonso seemed to be rather tardy, so that I believe that his heart had quite repented him of his first purpose. And if at this point there had been room for a bargain, I know he would have deemed it profitable to leave his gain to secure himself from loss. But while those two were in their struggle, Affonso's companions came upon them, and seized the Guinea by his arms and neck in order to bind him. And Stevam Affonso, thinking that he was now taken into custody and in the hands of the others, let go of his hair; whereupon, the Guinea, seeing that his head was free, shook off the others from his arms, flinging them [Pg 182]away on either side, and began to flee. And it was of little avail to the others to pursue him, for his agility gave him a great advantage over his pursuers in running, and in his course he took refuge in a wood full of thick undergrowth; and while the others thought they had him, and sought to find him, he was already in his hut, with the intention of saving his children and taking his arms, which he had left with them. But all his former toil was nothing in comparison of the great grief which came upon him at the absence of his children, whom he found gone—but as there yet remained for him a ray of hope, and he thought that perchance they were hidden somewhere, he began to look towards every side to see if he could catch any glimpse of them. And at this appeared Vicente Diaz, that trader who was the chief captain of that caravel to which the boat belonged wherein the others had come on land. And it appears that he, thinking that he was only coming out to walk along the shore, as he was wont to do in Lagos town, had not troubled to bring with him any arms except a boat-hook. But the Guinea, as soon as he caught sight of him, burning with rage as you may well imagine, made for him with right good will.

And although Vicente Diaz saw him coming on with such fury, and understood that for his own defence it were well he had somewhat better arms, yet thinking that flight would not profit him, but rather do him harm in many ways, he awaited his enemy without shewing him any sign of fear. And the Guinea rushing boldly upon him, gave him forthwith a wound in the face with his assegai, with the which he cut open the whole of one of his jaws; in return for this the Guinea received another wound, though not so fell a one as that which he had just bestowed. And because their weapons were not sufficient for such a struggle, they threw them aside and wrestled; and so for a short space they were rolling one over the other, each [Pg 183]one striving for victory. And while this was proceeding, Vicente Diaz saw another Guinea, one who was passing from youth to manhood; and he came to aid his countryman; and although the first Guinea was so strenuous and brave and inclined to fight with such good will as we have described, he could not have escaped being made prisoner if the second man had not come up: and for fear of him he[AW] now had to loose his hold of the first.[AX] And at this moment came up the other Portuguese, but the Guinea, being now once again free from his enemy's hands, began to put himself in safety with his companion, like men accustomed to running, little fearing the enemy who attempted to pursue them. And at last our men turned back to their caravels, with the small booty they had already stored in their boats.

[AQ] Canaga.
[AR] Grand.
[AS] Lit., would be.
[AT] Of God.
[AU] For a shield.
[AV] Affonso.
[AW] Diaz.
[AX] The Guinea.

CHAPTER LXI.

In which the author relateth some things concerning the River of Nile.

Meseemeth that since in this last chapter I have spoken of how our caravels arrived at the river of Nile, I ought now to tell you something of its marvels, so that our Prince may receive the greater honour for his mandate to our men to make booty upon the waters of the most noble river of the world. And about the greatness of this river there are marvellous testimonies, for these have spoken of it, to wit: Aristotle and Ptolemy, Pliny and Homer, Isidore, Lucan, and Paulus Orosius,[145] and many other learned men; but not even they knew how to give a full recital of its marvels. And in the first place, Paulus Orosius saith,[Pg 184]that the river appeareth to issue from the coast where the Red Sea beginneth, at the point which the Greeks call Mossylon Emporion;[146] and thence, he saith, it goeth towards the west and passeth through many lands, and maketh in the midst of its waters an isle called Meroë. And this city is in the lordship of Ethiopia, in which Moses was by command of Pharaoh with all the power of Egypt, even as Josephus Rabanus[147] and Master Peter write; and he saith that it was anciently called Saba, and, was the head of the kingdom of Ethiopia, but that after a long time Cambyses, who was king of that land, gave to that city the name of Meroë,[148] for love of one of his sisters, as Master Peter relateth. But Master Gondolfo[149] saith, in the ninth part of the book he wrote called *Pantheon*, that before it had that other name this place was called Nadabet, and that this was the first name the city had immediately after its foundation. And so the Nile, winding at this island, maketh its course toward the north, and thence turneth toward the south,[AY] and according to the description that he[AZ]hath, it overfloweth its banks at certain times of the year, and watereth all the plains of Egypt.

But Pliny relateth the story in another fashion, for he saith that the founts whence riseth this river of Nile are not certainly known to any man, and that the river goeth for a very long way through desert countries and through lands so hot that they would take fire

75

and blaze up if it were not for the river; and he saith also that many have toiled much to get to the knowledge of the place where this stream doth rise, but he who gained most knowledge of the same was the King Juba, who left it written that he had found that the river of Nile rose in a mountain called Atlas, which is in the land of Mauritania, at the furthest extremity of Africa towards the west, not very far from [Pg 185]the great sea,[BA] and that it riseth from a fountain where it maketh a great pool called Nullidom, in which breed certain fish, some called *Allaltetes*, and others*Coracinus*, and others *Sillurus*; and it is said moreover that the crocodiles breed there too.

And as to this, it is recounted that the inhabitants of the city of Caesarea,[BB]which is in that same land of Mauritania, took a crocodile[150] and put it in one of their temples called Eseo; and that for many years it remained there in testimony that the said crocodiles were to be found in that pool; and he relateth that it was found by some men of that land who examined the matter, and found it well proved that, according as it snowed and rained in the land of Mauritania, where that fountain is, in like manner rose or fell the Nile itself. And that after it issueth from that part and reacheth the land of the sands, it will not run over the surface of those sands nor through places altogether desert or miserable, but that it vanisheth there, and so floweth hidden beneath the sand for the space of many days. And they say, too, that after it arriveth at the other Mauritania Caesariensis, which is not a sandy land, it cometh up over the ground and there maketh another lake, in the which breed those same animals and creatures which breed in the other; and therefore men believe that all this water cometh from the Nile, and that after it floweth out from there and cometh to the other sandy districts which are beyond Mauritania and towards Ethiopia, it again disappeareth and runneth for the space of twenty days underground till it is within the land of Ethiopia. And here again it cometh up above the ground, showing clearly that it riseth from a fountain like that other in Mauritania, which is called Nigris, where also breed the same animals and other things that we have described before.

[Pg 186]And thenceforth it[BC] runneth ever above ground without any more hiding of itself beneath the soil, and parteth Africa from Ethiopia, and maketh great lakes from the which the men of that country derive their maintenance; and in the same way are to be found there all the creatures which breed in the other places of the said river. And from the place where it beginneth to run above ground without again taking its course subterranean, down to the place where it commenceth to divide itself, it is called Niger; and in this part its stream is already very great, and here it maketh of itself three parts, each one of which is a river by itself. And of these three rivers, one entereth Ethiopia and divideth the same in the middle, and this is called Astapus, that is to say, according to the language of that land, a water that runneth out of darkness. And this river watereth many islands which are so great that, in passing by the smallest of them, though it runneth in its course very briskly, it doth consume five days. But the noblest of these islands is that called Meroë, which we have named above; and the second branch of these three is that called Astaboras,[BD] the which in their language is as much as to say "an arm of the water which cometh out of darkness," and this taketh its course towards the left; the third of these three is called Astusapes, which meaneth "the water of the lake," and this also floweth towards the left; and these streams, so far as they flow separately, are called by these names that we have given. But when they are all joined together in one river, the stream taketh its own proper name, to wit, "the Nile;" but it is not called so before, though all these streams be one water. And when it leaveth the islands, it shutteth itself up in certain mountains, but in no part doth it flow so angrily and with such a rushing stream as when it [Pg 187]cometh to a place of Ethiopia called Catadupia,[BE] and thenceforth its bed is strewn with many great rocks for a long space. And these break it in its course, and the river goeth dashing through those rocks and maketh a very great noise therewith: so much so, that the learned say that no pregnant women dare dwell within two leagues of the same, in that the terror caused by this noise straightway maketh them to miscarry.

And coming forth from that multitude of great rocks, the strength of the waters is now broken, and the stream floweth as if wearied, and the current of the water is very gentle. And as soon as it entereth the plains of Egypt, it divideth many islands which have other names than those they used to have; and thence it maketh its way directly to the sea; but before that it formeth many lakes and marshes by which are watered all the plains of Egypt; and thereafter the river entereth the sea in one stream near the city which is called Damietta.

[AY] Lit., the midday.
[AZ] Gondolfo.
[BA] Atlantic.
[BB] Cherchel.
[BC] The Nile.
[BD] Astabores.
[BE] The Cataracts.

CHAPTER LXII.
Of the might of the Nile according to the Astronomers, and of its increase.

What man could decide the great contention there is among the learned concerning the source and power of this river: for Alexander, who was the most powerful of the Kings, to whom the province of Memphis in Egypt made prayer, conceived a grudge against the Nile, for that he was not able to learn the truth of the aforesaid source, though he was lord of the world. And this covetousness was not only in him, but it was also found among the [Pg 188]Kings of Egypt, and of Persia, and of Macedonia, and of Greece. But we will here describe in some small measure the course of this river, according to the Astronomers, who say that Mercury is the source of power over the waters, and that he hath influence over them; and that when he is in that part of the heaven where the stars of the sign of Leo are in conjunction with the stars of the sign of Cancer, or with the star Sirius, to wit, that which is called the Dog star,[BF][151]whence those days are called the Dog days, he poureth out flames full of fury from his mouth, and altereth thereby the circle of the year, and the weather also changeth, for then the summer endeth and autumn beginneth. And again, when the signs of Capricorn and Cancer are in conjunction, under which the outflow of the Nile is hidden, and when the star of Mercury is in conjunction with those signs, Mercury being lord of the waters, striketh on the mouths, that is to say, in those parts through which the Nile floweth, being under the fire of his constellation; then the Nile openeth its fount and floweth forth; and even as the sea waxeth with the waxing of the moon, so riseth the Nile as if Mercury commanded it, and increaseth till it covereth the land whence Egypt hath all its principal nutriment. And it doth not gather its waters together, nor return into its bed until the night hath as many hours as the day. And in old time there were some who said that the rising of this stream was chiefly because of the snows of Ethiopia, but this we find is not so, for the north doth not look upon those mountains of Ethiopia; no, not any one of the Bears of either pole, to wit, Ellice and Cynosure,[152] neither the greater nor the less, which bring the chill and are the cause of snows and frosts; nor doth the north-east wind,[BG] which bringeth the frost with it.

[Pg 189]And of this there is a good and sufficient testimony in the very colour of that same people of Ethiopia, whose blood is burnt by the great heat of the sun, which there hath the full power of its heat, and the breath of the south-west wind,[BH] which is the hottest of all winds; whence the men of that land have their colour exceeding black; and moreover, no river, whatever it be, that swelleth for reason of the snow or ice that hath recourse to it, is augmented except from the time of the entry of the summer season; for then the snow and ice begin to melt by reason of the heat; but the Nile doth not raise its waters so high, nor do they swell in its bed before the rising of that same Dog Star, nor do its waters reach outwards to their banks until the day is equal to the night, which is in the month of September, when the sun entereth into the sign of Libra. From all which it appeareth clearly that the Nile doth not follow the rule of any other waters; but when the sky becometh distempered in the midst of the great heat of the sun, the Nile issueth forth with the swelling of its waters, and this is under the belt of the mid-day, which is scorching hot.

And this it doth that the flame of the axis of the firmament, by reason of its increase, may not set fire to the land and burn it. And so the Nile is as it were a succour to the world, because when the mouth of Leo is kindled, and when Cancer burneth over its city of Syene in Egypt, then riseth this river against the mouths of the twain, to temper their fire, the which is a matter of the utmost need to the peoples of the earth.

And so it spreadeth its waters over the land, not to return to its bed till the sun shall have come to the time of autumn and lessened its strength, when the shadows begin to fall in the city of Meroe, where the trees cast no shadows in summer time, so directly passeth the sun[153] overhead [Pg 190]above everything. And so, in conclusion, to the great might of the Nile we may apply those words wherewith Bishop Achoreus[153a] spake of it to Caesar, as Lucan writeth: "Oh," said he, "great and mighty stream, which risest from the midst of the axis of the firmament, and venturest to raise thy waters over their banks against the sign of Cancer when that is in the fulness of its heat; thou who proceedest straight towards the north-east with thy waters, and takest thy course through the midst of the plain; thou who turnest thence to the west and again to the east; thou who dost reveal thyself sometimes in Arabia and sometimes in the sands of Libya, displaying thyself to the peoples of those lands, performing so many great benefits for them—of a truth the men of those regions could not dispense with thee or live without thee, and these are the first races of men that behold thee. Thy power is to issue forth at the solstices, the which do fall, the one in December and the other in June, and thou increasest in the alien winter which is not thine. To thee is it granted by nature to go through both the axes of the firmament, to wit: the axis of the north and that of the south; thy foam fighteth with the stars, so high dost thou cause it to rise by thy power; and before thy waves do all things tremble. What can I say of thee, except that thou art as it were the navel of the world: for even as the creatures which lie in the wombs of their mothers are governed by the navels of their bodies, a like comparison may be made of thy greatness in affairs of the earth."

[BF] Canicolla.
[BG] Blow upon these mountains.
[BH] Aurego.

[Pg 191]CHAPTER LXIII.
How the Caravels set forth from the river, and of the voyage which they made.

All these secrets and marvels did the genius of our prince bring before the eyes of the people of our kingdom, for although all the matters here spoken of concerning the marvels of the Nile[154] could not be witnessed by his own eyes, for that were impossible, it was a great matter that his ships arrived there, where 'tis not recorded that any other ship of these parts had ever come. And this may truthfully be affirmed according to the matters which at the beginning of this book I have related concerning the passage of Cape Bojador, and also from the astonishment which the natives of that land showed when they saw the first ships, for they went to them imagining they were fish, or some other natural product of the sea.[155] But now returning to our history, after that deed was thus concluded, it was the wish of all the three captains to endeavour to make an honourable booty, adventuring their bodies in whatsoever peril might be necessary; but it appeareth that the wind veered sharply round to south, wherefore it was convenient to set sail at once. And as they were cruising up and down in order to see what the weather purposed to do, the wind turned to the north, and with this they made their way towards Cape Verde, where Dinis Diaz had been the other year. And they went on as far as was possible for all the caravels to join them, except that of Rodrigueannes de Travaços, which lost its company and made thereafter that voyage which will be related.

And the five caravels being directly over against the Cape, saw an island, where they landed to see if it were peopled; they found that it was deserted, only they discovered there a great multitude of she goats. And of these [Pg 192]they took some to refresh themselves withal; and they reported that these were in no way different from the goats of our country, except that their ears were larger. From the same island also they took water and went on further, until they found another island, in the which they saw fresh skins of goats and other things, from which they understood that other caravels had gone on in front of them; and in further proof of this they found the Arms of the Infant carved upon the trees, and also the letters which composed his motto. "Of a surety I doubt," saith our author, "if since the great power of Alexander and of Cæsar, there hath been any prince in the world that ever had the marks of his conquest set up so far from his own land."

And by those signs, which those men of the caravels found there on the trees, they understood that some others had already gone on in front, and so they decided to turn back to their ships; and, as they afterwards discovered, it was the caravel of John Gonçalves Zarco, captain of the isle of Madeira, that had preceded them.

And because there were so many of those blacks[B] on land that by no means could they disembark either by day or night, Gomez Pirez sought to show that he desired to go among them on peaceful terms, and so placed upon the shore a cake and a mirror and a sheet of paper on which he drew a cross. And the natives when they came there and found those things, broke up the cake and threw it far away, and with their assegais they cast at the mirror, till they had broken it in many pieces, and the paper they tore, showing that they cared not for any of these things.

"Since it is so," said Gomez Pirez to his crossbowmen, "shoot at them with your bows that they may at least understand that we are people who can do them hurt, whenever they will not agree to a friendly understanding." But the [Pg 193]blacks seeing the others' intention, began to pay them back, launching at them also their arrows and assegais, some of which our men brought home to this kingdom. And the arrows are so made that they have no feathers, nor a notch for the string to enter, but they are all smooth and short, and made of rushes or reeds, and their iron points are long and some are made of wood fixed in the shafts, which are like the iron spindles with which the women of this country spin. And they use also other little harpoons of iron, the which darts are all equally poisoned with plants. And their assegais are each made with seven or eight harpoon-like prongs, and the plant they use is very venomous.

And in that island in which the arms of the Infant[156] were carved they found trees of great size, and of strange forms, and among these was one which was not less than 108 palms in circuit at the foot. And this tree[157] doth not grow very high, but is about as lofty as the walnut-tree, and from its middle bark they make very good thread for cordage, and it burneth like flax. The fruit is like a gourd, and its seeds are like filberts, and this fruit they eat green, and the seeds they dry. And of these there is a great abundance, and I believe they use them for their maintenance after the green faileth them. And some there were who said they saw there birds which appeared to them to be parrots.

So all the captains there agreed to make sail, with the intention of entering into the River of Nile, but no one was able to light upon it save Lawrence Diaz, that squire of the Infant's. And he, because he was alone, did not dare enter into the river, but he went with the little boat to the place where they took the blacks on the outward voyage; howbeit he turned back without doing anything worthy of mention. And since he did not fall in with the convoy again he came straight to Lagos. And in this wise Gomez Pirez lost the company of the other [Pg 194]caravels; and following his course towards Portugal, after taking in water at the isle of Arguim, he came to the Rio do Ouro,[158] and sailed as far up as the port where he had been the preceding year with Antam Gonçalvez and Diego Affonso, and there presently the Moors came, and in taking security of them he learnt there were no merchants there. But they sold him a black for the price of five doubloons, which he paid them by certain things he gave them in their stead. Also they brought him water on their camels, and gave him meat and made him a sufficiency of good reception; and above all they showed such confidence that without any hesitancy so many entered into the caravel, that he was not very well pleased, and would not consent that any more should enter; but at last, without causing them[B] any injury, he had them put on land, making an agreement with them that next year, in the month of July, he would return there, when he would find blacks in abundance, and gold, and merchandise by which he might gain much profit. Moreover, Gomez Pirez brought back from that voyage a great many skins of sea-calves, with the which he loaded his ship and so returned to the kingdom.[159]

[B] Guineas.
[B] The blacks.

CHAPTER LXIV.

Of how Lançarote and Alvaro de Freitas captured a dozen Moors.

It were unreasonable in our account of these caravels not to return to the place whereto we took them first; and since we have now described the return of some of them to the kingdom, we would recount the fortune of the rest, and we will speak at once of Lançarote and of Alvaro de Freitas. And it was so, that while Vicente Diaz was with both these captains—and I mean that same Vicente Diaz [Pg 195]who, as we have said already, was wounded by the Guinea upon the shore of the Nile—by chance he was parted from the company of the others; and inasmuch as it was night, he was not able to return very quickly to his friends. But while we leave him pursuing his way alone, it is fit that we should speak of the achievements of the others. Now they were not well content with the booty they had taken, and both of them determined to toil for the increase of their first gain, and so pursuing their way towards Tider, for there they thought they might yet light upon some matter of which they could make booty, they came to the point of Tira. And here they spake with their company, and said: that as they knew the land was peopled, it seemed good to them that they should go out of their ships and land and strive to see if they could obtain any gain. And on this motion there was no discussion, but all said they would do as it pleased him, for they well knew that they had such captains that none but profitable counsel could come from them.

The boats were at once made ready, and the captains embarked in them with their men, leaving the caravels guarded as was proper. And of those who were in the boats they disembarked some who were to go on by land; and the others, who remained in the boats, made their way under shelter of the land. And while both the one and the other party were going on their way, those on shore said that they had lighted on a track of men who had passed by that way, and also the track seemed to them to be fresh, and in it they discovered the footprints of women and children.

"Then let us follow after these," said the captains, "for since the track is so fresh it must be that they who made it are not very far off."

And as they had a good will for this action, and the track was clearly to be seen, they were led on a very great [Pg 196]distance, but they could not yet spy the Moors they sought; so that some there were who said that so distant an expedition was beyond reason and that they ought to turn back. But the others, more vehement in their covetousness for gain, did not pay any heed to the words of the former, and pursued their way none the less.

And as they went forward, not very far from there, while traversing a sandhill, they saw the Moors, who were journeying in a hollow. "Now," said those who there bore the office of captains, to these others, "you can show your good will by toiling in the pursuit of those foemen." And although our men were already somewhat wearied, it appeared to them as if they had only that moment issued from their ships, so great desire had they to come up with the enemy. And this desire they now put into practice very quickly, for the Moors were hardly able to issue forth before our men were up with them; and some, that endeavoured to offer a defence, in a brief space learnt the error of their sect, for without any pity our men killed them very speedily, in so much that there remained alive no more than twelve, whom they took back as their prisoners. And although the booty was not great in comparison of other spoil which had already been made in that land, yet were they all very glad of it; and this because the victory had been obtained by so few men rather than because of the share of gain that fell to the lot of each.

[Pg 197]CHAPTER LXV.

How Lançarote and Alvaro de Freitas and Vicente Diaz took fifty-seven Moors.

So having obtained that booty, small as it was, the captains made agreement to go straight to the Isle of Arguim, there to take in the water they needed, and to discuss the future of the voyage. And arriving at the said island—which they had first reconnoitred for the sake of security—as soon as they ascertained that the Isle was free from enemies, they all landed. And after they had taken a little rest they laid in their water, which gave them a singular pleasure, for one of the chief refreshments in which maritime folk delight, after they have been some time at sea, is good water, whenever they can obtain it. And so reposing there that night, on the next day, while they were on the point of holding a council, one began to say that it appeared to him that he saw a sail coming towards them, and when all looked in that direction they perceived it was a caravel. And this they supposed to be the ship of Vicente Diaz, which a little time before had parted company with them; and for this reason they put off their council, because they sought that all should join in it.

And when the caravel had come up to them, they asked Vicente Diaz to be so good as to land and take part in that council of theirs. "My friends," said he, "you will have patience till my people can take refreshment with the water of this island, for we have come here with a great desire for it." And having finished their refreshment, they began their council; and herein the captains put forward that their intent was to endeavour to make some further booty, for as to returning with so small a profit, that would be a reproach for persons such as they were.

[Pg 198]"Friends," said some, "your proposal would be good if the place were such that by toiling one might hope to receive some profit; but this land, as you know, is already turned upside down, and it hath been disturbed a thousand times, and the caravels go by it every day, so that there is not a Moor, however simple he may be, that dareth to set foot on all this land; but rather reason teacheth that they must have been terrified and fled from here as far as they could. Wherefore it appeareth to us that it would be well to content ourselves with the booty we have, and that we should make our voyage straightway to our own kingdom and not waste time in a matter which we so plainly know to be impossible of profit for us."

"Truth it is," said others, "that this land hath been roused even as you say, wherefore one of two things must needs be: Either the Moors are very far from here; or if they are here they will be so prepared as to be able to await any hostile attack that may be made upon them without fear, so that where we look for a capture they perchance may take us. And even if we pay heed to nothing else, consider what happened to the caravels of Lisbon, for they having obtained a cargo with which they could have very reasonably returned, sought to put all to the hazard of a venture, the result of which was as you have heard."

The third opinion, which was that of the captains and of some of the picked men, was delayed a little, but they maintained nevertheless, that the landing was not to be given up. "You know," said they, "how in the isle of Tider[160] were killed some Moors and others were taken, so that they cannot be counted at their former number, and the remainder are half conquered, for as you saw they fled before the points of our lances, as people who did not dare to try their strength against ours. But let us go and see if we can light upon any there, for if they are there it cannot be but that either of their flesh or their wool we shall[Pg 199]take some quantity. And if perchance the island is now void of inhabitants, we can then give sure news of this to the Infant our lord; and from this it would appear that our expedition was not without great profit, since the Moors were not content to fly from us once, but with the fear of us had altogether abandoned their huts and the land where they were born and lived."

Firmly stood by this opinion most of the chief men; yet the lower people nevertheless desired that no other matter should be undertaken, but that they should turn back to the kingdom. Howbeit they had to agree to the opinion of those who were worth more and understood better than they; and so they began presently to start on their expedition, and before night fell they arrived off the island, where they dropped their anchors, though not very close to it, and stayed there until they saw the sun had finished his daily toil.

Then when the sky was covered by the shades of night, they launched their boats and embarked in them and stationed themselves at the arm of the sea which ran on the land side, though in front of the said land there is another island called Cerina.[161] And so they landed on Tider, but did not find anyone, wherefore they turned back and retired to their boats and went forward so far that it was already sun rise.

And Lançarote issued forth from the side of Cerina and went along by land, ordering the boats to make their way by water; and when they saw that they found nothing, Lançarote said to the others that it would be well to go forward to a certain promontory, and all agreed with him. And while seeking to establish themselves and to gather themselves together for starting, Lançarote heard an ass bray.

"Meseemeth," said he to the others, "I hear the bray of an ass, as though some pleasure were in store for [Pg 200]us; for perchance it is God's will that we should not depart hence without booty." And because there was no doubt of what he had heard, he told them to await him there, and that he would go upon some sandhills to see what that could be. And while the others were waiting, he mounted up the sandhills, and from there looking round on all sides he saw the Moors where they stood, many more in number than our men. And these Moors were getting ready their asses and gathering up their baggage, as men who sought to leave that place, with little care of what in a few hours would overtake them. Truth it is that they were endeavouring to set out, but they deemed not it was upon so long a journey.

But Lançarote, as soon as he had seen them, descended very quietly from the place where he was, and came and gave the news to the others, and you know well how glad they would be when they heard it. "Now, God be praised," said he, "we have what we sought. The Moors are here, just ready to move away. They are more in number than we: if you will only labour the victory is ours. Strengthen your hearts and make your feet swift, for on the first encounter will depend the whole of our victory."

It were impossible to tell how great was the exultation then felt by all, for scarcely had Lançarote finished these words of his when all moved off at a run. Yet so well did they do this that they moved without noise till they were upon the sandhills, but when they arrived there they were not able to control their desires that urged them to cry out. And when they appeared over against the Moors they lifted up their voices, the which were not a whit less than the strength of each one availed; and when the Moors heard these they were very much affrighted and disordered. And now our men began to run forward, shouting out their accustomed cries, to wit, "St. James," [Pg 201]"Portugal," "St. George;" but the sound of these was not very pleasant to the enemy, so that they had not leisure to place their pack-saddles upon their asses. And those who had the packs upon their necks freed themselves from these burdens, and what was more noteworthy, some who had their children upon their shoulders, seeing that they could not save them, let them fall upon the ground, with how great a crash you may imagine. And so in this anguish they began to fly, not all together, nor by one road, but each one by himself, quite leaving behind their women and children, without any hope of remedy. Yet true it is that some there were, who though they perceived the manifest discomfiture of their party, had the courage to show some defence, the which were very quickly despatched from life. And finally of all the people there were taken fifty-seven; some others were killed and again others escaped. Oh, if only among those who fled there had been some little understanding of higher things. Of a surety I believe, that the same haste which they showed in flying, they would then have made in coming to where they might have saved their souls and restored their affairs in this life. For although it might appear to them that, living as they were, they were living in freedom, their bodies really lay in much greater captivity, considering the nature of the country and the bestiality of their life, than if they were living among us under an alien rule, and this all the more because of the perdition of their souls, a matter which above all others should have been perceived by them.

Of a surety, although their bodily eyes did not perceive any part of this good fortune of theirs,[BK] yet the eyes of the understanding, to wit of the soul pure and clean with unending glory, having received in this world the holy[Pg 202]sacraments, and departed from this life with some little portion of faith, would quickly be able to recognise the former error of their blindness.

Here did those three caravels make an end of that voyage and turned themselves back to the kingdom, not a little content with the advantage they perceived they had gained over the others their comrades in this meeting with their latest booty.

But now let us speak of those who are still at sea, in order to give you an account of their whole achievement.

[BK] In being taken captive.

CHAPTER LXVI.
How Rodrigueannes and Dinis Diaz joined company.

I am right sorry that in this history I cannot keep that order which reason demandeth, because the matter of the said history was so treated that many times it is necessary for me to make a chapter where else I could pass on with two words as at this present. For now, in order to join the caravel of Rodrigueannes with that of Dinis Diaz, it behoveth me to make a new rubric. Now these caravels having separated from the company of the others, went on seeking for them, and came together in so doing. And seeing how that of the other company they were not able to learn any more, the two then sailed together: but of what afterwards happened to them we will speak further on.

[Pg 203]CHAPTER LXVII.

How the five caravels returned to the kingdom, and of what they did beforehand.

Thus, as we have already said in our former chapters, these matters happened according as fortune gave them to happen. And in order that I may return with all the caravels to Lagos as I have promised, and as it is necessary, I desire in this present chapter to speak of those five, which separated themselves from the company of the rest after the invasion of the isle of Tider. For there was that honourable knight Sueiro da Costa, alcayde of Lagos, and four other captains, neighbours and natives of that place; and they, having agreed to turn back, as we have said, discussed among themselves the prosecution of their voyage, as it appeared to them that their first booty was a small matter, though an honourable, in comparison of their great toil and expense.

"We are not able," said some, "to alter our first opinion, in determining to make our return, both on account of the small size of our ships, and that we may not seem to be men of many opinions. But it would be well for us, nevertheless, to prosecute our voyage and try whether we can, on our course, obtain anything by way of adding to our booty, though in reason it must be little on account of the many visits which our ships have already made to this land. Still, we should not omit to try, and peradventure God may give us some good result. But in order to direct this matter with some foundation of reason, there is no other place so fitting, and where our toil may have such good hope of victory, as that arm of the sea which is at Cape Branco, and into this we will enter and see whither it leadeth. And it may be that, if it entereth far into the land, we may light on something near there [Pg 204]of which we may make booty: and if not, we need toil but little in that enterprise."

All agreed that what those first speakers had said was well spoken, and sailing in that direction they arrived at the said river. And herein entering a little space, they anchored their ships, and then letting down their boats, they began to endeavour themselves to reach the end of the river. And, following the course of this for four leagues, they arrived at the end of it.[162] And here they agreed to disembark to see if they could light upon any inhabited place where they could take some souls to add to the scantiness of their first booty. But they doubted in themselves of getting anything, as they knew that the land was prepared and had been so often invaded; only they toiled in this matter, constrained at least by the need of telling their companions that they had been on shore.

And landing thus they sent on ahead to reconnoitre the land, but they had not followed very far, when they saw before them a few huts. And upon these they rushed without waiting for any agreement, and there they came upon some few Moors, of whom they captured eight.

And seeking to learn from them if there were thereabouts any other settlement, and to this end threatening some of them, they were not able to learn anything but that in all this land there was no other settlement. And in this all the eight were agreed, after each one had been taken aside in turn. And for this reason it was needful for them to return to their ships, with the intention of now returning to their homes, without spending any more trouble in the matter, since they understood that they could not gain any further profit by more toil. And in agreement with this decision were all the others who belonged to the Caravels, except only the Alcayde of Lagos, who said that he still wished to return to Tider in order to make ransom of a Mooress, and of the son of a lord of [Pg 205]that place. And although he was counselled to the contrary, yet would he never abandon his design, howbeit afterwards he repented of it sorely. And arriving at the island, he began to make signs to the Moors, who had come down to the shore as soon as they saw the caravel sailing towards them.

And of them he had one Moor for his security while he surrendered the master of the caravel, and a Jew who was in his company. But when the Moors had them in their power, the Mooress, of whom the Alcayde sought to make the ransom, threw herself into the water, and like one practised in that kind of thing very quickly got to land and joined her relations and her friends. And on account of this the Moors considered that they ought not to give up the hostages without an advantage over what they at first had purposed; and finally they refused to surrender those whom they had until they[BL] should give them three Moors. Which matter, although it was a hard thing for the Alcayde to do, was yet condescended to by him, seeing the necessity of the case; howbeit he blamed himself in that he had not followed the first advice of his companions. And seeing how he could make no further profit in that ransom, he turned back to the Kingdom.

[BL] The Portuguese.

[Pg 206]CHAPTER LXVIII.

How the caravel of Alvaro Gonçalvez d'Atayde and that of Picanço and the other of Tavilla sailed in company, and of the Canarians that they captured.

We have told in other chapters how the caravel of Tavilla and the other of Picanço parted company with the others when they went to Guinea, where it befell that they agreed together to return to Portugal. And on their return voyage they met with the caravel of Alvaro Gonçalvez d'Atayde, whose captain was one John de Castilha, and on asking him whither he was going, he said that he was voyaging to Guinea. "But," said the others, "what availeth your going at such a time as this, for we have just come from there, as you see, and winter is beginning, and therefore if you pursue your journey further you will imperil your life and gain little honour and less profit; but if you think good to follow our advice, return with us and we will go to the island of Palma, and see if we can make a capture of some of those Canarians there."

And although John de Castilha had doubts about so returning, because it did not appear to him a sure thing from the accounts he had heard of the inhabitants of that island, how that they were difficult to capture, yet compelled by the reasons the others gave him, he had to return with them. And so, going all in company, they arrived at the island of Gomera, where, wishful to go on shore, they espied many Canarians, of whom they took security before wholly leaving their boats. The Canarians granted them this without any reluctance, like men whose wills were more inclined to do them service than to put difficulties in their way. And immediately came there two chiefs of that island, who said how they were servants of the Infant Don Henry (and not [Pg 207]without good reason, for they had previously been in the house of the King of Castile and the King of Portugal), and how in neither of them had they met with the favours they afterwards received from the Infant Don Henry; for while they were in his house they had from him a right excellent entertainment as long as they stayed there; and, in short[BM] he had clothed them very well, and sent them in his ships to their own land, on which account they were very ready to do him every service. "But," said they of the caravels, "we are also his men and servants, and by his command we left our country; wherefore if such is your mind, you have now the occasion of showing it right well, for we would go to the island of Palma and essay to take some captives, in the which your assistance would be very useful to us, if you would send with us some of these your subjects to aid and direct us, for we are unacquainted with the land, and have no knowledge of the ways of its inhabitants in their fighting." Now Bruco was the name of one of these chiefs, and the other's name was Piste, and they replied together that they were well pleased to toil in any matter that was for the service of the lord Infant Don Henry, and that they rendered many thanks to God for giving them the opportunity of showing what a good will they had for it; "and that you may see," said Piste, "the desire I have to serve him, I will accompany you and bring with me as many Canarians as you wish."

"It seemeth to me," saith the author, "that the gratitude of these men bringeth shame on many who had received greater and better things from this our Prince, and yet came not by a great way to so perfect a knowledge of it. Oh, what a dishonour for those who were brought up in his household, and whom he afterwards placed in [Pg 208]dignities and lordships, but who, clean forgetful of this, deserted him when their service was of need; and the names and deeds of these we will relate in the history of the Kingdom when we come to speak of the siege of Tangier."

And so that captain offered himself with his person and men, of whom he straightway had embarked in the ships as many as the captains wished to receive, and then they set sail forthwith, directing their course to the other Island of Palma, where they arrived when it was almost morning. And although reason would not have allowed them to land at such an hour, nevertheless they agreed together to go on shore forthwith. "For," said they, "we have already been perceived, and if we wait at all, our booty will be labour lost, for the Canarians will put themselves in safety, while if we land forthwith we shall be able to capture some; for although they are fleet of foot, yet there will be men among us that will follow them; and for sure the owners of those flocks who are wandering there before our eyes, will hasten up and get them in, for it is their custom to take almost as much toil about them as on their own behalf." And although such a resolve was perilous, yet it met with the approval of all of them; and so in a very short space they were all set on shore, as well the Portuguese as the Canarians.[BN] And as they were pursuing their way at no great distance from the beach, they perceived that the Canarians[BO] were flying, and as they commenced to follow them, one of the company said to the others: "Wherefore undertake a vain toil in running after those men? for however much you labour, you will not be able to come up with them; but rather let us follow those ewes and rams which are going up that crag, for of a surety the most part of those who are [Pg 209]with them are youths and women, and if we follow them well we are bound to capture some." And these words were scarcely finished when all our men began to run, leaving the other Canarians, whose track they had already commenced to follow up. But those shepherds entered with their flock into a valley so deep and so dangerous that it was easier to marvel at than to relate how any could make their passage through it.

But the Christians, both Portuguese and Canarians, followed them up with such zeal that just as the first began to enter into the valley, ours were already nigh unto them, and so all together they entered the valley, in such a way that the shepherds were obliged to take shelter among an expanse of rocky crags, the roughness of which was a marvellous thing; but much more marvellous was the ease with which the Canarians of that island made their way among those rocks, as though in sucking the milk from their mothers' breasts, they had commenced to walk in those places. And as the Psylli and Marmaridae,[BP] who live beyond the Libyan desert, know their sons to be sprung from their own bodies if straightway in their first boyhood they handle without fear the great poisons of that desert as they are offered to them by their fathers; so the Canarians of this island consider that their sons, if they are not born with this agility, have been generated by some wicked adultery.

But what about our countrymen, desirous to follow after them, for although they saw the roughness of the ground, yet they did not desist from pursuing them; and there a youth of noble heart, in running over those rocks, slipped from a very large and rough crag, and falling down, died. And think not that this misfortune happened only to that native of our realm, for many Canarians fell in the same way and died: for although Nature from [Pg 210]old time had given them to walk among those rocky hills, yet on account of the haste of their enemies, whom they perceived to be near them, and deeming that to be their last remedy, where the crags were roughest, thither with the better will they made their way, thinking that their foes would fear to pursue them.

And if that Diego Gonçalvez, a page of the Infant's household (of whom I have already spoken in the chapter where I related how he was the first to throw himself in and swim at the Island where they took the fifty-eight Moors), if he, I say, received praise for his excellent courage, I may truthfully increase it much more on this occasion unto him, as unto the man who before all others bore himself conspicuously on that day. And certainly with great reason may I here blame fortune for this youth, who had been rewarded by his lord the Infant with a recent marriage in the City of Lisbon, and had collected in his house a great abundance of wealth for the sustaining of his life, when a fire came upon it by the negligence of a servitor of his. And this burned all the things that he had, but fortune was so kindly to him that it left them some poor garments with the which they escaped from the said house. The toil of our men was great on that day, although not so much in the fighting. Yet that was perilous enough, especially on account of the multitude of stones with which the Canarians chiefly combat their enemies, for they are strong in the arm, and very deadly with their shots. And it is right hard for any one else to strike them, for so well do they know how to avoid blows, especially of anything thrown, that, marksman though a man be, only after a long time and through great good fortune is he able to hit them. And they carry other arms well according with their bestial mode of life, to wit, long lances with sharp horns at the heads instead of iron points, and others sharpened like them at the lower ends.

[Pg 211]But although the labour was so great, yet was it a beautiful thing to look upon; for anyone who had seen their skirmish, so disordered and confused, and in such a place—(the Christians engaged in capturing the Canarians and separating the flock from amongst them for the better securing of their booty, and the enemy busying themselves for the saving of their lives and of their flocks as best they could)—would say that such a sight was more delectable than any other that fell short of this ending. And so the booty of that day was seventeen Canarians, what of men and women, and among the latter they captured one who was of wondrous size for a woman, and they said that she was Queen of a part of that island. And after they had collected together their prisoners and the flock, they began to retreat towards their boats, but they were followed up by the Canarians so closely that they were obliged to leave them the greater part of the flock they had taken from them, and owing to this our men had much toil in their retreating.

[BM] They declared that.
[BN] Who were friendly.
[BO] Natives of Palma.
[BP] The text has "Sillos ou Marmorios."

CHAPTER LXIX.
How they took certain Canarians, despite the surety.

And when all were in their ships, they raised their sails and returned to the other island whence they had departed before; and because they had received much help from those first Canarians whom they had with them, they rendered great thanks to that Chief in the name of the Infant their lord for the toil that he had undergone for his service, and much more for the goodwill with which he had undertaken it, putting him in the hope of receiving for it many other and greater guerdons than those he had received before. And of a surety their promise was not in vain, for afterwards that Chief, who was called Piste [Pg 212]came to this kingdom, with others from that land, and they obtained many favours and much hospitality from the Infant, on account of which I can well believe they did not repent of their former toil. And of this I, who collected and put in order this history, can be a sure witness; for it happened that I was in the Kingdom of the Algarve in the house of this Prince[163] at the time when these Canarians were staying there, and I saw well how they were treated. And I believe that that Chief, and some of those who accompanied him, stayed so long in this kingdom, that they made an end of their lives there. And I have said already how John de Castilha, who was captain of that caravel of Alvaro Gonçalvez d'Atayde, did not arrive in Guinea as the others did, nor do I find that he made any other booty, but only those Canarians which they took there; and this seemed to him a very small thing with which to return to the Kingdom, especially as all the other caravels had a great advantage over him which he in his heart felt to be an injury. And so he imagined an ugly device by which he might make some increase in that little which he was carrying, and he began to treat with the others that they would be pleased to seize some part of these Canarians in spite of the sureties. And as covetousness is the root of all evils, though such a proceeding seemed devoid of reason to many, yet they had to consent to what John de Castilha on so many grounds showed them to be profitable. And because it seemed to them an ugly thing to take any of those men who had aided them so well, they moved from that place and went to another port. And there some Canarians, trusting in our men, went to the caravel, and these, I believe, were twenty-one in number, and with them they made sail to Portugal. But the Infant, having knowledge of this, was very wroth with those captains, and straightway he caused the Canarians to be brought to his own house, and had [Pg 213]them very nobly attired and returned to their own land. And there the natives bestowed much praise on the Prince for such a virtuous act, and were on this account much the more inclined to serve him. And of the first coming of these Canarians to this our Kingdom, and of many other things that passed concerning them, we will speak more fully in the general chronicle of the acts of our Kingdom.

CHAPTER LXX.
Of how Tristam of the Island[BQ] went towards Cape Branco.

We have already told how Tristam, one of the captains of the Island of Madeira, had armed a caravel to go in company with the others. And although he had a right good will to serve the Infant and much desired to profit himself (for he was abundantly covetous), yet such was his fortune that as soon as he passed Cape Branco, immediately the wind became contrary for him. And thereat he turned backwards; and although he afterwards toiled hard to return and pursue his first way, yet never again was he able to fill his sails save with a contrary wind, and with this he returned to the island from which he had started. Also Alvaro Dornellas, an esquire and servant of the Infant, and a good man and brave, armed another caravel, in the which he laboured hard to achieve some deed for his honour, yet was he never able to capture more than two Canarians, whom he took in one of those islands; and with them he sent back his caravel, giving the charge to an esquire to have it repaired for him and to return there against the next year. And further on we will relate something of the fortune of this esquire, in that he toiled greatly for his honour.

[BQ] Madeira.]

[Pg 214]CHAPTER LXXI.
Of how the men of Pallenço took the six Moors.

Dinis Diaz, as we have already said, armed a caravel of Don Alvaro de Castro and started at the beginning in company with Pallenço, who was taking out a pinnace, not that he intended to make use of it in aught save only in entering the river of Nile; for since it was an old one, he meant to abandon it whenever he should perceive it to be past service. And so the two, pursuing their voyage, came to the Isle of Arguim, and after they had taken in water, they agreed to continue so far on their way until they reached the land of the Negroes, according to the purpose with which they had set out from this Kingdom. And when they had already passed a good distance beyond the point of Santa Anna[164] and were becalmed one day, Pallenço said that it would not be an evil thing to land some men, who might essay to make capture of the Moors. "Wherefore is it," replied Dinis Diaz, "that men should be employed in such an adventure? Let us rather go straight on our way, for if God shall bring us to that land of Guinea, we shall surely find Moors more than sufficient to load our ships." True it is, as Dinis Diaz said, that many Moors were to be found there, but they were not so easy to capture as he thought; for, believe me, they are very brave men and full of artifices in their defence, and this you will see clearly in the next chapters when we shall speak of their combats. "Friend," replied Pallenço, "even though it happen that we take many Moors there, what shall we lose if God give us some here first? At any rate," said he, "it seemeth well to me that we should try if we can take them, and it might please God now for us to capture so many here [Pg 215]as to save us from voyaging further for this time." "Since it is so," said Dinis Diaz, "order it as you please." So Pallenço straightway made ready his pinnace to go on shore, and although the sea was very calm, yet there was a very great surf on the coast which never permitted the pinnace to touch the beach; but he, desirous of finishing what he had begun, said to his company: "You see, my friends, that the roughness of the sea near this coast will not allow us to touch the shore; nevertheless my will would be to land, but as I know not how to swim, it would be folly for me to dare such a thing. But if there are any amongst you that can go on shore by swimming, I will surely thank them much to do it, and afterwards you will not be without that praise which good men and true deserve for their valorous deeds." "It is true," replied some, "that we have a good will to do your pleasure, but two dangers will follow from it. The first is that we know not how we shall get on shore, for these waves here may pitch us about in such wise that we lose the mastery over our limbs and we shall perish very quickly, for such things have already happened on other occasions. The second danger is that, if we go on land and meet some people with whom perchance we ought not to fight without your aid, and if the sea is in such a state that you cannot reach the shore, what shall we do?" And as you see that where many men are, their opinions differ, so whilst Pallenço was listening to the reasons these men gave, others went apart and would not hear any part of that counsel, but suddenly appeared naked before Pallenço, prepared to throw themselves into the water. "Here we are," said they, "order us what to do, for death is the same in every part, and if God hath determined that we should die in His service, this is the best time in which to finish our lives." After this, admonished by their captain, they [Pg 216]made ready their clothes and arms as well as they could and fell to swimming; and so it pleased God that, rough as the sea was there, all twelve of them gained the shore as they had left the ships. Then they began to take their way along the beach, and they had not gone far when one of them who was in front spake to the others, telling them to be quiet, for that he saw the footprints of people, and the best was that they appeared to him to be recent. "Meseemeth," said he, "that we should go after them, for by the appearance of their footmarks, they ought not to be far off." "And for what," said the others, "did we adventure ourselves before our companions to leap into the sea, if we were to do otherwise?" Then they ordered three men to go in front and to keep their eyes on the track, and the others were to follow after them. And when they had gone in that expectation for the space of two leagues, they discovered a valley, and herein those men who were in the van caught sight of the Moors whose track they were following; but they seemed to them to be so few that, with the good will that was in them, they felt grieved, even though they had a greater assurance of victory. And so they turned their faces toward the others, who were coming behind, to advise them of the booty that was before them; and their words were brief, for scarcely had they begun to speak of "Moors" when the men behind were already beginning to run, and to raise their battle-cries as they ran; and the sound of these both warned and saddened their enemies. But for the last there was no other remedy save flight, for they had little care of their poor and scanty goods; and sure I am that those who escaped thence were slow to return with longing regret for their baggage. Now our men had commenced their chace early, and were already wearied by their landing from the pinnace and by their going along the road; therefore they were not able to follow much upon the track; and on [Pg 217]this account their booty was much diminished, for they captured no more than nine persons. "It would be well," said some, "were we to set aside six of our people to take these prisoners to the ships, and that the other six remaining should search through that thick undergrowth, for there perchance we shall find some[BR] in hiding." Accordingly those who were to return with the captives straightway separated from the others and began to bind their prisoners in the best way they could; but it seemeth that they did it not as well as the case required, although six were sufficient for[BS] nine, as you have already heard that others had previously convoyed many more without any contrary hap. And since women are usually stubborn, one woman of that company began to take it in conceipt to refuse to walk, throwing herself on the ground and letting herself be dragged along by the hair and the legs, having no pity on herself; and her over-great stubbornness compelled our men to leave her there bound, intending to return for her another day. And as they were going along in this contention, the others[BT] began to disperse, fleeing some to one side and some to another, and two of them got away, not counting the Mooress whom they had already left bound; and though our men laboured hard to catch them, they were not successful, for it appeareth that the spot was such that they were easily able to conceal themselves. And so they were forced to bring those six to the beach with many complaints of their ill fortune; and herein the others shared who arrived later without having found anything. Some among them still wished to return for the Mooress who had been left behind in bonds, but as it was very late and the sea was dangerous, they gave up the attempt, and afterward they had no opportunity, for the pinnace departed straightway; [Pg 218]and so remained the Mooress with her foolish stubbornness, strongly bound in that wood, wherein I believe she would meet with a troublous death, for those who escaped thence, being frightened by the first encounter, would not return that way very soon. And as these ships went on their course, the wind began to freshen and to blow very strongly, and so greatly were the said ships beaten about by the storm that the pinnace commenced to leak and to take in so much water that Pallenço perceived that it could not well voyage any further. For if it did, there was a doubt whether it would reach the place he desired, and also there might chance to come such a wind that the caravel would be separated from them, and their lives would be put in peril. So he said to Dinis Diaz that he should receive him into his ship, and also the rest of the crew, together with all the fittings and tackle of the pinnace, as well as much of the wood for fuel; and when these had been brought on board, they scuttled the pinnace and set forward on their voyage.

[BR] Natives.
[BS] I.e., to guard.
[BT] Captives.

CHAPTER LXXII.
Of what happened to Rodrigueannes de Travaços and Dinis Diaz.

We have already told how Rodrigueannes and Dinis Diaz sailed in company, but this is the fitting place where it behoveth us to declare certainly all that happened to them. And it was so, that they, sailing in company after the manner we have already told, which we believe was after the scuttling of the pinnace, came to Cape Verde; and thence they went to the islands,[165] and took in water, and knew for sure by the tracks all over them that other ships had already passed by that way. From there they [Pg 219]began to make proof of the Guineas, in search of whom they had come there, but they found them so well prepared, that though they essayed to get on shore many a time, they always encountered such a bold defence that they dared not come to close quarters. "It may be," said Dinis Diaz, "that these men will not be so brave in the night time as by day; therefore I wish to try what their courage is, and I can readily know it this next night." And this in fact was put in practice, for as soon as the sun had quite hidden its light, he went on shore, taking with him two men, and came upon two inhabited places which seemed to him so large that he thought it best to leave them, for his expedition was not in order to adventure anything, but only that he might advise his other comrades of what they should do. Then he returned to the ship and there described to Rodrigueannes and the others all that he had found. "We," said he, "should be acting with small judgment, were we wishful to adventure a conflict like this; for I discovered a village divided into two large parts full of habitations, and you know that the people of this land are not so easily captured as we desire, for they are very strong men, very wary and very well prepared in their combats, and the worst is that they have their arrows poisoned with a very dangerous herb. Wherefore it seemeth to me that we ought to turn back, for all our toil will be the cause of our death, if we should make an attempt upon these people." To this the others replied that it was well said, for they all knew that he spake the truth. Then they mended their sails and commenced to leave. Now Dinis Diaz said that he had seen one thing on that island that seemed to him a novelty, as far as his knowledge went, that is he saw, among the cows, two strange animals, very ugly in comparison with the other cattle; but as these two were going in company with them, I hold that they might perchance [Pg 220]be buffaloes,[166] which are animals in the nature of oxen. And it was so, that as those men were returning, Rodrigueannes, who was leaving that land ill-contented because he had found no opportunity of displaying the good-will he nourished to achieve some honourable action, said to Dinis Diaz that it seemed to him it would be well were they to send some of their men on shore, for it might happen that some Moors would come to seize the wood of the pinnace which they had left scuttled, and if they chanced on them, they could not fail to capture some. And as Dinis Diaz agreed with this, they put out their boats, in the which they dispatched twenty men to the shore. And clear it is that Rodrigueannes was not mistaken in his thought, for the Moors were already engaged in collecting that wood on the shore; and when they saw that the boats were coming to the land, they drew away a space from the beach, as men who said: "these are arrived in search of us, therefore let us seek out a way by which we may not only secure ourselves, but even do them hurt as well." So they threw themselves into two ambushes with the object of enticing our men away from the shore and employing their strength safely and without danger to themselves. Meanwhile the Christians landed, and halted for a space to order their movements, and this because they discovered such traces of the Moors that they thought they could not be removed far from there; yet they perceived by the number of the footmarks that the enemy was many more in number than their forces could cope with, and this made some ask that they should return, saying that it was not a thing to be attempted. But others said, "There is no help for it; we are already on shore, and it would be a disgrace were we to turn back; let the boats return, and let us go forward in search of our enemies, and let all our fortune rest in God's hand." And of the first twenty that were there six turned back [Pg 221]to the boats to take them to the ships, and the fourteen[BU] went forward as they found that the tracks led in the direction of the Upland. But their toil in marching was not long, for lo, the first ambuscade began to disclose itself, and in it there would be about forty Moors, who issued forth against them[BV] very eagerly, like men who felt they had victory in their grasp, as well by reason of their numbers, which were greater, as on account of the others who were lying in the other ambuscade, on whom they relied to come and aid them. But although the Moors came on thus boldly, the Christians did not turn their backs to them, but on the contrary made ready their weapons, and after the manner of fearless men awaited the coming of their foes. And after this there began a very fierce combat between them, in the which lances and arrows were not without employment, and they found neither harness nor coat of mail to stay their course. Now there were no stones on the field of which the Moors could much avail themselves; and as they were without armour and the Christians employed all their efforts in wounding and slaying them, the Moors began to feel themselves overmatched, and they withdrew from our men as far as they could. And in this fight a page of the Infant's Household, called Martin Pereira, toiled hard, and his shield was as full of the enemy's weapons as though it were the back of a porcupine when he lifteth his quills.

[BU] In text, Eighteen.
[BV] The Portuguese.

[Pg 222]CHAPTER LXXIII.
Of how those in the second ambuscade disclosed themselves, and how the Moors were vanquished.

The Moors did not draw off so far that the combat between the two sides continued any the less fierce, and the chief reason of this was that they expected succour from the second ambuscade, although it already seemed to them that it tarried more than was reasonable. However, there sallied forth at last twenty-five Moors, who lay in the said ambuscade, and their loud cries did much to revive the courage of their companions, and now you can understand how great would be the toil of our Christians, with their scanty numbers placed amid so many foes. Of a surety their fortitude showed itself very great on that occasion, for though they were already wearied, and so many fresh fighters came upon them, yet did they in no wise change their aspect which they had worn before, and so like good men and brave they began to fight, calling out one to the other that "damned was the man who turned back in such an affair as the present." And those Moors of the first combat, though they had previously shown signs of being vanquished, turned again very boldly to renew the struggle, the which was very fierce between them; but the Christians punished them so sorely that the enemy were already becoming fearful, and did not readily approach where our men had the greatest force. But this did not protect them, for the one or the other failed not to receive mortal wounds, with the which they very soon finished the term of their existence. And so it went on for a short while, until the Moors saw some of their comrades fall and almost the greater part wounded, and then they perceived that the longer they stayed there, the worse would be the hurt inflicted on them. Wherefore they began [Pg 223]to flee. And those who had remained in the caravels, although quite at the first encounter they saw their companions engaged in that fight, were encouraged to think that they would need no other assistance, save that which none of us can dispense with, to wit, that of our Lord God, and they were very joyous at the marvellous courage they perceived in those men. But after they saw how the other ambush came up, they feared much that they would not be able to stand against them, wherefore they endeavoured as speedily as they could to give them aid; but since the distance was great, they were not able to reach the scene of the combat very quickly. And in a short time the Moors were all fled, but our men did not follow up their track on account of the great toil they had gone through, for thereby they were greatly fatigued. And so they returned, with the others who were coming in their support, to take shelter in their ships and attend to their wounds, for few were without these, either great or small, according to the share of luck that befell each man. And the Moors, when they saw how the Christians were already returning, retraced their steps to the scene of the fight, intending to carry off one of those dead men who it seemeth was considered a noble amongst them; and our men perceiving their mind, turned back against them to renew the fight. But the enemy, warned by the hurt they had received before, left the dead man they were even then bearing off, and took to flight as fast as they could, so that it seemed to our men to be needful that they should return to their ships to give rest and cure to their weary and wounded.

[Pg 224]CHAPTER LXXIV.
Of how Rodrigueannes and Dinis Diaz returned to the kingdom,[BW] and of what befell them on their voyage.

And though it be that I have already told of noble and great deeds in this Chronicle, of a surety it is not without a cause that I add the toil of those fourteen men to the praise of all the good, for their merits are worthy of great honour among the living, and much more I believe before the face of that Eternal Lord (whose centre, as Hermes[167] saith, is in every part in an infinite manner and whose circumference is nowhere), for from Him shall their souls receive glorious bliss. And to make an end of the actions of these two caravels, I will say briefly that as soon as this fight was over, the captains agreed to return straight to the Kingdom. But when they reached the Cape of Tira, they both came to an accord to put on shore certain men, to see whether they could still make any booty, though they knew for certain that the land had been searched many times before. And so when these were landed, to the number of fifty, they began to make their way along the beach until they met with the footprints of men that led towards the interior, and as the tracks appeared recent, they informed their captains of it. And from them they received commandment to set aside some of their number who should go forward and follow up the track until they came upon the Moors who had made it. And as the land was very level, the Moors caught sight of our men from a distance and began to flee, and though the Christians ran hard after them they were never able to follow them; but it happened that two youths of the company met with a Moor whom they brought back with [Pg 225]them as an evidence of their great toil. And thence they forthwith made sail to Lisbon, where having paid to the Infant his due, they had of him honour and reward.

[BW] Of Portugal.

CHAPTER LXXV.

Of how the caravel of John Gonçalvez Zarco arrived at the land of the Negroes.

It still remaineth for me to relate the hap of the caravel of John Gonçalvez Zarco, who, to my thinking, bore himself in this affair more without hope of gain than any of the others sent there; for all those others, as you have already heard, had a mind to profit themselves, as well as to do service to the Infant. But this John Gonçalvez was noble in all his actions, and so he wished the world to know that for his Lord's service alone he disposed himself to have that voyage made. And therefore he armed a very fine caravel, and the captaincy of this he bestowed on his nephew, named Alvaro Fernandez, whom the Infant had brought up in his household, and he ordered him to have regard to no other profit, save only to see and know any new thing he could. And he was not to hinder himself by making raids in the land of the Moors, but to take his way straight to the land of the Negroes and thenceforward to lengthen his voyage as much as he could,[168] and endeavour to bring some new thing to the Infant his lord, such as he thought would give him pleasure. The caravel was well victualled and it was manned by men ready for toils, and Alvaro Fernandez was young in years and audacious. So they directed their voyage, determined to second the purpose of him who had dispatched them, and they went sailing over that great ocean sea until they reached the River of Nile,[169] and they knew it by the signs I have before mentioned, and took on board two pipes of water, one of which [Pg 226]they brought to the city of Lisbon. And I know not if Alexander, who was one of the monarchs of the world, drank in his days of water that had been brought him from so far. From hence they went forward until they passed Cape Verde, beyond which they descried an island[170] on the which they landed to see if they could meet with any natives, but they observed that caution in their own regard which they felt to be proper in such a place. And as they were going through the island, they found tame goats without any persons guarding them, or indeed dwelling in any part of that island, and then they took their refreshment of them; and we have already told how the others found their tracks when they came to those islands, for this Alvaro Fernandez was there first, and because the story could not be told in any other manner we have related it first of all in the way you have heard. Thence they went forward to the spot where the palm tree is, and that huge tree of which we have left an account in the other chapters, and here they found the arms of the Infant, with his device and motto. There they came to an agreement to go and lie near unto the Cape, for it might be that some canoes would come to them with which they could hold converse, at least by signs, for they had no other interpreter. And when they were as near to the Cape as it might be a third of a league, they cast anchor and rested as they had arranged; but they had not been there long when from the land there set out two boats, manned by ten Guineas, who straightway began to make their way direct to the ship, like men who came in peace. And when they were near, they made a signal asking security, which was granted them, and immediately without any other precaution, five of them went on board the caravel, where Alvaro Fernandez had them entertained as hospitably as he was able, giving orders to provide them with food and drink and all other good company that could [Pg 227]be made them. And after this they departed, giving signs of great contentment, but it seemeth that they had come with something different conceived in their minds. And as soon as they reached the land they told the rest of their fellows all they had found, and from this it seemed to them that they could easily capture them.[BX] And with this design there put off six boats with thirty-five or forty of their company prepared like men who meant to fight; but when they were near, they felt a fear of coming up to the caravel, and so they stayed a little distance off without daring to make an attack. And when Alvaro Fernandez perceived that they dared not come to him, he commanded his boat to be lowered and in it he ordered eight men to place themselves, from among the readiest that he found for the duty; and he arranged that the boat should be on the further side of the caravel so that it might not be seen by the enemy, in the hope that they would approach nearer to the ship. And the Guineas lay some way off until one of their boats took courage to move more forward and issued forth from the others towards the caravel, and in it were five brave and stout Guineas, distinguished in this respect among the others of the company. And as soon as Alvaro Fernandez perceived that this boat was already in a position for him to be able to reach it before it could receive help from the others, he ordered his own to issue forth quickly and go against it. And by the great advantage of our men in their manner of rowing they were soon upon the enemy, who seeing themselves thus overtaken, and having no hope of defence, leapt into the water, while the other boats fled towards the land. But our men had very great toil in the capture of those who were swimming, for they dived like cormorants, so that they could not get a hold of them; [Pg 228]yet they soon captured one, though not without some difficulty; but the capture of the second caused them to lose all the others. For he was so valiant that two men, very mighty as they were, could not drag him into the boat until they took a boathook and caught him above one eye, and the pain of this made him abate his courage and allow himself to be put inside the boat. And with these two captives they returned to the ship. And since Alvaro Fernandez saw that it was of no profit for him to remain in that spot, and that it might rather injure him, because they already had knowledge of him, he said that he wished to go on further to see if he could find some new thing to bring to the Infant his lord. And departing hence, they arrived at a Cape where there were many bare palm trees without palms, and they named this Cape of the Masts.[BY][171] And going forward on their course, Alvaro Fernandez made seven men embark in the boat and ordered them to row along the coast, and as they went, they caught sight of four Guineas seated by the water's edge; and as the men in the boat saw that they were not perceived by them, six of them leapt out and pursued their way, concealing themselves as much as they could until they were near to the Guineas, when they began to run to capture them. And it seemeth to me that these Guineas were archers who were going to kill their wild game in the hills with poison, even as the bowmen do in this our Spain.[BZ] And as soon as they caught sight of our men, they got up very hastily and began to flee, without having time to put arrows in their bows; but though our men ran a long way they could never take them, although at times they came close to [Pg 229]them, and the reason was that these men go naked and have only very short hair, so that it is not possible to capture them by it. And so they got clear of our men, who yet seized their bows and quivers and arrows, together with a quantity of wild boar's flesh that they had roasted. And among these animals that they found was one that looked like a hind,[172] which these Guineas were taking with a basket as a muzzle over its mouth to keep it from eating; and, so far as our men could see, they were using that animal as a decoy, that it might draw the other deer to them by its gentleness. And since they saw it so tame they would not kill it; and then they returned to their ships, where they took their resolve to come to the Kingdom, making their way straight to the Island of Madeira, and thence to the City of Lisbon. And there they found the Infant and received many bounties at his hands, in the which John Gonçalvez had no small share on account of the good will that had moved him to serve the Infant in that enterprise. And this was the caravel which in this year went further than all the others that voyaged to that land.

[BX] The Portuguese.
[BY] Cabo dos Matos.

[BZ] The word Spain is here used to designate the whole Peninsula, as was usual at that time.

CHAPTER LXXVI.
How the Author beginneth to speak of the manner of that land.

It is well that we should here leave these matters at rest for a space and treat of the limits of those lands through the which our people journeyed in the labours of which we have spoken, in order that you may have an understanding of the delusion in which our forefathers ever lived who were affrighted to pass that Cape for fear of those things of which we have told in the beginning of this book; and also that you may see how great praise [Pg 230]our Prince deserveth, by bringing their doubts before the presence not only of us who are now living, but also of all others who will be born in the time to come. And because one of the things which they alleged to be a hindrance to the passage into these lands consisted of the very strong currents that were there, on account of which it was impossible for any ship to navigate those seas, you now have a clear knowledge of their former error in that you have seen vessels come and go as free from danger as in any part of the other seas. They further alleged that the lands were all sandy and without any inhabitants, and true it is that in the matter of the sands they were not altogether deceived, but these were not so great as they thought; while as to the inhabitants, you have clearly seen the contrary to be the fact, since you witness the dwellers in those parts each day before your eyes, although their inhabited places are chiefly villages and very few towns. For from the Cape of Bojador to the kingdom of Tunis there will not be in the whole, what with towns and places fortified for defence, as many as fifty. They were no less at fault as regards the depth of the sea, for they had it marked on their charts that the shores were so shallow that at the distance of a league from the land there was only a fathom of water; but this was found not to be so, for the ships have had and have sufficient depth for their management, except for certain shoals, and thus dwellings[173] were made that exist on certain sandbanks, as you will find now in the navigating charts[174] which the Infant caused to be prepared.

In the land of the Negroes there is no walled place save that which they call Oadem,[175] nor are there any settlements except some by the water's edge, of straw houses, the which were emptied of their dwellers by those that went there in the ships of this land. True it is that the whole land is generally peopled, but their mode of living is only [Pg 231]in tents and carts,[176] such as we use here when our princes do happen to go upon a warlike march; and those who were captured there gave testimony of this, and also John Fernandez, of whom we have already spoken, related much concerning the same. All their principal study and toil is in guarding their flocks, to wit, cows and sheep and goats and camels, and they change their camp almost every day, for the longest they can rest in one spot will be eight days. And some of their chief men possess tame mares, of which they breed horses, though very few.

Their food consisteth for the great part of milk, and sometimes a little meat and the seeds of wild herbs that they gather in those mountains, and some who have been there have said that these herbs (but of them there are few)[177] seem to be the millet of that land. Also they eat wheat when they can obtain it, in the same way that we in this land eat confetti.[178] And for many months of the year they and their horses and dogs maintain themselves by no other thing except the drinking of milk. And those that live by the sea shore eat nothing save fish, and all for the most part without either bread or anything else, except the water that they drink, and they generally eat their fish raw and dried. Their clothing consisteth of a skin vest and breeches of the same, but some of the more honourable wear bournouses; and some pre-eminent men, who are almost above all the others, have good garments, like the other Moors, and good horses and good saddles, and good stirrups, but these are very few.

The women wear bournouses which are like mantles, with the which they only cover their faces, and by that they think they have covered all their shame, for they leave their bodies quite naked. "For sure," saith he who compiled this history, "this is one of the things by the which one may discern their great bestiality,[179] for if they had some particle of reason they would follow nature,[Pg 232]and cover those parts only which by its shewing ought to be covered, for we see how naturally in each one of these shameful parts it placeth a circle of hair in proof that it wished to hide them; and also some naturalists hold that if those hairs be let alone, they will grow so much as to hide all the parts of your shame." And the wives of the most honourable men wear rings of gold in their nostrils and ears, as well as other jewels.

CHAPTER LXXVII.
Of the things that happened to John Fernandez.

That we may assist in the knowledge of these matters, let us relate in this place the hap of John Fernandez[180] in this land during those seven months in which he stayed there in the service of the Lord Infant, as you have already heard. Now he, remaining there in the power of the relations of that Moor whom Antam Gonçalvez brought to this land, was conducted by them with his garments and biscuit and some corn that was left to him, and also his wearing apparel; and these things were all taken from him against his will, and he was only given a bournous like each of the other Moors wore. And the men with whom he thus remained were shepherds, and they departed to their country with their sheep, and he went with them.[181] And he reported that this country is all sandy, without any grass, except in the riverine lands or low-lying parts, where there is some grass from which the herds obtain their poor nutriment; but there are hills and mountains all of sand.[182] And this land runneth from Tagazza[CA][183] as far as the land of the Negroes, and it joineth with the Mediterranean Sea[Pg 233]at the extremity of the kingdom of Tunis and Momdebarque. And from there all the land is like this I have described, even from the Mediterranean Sea as far as the Negroes and Alexandria, all peopled by shepherd folk in greater or smaller numbers, according as they find pasturage for their flocks; and there are no trees in it save small ones, such as the fig-tree of Hell[CB] or the thorn, and in some places there are palms.[184] And all the water[185] is from wells, for there are no running streams, save in a very few spots, and the breadth of this land will be three thousand leagues and its length a thousand, and there is no noble place in it save Alexandria and Cairo.

Now the characters in which they write[186] and the language which they speak are not like those of the other Moors, but are clean different; yet they are all of the sect of Mohammed, and are called Arabs[CC] and Azanegues and Berbers.[187] And they all go in the manner I have already said, to wit, in tents with their herds, wherever it pleaseth them, without any rule or governance or law, for each goeth as he willeth and doeth what pleaseth him in so far as he hath power. They make war with the Negroes more by thieving than by force, for they have not so great strength as these last.[188] And to their land come some Moors and they sell them of those Negroes whom they have kidnapped, or else they take them to Momdebarque, which is beyond the kingdom of Tunis, to sell[189] to the Christian merchants who go there, and they give them these slaves in exchange for bread and some other things, just as they do now at the Rio do Ouro, as will be related further on. And 'tis well for you to know that in all the land of Africa which stretcheth from Egypt to the West, the Moors have no other kingdom than the kingdom of Fez, in the which lieth that of Marocco and of [Pg 234]Tafilet; and the kingdom of Tunis, in which is that of Tlemcen[CD] and of Bugia; and all the rest of the country is possessed by these Arabs and Azanegues, who are shepherds on horseback and foot, and who travel over the plains as I have already related. And it is said that in the land of the Negroes there is another kingdom called Melli, but this is not certain;[190] for they bring the Negroes from that kingdom, and sell them like the others, whereas 'tis manifest that if they were Moors they would not sell them so.

And returning to the hap of John Fernandez, who went off thus with those shepherds; He reported that, as he journeyed with them over those sands he oftentimes had not sufficient milk. And it fell out one day that two horsemen passed by there who were journeying in the direction of that Ahude Meymam, of whom we have already spoken before, and they asked this John Fernandez if he wished to go to the place where that Moor lived? "Well it pleaseth me," answered John Fernandez, "for I have heard that he is a noble man, and I would fain go to see and know him." So then the others placed him on a camel and they began to journey in the direction where they thought the Moor was, and they travelled so far that the water they were carrying fell very low, on which account they went three days without drinking. And he saith that they know not the place where any people dwell save by keeping their eyes on the heavens,[191]and where they see crows and *hussos francos*,[192] they judge there are people, for in all that country there is no fixed road save those that go by the sea coast. And that John Fernandez said that those Moors with whom he travelled guided themselves by the winds alone, as is done on the sea, and by those birds which we have already mentioned. And [Pg 235]they journeyed so far through that land, enduring their thirst, until they reached the place where was that Ahude Meymam with his sons and with others who accompanied him, in number as many as one hundred and fifty men. And to him John Fernandez made his reverence, and the Moor received him right well, and ordered him to be supplied with the food on which he supported himself, to wit, milk, so that at the time he was picked up by the caravels he was well nourished and of a good colour. He reported that the heats of that land are very great, and so is the dust of those sands, and the men on foot many, and therefore few on horseback, for the remainder who are not such as to travel on foot go on camels, of which latter some are white and make fifty leagues[193] in the day. And there is a great sufficiency of these camels, not of the white in particular, but of all colours, and there are also many flocks and herds, though the pastures be so few, as we have already noted. And he further saith that they have captive Negroes, and that the men of rank possess abundant gold, which they bring from that land where the Negroes live; and that there are in that land many ostriches[CE] and deer, and gazelles and partridges and hares, and that the swallows which depart hence[CF]in the summer go and winter there on those sands, and I believe this is on account of the heat; and other small birds go there as well, but he saith that the storks pass over to the land of the Negroes, where they abide through the winter.

[CA] In text "Tagaoz."
[CB] The *Palma Christi*.
[CC] In text "Alarves."
[CD] In text "Tremecam."
[CE] In text "Emas."
[CF] Portugal.

[Pg 236]CHAPTER LXXVIII.
Of the leagues that the caravels of the Infant went beyond the Cape, and of other things of all kinds.

It was the opinion among many people in Spain, and of other parts as well, that those great birds called ostriches did not hatch their eggs, but that as soon as they laid them on the sand they left them there; but it was found to be quite the contrary, for they lay twenty and thirty eggs and hatch them like other birds. And he[CG] reporteth that the things in that land, by which those who live by merchandise may gain profit, are those Negroes, whereof they have many whom they kidnap; and gold, which they get from the land of the latter; and hides, and wool, and butter, together with cheeses, of which there are many there; and also dates in great abundance, which are brought from another part, and amber, and the perfume of the civet, and resin,[194] and oil, and skins of sea-wolves, which are in great numbers in the Rio do Ouro as you have heard. And they could also obtain somewhat of the merchandise of Guinea, of which there are many kinds and very good, as will be recounted further on. And it was found that up to this era of 1446 years from the birth of Jesus Christ, fifty and one caravels had voyaged to those parts; but of the sum of the Moors that they captured we will speak at the end of this first book. And these caravels passed beyond the Cape[CH] four hundred and fifty leagues. And it is found that all that coast goeth to the south, with many promontories, according to what this our Prince had added to the navigating chart. And it should be understood that what had been known for certain of the coast of the great sea was six hundred[195]leagues, and to them are now [Pg 237]added these four hundred and fifty. And what was shown on the *mappemonde* with respect to this coast was not true, for they only depicted it at hazard; but this which is now placed on the charts was a matter witnessed by the eye, as you have already heard.[196]

[CG] Fernandez.
[CH] Bojador.

CHAPTER LXXIX.
Which speaketh of the Island of Canary and of the manner of living there.

Meseemeth I ought to give an account of many things in this book, for if I speak of them so briefly, those that read the history will remain still in desire and wishful to learn the details by which to perfect their knowledge. And since I told in the beginning of this book how the Infant Don Henry despatched an expedition to the Canary Islands, and afterwards how the ships sailed there to make some captures, I would now set forth the number of these islands and the manner of their inhabitants, and of their beliefs, and after that, everything that pertaineth to them. And, as I have found in ancient writings, in the time that the King Don Henry reigned in Castile, who was son of Don John the first, who was vanquished at the battle of Aljubarrota, a certain nobleman of France called Monsieur Jean de Béthencourt, who was a noble and Catholic man, and desired to render service to God, having learnt that these islands belonged to infidels, set out from his country with the purpose of subduing them. And coming into Castile he obtained ships and men, more than he brought, and he went against them and had great toil in their conquest; but at last he made subject three, and four remained to be subdued. And for that Monsieur Jean had now used all the provisions and money which he brought with him, he was [Pg 238]obliged to go back to his country with the intention of returning again to finish the conquest of the whole number; and in those three which he had already conquered he left as captain a nephew of his, called Monsieur Maciot.[197] But Monsieur Jean, when he arrived in France, returned no more to this land; some said because he fell ill of grave disorders which prevented him from returning to accomplish his good purpose; others again declared that he was kept back by the King of France on account of the wars in which he was engaged, in the which he needed his services; so the said Monsieur Maciot remained there for a time until he passed over to the Island of Madeira, as will be related further on. And the peopling of these three islands, at the time of the putting together of this book, was as follows: in the island called Lançarote there dwelt sixty men, and in that of Fuerteventura eighty, and in the other, called Ferro, there would be twelve men. And these are the three which were subdued by that great lord of France. And all their inhabitants are Christians, and carry out among them the divine offices, having churches and priests. But there is another island called Gomera, which Monsieur Maciot laboured to conquer with the aid of some Castilians whom he took in his company, and they were unable to perfect their conquest, although among those Canarians there are some Christians. And the number of its inhabitants will be seven hundred men, and in the other island of Palma there dwell five. And in the sixth island, which is that of Teneriffe or Inferno, because it hath on the top a chasm through which fire continually issueth forth, there dwell six thousand fighting men. The seventh island they call Grand Canary, in which there will be five thousand fighting men. These three islands, from the commencement of the world, have never been subdued, but many men have already been carried off from them, and by means of these nearly all [Pg 239]their manner of life hath been learnt. And because they seemed to me very different from the usage of other races, I would here discourse a little about it, so that those who have received such grace from the Lord that they are outside the tale of such bestiality, may praise the Lord for it, because it pleased Him that all things should be made in such different manners, and that those who are placed in the holy law of Christ, and for His love would suffer some hardness of life, may get them great courage to enable them to support it well, when they recollect that these others are men likewise and that they spend such a hard and rough life with pleasure and delight to themselves. Now of all these islands which I have already named Grand Canary is the largest, and it will be in circumference six-and-thirty leagues. Its people are not without cunning, but of little good faith; and they know that there is a God from whom those who work good will receive good, and those who work evil will receive evil. And they have two men amongst them whom they call kings, and one duke, but all the rule of the island is in the hands of certain knights, who cannot be less than one hundred and ninety in number, nor as many as two hundred. And when five or six of these are dead, the other knights meet together and select as many more of them who are also the sons of knights, for they must not choose others, and these they put in the place of those who are dead, so that the number may always be full. And some declare that these men are of the noblest birth recorded, for they have ever been of the lineage of knights without admixture of villein blood. And these knights know their creed, but the others know nothing of it, but say only that they believe what their knights believe. And they must violate all the virgin girls, and after one of the knights hath slept with the girl, then her father or he may marry her to whomsoever he [Pg 240]pleaseth. But before they sleep with them they fatten them with milk until their skin is wrinkled like that of a fig, for they hold that the thin girl is not as good as the fat one; and they say that so the womb is enlarged, enabling them to bear big children. And so, when she is stout, they exhibit her naked to those knights, and he who hath a mind to violate her, telleth her father that she is now fat enough. And her father or mother maketh her enter into the sea during some days for a certain time in each day, and she is then relieved of some of her excessive fatness, and then they take her to the knight, and when she hath been violated her father taketh her home.

These people fight with stones, and have no other arms save a short stick to hit with. They are very daring and strong fighters on the land, which is very stony, and they defend it well. All of them go naked and only wear a fork of coloured palm-leaves round about them by way of breeches, which hideth their shame, but many of them lack even this. They possess neither gold, nor silver, or money, nor jewels, nor any engines of warfare, save some things they make with stones, which they use in the place of hangers, and with which they also construct the houses wherein they dwell. They hold all gold and silver and every other metal in disdain, counting it folly in him who desireth them, and commonly there is none among them that hath a different opinion from the others. Neither care they for clothes of any kind, much or little; but rather they mock at the man who prizeth them, as they do with one who prizeth gold and silver, and all the other things I have mentioned; only they set great store on iron, which they fashion by the aid of these stones and make hooks of it to fish with. They have wheat and barley, but they are without the wit to make bread, and only make meal which they devour with flesh and butter. And they have many figs and dragon's blood trees, and dates, though poor [Pg 241]ones, and they have also herbs which they eat. And they possess moreover sheep and goats and a sufficiency of pigs. And they number five thousand fighting men, as I have said above. They only shave with stones. Some of them call themselves Christians; and after the Infant sent Don Fernando de Castro there with his fleet, in the which he carried two thousand and five hundred men and one hundred and twenty horses, many of them became Christians; and because Don Fernando was fearful that the victuals he carried would not last, he left without conquering them altogether. And afterwards the Infant wished to send another expedition there, but the King of Castile interfered in the matter, saying that the Islands belonged to his conquest, which of a surety is not so. And hereby this very pious undertaking, to wit, that this people might live under the law of Christ, still remained to be accomplished. But this fleet was dispatched there in the year of Christ one thousand four hundred twenty and four. The inhabitants of the island think it a great evil to kill flesh or skin it, and so if they get a Christian from abroad, they are rejoiced for him to be their butcher. And when they cannot obtain as many as they need for that trade, they seek out the worst men in the island for this charge, and the women will have nothing to do with these persons, and the men will not eat with them, for they hold them to be worse than lepers among us. They light fires by sticks, rubbing one against the other. The mothers suckle their children with disgust, so that the greater part of the rearing of their babies is done by the teats of she-goats.

[Pg 242]CHAPTER LXXX.
Which speaketh of the Island of Gomera.

The fighting of the men of the island of Gomera is done with small rods like arrows, sharp and burnt in the fire. They go about naked without any clothes, and have little shame at it; for they make a mockery of clothes, saying that they are but sacks in which men put themselves. They have only a small amount of barley and the flesh of pigs and goats, but little of all this. Their food is chiefly milk and herbs, like the beasts, and the roots of rushes, and rarely meat; they eat dirty and foul things such as rats, fleas, lice, and ticks, and consider them all as good viands. They possess no houses, but live in holes and huts. Their women are almost common, and when anyone cometh where another is, at once the latter giveth him his woman by way of hospitality, and him that doeth otherwise, they hold as a bad man.[198] Wherefore the sons do not inherit among them, but only their nephews, sons of their sisters. The greater part of their time they spend in dancing and singing, for their whole luxury consisteth in sport without work. They place all their happiness in the commerce of the sexes, for they have no teaching of a law, but only believe that there is a God. They will be seven hundred fighting men, who have a duke and certain headmen.

CHAPTER LXXXI.
Of the Island of Inferno or Teneriffe.

Meseemeth I find a betterment of life among those inhabitants of the island of Inferno, for they are well supplied with wheat and barley and vegetables, with many [Pg 243]pigs and sheep and goats, and they go clothed in skins; but they possess not houses, but only huts and dens, in the which they spend their lives. Also they draw in their privy parts, as horses do, who only extend them when they have to generate issue, or to make water. And they hold it to be as evil to act otherwise as we do in the case of those who go about without small clothes. Their fighting is done with staves made of the inner wood of the pine, fashioned like great javelins, very sharp, burnt in the fire, and dry. And they number from eight to nine bands, each with a king, whom they must always take with them, although death come to him, until the other who succeedeth to the lordship after him happeneth to die, so that they always have with them one dead and the other alive. And so, when the other dieth and there are two dead, and they have to abandon one according to their bestial ordinance, or more rightly I will say, custom, they bear him to a pit in which they throw him, and he who carrieth him on his neck exclaimeth as he throws him—"May he go to salvation." And these men are strong and daring, and have wives of their own, and they live more like men than some of these others; they fight one with the other, and in this all their principal care consisteth, and they believe that there is a God.

CHAPTER LXXXII.
Of the Island of Palma.

The inhabitants of this island of Palma have neither bread nor vegetables, but only sheep and milk and herbs, and maintain themselves on these; they know not to recognise God nor any faith, but only think they believe; like the other cattle they are very bestial; and they say they have certain among them who are called kings; [Pg 244]and their fighting is done with staves like the men of Teneriffe, except that where an iron head should be, they put a sharp horn, and another at the lower end, though not so sharp an one as that at the top. They have no fish, nor do the men of this island eat them; and, while those of all the other islands do just the contrary, seeking means to capture them and making use of them in their housekeeping, these men only do not eat fish nor are they at the pains to capture them. And the number of inhabitants will be five hundred men, which is a great marvel, that being so few they have never been conquered from the beginning of the world; and from this it is evident how all things are only as God willeth them to be, and at the times and within the bounds that please Him.

CHAPTER LXXXIII.
Of how the Island of Madeira was peopled, and also the other Islands that are in that part.

Since I have related, in the fifth Chapter of this work, where I spoke of the especial things which the Infant performed for the service of God and the honour of the realm, how that among the other matters accomplished by him was the peopling of these islands, I would here tell briefly of the said peopling, and the more particularly as in the past few chapters I have spoken of the Canary Islands. Now it was so, that in the household of the Infant there were two noble esquires, brought up by that lord, men young in years and fit for great deeds. And after the Infant returned from raising the siege of Ceuta, when the united power of those Moorish Kings had encircled it, these men begged him to put them in the way to perform some honourable deed, like men who desired it much, for it seemed to them that their time was ill spent [Pg 245]if they did not toil in some undertaking with their bodies. And the Infant, perceiving their good wills, bade them make ready a vessel in which they were to go on a warlike enterprise against the Moors, directing them to voyage in search of the land of Guinea, which he already had purposed to discover.[199] And since it pleased God to ordain such a benefit, both for this Kingdom and also for many other parts, He guided them so that, even with the weather against them, they reached the island that is now called Porto Santo, being nigh to the island of Madeira, the which may be seven leagues in circumference. And so they remained there for some days and right well examined the land,

and it seemed to them that it would be a very profitable thing to people it. And returning thence to the Kingdom, they spoke of it to the Infant, and described the goodness of the land and the desire they had as to its peopling; and this pleased the Infant much, and he straightway took order for them to obtain what was needful to enable them to return to the said island. And as they were busied in the work of making ready for their departure, there joined himself to their company Bartholomew Perestrello, a nobleman of the household of the Infant Don John; and these men, having all their things ready, set out on their voyage to the said island. And it happened that among the things they took with them to stock the said island was a she-rabbit, which had been given to Bartholomew Perestrello by a friend of his, and the rabbit went in a hutch pregnant, and it came about that it gave birth to young on the sea, and so they took all these to the island. And when they were lodged in their huts, to make ready houses for themselves, they set free that female rabbit with her young to breed; and these in a very short time multiplied so much as to overspread the land, so that our men could sow nothing that was not destroyed by them.

[Pg 246]And it is a marvel how they found in the year following their arrival, that although they killed a very great quantity of these rabbits, there yet remained no lack of them. Wherefore they abandoned that island and passed over to the other isle of Madeira, which will be forty leagues in circumference, and twelve leagues distant from Porto Santo; and there stayed the two, to wit, John Gonçalvez and Tristam, and Bartholomew Perestrello returned to the kingdom. This second island they discovered to be good, especially in very noble flowing waters, which are made to irrigate what part they will; and there they began to make very great sowings, from the which they obtained most abundant crops. From that time they saw that the land had good air and was healthy, and they found many birds, which in the beginning they were wont to capture in their hands, and they discovered many other good things in the said island. So they let the Infant know all this, and he straightway laboured to send there other people and ornaments for a church, and clerics, so that in a very brief space a great portion of that land was put to use. And the Infant, considering how those two men were the pioneers of this settlement, bestowed on them the chief governance of the island, to wit, on John Gonçalvez Zarco, who was a noble man and had been made a knight at the siege of Tangier in a battle that the Infant won there upon a Thursday, of which the history of the Kingdom maketh a fuller mention. And this John Gonçalvez had already been present at very great actions, and especially at the raising of the siege of Ceuta and the overthrow of the Moors that took place on the day of arrival. And to this man the Infant gave the governance of the portion of the island called Funchal, and the other part called Machico[C1][200] he bestowed on Tristam, who also was dubbed [Pg 247]a knight in a foray that was made at Ceuta; and he was a very daring man, but not so noble in every other respect as John Gonçalvez. And the beginning of the peopling of this island took place in the year of the birth of Jesus Christ one thousand and four hundred and twenty; and at the time of the making of this history it was peopled reasonably well, for there were in it one hundred and fifty inhabitants, besides other persons such as traders and unmarried men and women and youths, and boys and girls who had been born on the said island, as well as clerics and friars, and others who came and went for their merchandise and for those things which they cannot dispense with in that island. And in the year one thousand and four hundred and forty-five the Infant despatched a knight called Gonçallo Velho,[201] who was a Commander of the Order of Christ, to go and people other two islands that are distant from those one hundred and seventy leagues to the north-west. And one of these the Infant Don Pedro began to people with the approval of his brother; but his death followed shortly, therefore it remained afterwards for the Infant Don Henry to continue this work. And to this island Don Pedro had assigned the name of St. Michael, on account of the singular devotion which he had ever felt to that Saint. And the Infant Don Henry also caused to return to the island of Porto Santo, for the purpose of peopling it, Bartholomew Perestrello, the same man who had first voyaged there with John Gonçalvez and Tristam; but owing to the multitude of rabbits, which are almost without end, no tillage is possible there, but many cattle are reared there, and dragon's blood is also collected there and brought for sale to this Kingdom, and taken to many other parts as well. And he turned out cattle on another island which lieth seven leagues from the island of Madeira, intending to have it peopled like the other, and [Pg 248]its name is Deserta. And of these seven islands, four are as large as that of Madeira and three are smaller. And for the profit of the Order of Christ, whose governor the Infant was at the time of the said peopling, he gave the said Order all the revenues ecclesiastical of the island of Madeira and of Porto Santo and all the revenues both ecclesiastical and temporal of the other island, of which he made Gonçallo Velho Commander. And beside all this he bequeathed to the said Order the tithes and half the sugar produce of the Island of St. Michael.

[CI] In the text, "Machito."

CHAPTER LXXXIV.

Of how the Infant Don Henry required of the King the right over the Canaries.

In the year 1446 the Infant began to make ready his ships to return to the said conquest, but before doing aught in the same, he requested the Infant Don Pedro, his brother, who at that time was ruling the Kingdom in the name of the King, to give him a Letter forbidding all the subjects of these realms from daring to go to the Canary Islands, to make war or treat of merchandise, without the command of the said Infant. This letter was granted him, and beside this he was privileged to enjoy a fifth of whatever should be brought from there; and this was very rightly given him, considering the great expense which that noble Prince had incurred in the matter of the said conquest. And though we found the substance of that letter set forth in the former book written by Affonso Cerveira, by aid of which we prosecute this history, yet we care not to transcribe it, for it is no new thing to any one of experience to see such writings, and well we know that their style would rather induce weariness in readers, so trite is it, than the desire to see their accustomed reasonings.[201a]

[Pg 249]## CHAPTER LXXXV.

Of how the caravel of Alvaro Dornellas returned, and of the Canarians that he took.

Now in this chapter it behoveth us to return to the action of Alvaro Dornellas, about whom we wrote that he stayed in the Canary Islands. And he let himself remain there out of shame, for it seemed to him that he would be blamed if he were to turn back to the kingdom without any booty, by means of which some portion of his toil might be known. And it was so, that Affonso Marta brought his caravel, as we have told, and this was despatched to the Madeira Islands. For here the said Alvaro Dornellas ordered him to take in provisions against the price he should receive for the sale of two Canarians that he forwarded in her, and he remained to pay those persons from whom he had borrowed them in merchandise equal in value. But by the chance of the weather he failed to make the Islands, and was forced to enter the river-mouth at Lisbon, where at that season was one John Dornellas, an esquire of the King, a man of noble birth, brought up in the household of the King Don John and the King Don Edward, and a cousin of this Alvaro Dornellas of whom we are speaking, who had an equal share with him in the ownership of the said caravel. And both were of one mind to go in her, only they accorded not as to the date of their first departure, when John Dornellas received command of the King, ordering him to abstain for the time from making the said voyage, for so it was necessary for his service. And when that esquire saw how the caravel came, he knew the necessity in which his cousin must be, and he at once had provisions and men got ready in haste so that the ship [Pg 250]might be furnished, and he also took merchandise, by means of which he thought his cousin might satisfy his debt in respect of the captives he had taken. Now this John Dornellas was a man of courage, and longed to accomplish great actions, and so he made his voyage with despatch, although it was at great expense to himself, and arrived in a short time at that island where his cousin was, namely, the one called Fuerteventura. And Alvaro Dornellas arrived there as soon as he knew of his coming, and taking aside his cousin, he said to him: "In that I have informed these Castilians that this caravel is all mine (which I said that they might have cause to help me better in my actions, thinking that you would not come to this land, and also more especially that I might fit out by their help a pinnace that is here), I beg of you, even though this thing may be in some part a lessening of your honour, that for my sake you will be pleased to endure it, and advise all[CII] to say none the less that the ship is mine, and that as a thing of mine it arrived here, with all it containeth. And from this moment, dear cousin, it remaineth for you to command me in some other matter, albeit a greater one, at a future time; and you may be well assured that, beside the reasons I have, if I receive this favour of you, I shall perform it with such good will as you shall see." "By God, cousin," replied John Dornellas, "though it be somewhat of a hardship for me to lessen my honour, being the man I am and with the upbringing I have had, yet I am well pleased to put all out of sight in order to do your will, although some of the men who come with me are persons of such rank that they have accompanied me here more out of friendship than from hope of profit. For here I have Diego Vasquez Portocarreiro, an esquire of the King our lord, and other[Pg 251]good men; but I will endeavour what I can in the business." And this in fact he did, so that all ended as Alvaro Dornellas desired. But this much you ought to know, that he acted afterwards quite contrary to what his words showed. For but little time had passed when John Dornellas perceived his deceit, and on account of this they were henceforth in very great contention, and almost came to slaying one another over it, but the matter is not fit unto this place. And so when both men came to this first agreement, they straightway armed the pinnace, and arrived in company at the Island of Gomera, where Alvaro Dornellas, as the captain, spake with the chief men of the island and asked them, on behalf of the Infant Don Henry, that they would give him some assistance to go to the island of Palma to make some captures. And they with good will granted him as much as he required. And so taking some of those Canarians to aid them, they reached a port of the island of Palma, where they landed and at once concealed themselves in a valley, because it was in the day time and they feared to be discovered. But as soon as night fell, they began to journey through the island without any guide or sure path by which to direct them to any certain part, but only at any venture that God might be pleased to ordain for them, until they arrived at a place where they heard the barking of dogs, and knew by this that they were nigh to an inhabited spot. "Now that we are already sure of that we seek," said some, "let us rest here in this valley, and very early, God permitting, we will go against them, for our going now might bring to us rather injury than benefit." And so they reposed there until they saw it was time to attack their foes, and then they charged them with such vigour that in a very brief space they captured twenty. And since the Canarians gave them much trouble in their attempts to deliver their [Pg 252]relations and friends, and also to avenge others who were left for dead, John Dornellas said to his cousin that he should take the captives and go on in advance with them, and he would hold in check the others, so that they might not diminish the booty; and in this stay, although they were hard pressed, yet they availed to escape from them, leaving fifteen of them dead in that valley, and none of the Christians died, and only two were wounded. And so they returned to the island of Gomera, where Alvaro Dornellas was compelled to stay, while his cousin departed to the Kingdom. But such lack of provisions overtook them that they looked for no other remedy than to eat some of those captives, as they felt they could be saved in no other way. However, it pleased God that before they came to this extremity, they made the port of Tavira,[CK] which is in the kingdom of the Algarve.[202]

[CJ] Your men.

[CK] The text has the old form, "Tavilla."

CHAPTER LXXXVI.

Of how Nuno Tristam was slain in the land of Guinea, and of those who died with him.

Ah, in what brief words do I find enregistered[202a] the record of the death of such a noble knight as was this Nuno Tristam, of whose sudden end I purpose to speak in the present chapter. And of a surety I could not pass it by without tears, did I not know, almost by divine forecast, the eternal delight his soul tasteth, for it seemeth to me that I should be reckoned as covetous by all true Catholics were I to bewail the death of one whom it hath pleased God to make a sharer in His immortality. And of a surety, inasmuch as he was the first knight who by himself bestowed that honour[CL] on another in that land, and as [Pg 253]I made a commencement of this book with an account of the booty he obtained, so did I feel almost resolved to conclude it with his death, giving to his divine soul the primary seat of celestial glory as the firstfruits of all the others who for God's sake were to meet their end in that land. Now this noble knight was perfectly informed of the great desire and purpose of our virtuous Prince, being one who from such an early youth had been brought up in his household; and seeing how the Prince was toiling to send his ships to the land of the Negroes and much further yet, if he might accomplish it; and hearing that some caravels had already passed the river of Nile, and the things that were reported from there; it seemed to him that if he were not to make himself one of that elect company and to render service to the Infant his lord in that land in any good thing that might be done or encountered there, he could not obtain the name of a good man and true. Wherefore he straightway made him ready a caravel, and having it armed, he began his voyage and stayed not in any part, but pursued his course toward the land of the Negroes. And passing by Cape Verde, he went sixty leagues further on and came unto a river, in the which it seemed to him that there ought to be some inhabited places. Wherefore he caused to be launched two small boats he was carrying, and in them there entered twenty-two men, to wit, ten in one and twelve in the other. And as they began to take their way up the river, the tide was rising with the which they entered, and they made for some habitations that they espied on the right hand. And it came to pass that before they went on shore, there appeared from the other side twelve boats, in the which there would be as many as seventy or eighty Guineas, all Negroes, with bows in their hands. And because the water was rising, one of the boats of the Guineas [Pg 254]crossed to the other side and put on shore those it was carrying, and thence they began to shoot arrows at our men in the boats. And the others[CM]who remained in the boats bestirred themselves as much as they could to get at our men, and as soon as they perceived themselves to be within reach, they discharged that accursed ammunition of theirs all full of poison upon the bodies of our countrymen. And so they held on in pursuit of them until they had reached the caravel which was lying outside the river in the open sea; and they[CN] were all hit by those poisoned arrows, in such wise that before they came on board four of them died in the boats. And so, wounded as they were, they made fast their small boats to the ship, and commenced to make ready for their voyage, seeing their case, how perilous it was; but they were not able to lift their anchors for the multitude of arrows with which they were attacked, and they were constrained to cut the cables so that not one remained. And so they began to make sail, leaving the boats behind, for they could not hoist them up. And it came to pass that of the twenty-two men that left the ship only two escaped, to wit, one André Diaz and another Alvaro da Costa, both esquires of the Infant and natives of the City of Evora; and the remaining nineteen[CO] died, for that poison was so artfully composed that a slight wound, if it only let blood, brought men to their last end. And there died that noble Knight Nuno Tristam,[203] very desirous as he was of this present life, in that there was no place left him to buy his death like a brave man. And there died also another Knight called John Correa and one Duarte Dollanda and Estevam Dalmeida and Diego Machado, men of noble birth and young in [Pg 255]years, brought up by the Infant in his household; as well as other esquires and foot soldiers of the same upbringing; and seamen and others of the ship's company.

Suffice it to say that they numbered in all twenty-one,[203a] for of the seven that had remained in the caravel two were also wounded as they were trying to raise the anchors. But whom will you have to make ready this ship that she may pursue her voyage and depart from among that evil race? for the two esquires who remained, as we said, did not wholly escape from that peril, for being wounded they came near unto death, and lay ill quite twenty days, not being able to render any aid to the others who were toiling to direct the caravel. And these latter were not more than five in number, to wit, a sailor lad very little acquainted with the art of navigating, and a boy of the Infant's household called Airas Tinoco, who went as purser, and a Guinea boy who had been captured with the first prisoners taken in that land, and two other boys, both quite young, who were living with some of those esquires that died there. Of a surety, compassion is due to their great toil at that hour. They went weeping and sorrowing for the death of such a captain and of the others their comrades and friends, and were from that time in fear of the hateful enemies they knew to be near them, from whose deadly wounds so many and such brave men had died in a very brief space. And especially they sorrowed because they found so slight a remedy whereby to seek their safety; for the sailor lad, in whom they were all putting their hope, confessed openly his scant knowledge, saying that he knew not how to direct the course of a ship or to work at anything of that kind in such wise as to be serviceable; but only if directed by another he would do what he could, as he was bidden. O, Thou great and supreme succour of all the forsaken and afflicted, who dost never desert those that cry out to [Pg 256]Thee in their most great necessity, and who now didst hear the cries of these men who made their moan to Thee, fixing their eyes on the height of the clouds and calling upon Thee to hasten to their aid; clearly didst Thou show that Thou heardest their prayers when in such a brief space Thou didst send them heavenly aid. For Thou didst give courage and understanding to a youth who had been born and brought up in Olivença, an inland town far removed from the sea; and he, enlightened by divine grace, piloted the ship, and bade the seaman steer directly to the north, declining a little to the east, namely, to the wind that is called north-east, for he thought that there lay the kingdom of Portugal, towards which they wished to make their voyage. And as they were going thus on their way, after a part of the day was over, they went to see Nuno Tristam and the other wounded men, and they found them dead, so that they were obliged to throw them into the sea; and on that day they threw in fifteen, and four remained in the boats, and two they threw in the next day. But I write not of the feelings that would be theirs when they cast those bodies upon the multitude of waters, burying their flesh in the bellies of fish. But what importeth it to us if our bodies lack sepulture? since in our own flesh we shall see our Saviour, according to the determination of Holy Scripture, for it is the same thing whether we lie in the sea or the land, and whether we be eaten of fishes or of birds. Our chief concern is in those works of ours by which after our death we shall find the truth of all these matters that here we see in figure; and since we all believe and confess that the Pope is our Chief Vicar and Supreme Pontiff, through whose power we shall be able to receive absolution or condemnation, according to the authority of the Gospel, we are as true Catholics bound to believe that those whom he shall absolve, if they fulfil the conditions of his decree, [Pg 257]will be placed in the company of the saints. Therefore we can say with justice to these men: "Beati mortui qui in Domino moriuntur." And moreover, all who read this history will obtain a reward from God, if they make a memorial of the death of these men in their prayers, for inasmuch as they died in the service of God and their lord, their death is happy. Now this youth whom I have mentioned was that same Airas Tinoco of whom I spoke above, and in him God put such grace that for two months together he directed the course of that ship; but all were doubtful what their end would be, for in all those two months they never caught sight of land. And at the end of this time they sighted a pinnace which was on warlike business, and they had great fear at the sight, for they thought it belonged to Moors; but after they found it pertained to a Galician pirate whose name was Pero Falcom, a new joy came upon them, and much more so when they were told that they were off the coast of Portugal, opposite a place belonging to the Master-ship of Santiago, called Sines.[204] And so they arrived at Lagos, and thence they went to the Infant to tell him of the tragical fortune of their voyage, and laid before him the multitude of arrows by the which their companions had died. The Infant had great displeasure at the loss of these men, for wellnigh the whole number of them had he brought up, and although he well believed that their souls had found salvation, yet could he not prevent a sorrow for that humanity which was brought up in his presence for the space of so many years. And so, like a lord who felt that their deaths had come to pass in his service, he afterward had an especial care of their wives and children.

[CL] Of knighthood.
[CM] Guineas.
[CN] Our men.
[CO] Not counting Tristam himself.]

[Pg 258]CHAPTER LXXXVII.
Of how Alvaro Fernandez returned again to the land of the Negroes, and of the things he accomplished there.

One of the signs by which a noble heart is recognised is that it hath no contentment in small matters, but ever seeketh some betterment, that its honour may be increased among the deeds of the noble both in its own land and outside it. And this may we justly say of John Gonçalvez, captain of the island;[CP] for he, not satisfied by the other voyage that his ship had made in the previous year to the land of the Negroes, made ready once more to dispatch there that same Alvaro Fernandez with his caravel well armed, and charged him to make his way still further onward to the utmost of his power, and to toil for some booty which by its novelty and greatness might give testimony of the good will he had to serve that

103

lord who had brought him up. Now Alvaro Fernandez undertook this matter as an honourable burden, like one who had no less desire[CQ] to carry through the mandate which his uncle had laid upon him. And when the ship had been provisioned, they made their voyage straight to Cape Verde, whereat in the past year they had captured the two Guineas of whom we have spoken in another place, and thence they passed on to the Cape of Masts,[205] and made a stay there to put some men on shore. And for the sole purpose of seeing the land, seven of them joined together, and these, when they had been landed upon the beach, discovered the footprints of men leading along a certain path. And they followed them up and reached a well where they found goats, which it seemeth the Guineas had left there, and this [Pg 259]would be, I think, because they perceived that they were being followed. The Christians went so far and no further, for they dared not pursue their course, and returning to their caravel, they voyaged on, and putting out their boat, found on land some elephant's dung of the bigness of a man, according to the judgment of those that saw it; and because it seemed not a place wherein to make booty they returned again to their caravel. And so journeying along the sea coast, in a few days they went on shore again, and came upon a village, and its inhabitants issued forth like men who showed they had a will to defend their houses, and among them came one armed with a good buckler and an assegai in his hand. And Alvaro Fernandez seeing him, and judging him to be the leader of the band, went stoutly at him, and gave him such a great wound with his lance that he fell down dead, and then he took from him his shield and assegai; and these he brought home to the Infant along with some other things, as will be related further on.

Now the Guineas, perceiving that man to be dead, paused from their fighting, and it appeared to our men to be neither the time nor the place to withdraw them from that fear. But rather they returned to their ship and on the next day landed a little way distant from there, where they espied some of the wives of those Guineas walking. And it seemeth that they were going nigh to a creek collecting shell-fish, and they captured one of them, who would be as much as thirty years of age, with a son of hers who would be of about two, and also a young girl of fourteen years, who had well-formed limbs and also a favourable presence for a Guinea; but the strength of the woman was much to be marvelled at, for not one of the three men who came upon her but would have had a great labour in attempting to get her to the boat. And so one of our men, seeing the delay they were making, [Pg 260]during which it might be that some of the dwellers of the land would come upon them, conceived it well to take her son from her and to carry him to the boat; and love of the child compelled the mother to follow after it, without great pressure on the part of the two who were bringing her. From this place they went on further for a certain distance until they lighted upon a river,[206] into the which they entered with the boat, and in some houses that they found they captured a woman, and after they had brought her to the caravel, they returned once more to the river, intending to journey higher up in order to try and make some good booty. And as they were pursuing their voyage thus, there came upon them four or five boats of Guineas prepared like men who would defend their land, and our men in the boat were not desirous to try a combat with them, seeing the great advantage their enemies had, and especially because they feared the great peril that lay in the poison with which they shot. And so they began to retreat to their ship as well as they could, but seeing how one of those boats was much in front of the others, they turned round upon it, but it retired towards its companions, and as our men were trying to reach it before it escaped (for it seemeth that it was already distant a good way from the company) their boat came so near that one of those Guineas made a shot at it and happened to hit Alvaro Fernandez with an arrow in the leg. But since he had already been warned of its poison, he drew out that arrow very quickly and had the wound washed with urine and olive oil, and then anointed it very well with theriack, and it pleased God that it availed him, although his health was in very troublous case, for during certain days he was in the very act of passing away from life. The others on the caravel, although they saw their captain thus wounded, desisted not from voyaging forward along that coast until they arrived at [Pg 261]a narrow strip of sand stretching in front of a great bay, and here they put out their boat and went inside to see what kind of land they would find; and when they were in sight of the beach they saw coming toward them full 120 Guineas, some with shields and assegais, others with bows.

And as soon as they came near the water these began to play and dance like men far removed from any sorrow; but our men in the boat, wishful to escape from the invitation to that festival, returned to their ship. And this took place 110 leagues beyond Cape Verde,[207] and all that coast trendeth commonly to the south. And this caravel went further this year than all the others, wherefore with right good will a guerdon of 200 doubloons was granted unto it, that is to say 100 which the Infant Don Pedro, who was then Regent, ordered to be given, and another 100 which it obtained from the Infant Don Henry. And had it not been for the illness of Alvaro Fernandez, by which he was much disabled, the caravel would have gone further still, but it was obliged to return from that last place I have mentioned, and it came straight to the Isle of Arguim, and thence to the Cape of the Ransom, where they found that Ahude Meymam of whom we have already spoken at times in this history. And although they did not carry an interpreter, yet by making signs they obtained a negress, whom the Moors gave them in exchange for some cloths they brought with them, and had they not brought so little they could have obtained much more, judging by the desire that the Moors showed. And thence they made their voyage towards the Kingdom, where they received the doubloons as I have already said, together with many other guerdons from the Infant their lord, who was very joyful at their coming on account of the advance they had made in their expedition.

[CP] Madeira.

[CQ] Than his uncle.

CHAPTER LXXXVIII.

Of how the nine caravels departed from Lagos, and of the Moors they captured.

Although the news of the death of Nuno Tristam caused in many people of our Kingdom a great fear of following up the war they had commenced; for the one party said to the other that it was a very doubtful matter to undertake fighting with men who so plainly carried death about with them; yet there were not wanting men to attempt the enterprise with good will. For manifest as the danger was, yet sufficient for all things were the hearts of those who would fain earn the name of good men; and especially were they moved to this by the knowledge they had of the Infant's desire and by seeing the great increasements that he made to those who toiled thereat, for, as Vegetius saith, "Men are valiant where valour is rewarded." And so in this year certain captains, with nine caravels, were moved to go to that land of the Negroes; and of these the first was Gil Eannes, a knight who dwelt in the town of Lagos. And the second was a noble esquire brought up in the Infant's household from early boyhood. Now this was a very bold youth, and none the less endowed with many other good qualities, and you will find his deeds writ more fully in the Chronicle of the Kingdom, and especially where it speaketh of the great deeds that were achieved in Ceuta; and this man's name was Francisco Vallarinho. The third was that Stevam Affonso of whom we have already spoken in other places of this our history, and he had under his captaincy three caravels. There was Laurence Diaz, of whom we have also spoken ere now, and Laurence Delvas and John Bernaldez, a pilot, each of whom brought his caravel. And there was moreover in this company a caravel belonging to the Bishop of Algarve, which an esquire of his commanded. And these,[CR] by the Infant's ordinance, went to the Island of Madeira to take in their supplies; and from the said Island there departed, with these caravels that went from this land,[CS] two ships, to wit, one commanded by its owner, Tristam, one of the captains who lived in the isle, and another in which sailed Garcia Homem, son-in-law to John Gonçalvez Zarco, the other captain. And so making their voyage all together, they arrived at the Island of Gomera, and here they landed the nineteen Canarians who had been captured in spite of the sureties, as you have heard further back; and they also took up certain men who had remained there belonging to the Infant's household and to the Island of Madeira. "Now," said those on the ships to the Canarians of that island, "we would fain try our fortune in the Island of Palma, if perchance we can make any booty wherewith to do service to the Infant our lord; and we would know for our better despatch if it will please you to give us some of your men who are ready to help us." "You know already," replied the Canarians by means of their interpreters, "that everything which is for the service of the Infant we will do with all our power." And true it is that they all went to the said island; but their going availed them nought, because the Canarians were already forewarned by sight of the caravel of Laurence Diaz, which had arrived there some days before. And after the great labour they had gone through in this affair, the two caravels of the Island returned, perceiving that they could not make any booty. But Gil Eannes, that knight of Lagos, and the others, pursued their voyage until they arrived sixty leagues beyond Cape Verde, where they met with a river which was of a good width, and into [Pg 264]it they entered with their caravels;[208] but that entry was not very profitable for the Bishop's caravel, forasmuch as it chanced to touch on a sand-bank and sprang a leak, in such wise that they could not get it off any more; but the crew escaped with everything they cared to take from it. And while some were occupied with this, Stevam Affonso and his brother went on shore; but the inhabitants were in another part, and intending to go in search of them they departed from there, guiding themselves by the glimpse of a track they found near the place. And after pursuing their way for some little distance they said they found much of the land sown, and many cotton trees and many fields sown with rice, and also other trees of different kinds. And he[CI] said that all that land seemed to him like marshes.

And it appeareth that Diegaffonso had gone on in front before the others, and with him fifteen of those who had a pre-eminent desire to achieve some deed, among whom was a youth of the Infant's household called John Villes, who was with them as purser. And as they were entering into a very thick grove of trees, the Guineas issued out against them from one side with their assegais and bows, and came as near them as they could, and Fortune so willed it that of the seven who were wounded five died straightway on the spot, of whom two were Portuguese and three strangers. And as the affair was at this point, Stevam Affonso arrived with the others who were coming behind. And he, seeing the perilous place they were in, brought them all back as best he could, and in this retirement they had not a little trouble, because the Guineas were numerous and carried hurtful weapons, even as you perceive those were which in such a brief space killed our men. And at this time four youths who were brought [Pg 265]up in the Infant's household received a pre-eminent meed of praise, and the chief of them was that Diego Gonçalvez, a noble esquire, of whose manly parts we have already left an account in other places. Another was one Henry Lourenço, who was also a youth desirous of toil for the increase of his honour. And of the other two one had for his name Affonseannes, and one Fernandeannes. And as soon as they arrived at their caravels they held a council and agreed to return, seeing that they were already discovered, and that their ships were overflowing with the crew they had taken from the Bishop's caravel. But although they gave this reason, I hold that the principal cause of their departure was the fear of their enemies, whose terrible manner of fighting was such as to strike any man of understanding with great terror. For it cannot be named true courage, unless they had some other and greater need of fighting, willingly to enter into combat with men who they knew had the power to do them so much injury. And there remained the bodies of those dead men among the thickness of the trees, and their souls departed to see the things of the other world; and may it please God, if they are not yet in His holy kingdom, to take them to Himself. And for pity's sake, all ye others that hold the Christian faith, say your prayers for them, for in asking for them ye ask for yourselves also. And the caravels returning as they had arranged, arrived at the Island of Arguim to provide themselves with water, of which they had need. And then they determined to go to the Cape of the Ransom,[209] where they went on shore and found the track of some Moors. And although by reason of the heat a journey by land was very perilous, yet considering that they were returning without booty to the kingdom, they felt constrained to adventure the risk, and so they began to follow up that track until after two leagues they reached the Moors and [Pg 266]with little labour captured eight and forty of them. And thence they resolved to make their way straight to the Kingdom; and so in truth did all save only Stevam Affonso, who sailed to the Island of Palma, where he went on shore with the greater part of those he brought with him. And there they happened to light at once upon some Canarians, of whom they took two women; but this was not fated to pass without a very harmful return on the part of the enemy. For they turned upon our men as they were carrying off the booty, and attacked them so boldly that there were some there who would willingly have left a part of that spoil to any who would have secured them from destruction. But that bold and good esquire Diego Gonçalvez, forgetting not his courage, stoutly took a crossbow from the hands of one of those archers there, and also the bolts and quiver, and placing himself among our men shot at the Canarians; and so much did he toil in the using of his arrows that in a very brief space he killed seven of those enemies. And among them there died one of their kings, who was recognised by a palm he carried in his hand, for it seemeth that their custom is for a king to have that pre-eminence among the others. And as you know that with all men it is a natural thing that when the chief dieth all the others do fly, so those men, seeing their captain to be dead, ceased from their fighting, giving place to our men that they might put themselves in safety; and so they came to the Kingdom with their booty, although one of those Canarian women died before they disembarked at the town of Lagos.

[CR] Caravels.
[CS] Portugal.
[CT] Stevam.

[Pg 267]CHAPTER LXXXIX.

How Gomez Pirez went to the Rio do Ouro, and of the Moors that he captured.

When this year of 1446 arrived, Gomez Pirez remembered what he had said to the Moors when he came to the Rio do Ouro in the year preceding; and forasmuch as he could not pass to that land without the licence and aid of the Infant, he began to require of him that he would assist him to go whither he had promised the Moors to return. And omitting some other reasonings that passed between them the Infant granted him the said licence and made him ready two caravels, that is to say, one decked and the other a fishing-boat, in which were twenty men (or with Gomez Pirez one and twenty), and among them was a youth of the Infant's household called John Gorizo, who had it in charge to write down all the receipts and expenses with the Moors.[210] And it was already the accustomed thing for all the ships that were sent out by the Infant, when they left this realm, to go first of all to the Island of Madeira to take in their victuals; and so soon as they arrived there Gomez Pirez spake with that purser and said that he would depart immediately towards the Rio do Ouro in the smaller caravel; and that John Gorizo should remain in the other and take in the things they had to carry; and that when the latter arrived there he[CU] would have arranged his traffic with the Moors. And so the first caravel departed, and arrived at the entering in of the Rio do Ouro, where they lay on their anchors for a space. "Let us go," said Gomez Pirez to the men he brought with him, "to the end of this river, where I promised the Moors the year before that I would come and traffic, for [Pg 268]there is no reason in our staying here, since the Moors appear not." And so they made their voyage thither and arrived at a port called Porto da Caldeira,[211] where they cast anchor. And in order that the Moors might have knowledge of their coming, on the day after their arrival Gomez Pirez bade them make a small smoky fire on a hill that was near the port. And when he saw that they came not on that day he had another made, and others also by night and by day until, after three days were passed, the Moors began to arrive, and Gomez Pirez began to speak with them by means of his interpreters, asking them to have some Guineas brought there, in exchange for whom he would give them cloth. "We," replied they, "are not merchants, nor are there any near here, but they are all engaged in trafficking in the Upland; yet, if they knew it, they would make great endeavour to come here, for they are men well supplied both with Guineas and gold, as well as some other things with which you might be well content."[212] Then spake Gomez Pirez to some of those men, and asked them to go and summon them, saying he would give them a certain fee for it; but the Moors received the money and pretended they were going to call them, but in the end they would never put themselves to the trouble of it, although Gomez Pirez waited there for the space of one-and-twenty days. And so full of trust were the Moors toward our men that five or six of them willingly entered into the caravel, and meanwhile there arrived the other ship of John Gorizo, which had remained in the Island. And when the one-and-twenty days were passed, and Gomez Pirez perceived how the Moors were cheating him, and how they would not go and summon the merchants, he said to them that until then he had granted them security in the name of the Lord Infant his lord, but that since they did not deal straightly, from henceforth they were to beware of him and to consider the security as ended. [Pg 269]And so forthwith he drave out all the men he had in the caravel, and made sail forthwith, moving away four leagues from thence to the other side of the river; and on the day after he had

107

arrived there, he saw two Moors coming towards the beach, and these by his command were captured in brief space. Gomez Pirez spake with them apart, and asked them if they had news of any other Moors being at hand. "We know," replied they, "that ten are gone to an island that is at the end of this river, and that there is an inhabited place near there in which there will be some forty or fifty souls." "Now, since this is so," said Gomez Pirez to John Gorizo, "make you ready six of your other men and take one of these boats and go on shore in search of those Moors who are in the island, as this man telleth me; and be careful," added he, "that you find a way to seize them before they throw themselves into the water, because I hear that all are very expert swimmers, and they might escape you if you were not advised of this."

So these men departed, and Gomez Pirez had another boat made ready, in the which he put eleven men with himself and went on shore, and there he spake to them in this wise: "My friends, you well know how we are come to this part chiefly to do service to God, and then to the Lord Infant our master, and all this not without a profitable return for ourselves. And because I have learned that in front of that island whither I despatched those other companions of ours, there is a village containing some forty or fifty souls, the most that can fight therein will number from twenty to five and twenty, and I truly believe that if we go against them as we ought, we shall make a great booty among them without grave peril to ourselves. Wherefore my advice is that we set out against them forthwith, so that if any of those on the island escape, they may not be able to give the news [Pg 270]of our coming to warn our foe and to cause him to flee. And this I make known to you as a man who desireth your counsel and approval." "What needeth there," replied the others, "any more talking or taking of counsel, but rather go you whither you wish, and God be with you. We will follow as we ought; for in regard to a man of such authority, and one who hath seen and passed through so many dangers both on sea and land, it would be matter of scorn if any of us were to think of correcting what you had determined." Now let us leave these men in their good purpose and speak of the six who went to the island; for these put all their energy in rowing their boat to arrive at that Island before the tide ebbed, because the Moors could easily escape at low water. And when they came near it, they agreed that four of them should go on shore and that two should proceed in the boat along the land, so that if the Moors attempted to throw themselves into the water, they could easily seize them, and also that if it were needful for them to leap forth and help their companions, they could do so. And as the four were making their way by land, the Moors caught sight of them, and either because they were men of courage or because they thought they had an advantage, they straightway rushed upon the Christians, hurling their assegais at a very short distance from them. These our men received upon their shields, and then they came to close combat, in which the four men had the better of the enemy, but the two men who were in the boat seeing clearly the toil of their companions, sprang upon land to aid them, and their coming was a sign of defeat for the foe, who began at once to retire and then altogether took to flight. And of the ten, which was the number of the Moors, two who tried to throw themselves into the water were drowned forthwith, either because they knew not well how to swim or for some other hindrance. And [Pg 271]when the Christians saw that they were throwing themselves into the water, they leapt into their boat, and so inside and out they captured the eight. And when they had them bound, John Gorizo said to the others: "Let us go to the land whither we saw Gomez Pirez faring in the other boat, for he departed immediately after us, and of a surety it was only because he willed to attack the village which the Moors told him was situate there. And since we have now accomplished our undertaking, let us go and aid him, for perchance he will need our help, or at any rate they will at least know our good will." And this John Gorizo said, because when they were going to the Island, they well perceived the course that the other boat was taking. And all held this counsel to be good; and so leaving these men now to follow their way to where Gomez Pirez goeth, let us speak of the fortune of the others.

[CU] Pirez.

CHAPTER XC.
Of the Moors that Gomez Pirez took in the other village.

Returning now to the deed of Gomez Pirez, let us suppose that council to be ended and consider that they are faring on their way, guided by those Moors whose words persuaded them to leave their ship. And it was so, that as they were already going near unto where they were told the village stood, they espied the Moors coming out of their encampment, and Gomez Pirez, catching sight of them, shouted lustily to the others to pursue them. "Run," said he, "for all our victory is in the speed of our feet, as you see that the foemen are beginning to make them ready." And his command was more than enough in their ears, for hardly had he uttered the first word, when they were already among the Moors, and crying [Pg 272]out "Santiago" and "Portugal," in a very brief space they leapt into the middle of the village, and there at the first onset seized one and twenty of those people, what of men, women, and children. But I believe the most of these would be such as could not flee, for of the twelve Christians who reached that place, four separated themselves from the rest and ran after those that were flying; yet their toil availed them little, for they could never come up with them to take them, and at last their strength commenced to fail and they started to turn back. And as they were returning to their ships, well content with their victory, they met with the others who were coming to their aid, and there was united an almost equal joyfulness, for each party on its side was content with the victory it had gained, and much more because this had been without any loss. And so they went to their ships, where they took rest with the victuals they had, offering one to the other with a right good will, as is done in places where the like meetings take place, for a common proverb saith: "A poor man hath joy in a little." Gomez Pirez would not allow himself altogether to rest upon this victory, and content himself with what he had already gained, but while the others were in converse he took aside one of those Moors and asked him if he knew of any inhabited place near at hand. And he replied that he only knew one, but it was six leagues off, and this would hold not less than a hundred souls. "It were all one," said Gomez Pirez, "if there were three hundred of them, for we will go on all the same, since we are at the matter;" and so he ordered sail to be made on the sudden, and directed his ships whither the Moor pointed out to him that the village lay. And when he perceived that he was already four leagues from the place he had left, he had his boat put on shore with seventeen men of those he thought the best and the most daring, and three he left to guard the caravels. And [Pg 273]then he had the Moor put in front as a guide. And because it seemeth they went by night, and the Moor knew not certainly where the place lay, but could only make guess of it, they would have passed it by, had it not been for the barking of a dog, by whose voice they discovered the place where the Moors were lying and turned back on them. But when they had reached the village, morning commenced to break, so that part of the Moors were already gone afield. However, with their accustomed cry, they came upon the place, and though the Moors defended themselves, they captured one and thirty of them; and I think this would be because it appeareth that the greater and principal men were already away, and the others that remained were old men and women and children. And they straightway asked of these what had become of the others who had departed thence? "They are," answered they, "three leagues from here toward the sea-shore, whither they went in search of food for themselves and for us." "Well, then," said Gomez Pirez, "my purpose is that we should go against them, for since we have already undertaken this toil, we should err if we did not make an end of it; wherefore eat something if you have it with you, that you may take some refreshment, and let us use one of these men to direct us to where these Moors are." True it is there were some there who would willingly have rested, if the contrary reasonings of the captain and of other some who agreed with his design had not prevented them. "Take two men of this company," said Gomez Pirez to John Fernandez (that good esquire of whom we have already told you how he went seven months in that land), "and conduct these Moors to the ships, and we will go in search of the others who left here before we arrived to-day."

[Pg 274]CHAPTER XCI.

Of what happened to John Fernandez when he was taking along the Moors.

Now as John Fernandez was going on his way with his prisoners in front of him, feeling not very sure that he would not find some foemen who perchance would make him lose his booty; and as he was looking around him on every side, for the land was level;[213] he happened to espy, some distance off, five persons coming towards him. And he was very glad at the sight, because it appeared to him that they were coming straight for him; but he began to ponder thereon. "Now," said he to the others, "you can see those Moors there how they are coming straight for us. Meseemeth they are five while we are three, and one of us must needs guard the prisoners; so do you," quoth he to John Bertollomeu, "remain with them in the rear, and Lourenceannes and I will move on towards those who are coming, and we will go straight against them. For the further off we fight from these prisoners so much the more will it be to our advantage, since it might happen that they would mingle with those we have and it would be an occasion for some of the last to get free." And on this they began to pursue their way straight toward those who came against them, thinking they were fighting Moors, but they found it quite otherwise, for all five were women, and these they took with right good will, as something that increased their capital without toil; and then they conducted them with the others to their ships.

[Pg 275]CHAPTER XCII.

How Gomez Pirez and the others who were with him took the other Moors.

So Gomez Pirez pursued his voyage, as you have heard he had said to the others after they reached the village; and when he was now distant a good space from the place where they had made their booty, he caught sight of a Moor coming on an ass; and it appeareth that he had left the spot where the other Moors remained. But as soon as the Moor caught sight of our men he threw himself from his ass and began to turn back, running to where he had left his companions. And since the land was level, and the Moor was fresh, and had sight of our men coming a long way off; because of all this the Christians could not follow him, being greatly wearied from the toil and loss of sleep they had now had for two days. But they kept him in sight as long as they were able, and at the end they were obliged to lose him, yet they failed not to keep a straight course until they reached the huts of a village, where it seemeth the other Moors were, and in it they found no one; and this would be about the hour of terce. And as they were gazing around the moorland as far as their eyes could reach, they perceived the Moors who had set out from thence; and tired as they were, they followed after them by the space of a league and a half, when they came upon them by the sea, near which they had retreated to some very great rocks;[214] and our men laboured to seek them out, but many as they were, yet on account of the difficulty of the place, they could not capture more than seven. And so they persevered in this toil all that day until nearly nightfall, but over and above their weariness, they sorely felt hunger and thirst, for which they had no remedy. [Pg 276]And when they had searched all the places they deemed likely for anyone to hide in, they agreed to turn back. And true it is that some declared it would be well for some of them to remain there that night, to see if those Moors would come out, who were lying hid, but there was no one who dared to remain, so weakly did they feel their bodies to be; but rather they determined one and all to turn back to their caravels. And it seemeth that it pleased our Lord God to have a mind to their weakness, for He ordained that they should meet upon that path, by the which they were going, two camels already saddled. And this was a great help to their repose, for they took it in turn to ride them until they came to their ships, where they found they had a booty of nine-and-seventy souls.

On the next day it was agreed among them that inasmuch as their ships were not able to lodge so many Moors on account of the salt they were carrying from this realm—and this was in order to salt the skins of the sea-calves lest they should have no other booty, or perchance it was to enter into ransoming with the Moors—therefore they should throw all that salt overboard, as in fact they did. And they were minded still to depart and run down that other coast, and on account of a storm that came upon them, they determined there to caulk their ships that they might the better encounter the fortunes of the sea as they returned. And when their ships had finished their repairing, Gomez Pirez took aside one of those Moors to know where there might be any other Moors that he could capture; but although the Moor told him where lay certain villages and they went to them, directing their course toward the south, they found neither Moor nor Mooress in them nor any other creature. And so they made their way by certain places where the Moor thought they would find them, until they were right well assured that the Moors had knowledge of them, and [Pg 277]that it would be lost labour for them to go further in their search. Wherefore they agreed to turn back to the Kingdom, seeing that their food was failing them, and especially their water, of which they could have no fresh supply in that land. And so they directed their voyage until they returned to Lagos, on the borders of which the Infant was staying at a place that is called Mexilhueira.

CHAPTER XCIII.
Of the caravel that went to Meça, and of the Moors that it found.

In the following year, which was 1447 from the birth of Christ, the Infant considering that the Moors would not enter into trafficking at the Rio do Ouro, and that even though they had been minded to do it aforetime, yet now their good will would be altogether lacking on account of the Moors who had been captured by Gomez Pirez, as you have heard at length, wished to make trial if perchance the matter might better be accomplished by trafficking at that place which is called Meça.[215] And that he might also obtain a better knowledge of that land, he straightway ordered them to make ready a caravel of an esquire of his called Diego Gil, the which was a man who had right well served him in the wars of the Moors both by land and by sea. And after he had taken order for these things, he had tidings that a merchant of Castile, named Marcos Cisfontes, was possessed of twenty-six Moors, from that place, who were already ransomed in exchange for certain Guineas. And in order that his ship might have some cargo on its outward voyage, he let the said merchant know that, if it pleased him, his Moors should be transported to that place in the caravel which he had made ready, if only he would give him a certain part of his profits in the said ransom. [Pg 278]And to say truth, it was not so much the hope of gain from those men, as for two other reasons, that the Infant was content to do this—in the first place that he might have a better opportunity of seeing the land and knowing in what manner they would enter into the traffic of merchandise; and in the second place, that he might bring from thence those Guineas,[216] for he believed they would receive the faith of Christ. That merchant was right well pleased with the terms the Infant sent to offer him, and so the caravel was immediately got ready and the cargo embarked, and the ship made its voyage straight to Meça, where they talked much about the trafficking, but could not bring anything to an agreement. Wherefore John Fernandez, that esquire who had remained for those seven months among the Moors of the Sahara, as you have already heard, spake to Diego Gil and to Rodrigueannes, another esquire whom the Infant was sending there to carry out the trafficking, and also to a Castilian merchant who was there to ransom the Moors. And he said: "If you are willing, I will go on land to arrange this ransom." And taking his sureties, he went amongst them, and bargained in such wise that he had fifty-one Guineas brought to the caravel, in exchange for whom eighteen Moors[217] were given. And then it came to pass that the wind arose with such force from the side of the South that he was obliged to raise sail and return to the Kingdom. Then there was brought to the Infant a lion, which he afterwards sent to a place in Ireland which is called Galway, to a servitor of his who dwelt in that land, for they knew that never had such a beast been seen in that part. And so John Fernandez remained until another ship returned for him. And in this same year Antam Gonçalvez returned to the Rio do Ouro to see if he could persuade the Moors to come to traffick, but his going there turned out to be very dangerous. For as he was lying on his[Pg 279]anchors up the river, the Moors straightway came down to the beach. And among them was one who clearly showed that he held lordship over them, and of him Antam Gonçalvez received sureties; but he warned him that he was not to trust the others except when he himself was present. And it was so, that when that Moor was distant from there, because the other Moors showed signs of confidence to the Christians, Antam Gonçalvez willed to go on land, thinking moreover that the Moor who had given him security would be there. And as soon as he came near the shore, and saw not that captain or lord of the enemy, he would not land. But as he could not well speak with them, being at a distance, he had the boat pulled very near the beach, and there the foemen clearly discovered the hidden guile that was in them, for they hurled their assegais like men who would fain display the mortal enmity they felt for our people. And had it not been for the great hardihood of Antam Gonçalvez, he had there met his end in a brief space with all his company. But as it was, he had the boat rowed off very lustily, though this could not be accomplished except with much labour, for the multitude of assegais that fell upon them. But it pleased God that they escaped out of that place and left some of those Moors wounded; and of the Christians one was wounded in such wise that within a few days he made his end, whenas the ship was already at sea.

And in this same year there went another caravel of a servitor of the Infant, whose name was George Gonçalvez, in which voyaged the said Gonçalvez and another; and they brought back from the Rio do Ouro much oil and many skins of sea-calves. And in this chapter the affairs of this year come to an end, for we find no other deeds in it that are worthy of being recounted.

[Pg 280]CHAPTER XCIV.

How Vallarte went to the land of Guinea, and the fashion of his remaining there.

The fame of the affair having spread through the different parts of the world, it arrived at the Court of the King of Denmark and Sweden and Norway;[218] and as you see how noble men venture themselves with the desire to see and know such things, it came to pass that a gentleman of the household of that Prince, covetous of seeing the world, received his license and came to this realm. And staying for a time in the house of the Infant, he came one day and asked him that he would be pleased to arm him a caravel and put him in the way to go to the land of the Negroes. The Infant, as he was easily moved to anything wherein a good man might gain for himself honour or increase, straightway ordered a caravel to be armed as completely as might be, and told him to go to Cape Verde and see if they could obtain sureties from the King of that land, for he was informed that this man was a very great lord; and he was to convey the Prince's letters to him and also to tell him certain things from himself for the service of God and His holy faith. And all this because they assured him the said King was a Christian; and the conclusion of all was, that if he did truly hold the law of Christ, it would please him to aid in the war against the Moors of Africa, in the which the King Don Affonso, who then reigned in Portugal, and the Infant in his name, with the others their vassals and countrymen, were continually toiling. All things were very quickly ready, and that esquire, who was named Vallarte, embarked in his ship, and with him a Knight of the Order of Christ called Fernandaffonso, who was of the Infant's service and upbringing, [Pg 281]and was sent by him in that caravel because Vallarte was a foreigner and knew not so well the customs and ways of the ship's company. And he came in order that he might direct the sailors and other matters that pertained to the governance of the vessel, and also that he might be as it were an envoy, if they chanced to see that King. And therefore he took two natives of that land as interpreters; but the chief captaincy belonged to Vallarte. And after enduring great toils on the sea, they made such a voyage that six months after the day that they first left Lisbon, they reached the Island of Palma that is in the land of the Negroes near Cape Verde. And there they took counsel about the manner in which they should henceforth act, according to the regulations they carried with them from the Infant; and then they sailed forward because that was not yet the port where they had to rest. And when they were at the extremity of the cape, in a place which among the natives of that land is called Abram, they had their boat put out and went on shore, and Vallarte went in it with some others and they found many of those Negroes already there. And Vallarte asked them to give him one of their people and he would give them one of his, so that there might be security between them and they could have their parleying; but they made reply that such a thing they could not do without the leave of a knight who lived there as a governor of that land, whose name was Guitanye. And he, as soon as he knew of this requirement, came there and was well pleased to grant what Vallarte asked. And as soon as one of these Negroes had reached the caravel, Fernandaffonso, who knew our Portuguese language best, began to speak with him, saying as follows: "The reason why we required of you to come to this ship was that you might tell your lord, by our authority, how we are the subjects of a great and powerful [Pg 282]Prince of Spain, who is at the limits of the west, and by whose command we have come here to converse on his behalf with the great and good King of this land." And they caused him to read one of the letters they were carrying, the which was declared to him by one of their interpreters, so that he might repeat it to that knight who had sent him there. "How much soever," quoth he, "you desire to see Boor, who is our great King, you cannot for the present have a message from him, for it is certain that he is very distant from here, busied in making war upon another great lord who willeth not to obey him." "And if he were still in his house," said Fernandaffonso, "in how many days could they go to him with our message and also return with the reply?" "From six to seven days would be the greatest delay," replied the Guinea. "Then," said Fernandaffonso, "it would be well for you to tell this knight with whom you live to send a man there with the message, and to let him know all that I have already told you, and if your lord will do after this wise he will render a great service to his king and bring much profit to his land." "Now," said the Guinea, "I will tell all very truly to Guitanye."

Then they presented him with victuals, of the which he ate and drank, and afterward gave him one of the letters they brought, for him to show it to his lord; and this, he was to say, contained what they had told him, and he was to bear it as a token of friendship. But already when that Guinea reached the land, where was the knight who had despatched him, another like unto him was there named Satam, and another known as Minef, who had arrived there a little time before. And of this last the foulness was extreme, and those who were there said that nothing more foul could be painted, and his apparel was no great testimony to his honour, for he appeared there very ill-clad, although he had a greater[Pg 283]power than some of the others. And whilst that Guinea was telling the knight of his embassy, the boat lay near the beach waiting for a reply, the which was very difficile to come at because the Guineas crowded round the man who came from the caravel, with a mind to know what he said, and also with desire to see the letter he bore, so that the knights were put to great trouble to remove them from there for a space. And in the end they could get no reply in all that day, although the knight went far into the water to speak with those in the boat, for such was the multitude of Guineas that they would never let him finish, and so all was left over for the next day, on which the boat went ashore very early. But the knight was already there in a canoe wherewith he would have journeyed to the caravel, but when he saw the boat coming he returned ashore. And he had a she-goat brought, and a kid, and paste, and boiled flour with butter, and bread with meal, and corn in the ear, and an elephant's tooth, and some seed of which that bread was made, and milk, and palm wine. And there happened to be there a knight who had arrived that same night, called Amallam, and he was the son of an uncle of that Guitanye by whose favour he had received that land, and it seemeth he would fain have spoken with those in the boat, but the Guinea would not allow him, saying that it was not right, as he had commenced the matter. And on this account he advised our men to return and take away those things for their refreshment, and after they had eaten to come back; and in the meanwhile they would hold their council. But if before this they were divided in mind through their conversing, they were much more so in the afternoon; and because we should have to be very prolix were we to recount minutely all that passed between one and the other in their parleying, let it suffice to say that this knight Guitanye went several times to the caravel, [Pg 284]making the journey in a canoe and taking four men with him. And he talked with our men concerning the traffic, and said that he was able to set everything in order, because that, when King Boor bestowed land on a knight, the latter could do therewith like the king himself, so that whatever he did, the king held it as well done. Howbeit, our men said that they carried orders to do nothing until they should have first spoken to that king, and upon this matter there passed much reasoning, and the end was that he should nevertheless send to the house of the king with their message. And whilst they were tarrying for the messenger who was there, that Guitanye went to the ship in all security, taking with him of the best viands that he had, with elephant's teeth, and certain other things, and he also received drink-money, and cloth, with other precious articles that our men gave him, and he showed himself to be very content with their converse. And one day they came to ask him that he would have an elephant killed for them, to strip off its skin, and teeth, and bones, with some part of the flesh, to which the Guinea replied that this could be accomplished without great toil. "Then," said Vallarte, "if you will put us in the way to this, for each one of us two that returneth here, you shall have a tent of linen cloth, in the which from twenty-five to thirty men can lodge, and so light that one can carry it on his neck." And our men went many times to the land with him and were at his call, but not so near that they could capture them. And it happened once on a time that the boat was near to the shore and with the rush of the sea it touched on the dry land, whereupon those in it were much affrighted; and when the knight perceived it, he told them to be of good courage, for all those were his men, and they would do them no displeasure; and so in everything that

Guinea knight [Pg 285] showed himself to be a true man. But Fortune, aided at times by the ill counsel of some, ordained matters in such wise that our men had not so agreeable an end to this commencement. For it was so, that whilst that Guitanye was in search of the elephant as he had promised, Vallarte, like a man of little discretion, would go on shore one day, for it seemeth that for some time they had called him. And true it is that he was told beforehand that he should abstain from going, yet he must needs land, as a man summoned by Fortune to witness the hour of his great trouble. And as he was near the shore, there appeared a Negro carrying a gourd with wine or water, and pretending that he was desirous to give it him; and Vallarte bade those who were rowing to draw near; and although some said to him that such an approach was unwise, yet they had to obey his orders, to the great injury of all. For as the boat was being taken into shore they went so near the land, to take the said gourd from the negro, that it touched ground. And whilst Vallarte was looking at a multitude of those Negroes who were lying under the shade of a tree, one of the interpreters they carried, called Affonso, made as though he would take the gourd and let himself slip out. And when the others perceived this and tried to bring the boat back, there came upon them a wave and overturned it altogether; and then the Negroes hastened up very lustily and fell in a body on the boat, hurling their assegais. So that of all the number who set out from the caravel in that journey, there returned not to the ship more than one, who threw himself into the water and swam; but we find not what end the others had, inasmuch as that man who came away by swimming said that he only saw one slain, and that when he looked behind him, yea, three or four times, he always saw Vallarte seated on the poop of the boat. But at the time when we were writing this history, there came into the Infant's [Pg 286] power some captives who were natives of that part, and they said that in a castle very far inland were four Christians, of whom one was dead already, but the other three were still living, and some held that these would be the lost men, according to the tokens that the Negro gave. And Fernandaffonso, considering this untoward event, and also that he had no boat wherewith he could return on shore to gain news of the others, had his anchors raised and returned to the Kingdom.[219]

CHAPTER XCV.

How Antam Gonçalvez went and received the Island of Lançarote in the Infant's name.

Of so well tried a usance in that land of the Moors were now the dwellers in Lagos, that not only were they content to go there and make war on the inhabitants, but there were some even who, not satiate with fishing in the accustomed places of their fathers and grandfathers, essayed to go and fish in the seas of that coast. And they sought license of the Infant and promised him a certain sum for it, that he would let them pass there and set in order their fishery. And I believe that this was not required in vain, for it may well be conceived that some of those who had gone there before had perceived the sea to be so replete with fish that they were moved to make such a request. Wherefore having arranged with the Infant for a certain quantity of money which they had to give him for the right which belonged to him there, they directed their expedition, sailing on their course until they reached a place called the Cabo dos Ruyvos.[220] And here they began to set in order their fishery, and of the fish they found a very great abundance. And when they had been there for some [Pg 287] days and already had a good part of their fish dried, and another portion set upon poles to dry it, the Moors came upon them, very wroth at such daring, and they almost killed the fishermen, and this in fact they would have done if it had not been for their good diligence in retreating. So that in the end they turned all their anger upon the fish that was spread out to dry, and this they cut in pieces with their arms with no less anger than they would have done to their foemen if they could have reached them. And two of those fishermen were wounded in that retirement, though not with dangerous wounds, but only with such that they were healed of them in a very brief space. And they turned back to their native town, not repenting them of their voyage, for they brought with them sufficient gain in the fish that they had already dried and packed in their ship in precaution against the fortune that afterwards happened to them. And in this year the Infant, who was desirous to follow up much further his first design, seeing that for matters to come to better perfection he needed one of the Islands of Canary, contracted with that Monsieur Maciot, of whom we have already spoken, who had the lordship of the Island of Lançarote, to give it up to him. And he, satisfied by a present or fixed rent for every year, gave up the said Island with all its seigniory to the Infant, and the latter made chief captain thereof that noble knight Antam Gonçalvez, first of all; and he went and took possession of the said Island in his name, and remained therein some time animating its inhabitants to the service and obedience of his lord with such benignity and sweetness that in a very brief space his virtue was confessed of all.

[Pg 288]CHAPTER XCVI.
Wherein the Author declareth how many souls were brought to this Kingdom from the beginning of this Conquest.

At the commencement of this book I assigned five reasons by which our high-souled Prince was moved to send his ships so often in the toil of this Conquest, and because me seemeth I have given you a plentiful understanding of the first four in the chapters wherein I spake of the different parts into which those Eastern lands may be divided, it remaineth for me to tell of the fifth reason, and to fix the certain number of the souls of infidels who have come from those lands to this, through the virtue and talents of our glorious Prince. And I counted these souls and found they were nine hundred twenty and seven, of whom, as I have said before, the greater part were turned into the true path of salvation.[221] See now how numerous would be the generation that could issue from these, and what taking of a city or of a town could yield greater honour than that of which I have spoken up to now; for leaving out these first and those who have descended, and until the end of the world may descend, from them, many more came afterwards, as in the following book you will learn. For it was needful that we should here make an end at the deeds of this year 1448 from the birth of Christ; because at this time the King Don Affonso of Portugal, 5th of that name and 12th in the number of Kings, had the entire rule of his kingdoms, being then of the age of 17 years, and married to the very virtuous and illustrious princess, the Queen Donna Isabel, who was daughter to the Infant Don Pedro, Duke of Coimbra and Lord of Montemor, the same that in the past years had governed the Kingdom in the King's name, as in some parts of this history we have recorded, and as you will find much more perfectly in the[Pg 289]general Chronicle of the Kingdom. So considering how that all other things, as it were, became new with the new ruler, it appeared to us fitting that all books of his acts and histories should here commence. And, moreover, as it seemeth to us that the volume we have already written is of reasonable size, we have here made an end, intending, as hath been said, to make another book that shall reach to the end of the Infant's deeds, although the matters that follow were not accomplished with such toil and bravery as in the past. For after this year, the affairs of these parts were henceforth treated more by trafficking and bargaining of merchants than by bravery and toil in arms.[222]

CHAPTER XCVII.
In which the Author putteth a final conclusion to his work.

Every work to be perfect requireth to be placed in the ternary number, that is to say, it must have a beginning, a middle, and an end; and for the more perfect understanding of this, it is well we should know that there are three ternaries in the General Universal of the world, and the first of these we call "super-excellent," and we can find no certain name to signify its perfection to us, for it is unknown of sensuality, and common natures cannot understand it; but an obedient faith, with great humility, rendered more lively by the grace of God, placeth in it a steadfast strength. And therefore that philosopher and theologian, Albert the Great,[223] in the 1st chapter of the *Celestial Hierarchy*, giveth three degrees of understanding by which God may be known.

And the first he compareth to the birds that fly by night, such as bats, owls, and other such, whose sight can in no way endure the sun's brightness; which also the prince [Pg 290]of philosophers affirmeth in his *Metaphysics*, saying that our understanding is such (compared to the things that in their essence, as far as Nature runneth, are manifest) as the eye of the owl or bat in comparison with the brightness of the Sun. For such a vision have those who involve themselves in the desires of the earth, placing all their affection in what they receive from the images that are felt, and by this obstruct their understanding, so that it knoweth nothing of the Divine Being. And in the second he maketh comparison of the other birds that have a stronger sense and endure the heat of the Sun, but when they regard its splendour their eyes do constantly tremble; and in this manner do some act, who, withdrawing themselves far from external objects follow after Speculation by Understanding, and removing their minds far from Materiality see the Deity from afar with trembling; but as they desire to understand with human reason, it faileth them frequently and they fall into error, even as fell a part of the great philosophers who were not illumined by the light of Faith. The third vision is possessed by the beauteous eagles, which can gaze with the organ of vision upon the resplendent orb of this Planet, and by these we may principally understand those that read in the book of life and know all things as far as their understanding extendeth without other investigation. And so the men, who in the knowledge of God wish to obtain entire strength, subdue themselves to the Holy Gospel, and taking solace from what they understand, adore with humble and great reverence that which by subtlety they cannot embrace, and faithfully confess with the Doctor Saint Thomas in the ninth article of the 10th question of the book called *De Potentia Dei*, that in God there is one real circle wholly enclosed in a perfect ternary, because He comprehendeth Himself and speaketh and begetteth an Eternal Word in which He vieweth [Pg 291]Himself and all things. And from the Father and Son there is breathed forth a tender issue by which the Divine essence is beloved and all that proceedeth from it. And so where was the Commencement of Understanding, there the Loving Will maketh its End. And we have an example of this in ourselves; for, if we consider what we understand, a certain knowledge is generated in the soul, and then the understanding offereth to the will that it may freely take what pleaseth it most; and it, receptive of the tender object, inclineth by affection to that by which the understanding was first moved.

In this manner is finished the circle which is super-spiritual and infinite in height, and in itself cannot proceed beyond the ternary in which it endeth. The second circular ternary is that of nature which includeth in it all the creatures, and it may be imagined in this wise: let us take some fountain that never faileth, from which a certain river taketh its birth, and following its course according to the vigour that it received in the commencement, it returneth to that fount at last from which it originally proceeded. And so all things have their commencement in the Lord God, the general cause and continuing in the Life they receive from Him, they have their last end in that from which they had their first beginning.

And by this ternary (which is in them of beginning, middle, and final end), saith the Philosopher, in the book that he made in which he discoursed of the Heaven and the World, that the ternary is the number in everything, and that it encloseth in itself the like perfection and middle and certain end, and that from it no creature is exempt. And on this account it was anciently established that God should be praised as a ternary.

The third ternary circle we call Moral, and it belongeth to the works that are done by us, the which commence in the credit that the Lord God willeth to give them, [Pg 292]for He doeth them chiefly, and we are instruments set in the midst, which He useth at His pleasure, working His will and accomplishing them as He pleaseth; and for the confirming of this it is written in the Gospel of St. Luke that if we do all that is commanded of us, we may know that we are unprofitable servants, for we only perform that to which we are constrained. And of a certainty all that we can do is vanity, since it can be accomplished without us, and we deserve nothing in it except as far as it pleaseth the Creator to grant us of His mercy, by doing us the excellent favour of making use of us in His actions, and willing that we be instruments in some of the things that He doeth. And this pleaseth His goodness, because He findeth in us some work of His by which we may earn a good reward. And therefore wise men perceiving this infinite mercy, that maketh them to be what they are, and understanding that all good works proceed from Him by His imperial pleasure, confess that they deserve nothing for what they may do; and they labour to fulfil this circle, so that their every act may terminate in that beginning where it commenced.

* * * * *

And because you, most high and excellent Prince, among mortals, and according to my thinking, most virtuous lord, chiefly for the sake of thanksgiving didst order me, Gomez Eannes de Azurara, your servant and creature, and through your munificence, Knight and Commander in the Order of Christ, to compose this book, with good reason it seemeth fit that in thanksgiving I should make an end of it. And since the Apostle Saint Paul teacheth us in all things to give thanks to God, as is contained in the Epistle which he sent to the men of

Thessalonica; so, making the circle of my work, I put the final term in that Helper who was invoked by my will in the commencement; and I offer to the Infinite Personal Ternary whatsoever thanks I can, for I [Pg 293]have not the power to give as many as I owe: firstly, to the Father super-essential, from whom universally proceed all things, to Him I give thanks for the talent he gave me to commence this work; and then to the Son super-spiritual, who had no commencement of being, to Him I give thanks for the help He bestowed on me to continue what I had commenced; and then to the Holy Spirit super-natural, from whom we have all good things by His benevolence, to Him I give thanks for the inspiration by which He moved your Highness to lay this command upon me and not on any other of your countrymen and subjects, of whom you could have had many. And jointly to all the Three Persons who compose the Ineffable Trinity and Super-essential Unity, our one only true Lord God, I offer thanks for the ending, because all things have concluded better than I thought before.

* * * * *

And this work was finished in the Library that this King Don Affonso made in Lisbon, on the 18th day of February, being written in this first volume by John Gonçalvez, Esquire and Scrivener of the books of the said Lord King. And to this lord may the most infinite, benign, and merciful God ever grant increase of good works and virtues better and better all the days and years of his life, and give him the fruit of His blessing that he may ever render Him thanks and praise, because He is his Maker and Creator. In the year of Jesus Christ 1453.

DEO GRACIAS.

[Pg 294]
[Pg 295]

NOTES.

[N.B.—*The page references are to the Hakluyt Society's translation*].

1 (p. 2). *St. Thomas, who was the most clear teacher among the Doctors of Theology*, i.e., St. Thomas Aquinas, greatest of the Schoolmen ("Doctor Angelicus"); born at Rocca Secca, near Aquino, 1225 (according to some 1227); Professor of Theology at Cologne 1248, at Paris 1253 and 1269, at Rome 1261, etc., at Naples 1272 (Doctor of Theology, 1257). Died at Fossa Nuova, in the diocese of Terracino, 1274; canonised 1323; declared a Doctor of the Church, 1567; author, among many other writings, of the *Summa Theologiae*, the greatest monument of Roman divinity. Aquinas completed the fusion of the re-discovered Aristotelian philosophy with church doctrine, which in the earlier Middle Ages had been hampered by the imperfect knowledge of Aristotelian texts in the Latin world, but which had for some time been preparing, *e.g.*, in the work of Peter Lombard (d. 1164), and even earlier. Aquinas also marks the temporary intellectual victory of the Church, in the thirteenth century, over the free-thinking and disruptive tendencies which had shown themselves so threatening in the twelfth. See K. Werner,*Thomas von Aquino*, Regensburg, 1858-59; Feugueray, *Essai sur les doctrines politiques de St. T. d'A.*, Paris, 1857; De Liechty, *Albert le grand et St. T. d'A.*, Paris, 1880. Encken,*Die Philosophie des T. von A.*, Halle, 1886.

2 (p. 3). *When the King John ... went to take Ceuta*, viz., in 1415, in company with his sons, Edward (Duarte), Pedro, and Henry, and a force of 50,000 soldiers. See especially Oliveira Martins, *Os Filhos de D. João I* (1891), ch. ii; Azurara's *Chronica de Ceuta*; Mat. Pisano, *De bello Septensi*; Major's *Henry Navigator*, 1868 ed., pp. 26-43; "Life" of the same, in *Heroes of the Nations Series*, ch. viii.

3 (p. 4). *Duke John, Lord of Lançam*.—On this Santarem has the following: [The Duke of whom our author speaks was probably John of Lançon, one of the Paladins of Charles the Great, concerning whose deeds there exists a MS. poem of the thirteenth century in the Collection of MSS. in the Royal Library of Paris (No. 8; 203). This reference cannot be to John I, Duke of Alençon, seeing that it does not appear that any history of his deeds was ever written].—S.

4 [Pg 296](p. 4). *Deeds of the Cid Ruy Diaz.*—[Here our author probably refers to the poem of the Cid, copies of which were spread through Spain from the twelfth century (see the*Coleccion de Poesias castellanas anteriores al siglo* XV, Madrid, 1779-90). In the time of Azurara there was no *one* chronicle of the Cid's deeds; see Herder, *Der Cid nach Spanischen Romanzen besungen* 1857(-59), who translates eighty romances published on this subject; Southey's *Chronicle of the Cid*, London, 1808].—S. See also *The Cid* (H. B. Clarke) in *Heroes of the Nations Series*; R. P. A. Dozy, *Hist. Pol-Litt. d'Espagne, Moyen-âge*, i, 320-706; *Le Cid ... Nouveaux Documents*, 1860; J. Cornu, *Etudes*, 1881 (*Romania*, x, 75-99); Canton Zalazar, *Los restos del Cid*, 1883.

5 (p. 4). *The Count Nunalvarez Pereira.*—The "Holy Constable," one of the Portuguese leaders in the Nationalist rising of 1383-5, which set the House of Aviz on the Portuguese throne. Azurara is credited with the (doubtful) authorship of a work on the miracles of the Holy Constable. See the Introduction to vol. i of this Edition, pp. liii-liv, and Oliveira Martins' *Vida de Nun'Alvares*, Lisbon 1893; also the latter's *Os Filhos de D. João I*, chs. i, ii; Major's *Henry Navigator*, pp. 11, 13, 14, 16, 17, 21, 78.

6 (p. 5). *Pillars of Hercules*, or Straits of Gibraltar; called by some Arabic geographers (*e.g.*, Mas'udi) the Strait of the Idols of Copper. The conquest of Ceuta in 1415 gave Portugal a great hold over this "narrow passage," and in 1418 Prince Henry aspired to seize Gibraltar, which would have made his country complete master of the same, but his project was discountenanced by his father's government. We may refer to Galvano's story of a Portuguese ship starting from here, shortly after 1447 (?), being driven out to certain islands in the Atlantic; to the Infant's settlement at Sagres being in tolerable proximity; and to Azurara's (and others') reckoning of distances along new-discovered coasts from the same. See Azurara, *Guinea*, ch. v.

7 (p. 5). *The Church of Santiago*, i.e., St. James of Compostella, in Galicia.—[In this passage our author refers to the celebrated diploma of King D. Ramiro about the battle of Clavijo, though he does not cite that document, and also to the *Chronicle of Sampiro*. On these two documents the reader can consult Masdeu, *Historia Critica de España*, tom. xii, p. 214, etc.; tom. xiii, 390; and tom. xvi—Voto de S. Thiago Suppl. 1.].—S.

8 (p. 7). *Sentences of St. Thomas and St. Gregory*, i.e., of St. Thomas Aquinas and Pope (St.) Gregory the Great (A.D. 590-604).

9 (p. 7). *Garamantes, etc.*—Properly the inhabitants of Fezzan—"Garama," or "Phazania" in classical language. Γαράμαντεσ ... ἔθνοσ μέγα ἰσχυρῶσ says Herodotus (iv, 183). Yet like the Nasamones and other nations of this part, they are apparently conceived of by H. as a people confined to a single oasis of the desert. The Garamantes' land, H. adds, is thirty days' journey from the Lotos Eaters on the North coast of Africa, which is about the true distance from Mourzuk, in Fezzan, to Tripoli (see the journeys of Captain Lyon in 1820, and of Colonel Monteil in 1892). The oasis, ten days' journey beyond the Garamantes, inhabited by the Atarantes or Atlantes, may be the Herodotean conception of Tibesti.

Compare the story, in Herodotus, ii, 32, 33, of five Nasamonians, [Pg 297]from the shore of the Great Syrtes, crossing the deserts to the south of Libya to an inhabited region, far west of their home, with fruit trees, extensive marshes, a city inhabited by Black People of small stature, a river flowing from west to east containing crocodiles: probably either the modern Bornu or one of the Negro states on the Middle Niger.

Pliny (*Hist Nat.*, v, 5, §36) records the conquest of the Garamantes by Cornelius Balbus in B.C. 20, when the Romans captured Cydamus (Ghadames in south-west Tripoli) and Garama ("clarissimum oppidum," the Germa of the present day, whence the name "Garamantes").

In the time of Vespasian the more direct route from Œa or Tripoli to Phazania was discovered (Pliny, *l. c.*). In the reign of Tiberius, during the revolt of Tacfarinas in Numidia, the Garamantes supported the rebel, and after his defeat sent to Rome to sue for pardon, an unusual embassy, as Tacitus remarks ("Garamantum legati, raro in urbe visi"). From Fezzan, in later days (about time of Trajan?) started the remarkable expeditions of Septimius Flaccus and Julius Maternus to the "Ethiopian land" (Sudan) and Agisymba (Region of Lake Chad?) in the south, which reached inhabited country after a march of three and four months

respectively across the desert (see Ptolemy, i, 8, §5, from Marinus of Tyre, now lost except in Pt.'s citations). The original conquest by Balbus is probably referred to in Virgil's *Æneid VI*, 795, in the prophecy of Augustus' triumphs:—
"Super et Garamantes et Indos Proferet imperium."
The Ethiopians ... under the Shadow of Mount Caucasus is an extreme instance of the mediæval geography met with so frequently in Azurara, as no African "Mt. Caucasus" has ever been identified, even as a barbarous misnomer for one of the African ranges; while Ethiopia, however confused the reference, always starts from the ancient knowledge of the Sudan, and especially the Eastern or Egyptian Sudan (see below).

The Caucasus, here used, perhaps, like "Taurus," or "Alps," in the general sense of "lofty mountains," was a great centre of mediæval myth. Here was situated, according to most authorities, the wall of Alexander, when with an iron rampart he shut up Gog and Magog, and "twenty-two nations of evil men" from invading the fertile countries of the south (see *Koran*, chs. xv, xviii; the Arabic record of "Sallam the interpreter," sent to the Caucasus about 840 by the Caliph Wathek-Billah; Ibn Khordadbeh, c. 880; St. Jerome*On Genesis*, x, 2, and *On Ezekiel*, xxxviii-ix; St. Augustine, *De Civitate Dei*, xx, 11; St. Ambrose, *De Fide ad Gratianum*, ii, 4; St. Isidore, *Origines*, ix, 2; xiv, 3; and the*Commentaries* of Andrew and Aretes of Caesarea *On the Apocalypse* of A.D. *c.* 400 and*c.* 540; *Dawn of Modern Geography*, pp. 335-8, 425-434).

10 (p. 7). *Indians of Greater and Lesser India* is a regular mediæval term for the inhabitants of India proper and of south-western Asia, sometimes including Abyssinia. Another frequent division was threefold: India Prima, Secunda, Tertia, or Greater, Lesser, and Middle, as in Marco Polo, Bk. III, chs. i, xxxviii-xxxix. Most commonly, Greater India means India west of Ganges; Lesser India corresponds to the classical*India extra Gangem*, or Assam, Burma, Siam, etc.; and Middle India stands for Abyssinia, and perhaps for some parts of the Arabian coast, as far as the Persian Gulf.

[Pg 298]On this passage we must also notice the following MS. notes:—

[α. *Garamantes, Ethiopians and Indians*.—It must be understood that these are three peoples, as saith Isidore in his sixth book [*i.e., of the Etymologies* or *Origins of St. Isidore of Seville, written c. A.D. 600*], to wit, the Asperi, Garamantes and Indians. The Asperi are in the west, the Garamantes in the middle, the Indians in the east. He reckoned with the Garamantes, the Tregodites [*Troglodytes or Trogodites*] because they are their neighbours. Alfargano [*Mohammed Alfergani, or of Ferghanah on the Upper Oxus, a great Mohammedan geographer of the ninth century, author of a "Book of Celestial Movements" translated into Hebrew and from Hebrew into Latin, which also described the chief towns and countries of the world*] placed Meroe, which is Queen of the Nations, between the Nubians and the Indians. The Garamantes are so called from Garama, which is the capital of their Kingdom, and the castle of which standeth between Inenense and Ethiopia, where is a fountain which cooleth with the heat of the day, and groweth hot with the cold of the night. Ethiopia is over against Egypt and Africa, on the southern part thereof; from the east it stretcheth over against the west even to the Ethiopian Sea. And because much of the people of these three nations are Christians, and because they desired to see the world, they came to these parts of Spain, where they received great gifts from the Infant, on account of which the author hath given this description in his chapter thereupon.

β. *Caucasus*.—This mount is so called from Candor, the which stretcheth from India to Taurus, in its length, through various peoples and tongues, and therefore is variously named. Some say that Mt. Caucasus and Mt. Taurus are all one, but Orosius reproveth this opinion.] On the fountain of Garama, cf. Solinus, xxx, i.

11 (p. 7). *To visit the Apostle*, viz., St. James of Compostella, patron saint of Spain, and traditionally the "Apostle" of that country. Santiago de Compostella was once the capital of Galicia; it lies 55 kilometres south of Coruña, on the north bank, and near the source, of the River Sar, which flows into the Ulla. The town is built round the Cathedral, which claims to possess the body of St. James. A star was said to have originally shown the place of this relic, hence "Compostella" (Campus stellae). The body of the great church was commenced in 1082 and completed in 1128; the cloisters were finished in 1533. An earlier church of the

later ninth century had been destroyed in 997 by the Arabs under the famous "hagib" Almanzor, who also restored Barcelona to the Western Caliphate, and nearly crushed all the Christian kingdoms of Spain. For centuries Compostella was the most famous and fashionable place of pilgrimage, next to Rome, in Europe. It is referred to in Chaucer, Prologue to *Canterbury Tales*, l. 466, in the description of the "Wife of Bath:"
"At Rome she haddé been, and at Boloyne In Galice at Saint Jame, and at Coloyne."
12 (p. 8). *Ancient and venerable city of Thebes.*—Here we have again a MS. note.

[We must understand that there are two cities of Thebes—the one in Egypt and the other in Greece. That in Greece was the selfsame which in the time of Pharaoh Nicrao (*Necho,see Herodotus, ii*, [Pg 299]*158-9: Josephus Antiq. Jud.*) was called Jersem, as saith Marco Polo, whence came the Kings of Thebes who reigned in Egypt C I R (*190*) years. And this was one of the places which were given to Jacob, by the countenance of his son Joseph, when by the needs of hunger he went with his eleven sons to Egypt, as it is writ in Genesis. And Saint Isidore saith in his xvth book (*of Origins*) that Cadmus built Thebes in Egypt, and that he, passing into Greece, founded the other and Grecian Thebes, in the province of Acaya (*Achaia*), the which is now called the land of the Prince of the Amoreans.]

It is not necessary to dwell on the additional confusion furnished by this "explanation"—Thebes given to the Israelites (as part of Goshen?), Cadmus building the Egyptian Thebes, Achaia for Bœotia, and so forth; but the point really noticeable is that in Azurara's text the "dwellers on the Nile who possess Thebes" came in here as "wearing the Prince's livery:" *i.e.*, the negroes of the Senegal are supposed to live on the western branch of the Nile, which mediæval conceptions obstinately brought from Egypt or Nubia to the Atlantic, and which Prince Henry's seamen thought they had discovered when they reached the Senegal; just as later in the Gambia, the Niger, and the Congo, other equivalents were imagined for the Negro Nile of Edrisi, and the West African river-courses of Pliny and Ptolemy. Cf. chs. xxx, xxxi, lx-lxii, of this Chronicle.

13 (p. 8). *Wisdom of the Italians ... labyrinth.*—Here we have another original MS. note. [Labyrinth is so much as to say anything into which a man having entered cannot go out again (*so Prince Henry, in Azurara, vol. i, p. 8 (ch. ii), has "entered a labyrinth of Glory"*). And therefore, saith Ovid, in his *Metamorphoses*, that Pasiphaë, wife of Minos, king of Crete, conceived the Minotaur, who was half man and half bull. The which was imprisoned by Daedalus in the Labyrinth into which whatsoever entered knew not how to come out, and whosoever was without knew not how to enter. And of this Labyrinth speaketh Seneca in the *Tragedy*, where he treated of the matter of Hippolytus and Phedra].

Azurara's reference to the distinctive virtues of the four great peoples here noticed is interesting, especially from the fact that Prince Henry's mother was an Englishwoman; that the Emperor (now a purely German sovereign, though still in name "holy and Roman"), invited him to enter his service (see ch. vi); that the Pope (like Henry VI (?) King of England) made him similar offers; that his scientific and practical connections with Italy were very important; and that his sister Isabel was married to the Duke of Burgundy. "The wisdom of the Italians" was nowhere more conspicuous at that time than in geography. Italians initiated the great mediæval and renaissance movement of discovery both by land and sea (cf. John de Plano Carpini, Marco, Nicolo, and Matteo Polo, Malocello, Tedisio Dorio, the Vivaldi, the Genoese captains and pilots of 1341, precursors of Varthema, the Cabots, Verrazano, and Columbus). Italians also constructed the first scientific maps or Portolani (existing specimens from 1300 show out of 498 examples 413 of Italian origin, including all the more famous and perfect). Lastly, Italians probably brought the use of the magnet to higher efficiency; though they did not "invent" the same, it is likely that they were the first to fit the [Pg 300]magnet into a box and connect it with a compass-card. "Prima dedit nautis *usum* magnetis Amalphis."

Also, we may recall that the Infant Don Pedro, Henry's brother, brought home from Venice in 1428 a map illustrating a copy of Marco Polo (see p. liv of the Introduction to this volume), and that the most important map-draughtsmen of the Prince's lifetime were Andrea Bianco, Fra Mauro, and Gratiosus Benincasa. From 1317, when King Diniz appointed the Genoese Emmanuele Pesagno Admiral of Portugal, and contracted for a regular supply of Genoese pilots and captains, down to the Infant's earlier years, when the

Genoese tried to secure a "lease" of Sagres promontory as a naval station, and even to the time when the Venetian Cadamosto sailed in his service (1455-6), and Antoniotto Uso di Mare and Antonio de Noli were to be found in the same employment, the connection between Portuguese and Italian seamanship was very close—a relationship almost of daughter and mother.

14 (p. 9). *From the islands thou didst people in the Ocean*, etc. ... *wood from those parts.*

Here Azurara gives some references to the products raised in the newly-colonised groups of "African Islands"—corn, honey, wax, and especially wood, on which Santarem remarks:—

[This interesting detail shows that the wood (Madeira) transported to Portugal from the islands newly discovered by the Infant D. Henrique, chiefly from the isle of Madeira, was in such quantity as to cause a change in the system of construction of houses in towns, by increasing the number of storeys, and raising the height of the houses, thus bringing in a new style of building instead of the Roman and Arabic systems then probably followed. This probability acquires more weight in view of the system of lighting at Lisbon ordered by King Ferdinand, as appears from a document in the Archives of the Municipality of Lisbon. So this detail related by Azurara is a very curious one for the history of our architecture.]—S.

15 (p. 9). *Dwellers in the Algarve (Alfagher)*, i.e., the extreme southern portion of Portugal, including Cape St. Vincent, the cities of Lagos, Faro and Tavira, and Sagres (off C. St. V.), the special residence of the Prince himself. Later, the plural title "Algarves" was applied to this Province, in conjunction with the possessions of Portugal on the North African coast immediately fronting the Spanish peninsula, viz., Ceuta, "Alcacer Seguer," Anafe, Tangier, Arzila, etc.

16 (p. 10). *Moors ... on this side the Straits and also beyond.*—Moors who on "this side the Straits" had "died" from Prince Henry's lance might be difficult to find; but of "those beyond" the reference is more particularly to the conquest of Ceuta, 1415; the relief of the same, 1418; the abortive attempt on Tangier, 1437; and the raids upon the Azanegue Moors between Cape Bojador and the Senegal, *c.* 1441-1450. The African campaign of 1458, which resulted in the capture of Alcacer the Little, cannot, of course, be included here.

17 (p. 10). *That false schismatic Mohammed.*—In the ordinary style of mediæval reference, as followed by Father Maracci and the older [Pg 301]European school of Arabic learning. The progress of the Moslem faith in North Africa was rapid in the Mediterranean coast zone, but comparatively slow in the Sahara and Sudan. See Introduction to vol. ii, pp. xliii-lix, and W. T. Arnold, *Missions of Islam.*

18 (p. 11). *Duchess of Burgundy.*—The Infanta Isabel, Prince Henry's sister, was niece of a King of England, viz., as Santarem says, of Henry IV, son of John, Duke of Lancaster. [By this connection our Infant was a great-grandson of Edward III, and at the same time a descendant of the last kings of the Capetian house, and likewise allied to the family of Valois. The Infanta Donna Philippa was married to the Duke of Burgundy, Philip the Good, on January 10th, 1429. She was not only endowed with very eminent qualities, but was also of rare beauty. She had great influence on public affairs. The Duke, her husband, instituted the celebrated order of the Golden Fleece to celebrate this marriage. This princess died at Dijon, December 17th, 1472. From this alliance came many descendants. She was equally beloved by her brothers, and especially by King D. Edward (Duarte), who, in his *Leal Conselheiro* (ch. xliv, "Da Amizade"), speaks of the great affection and regret which he felt for her. The festivities which took place at Bruges on her arrival were among the most sumptuous of the Middle Ages].—S.

19 (p. 12). *The Philosopher*, i.e., Aristotle, in Azurara's day regarded among Christians as the "master of them that knew." The transformation of Aristotle into a storehouse of Christian theology was a long process, which was perhaps most completely successful in the hands of Thomas Aquinas.

20 (p. 14). *As in his Chronicle*, i.e., *The Chronicle of the Reign of Affonso V, the African*, attributed by Barros and Goes to Azurara himself, and perhaps embodied (partially) in Ruy de Pina's existing chronicle of the monarch. (See Azurara, Hakluyt Soc. ed., vol. i, Introduction, pp. lxi-lxiii.) We must notice that a little earlier (p. 13, top of our version), on

Azurara's reference to Prince Henry as an "uncrowned prince" (cf. Azurara, vol. ii, Introduction, p. xix). Santarem remarks:

[This detail, recorded by Azurara, a contemporary writer, shows the error into which Fr. Luiz de Souza fell in his *Historia de S. Domingos*, liv. vi, fol. 331, by saying that the Infant was elected King of Cyprus: an error which José Soares da Silva repeated in his*Memorias d'El Rei D. João I*; whereas if the words of Azurara were not sufficient to demonstrate the contrary, the dates and facts of history would prove the errors of those authors. As a matter of fact, the kingdom of Cyprus, which Richard, King of England, took from the Greeks in 1191, was immediately ceded by that Prince to Guy of Lusignan, whose posterity reigned in that kingdom till 1487; and as our Infant was born in 1394 and died in 1460, it was not possible for him to be elected sovereign of a kingdom ruled by a legitimate line of monarchs. Besides this, in the list of the Latin or Frank Kings of Cyprus, the name of D. Henry is not found. It is to be presumed that Fr. Luiz de Souza confounded Henry, Prince of Galilee, son of James I, King of Cyprus, with our Infant D. Henry.]—S.

Also, on the words *Atlas the Giant* (middle of p. 13 in our version), there is another original MS. note:

[Atlas was king of the land in the west of Europe and of that in the [Pg 302]west of Africa, brother of Prometheus, that great wise man and philosopher descended from Japhet, the giant. And this Atlas was considered the greatest astrologer living in the world at his time. And his knowledge of the stars made him give such true forecasts of matters which were fated to happen, that men said in his time that he sustained the heaven upon his shoulders. And as Lucas saith, he was the first who invented the art of painting in the city of Corinth, which is in Greece.]

On this Santarem remarks:—

[Here our author mixes up all the historical and mythological traditions from Greek and Latin authors relative to Atlas. Diodorus Siculus and Plato are not cited by Azurara, who, however, relates that Atlas was king of the West of Europe and of the West of Africa; but he forgets to say that he reigned over the Atlantes, as Herodotus says, and confounds Prometheus with "Japhet," whose son he was, viz., according to Apollodorus, Diodorus Siculus, and all the ancient writers. Diodorus says in effect that Atlas had taught astronomy to Hercules, but our author confounds the three princes of this name, and made a mistake in citing Lucas de Tuy (continuer of the *Chronicle* of Isidore of Seville) as saying that Atlas was the first who invented the art of painting in the city of Corinth. The origin of this art was unknown to the ancients. It is true that Sicyon and Corinth disputed the glory of the discovery, but the discoverer according to most of the ancient authors was Cleanthes of Corinth and not Atlas, as Azurara says. According to others, the discovery was due to Philocles the Egyptian.]—S.

The Atlas chain of N. Africa has been the subject of persistent exaggeration. The Greek pillar of heaven (derived from Carthaginian? seamen) probably referred to Teneriffe. No summit in the Atlas range answers to the legend. Though Miltsin rises to 11,400 feet, neither this nor any other peak can be supposed to represent the idea of towering height embodied in the story. We may notice the enormous over-proportion of the Atlas in some of the most important maps which Prince Henry and his seamen had to consult (*e.g.*, Dulcert of 1339, the Catalan of 1375). See Introduction, vol. ii, pp. cxxiii-iv, cxxvi.

21 (p. 14). *Tangier ... the most perilous affair in which he ever stood before or after*, viz., in 1437. The conquest of Ceuta (aided perhaps by the earlier discoveries of Prince Henry's seamen) had made some in Portugal eager for more African conquests, and in 1433 King Duarte (Edward) on his accession was induced by his brothers Henry and Ferdinand, against the opinion of his next brother Pedro, to take up the project of an attack on Tangier. The Papal Court gave only a very doubtful approval to the war, but on August 22, 1437, an expedition sailed for Ceuta. Tetuan was captured, and on September 23 Prince Henry began the siege of Tangier, but his attacks on the town were repulsed; the Portuguese were surrounded by overwhelming forces which had come down from Marocco, Fez, and Tafilet for the relief of the city; and on October 25 the assailants surrendered with the honours of war, on condition that Ceuta should be given up with all the Moorish prisoners then in Portuguese hands, and that the Portuguese should abstain for 100 years from any further attack upon the Moors of

this part of Barbary. Prince Ferdinand was left with twelve nobles as hostages for the performance of the treaty. The convention was repudiated in Portugal, and Ferdinand, the [Pg 303]"constant Prince," died in his captivity June 3, 1443. Like Regulus in Roman tradition, he advised his countrymen against the enemy's terms of ransom,

"Lest bought with price of Ceita's potent townTo public welfare be preferred his own."Camöens: *Lusiads*, iv, 52 (Burton).

22 (p. 14). *Because Tully commandeth.*—It is characteristic of Azurara's school and time that he should declare his preference for truthful writing because a great classic recommended the same.

23 (p. 15). *College of Celestial virtues.*—Contrasted with the previous reference, this gives a good idea of Azurara's mental outlook—on one side towards Greek and Latin antiquity, on another to the Catholic theology. The Christian side of the Mediæval Renaissance had not, in Portugal, been overpowered by the Pagan. We may remember, as to the context here, that on the capture of Ceuta the chief mosque was at once turned into the Cathedral.

24 (p. 16). *Districts of the Beira ... and Entre Douro e Minho.* The three northern provinces of Portugal:—The Beira, comprising most of the land between the Tagus and the Douro (except the S.W. portion); the Tral (or Traz) os Montes, the N.E. extremity; and the Entre Douro e Minho, the N.W. extremity of the Kingdom. Here was the cradle of the state—for the principality granted in 1095 by Alfonso VI of Leon to the free-lance, Henry of Burgundy, was entirely within the limits of these provinces, and was at first almost entirely confined to lands North of the Mondego, being composed of the counties of Coimbra and Oporto.

25 (p. 16). *The two cities,* viz., The citadel and the lower town of Ceuta, which together covered the neck of a long peninsula running out some three miles eastward from the African mainland, and broadening again beyond the eastern wall of Ceuta into a hilly square of country. The citadel covered the isthmus which joined the peninsula to the mainland. East of the citadel was Almina, containing "the outer and larger division of the city, as well as the seven hills from which Ceuta derived its name," the highest of which was in the middle of the peninsula, and was called El Acho, from the fortress on its summit. "On the north side of the peninsula, from the citadel to the foot of this last-mentioned hill, the city was protected by another lofty wall." According to some, the old name of *Septa* was derived from the town's seven hills; it was ancient, being repaired, enlarged and re-fortified by Justinian in the course of his restoration of the Roman Empire in the Western Mediterranean.

26 (p. 17). *A duke ... in the Algarve,* viz., Duke of Viseu and Lord of Covilham. His investiture took place at Tavira in the Algarve, immediately on the return of the Ceuta expedition. Together with his elder brother Pedro, whom King John at the same time made Duke of Coimbra, Henry was the first of Portuguese dukes. This title was introduced into England as early as 1337, and the Infant's mother was the daughter of one of the first English dukes, "old John of Gaunt, time-honoured Lancaster."

[Pg 304]27 (p. 17). *The people of Fez ... of Bugya.*—This Moslem league of 1418 against Portuguese Ceuta comprised nearly all the neighbouring Islamic states (1) Fez—the centre of Moslem culture in Western "Barbary," a very troublesome state, politically, to the great ruling dynasties in N.W. Africa—contained two towns at this time, called respectively the town of the Andalusi, or Spaniards—from the European (Moslem) emigrants who lived there—and the town of the Kairwani, from Kairwan ("Cairoan"), the holy city of Tunis. The founder of the greatness of Fez was Idris, whose dynasty reigned there A.D. 788-985. It was captured by Abd-el-Mumen ben Ali, the Almohade, in 1145. It was also besieged in 960, 979, 1045, 1048, 1069, 1248, 1250. See Leo Africanus (Hakluyt Soc. ed.), pp. 143-5, 393, 416-486, 589-606. (2) *Granada* was still a Moslem Kingdom, as it remained till its capture by Ferdinand and Isabella in 1492. It was now (1418) ruled by the successors of Mohammed-al-Hamar, who in 1236 gathered the relics of the western Caliphate into the Kingdom of Granada. In 1340 the Granadine attempt, in alliance with Berber help from Africa, to recover southern Spain for Islam, had been defeated in the great battle of the Tarifa, or Salado (one of the first engagements where cannon were used); but Granada still (in the fifteenth century) retained considerable strength. (3) *Tunis.*—Leo Africanus mentions its capture by Okba (Akbah) in the seventh century A.D., by the Almoravides in the eleventh century, and by Abd-el Mumen ben Ali, the Almohade, in the twelfth century. It was unsuccessfully attacked at times by those states whose trade with it was most important, *e.g.*, by Louis IX of France in his crusade of 1270; by the Genoese, 1388-90; by the Kings of Sicily, 1289-1335; and by other foreign states; but remained for the most part independent, from the breakup of the Almohade empire till its capture by Barbarossa for the Ottomans in 1531. See Leo Africanus, pp. 699, 716, 753. (4) *Marocco*.—The city of Marocco was founded, A.D. 1070-2 according to some, 1062-3 according to others (A.H. 454), by Yusuf Ibn Tashfin, the Almoravide. Under both Almoravides and Almohades its greatness steadily increased. Abd-el-Mumen ben Ali took it for the latter, and under his grandson, Yakub Almansor, it became the Almohade capital (A.D. 1189-90). The Beni-Merini succeeding to power in these parts in the thirteenth century, removed the seat of government to Fez (1269-1470). See Leo Africanus, pp. 262-272, 351-359. Early in the sixteenth century the Portuguese, under Nuno Fernandez d'Ataide, Governor of Safi, attacked Marocco without success. A district called Marocco was much older than the city. "Marakiyah," in Masudi (iii, p. 241, Meynard and Courteille), is used of a district to which the Berbers emigrated. (5) *Bugia, Bougie*, anciently also *Bujaïa* and *Bejaïa*, a very ancient city. Carthage had a settlement here; Augustus established a Roman colony with the title of Colonia Julia Augusta Saldantum ("Saldaa"). It fell into the power of the Vandals in the fifth, of the Arabs in the sixth, century; and during the earlier Caliphate it carried on a considerable trade, especially with the Christian states of the Western Mediterranean. This trade continued to flourish during the later Middle Ages; and we may instance, not only the favourable descriptions of Edrisi (*c.* 1154) and of Leo Africanus (1494-1552), but also the Pisan commerce (of about 1250-64) both in merchandise and in learning, with this city, as well as the Aragonese treaties of 1309 and 1314, and the Pisan embassy of 1378, as a few examples out of many. [Pg 305]In 1068, En-Naser having restored and embellished the town, made it his capital, re-naming it En-Naseria; Abd-el-Mumen ben Ali subjected it to the Almohade empire in 1152; in 1509 Count Peter of Navarre seized it, and the Spaniards held it till 1555. From 1833 it has been a French possession. See Edrisi (Jaubert), vol. i, pp. 202, 236-8, 241, 245-6, 258, 269; Leo Africanus, Hakluyt Soc. edn. pp. 126, 143-4, 699, 700, 745, 932.

28 (p. 17). *Chance of taking Gibraltar ... did not offer itself to him*.—This project is especially notable in the light of later history, as of the years 1704, 1729, 1779-82, and of earlier times, *e.g.*, 710. Prince Henry seems to have been one of the few men who valued aright (before quite modern times) the position from which the Arabs advanced to the Conquest of Spain, and from which the English obtained so great a hold over the Mediterranean. It was only in the later sixteenth century that one can discover anything like a widespread perception of Gibraltar's importance.

29 (p. 18). *Canary Islands*.—Here Azurara probably refers to the projects of 1424-5, though his words may apply to Henry's efforts in 1418, or in 1445-6, to acquire the Canaries for Portugal (see Introduction to vol. ii, p. xcvi-xcviii).

The "great Armada ... to shew the natives the way of the holy faith" is very characteristic of Azurara.

30 (p. 18). *Governed Ceuta ... left the government to King Affonso at the beginning of his reign*.— On this, Santarem has the following note:—

[The 35 years during which the Infant governed Ceuta must be understood in the sense that during the reigns of his father and brother and nephew (till Affonso V reached his majority) he directed the affairs of Ceuta, but not that he governed that place by residing there. The dates and facts recorded show that we must understand what is here said in this sense, seeing that the Infant, after the capture of that city (Ceuta) in August 1415, returned to the Kingdom (of Portugal); and there was left as Governor of Ceuta D. Pedro de Menezes, who held this command for twenty-two years (*D. N. do Leão*, cap. 97). The Infant returned to Africa in 1437 for the unfortunate campaign of Tangier. After this expedition he fell ill in Ceuta and stayed there only five months, and thence again returned to Portugal, and spent the greater part of his time in the Algarve, occupied with his maritime expeditions. He went back for the third time to Africa with King D. Affonso V for the campaign of Alcacer in 1456, returning immediately afterwards to Sagres.

Beyond this, it should be noticed that the sons of King D. John I had charge of the presidency and direction of various branches of State administration. D. Duarte (Edward) was, in the life of the King his father, entrusted with the presidency of the Supreme Court of Judicature and with the duty of despatching business in Council, as is recorded by him in detail in ch. xxx of the *Leal Conselheiro*. The Infant D. Henry had charge of all African business, and so by implication of everything relating to Ceuta.

Finally, the sublime words of King D. Duarte to D. Duarte de Menezes, when he said, "If I am not deceived in you, not even to give it to a son of mine will I deprive you of the captaincy of Ceuta" [Pg 306](Azurara, *Chronica de D. Duarte*, ch. xliii), show that the Infant D. Henry was not then properly Governor of Ceuta; although he was formally appointed to that post on July 5th, 1450, he never actually occupied it (see Souza, prov. of Bk. v, No. 51).]—S.

31 (p. 18). *The fear of his vessels kept in security ... the merchants who traded between East and West.*—This important detail has not been noticed sufficiently in lives of D. Henry. If Azurara really means that the Infant's fleet preserved the coasts of Spain from all fear of the piracy which then, as later, endangered the commerce of the Western Mediterranean, we can only regret that no further details have come down to us about this point. For such a task the Prince must have maintained a pretty large navy: though it is noticeable that piracy seems to have been worse on the so-called Christian side in the mediæval period; and not till after the fifteenth century, and the establishment of Turkish suzerainty, was it as bad on the Moslem side (see Mas Latrie, *Relations de l'Afrique Septentrionale avec les Chrétiens au Moyen Age*, passim, and especially pp. 4, 5, 61-2, 117, 128-30, 161-208, 340-5, 453, 469, 534). The forbearance of the Barbary States with Christian freebooting from the eleventh century to the sixteenth, their tolerance of Christian colonies in their midst, and the special favours constantly shown to individual Christians, would surprise those who think only of Algerine, Tunisian, or Maroccan piracy and "Salee rovers." Roger II of Sicily is a striking exception to this disgraceful rule. In the earlier Middle Ages, some of the Christian Republics of Italy even joined Moslems in slave-raiding upon other Christians (see *Dawn of Modern Geography*, pp. 203-4).

32 (p. 18). *Peopled five Islands ... especially Madeira* (see Introduction to vol. ii, pp. xcviii-cii).

33 (p. 19). *Alfarrobeira, where ... Don Pedro was ... defeated.*—D. Pedro, the eldest of the uncrowned sons of King John I, was famous for his journeys in Europe, ending in 1428, when he returned from Venice with many treasures, among others a MS. copy of Marco Polo, and a map of the traveller's route (see Introduction to vol. ii, p. liv). He was still more famous for his wise government of Portugal as Regent for his young nephew, Affonso V, 1439-47. He took part in the campaign of Ceuta, 1415; advised vainly against the Tangier campaign of 1437; married his daughter Isabel to the King in 1447 (May); was worried into a semblance of rebellion, 1448-9, and was killed in a battle at the rivulet of Alfarrobeira, between Aljubarrota and Lisbon, in May 1449.

On his companion, the Count of Avranches ("Dabranxes" in Azurara), Santarem has a note remarking that he, D. Alvaro Vaz d'Almada, was [made a Count (of Avranches) in Normandy, by gift of the King of England (Henry V), after the battle of Azincourt, when he was also created a knight of the Order of the Garter.]

He was sometimes called, in the affected Renaissance fashion of the time, the "Spanish Hercules;" but he also had fallen into disfavour with Affonso V. He escaped from imprisonment at Cintra, joined D. Pedro in Coimbra (the latter's dukedom), and marched with him to his death (see Introduction to vol. ii, pp. xvi-xviii).

[Pg 307]34 (p. 19). *Order of Christ ... Mother-convent ... Sacred uses.*—Prince Henry was Grand Master of the Order of Christ, founded by King Diniz in 1319, in place of the Templars, whose property in great measure it inherited (see Introduction to vol. ii, p. xviii-xix).

The mother-convent of the Order of Christ was at Thomar, in the (Portuguese) province of Estremadura, 45 kilometres N.N.E. of Santarem, or a little N.W. of Abrantes, and is noticeable for its sumptuous architecture. It was founded originally as a house of the Templars by Donna Theresa, mother of Affonso Henriques, first King of Portugal; it was enlarged and rebuilt in 1180 and 1320. At the latter date it passed, with the reconstitution of Diniz, from the Templars to the Order of Christ.

35 (p. 19). *St. Mary of Belem ... Pombal ... Soure ... Chair of Theology ... St. Mary of Victory ... yearly revenue* (and see next sentence of text).—This is the *locus classicus* on the benefactions of the Prince (see Introduction to vol. ii, pp. cvi-cix).

St. Mary of Belem, "near the sea at Restello," a chapel where the Infant's mariners could pay their devotions the last thing before putting out to sea from Lisbon, or return thanks after a voyage, was superseded by the more sumptuous edifice of Kings Emanuel and John III, known as the Jeronymos, and named "the Lusiads in stone," which, with the exception of Batalha, is the noblest of Portuguese buildings. Da Gama, however, when starting for and returning from India, had only Prince Henry's little chapel available.

Pombal, in Estremadura, and Soure, in Beira, are both a little S.W. of Coimbra: Pombal being further in the direction of Leiria.

36 (p. 20). *Ready to go to Ceuta ... desisted.*—This abortive African expedition belongs to the reign of Affonso V, and apparently to the years immediately subsequent to the Tangier disaster of 1437 (see Introduction to vol. ii. pp. xvi-xvii).

37 (p. 21). *The Infant's town ... So named ... by writing.*—The settlement at Sagres. On this Santarem has the following notes:—

[α. We see by our author's account what was the state in 1453 of the town of which the Infant had laid the foundations in 1416, and to which at first was given the name of "Tercena Naval" (Naval Arsenal), from the Venetian word "Darcena," an arsenal for the construction and docking of galleys; it afterwards received the name of Villa do Infante (the Infant's town), and later on that of Sagres—derived from Sagro, Sacrum, the famous Promontorium Sacrum of the ancients, according to D. Francisco Manoel, *Epanaphoras*, p. 310. It should be noted that the celebrated Cadamosto, who had speech with the Infant in 1455, at Cape St. Vincent, does not give the name of the town, though he speaks of the interview which he had with him (Henry) at Rapozeira].

[β. In writing "Callez" for "Cadiz" in this paragraph, our author follows the corrupt nomenclature of the authors and MSS. of the Middle Ages, which altered the name of that city from the Gades of Pliny (v, 19), Macrobius, Silius Italicus (xvi, 468), Columella (viii, ch. xvi), a form more like the primitive Gadir (a hedge) in the Phœnician or Punic language. The corrupt terms Calles, Callis, etc., [Pg 308]are, however, met with even in documents of the sixteenth century. See the letters of Vespucci in the edition of Gruninger (1509)].

[γ. As to this reference to the Genoese (desiring to buy Sagres from Portugal), the meaning must be that they offered great sums of money for the concession of a place in the new town for the establishment there of a factory, and perhaps of a colony, similar to those they possessed in the Black Sea, as especially Caffa (now Theodosia, in the Crimea), or Smyrna in the Archipelago. It is, however, improbable that they proposed to the Infant the cession of a town of which he did not hold the sovereignty. The Republic of Genoa had preserved very close relations with Portugal from the commencement of the monarchy, and could not be ignorant that even the Sovereigns of the country were not able to alienate any portion of the land without the consent of the Cortes (on this subject see Part III of our *Memorias sobre as Cortes*). Howsoever the case may have been, the detail referred to by our author illustrates the prudence of the Portuguese Government of that time in having resisted such a proposal, in view of the fact that the Republic of Genoa had by its immense naval power obtained from the Moorish and African princes the concession of various important points in Asia and Africa; and had also procured from the Greek Emperors the cession of the suburbs of Pera and Galata in Constantinople, and the isles of Scios, Mitylene (Lesbos), and Tenedos in the Archipelago. The reader will find it worth his attention that Portugal refused to accede to a similar offer when the Emperors of the East and of Germany, the Kings of Sicily, Castile, Aragon, and the Sultans of Egypt constantly sought the alliance of that Republic and the protection of its powerful marine. True it is that the power of Genoa had already then begun to decline and to become enfeebled, but none the less important are the details given by Azurara and the observations which we have offered for the consideration of the reader].

As to the connections of Genoa with Spain, we may add the following:—

Genoese relations with Barcelona became active in the twelfth century. In 1127 the Republic concluded a commercial treaty with Count Raymond Berenger III, and formed an offensive and defensive alliance with the same Prince in 1147. As a result, the allies took Almeria and Tortosa. In this conquest two-thirds went to the Count, one-third to the Genoese. In 1153 they sold their new possessions to Count Raymond for money and trading rights; but in 1149 they concluded a treaty of peace and commerce with the Moorish King of Valencia, and in 1181 a similar treaty with the King of Majorca. As early as 1315 the Genoese had begun a direct trade by sea with the Low Countries, passing round the Spanish coast. After the conquest of Seville by Ferdinand III they also obtained important trade privileges in that city, especially those enjoyed by a grant of May 22nd, 1251. By this time they had ousted all their Italian rivals in the trade of the Western Mediterranean, and there held a position analogous almost to that of Venice under the Latin empire of Constantinople. In 1267 all the Genoese consuls in Spain were put under a Consul-General at Ceuta. In 1278 Genoa concluded a treaty of peace and commerce with Granada. In 1317 the Genoese, Emmanuel Pessanha (Pezagno), became Lord High Admiral of Portugal: Genoese captains and pilots were employed in the Spanish exploring voyage to the Canaries in 1341; and a regular [Pg 309]contingent of Genoese pilots and captains was maintained in the Spanish service. See Introduction to vol. ii, p. lxxx.

38 (p. 22). *Jerome ... Sallust ... so high a charge.*—Here again is the truly characteristic mingling of sacred and profane learning, both almost equally authoritative to his mind, in Azurara. Cf. Sallust, *Catiline,* chs. ii, viii, li; especially viii.

39 (p. 22). *Phidias ("Fadyas") ... the philosopher ... chapter on wisdom.*—Here Santarem has the following notes:—

[α. The "height" of which Azurara speaks is the Parthenon, or Temple of Minerva, in Athens. The famous statue of that goddess, in gold and ivory, was made by that famous sculptor (Phidias), and placed by the Athenians in that magnificent temple]. Cf. Pliny,*Nat. Hist.,* Bk. xxxiv, ch. xix.

[β. The philosopher is Aristotle. It is not unworthy of note that our author cites Aristotle in this place, and prefers his authority to that of Pausanias. This preference, which may also be frequently observed in the *Leal Conselheiro* of King D. Duarte, proves the great esteem in which the works of the Stagyrite philosopher were held among our ancestors (as well as in other nations) during the Middle Ages. Our learned men followed him in preference to Pausanias, even when treating of the antiquities of Greece].

40 (p. 23). *Great Valerius.*—Here again Santarem:—[This author, cited by Azurara, is Valerius Maximus, a writer of the time of Tiberius, who wrote *De dictis factisque memorabilibus* in nine books. He was a native of Rome, and therefore Azurara says, "of thy city."] Azurara is not mistaken, as Santarem suggests, in assuming that the Roman author did not only deal with the deeds of his compatriots but also described those of foreigners. Of the main divisions of V.'s work, the first book is devoted chiefly to religious and ritual matters, the second to various civil institutions, the third and three following books to social virtues; the seventh book treats of many different subjects. This treatise was very popular in the Middle Ages, and several abridgments were made, one by Julius Paris.

41 (p. 24). *What Romulus ... Manlius Torquatus ... Cocles ("Colles") ... diminishing of his praise.*—On this Santarem remarks: [T. Manlius Torquatus, the dictator, is here seemingly referred to; on whom see *Livy,* vii, 4, and *Plutarch,* i].

The contrast of Cæsar's gaiety with the strictness of Henry's life refers us to ch. iv (beginning), pp. 12, 13, of this version. Azurara had but a very inadequate conception (supplement from Cadamosto, Pacheco Pereira, and Barros) of the real scope of Henry's life-work, and his remarks sometimes sink into mere flattery; but the comparisons he makes here are not misjudged. The Infant was really one of the men who, like Cæsar, Alexander, Peter I of Russia, or Mohammed, force us to think how different the history of the world would have been without them.

42 (p. 24). *Captain of their Armies.*—Here Santarem:—[This detail is so interesting for the history of that epoch, that we judge it opportune to indicate here, for the illustration of

our text, the names of these sovereigns. The invitation given by the Pope (as recorded here) [Pg 310]to the Infant could only have taken place after the taking of Ceuta, a campaign in which the Prince acquired immortal glory, having commanded the squadron and been first of the princes to enter the fortress. In view of this, it appears to us that only after 1415 could this proposal have been made by the Pontiff; and also it seems as if the offer must have been made to him before the unfortunate campaign of Tangier in 1437, during the time in which the Infant was exclusively occupied with the business of the Kingdom and of Africa, and with his expeditions and discoveries. From this it appears likely that the Pope who invited him to become general of his armies was Martin V, and the year of the invitation 1420 or 1421, after the embassy which, the Greek Emperor, Manuel Palaeologus, sent to the Pontiff to beg for aid against the Turks. The Emperor of Germany of whom Azurara speaks was Sigismund (Siegmund), who, by reason of his close relations with the Court of Lisbon, and with the ambassadors of Portugal at the Council of Constance, could appreciate the eminent qualities of the Infant, and form the high opinion of him which he deserved. Lastly, the Kings of Castile and England of whom Azurara speaks must be D. John II, and Henry V.]— S. Santarem is probably wrong here. "Henry VI" should be read for "Henry V;" see Introduction to vol. ii, p. xv.

43 (p. 25). *Discipline ... clemency.*—Azurara here imitates somewhat the formal disputations of Seneca and Cicero. We may especially compare Seneca's *De Ira, De Providentia,* and *De Clementia ad Neronem Caesarem libri duo*; also, but with rather less close a parallelism, the same writer's *De Animi tranquillitate, De Constantia Sapientis.* The Elder Seneca's rhetorical exercises, *Controversiarum libri X,* and*Suasoriarum Liber,* were also, as far as the form goes, models for such discussions as are here conducted. Azurara's point, of course, is that, of the two extremes, Prince Henry leaned rather to "clemency" than to "discipline;" and though he by no means neglected the latter, he was content rather to err in generosity than in severity. Precisely the opposite is the view of some modern students: *e.g.,* Oliveira Martins, *Os Filhos de D. João I,* especially pp. 59-63, 210-1, 267-270, 311-346.

44 (p. 26). *St. Chrysostom ... something to asperse.*—As to the Prince's critics, though in a slightly different sense, cp. what Azurara says in ch. xviii (beginning). The modern criticisms of the Infant's conduct may be read in O. Martins (*Os Filhos,* as cited in last note). According to this view, the Infant's genius was pitiless: he cared little or nothing for the captivity and torture of D. Fernando the Constant, who died in his Moorish prison after the disaster of Tangier; for the broken heart and premature end of D. Edward; or for the fate of D. Pedro. As little did he care for the misery of the Africans killed or enslaved by his captains, or for the unhappy life of Queen Leonor, mother of Affonso V. Not only was he indifferent to these sufferings, but indirectly or directly he was the efficient cause of the same. This extreme view, as regards the slave-raiding, is much weakened by Cadamosto's testimony, and Azurara's own admission in ch. xcvi (end) of this Chronicle (see Introduction to vol. ii, p. xxv). The truth seems to lie between Azurara and Martins: between the conceptions of Henry as a St. Louis and as a Bismarck.

[Pg 311]45 (p. 26). *Seneca ... first tragedy.*—This is the *Hercules Furens* of the great—or younger—Seneca, the philosopher.

46 (p. 27). *St. Brandan ... returned.*—On this Santarem writes:—

[The voyage of St. Brandan, to which Azurara refers, is reputed fabulous, like the island of the same name. According to this tradition, it was said that St. Brandan arrived in the year 565 at an island near the Equinoctial(?). This legend was preserved among the inhabitants of Madeira and of Gomera, who believed that they were able to see Brandan's isle towards the west at a certain time of the year. This appearance was, however, the result of certain meteorological circumstances. Azurara became acquainted with this tradition of the Middle Ages from some copy of the MS. of the thirteenth century, entitled *Imago Mundi de dispositione Orbis,* of Honorius of Autun; and this circumstance is so much the more curious as Azurara could not have been acquainted with the famous Mappemonde of Fra Mauro, which was only executed between the years 1457-9; and still less with the Planisphere of Martin of Bohemia (Behaim), which is preserved at Nuremburg, on which appears depicted at the Equinoctial a great island, with the following legend: *In the year 565 St. Brandan came with his ship to this island.*The famous Jesuit, Henschenius, who composed a critical examination of the life of St. Brandan, says of it:—"Cujus historia, ut fabulis referta, omittitur."] The Bollandists speak with equal distrust of the Brandan story.

To this we may add:—It is possible Azurara may have read the original *Navigatio Sti. Brendani*. The legendary voyage of Brandan is usually dated in 565, but this is probably a mere figure of speech. He was supposed to have sailed west from Ireland (his home was at Clonfert on the Middle Shannon) in search of Paradise, and to have made discoveries of various islands in the Ocean, all associated with fantastic incidents: as the Isle of St. Patrick and St. Ailbhé, inhabited by Irish Cœnobites; the isle of the Hermit Paul, at or near which Brandan met with Judas Iscariot floating on an iceberg; the Isle of the Whale's Back, and the Paradise of Birds; to say nothing of the Isle of the Cyclops, the Mouth of Hell, and the Land of the Saints—the last encircled in a zone of mist and darkness which veiled it from profane search. It is more than probable that the Brandan tradition, as we have it, is mainly compiled from the highly-coloured narratives of some Arab voyagers, such as Sinbad the Sailor in the Indian Ocean, and the Wanderers (Maghrurins) of Lisbon in the Atlantic (as recorded in *Edrisi*, Jaubert, ii, 26-29), with some help from classical travel-myth; that it is only in very small part referable to any historical fact; that this fact is to be found in the contemporary voyages of Irish hermits to the Hebrides, Orkneys, Shetlands, Faroes, and Iceland; that a certain special appropriateness may be found in the far western Scottish island of St. Kildas (Holy Culdees) or the islet of Rockall; and that some of the matter in the Brandan story is derived from the travels of early Christian pilgrims to Palestine, *e.g.*, Bernard the Wise,*c.* 867. It is important to remember that the tradition, though professing to record facts of the sixth century, is not traceable in any MS. record before the eleventh century; but, like so many other matters of mediæval tradition, its popularity was just in inverse proportion to its certainty, and "St. Brandan's isle" was a deeply-rooted prejudice of the twelfth, thirteenth, [Pg 312]fourteenth, and even fifteenth centuries. Down to the middle of the sixteenth century it usually found a place on maps of the Western Ocean, usually due west of Ireland (see *Dawn of Modern Geography*, pp. 230-240, and references in same to other works, p. 239, *n.* 2, especially to De Goeje's *La légende de Saint Brandan*, 1890; Avezac's *Iles fantastique de l'Océan Occidental*, 1845; Schirmer, *Zur Brendanus Legende*, 1888; and the study of *Schröder*, 1871). We may note that Azurara is (for his time) somewhat exceptional in his hesitating reference to the Brandan story; but of course his object led him, however unconsciously, to minimise foreign claims of precedence against the Portuguese on the Western Ocean. As far as Brandan goes, no one would now contradict the Prince's apologist; but more formidable rivals to a literal acceptance of the absolute Portuguese priority along the north-west coasts of Africa are to be found in Italian, French, and Catalan voyagers of the thirteenth and fourteenth centuries, one of which is perhaps alluded to here by Azurara. For "the two galleys which rounded the Cape (Bojador) but never returned" were probably the ships of Tedisio Doria and the Vivaldi, who in 1291 (*aliter* 1281) left Genoa "to go by sea to the ports of India to trade there," reached Cape Nun, and, according to a later story, "sailed the sea of Ghinoia to a city of Ethiopia." In 1312, we are told, enquiry had failed to learn anything more of them (see Introduction to vol. ii, pp. lxi-lxiii).

47 (p. 28). *Power of ... Moors in ... Africa ... greater than was commonly supposed* (see Introduction to vol. ii, pp. xlv-lix).

48 (p. 30). *King and Lord.*—With this astrological explanation compare what Azurara says about the death of Gonçalo de Sintra, ch. xxviii, p. 92.

49 (p. 31). *A fathom deep ... ever be able to return ...* (see Introduction to vol. ii, pp. v, viii-x, lxiv, lxx).

Here Santarem has the following notes:—

[α. This passage shows that the Portuguese mariners already, before the expedition of Gil Eannes, knew that beyond Cape Bojador the great desert of the Sahara was to be met with, and that the land was not less sandy than that of "Libya." This last term of Plinian geography, and the circumstances which the author relates in this chapter, show that before these expeditions our seamen had collected all the notices upon that part of the African continent found in the ancient geographers, and in the accounts of the Moors of the caravans which traversed the great desert. This is confirmed by what Azurara says in ch. lxxvii, as we shall see in due course].

[β. The reader will observe from this passage that in spite of the hydrographical knowledge which our mariners had already obtained of those coasts, from their imperfect understanding of what are called the Pelagic currents, those sailors of the fifteenth century still feared the great perils which the passage of that Cape offered to their imagination. Azurara makes clear to us here how powerful, even at this epoch, was the influence of the traditions of the Arabic geographers about the Sea of Darkness, which according to them existed beyond the isles of Kalidad (the Canaries), situated at the extremity of the Mogreb of Africa. See Edrisi, Backoui, and Ibn-al-Wardi. Lastly, on the superstitious and other fears of mediæval [Pg 313]navigators, the reader can consult the *Itinera Mundi* of Abraham Peritsol, translated from Hebrew into Latin by Hyde]. Cf. Introduction to vol. ii, p. x. Cape Bojador, in N. lat. 26° 6' 57", W. long. (Paris) 16° 48' 30", is thus described by the most recent French surveys: "Viewed from the north there is nothing remarkable, but from the west there appears a cliff of about 20 metres in height. A little bay opens on the south of the Cape."

50 (p. 32). *Virgin Themis ... returned to the Kingdom very honourably.*

On the first words there is this original MS. note:—[It is to be understood that near to Mount Parnassus, which is in the midst between east and west, are two hill tops, which contend with the snows. And in one of these was a cave, in which in the time of the Heathen, Apollo gave responses to certain priestly virgins who served in a temple which was there dedicated to the said Apollo. And those virgins dwelt by the fountains of the Castalian mount. And among these virgins was that virgin Themis, whom some held to be one of the Sibyls. And it is said that those virgins were so fearful of entering into that cave, that, save on great constraint they dared not do so—according as Lucan relateth in his fifth book and sixth chapter, where he speaketh of the response which the Consul Appius received, on the end of the war between Cæsar and Pompey.]

On this Santarem remarks:—

[Both in this note and in those on pp. 10, 11, 12, and 21 (= pp. 7-8, 13, of this version), which are met with in our MS., and are in the same script, there prevails such a confusion of thought that we hesitate in supposing them to have been written by Azurara. These notes, so far from illustrating the text, themselves call for elucidation. Here the writer follows the opinion of the ancients as to the position of Parnassus, viz., that it was situated in the middle of the world, though, according to Strabo, it was placed between Phocis and Locris. As to its "contending with the snows," the writer of this note, who quotes Lucan, seems to have taken this passage from Ovid rather than from the *Pharsalia*. See Ovid, *Metamorphoses*, I, v, 316-7; Lucan, *Pharsalia*, V, v, 72-3. The cave is the Antrum Corysium of the Poets. See the *Journey to Greece* of the famous archæologist Spon. The passages referred to as from Bk. V of the Pharsalia are those beginning with the lines— *Hisperio tantum ...* and v, 114, *Nec voce negata ...* together with line 120, *Sic tempore longo*, and the following lines.]

On the "honourable return" of these caravels, with "booty of the Infidels," from the Levant Seas, we may compare the text on p. 18, and note (31) to the same. Here Santarem remarks:—

[The attempts made by the Portuguese seamen to pass the Cape began before the fifteenth century. Already, in the time of King Affonso IV, the Portuguese passed beyond Cape Non, *i.e.*, before 1336 (?). The documents published by Professor Ciampi in 1827, and discovered by him in the *MSS. of Boccaccio* in the Bibliotheca Magliabechiana in Florence, as well as the letter of King Affonso IV to Pope Clement VI attest that fact. See the *Memoir* of Sr. J. J. da Costa de Macedo, in vol. vi. of the Memoirs of the Royal Academy of Sciences of Lisbon, and the additions published in 1835. As for the attempts made in the Prince's time by ships that he sent into those latitudes to pass beyond Cape Bojador, if we admit the number [Pg 314]of twelve years which Azurara indicates, and if this is taken together with the date 1433, which he fixes for the passage effected by Gil Eannes(?), the result is that these attempts began only in 1421; and so Azurara did not admit that the expedition of 1418 (or of 1419), which went out under J. G. Zarco, had for its chief object the passage of the

Cape at all. But from Barros it is seen that Zarco and Vaz went out with the object of doubling the Cape, but that a storm carried them to the island they discovered, and named Porto Santo (*Decades I*, ch. 2, and D. Franc. Manoel, *Epanaphoras*, p. 313]. The statements of part of this note are loosely worded. See Introduction to vol. ii, on the voyage of 1341, on the earlier claims of Affonso IV, and on the rounding of Bojador.]

Also, on Azurara's use of *Graada* for *Granada*, Santarem remarks: [On the origin and etymology of this word, see Cortes y Lopez, art. *Ebura quae Cerialis. Dic. Geograf. Hist. de la Esp. Ant.*, II., 420, etc.].

And on the "Granada" and "Levant" expeditions, the same editor remarks: [The details of these expeditions prove the activity of our marine at the beginning of the fifteenth century, and its system of training, which enabled it to cope better with the perils of Ocean voyages, and in naval combats with Arabs and Moors to protect the commerce of the Christian nations in the Mediterranean]. Cf. note 31 to p. 18 of this version.

51 (p. 33). *Gil Eannes ... touched by the self-same terror.*—As to Gil Eannes, Santarem remarks:—[Barros also says he was a native of Lagos, and was the man who so named "Bojador" from the way it jutted or bulged out (*Decades I*, 6)]; This last statement is quite untrue; [cf. an Atlas of which Morelli and Zurla treat in their *Dei Viaggi et delle Scoperte Africane da Ca-da-Mosto*, p. 37, on which is the inscription "*Jachobus de Giraldis de Venetiis me fecit anno Dmi* MCCCCXVI;" as well as another atlas of the fourteenth century, on which two the Cape appears as (1) *Cabo de Buider*, and (2) *Cavo de Imbugder*, cf. Zurla's *Dissertazione*, p. 37.]. Also, see Introduction to vol. ii, pp. x, lxiv, lxviii-lxx.

52 (p. 33). *Needle or sailing chart.*—See Introductory § on History of Maps and Nautical Intruments in Europe up to the time of Prince Henry, vol. ii, pp. cxvii-cl, and especially pp. cxlvii-cl.

53 (p. 34). *Barinel ... Barcha ... anything worth recording.*—[A Varinel or Barinel was an oared vessel then in use, whose name survives in the modern Varina; so Francisco Manoel, *Epanaphoras*, p. 317, etc.].—S. See Introduction to vol. ii, pp. cxii-cxiii.

On the *Footmarks of men and camels* Santarem remarks.—[To this place our sailors gave the name of Mullet Bay (Angra dos Ruivos), from the great quantity of these fish that they found there. The bay appears with this name in the Map of Africa in the splendid Portuguese Atlas (unpublished), dating from the middle of the sixteenth century, in the Royal (National) Library at Paris (R. B. No. 1, 764)].—S. See Introduction to vol. ii, p. x. Ruivos is variously rendered "Mullet," "Gurnet," "Roach." The original meaning is simply "red[fish]."

54 (p. 35). *Went up country 8 leagues, etc. ... anchorages.*—[Our men named this place Angra dos Cavallos (cf. Barros *Decades I*, i, 5; [Pg 315]Martines de la Puente, *Compendio de las Historias de las Indias*, ii, 1). This place-name is marked in nearly all the sixteenth and seventeenth century maps of Africa].—S.

55 (p. 36). *Two things I consider ... saith he who wrote this history.*—Though these phrases, "our author," "he who wrote this history," are certainly applied by Azurara to himself in some instances, there is also sometimes a suggestion of the previous writer on the Portuguese *Discovery and Conquest of Guinea*, viz., Affonso Cerveira, a seaman in Prince Henry's service (see Introduction to vol. ii, p. cx). Here, we fancy, a passage of Cerveira's work is referred to. The loss of the latter is deplorable. It evidently contained all the facts and documents given by Azurara, and some omitted by him (see ch. lxxxiv of this Chronicle, end). Azurara added the reflections and the rhetoric, but followed Cerveira's order of narrative closely (see especially ch. lxvi).

56 (pp. 37-8). *Sea-wolves ... Port of the Galley ... nets ... with all other cordage.*—[These Seawolves are the *Phocæ Vitulinæ* of Linnæus. Cf. the *Roteiro* of Vasco da Gama's First Voyage, under December 27th, 1497, p. 3 of Port. text "Achamos muitas baleas, e humas que se chamam *quoquas* e Lobos marinhos."]—S.

[The *Port of the Galley* is so named in the Portuguese Atlas above referred to (Paris:*Bibl. Nat.*, i, 764, of the sixteenth century), and in the Venetian maps of Gastaldi (1564); cf. Barros, *Decades I*, v, 11, who says, "Ponto a que ora chamâo a pedra da Galé"].—S.

On the "nets ... with all other cordage," cf. Barros, *Decades I*, ch. v, fol. 11: "No qual logar achou humas redes de pescar, que parecia ser feito o fiado dellas, do entrecasco d'algum pao, como ora vemos o fiado da palma que se faz em Guiné."

57] (pp. 38, 39). *Rio d'Ouro ... discords in the Kingdom.*—[On old unpublished Portuguese maps we find marked between Cape Bojador and the Angra dos Ruivos, the following points: *Penha Grande, Terra Alta,* and *Sete-Montes,* besides the *Angra dos Ruivos,* being all of them probably points where the Portuguese had landed].—S. See Introduction to vol. ii, pp. x-xiii, lxi-lxxi.

[The events which interrupted the Infant's expeditions and discoveries from 1437 to 1440 may be briefly indicated. The Infant returned to the Algarve after the expedition to Tangier (1437), and was there in September of the following year, when King Edward fell ill at Thomar. On the King's death, the Prince was at once summoned by the Queen, and charged by her to concert with the Infant D. Pedro, and with the grandees of the realm, some means of grappling with the difficulties of the Kingdom. The Infant convoked these persons, who decided that the Cortes ought to be assembled to pass the resolutions they judged expedient.

The Prince thought that D. Pedro ought to sign the summonses; but as he refused to do this, they were all signed by the Queen, with the proviso that such signature should hold good only till the Assembly of the Estates should settle the question.

At the same time the Infant, on account of his accustomed prudence, was chosen mediator between the Queen and D. Pedro. At his proposal, discussed in various conferences, the Queen was [Pg 316]charged with the education of her children and the administration of their property; while to the Infant D. Pedro was given the administration and government of the Kingdom, with the title of Defender of the Kingdom for the King (*Ruy de Pina,* ch. xv).

But, as a large party did not agree to this, and so public disorder increased, Henry sought to conciliate the different parties by getting their consent to an Accord, published November 9th, 1438, providing:—

1. That the education of the King while a minor, and of his brothers, and the power of nominating to Court Offices, should rest with the Queen; and that a sum should be paid her sufficient to defray the expenses of the Royal Household.

2. The Royal Council was to consist of six members, who should be charged in turn and at definite periods with such business of state as was within their power to decide, conformably to the regulations of the Cortes.

3. Besides this Council there was to be elected a permanent deputation of the Estates, to reside at the Court, composed of one prelate, one fidalgo, and one burgess or citizen, to be elected, each by his respective estate, for a year.

4. All the business of the Royal Council was to be conducted by the six councillors and the deputation of the Three Estates under the presidency of the Queen, with the approval and consent of the Infant D. Pedro.

If the votes were equal, the business in question was to be submitted to the Infants, the Counts, and the Archbishop, and to be decided by the majority.

If the Queen agreed with the Infant D. Pedro, their vote was to be decisive, even though the whole Council should be against them.

5. All the business of the Treasury, except what belonged to the Cortes, was to be conducted by the Queen and the Infant: decrees and orders on the subject were to be signed by both, and the Controllers of the Treasury were to be charged with their execution.

6. It was settled that the Cortes should be summoned every year to settle any doubts which the Council could not decide for themselves, such as "the [condemnation to] death of great personages, the deprivation of state servants from great offices, the [confiscation or] loss of lands, the amendment of old or the making of new laws and ordinances; and it was also agreed that future Cortes should be able to correct or amend any defect or error in past sessions" (*Ruy de Pina,* ch. xv). The Queen, however, being induced by a violent party to resist, refused to agree to these resolutions, in spite of the vigorous efforts of D. Henry. This produced great excitement, and in the Cortes it was proposed to confer the sole regency on D. Pedro. It should be noted that Prince Henry expressed his disapproval of all the

resolutions of the municipality of Lisbon and other assemblies, declaring that they illegally tried to rob the Cortes of its powers. Equally plain was his indignation when he learned that the Queen had fortified herself in Alemquer, and had invoked the aid of the Infants of Aragon.

He did not hesitate to go to Alemquer in person, and induce the Queen to return to Lisbon, in order to present the young King to the Cortes (1439); and such was the respect felt for him (Henry) that the Queen, who had resisted all other persuasions, yielded to the Infant's.

[Pg 317]In the following year the divisions of the Kingdom compelled the Infant to occupy himself with public business, the conciliation of parties, and the prevention of a civil war.]—S.

58 (p. 39). *Chronicle of D. Affonso.*—This chronicle, according to Barros and Goës, was written by Azurara himself as far as the year 1449, and continued by Ruy de Pina. It is cited by Barbosa Machado. See Introduction to the first volume of this translation, pp. lxi-ii.

[58A (p. 43). *Those on the hill.*—This hill is also marked in the unpublished Portuguese maps in the National Library at Paris, and is situated to the south of the Rio do Ouro.]—S.

59 (p. 44). *The philosopher saith, that the beginning is two parts of the whole matter.*—Here, and in the two following notes, it is very difficult to suggest any classical reference which corresponds closely enough with Azurara's language; but cf., in this place, Aristotle, *Ethics*, Bk. I, ch. vii, p. 1098^{b}7; *Topics*, Bk. IX, ch. xxxiv, p. 183^{b}22 (Berlin edn.).

60 (p. 44). *Roman History.*—Cf. Valerius Maximus, Bk. II, cc. 3, 7; St. Augustine, *De Civitate Dei*, Bk. II, cc. 18, 21; Bk. V, c. 12.

61 (p. 45). *That emulation which Socrates praised in gallant youths.*—Cf. Xenophon,*Memorabilia*, Bk. I, c. 7; Bk. III, cc. 1, 3, 5, 6, and especially 7; also Plato, *Laches*, 190-9;*Protagoras*, 349-350, 359. On the history that follows, cf. D. Pacheco Pereira,*Esmeraldo*, cc. 20-33. Pereira must have had a copy of this Chronicle before him, for in places he transcribes *verbatim*; see *Esmeraldo*, c. 22.

62 (p. 47). *"Portugal" and "Santiago."*—The latter war-cry is of course derived from St. James of Compostella, which being in Gallicia was not properly a Portuguese shrine at all. All Spanish crusaders, however, from each of the five Kingdoms, made use of this famous sanctuary. See note 11, p. 7 of this version.

63 (p. 48). *Port of the Cavalier.*—[This is marked in two Portuguese maps of Africa in Paris, both of the sixteenth century, as on this side of Cape Branco, which is in 20° 46' 55" N. lat.]—S.

64 (p. 49). *Azanegues of Sahara ... Moorish tongue.*—[Cf. Ritter, *Géographie Comparée*, III, p. 366, art. *Azenagha*. Ritter says they speak Berber. On this language see the curious article, *Berber*, by M. d'Avezac, in his *Encylopédie des gens du Monde*. On the Azanegues, Barros says (*Decade I*, Bk. I, ch. ii): "The countries which the Azanegues inhabit border on the negroes of Jaloff, where begins the region of Guinea."*Sahará* signifies desert. Geographers spell Zahará, Zaara, Ssahhará, Sarra, and Sahar. The inhabitants are called Saharacin—Saracens—"sons of the desert" (cf. Ritter,*Géographie Comparée*, III, p. 360), a term immensely extended by mediæval writers—thus Plano Carpini expects to find "black Saracens" in India. On the etymology, cf. Renaud's *Invasions des Sarrasins en France*, Pt. IV, pp. 227-242, etc. He confirms Azurara's statement that the Sahara language differed from the Moorish—*i.e.*, it was Berber, not Arabic—and he refers us to the Arab author Ibn-Alkûtya, in evidence of this.]—S.

[Pg 318]The "Other lands where he learned the Moorish tongue" were probably Marocco, or one of the other Barbary States along the Mediterranean littoral, where Arabic was in regular use. This language stopped, for the most part, at the Sahara Desert. Santarem's derivation of the word "Saracen" is much disputed.

65 (p. 50). *Lisbon Harbour* ... —Here, perhaps, Azurara refers to the broad expanse of the Tagus, opposite the present Custom House and Marine Arsenal of Lisbon. "The broad estuary of the Tagus gives Lisbon an extensive and safe harbour." From the suburb of Belem up to the western end of Lisbon, the Tagus is little more than a mile in width, but opposite the central quays of the city the river widens considerably, the left, or southern, bank turning suddenly to the south near the town of Almada, and forming a wide bay, reach, or road

about 5½ miles in breadth, and extending far to the north-east. "In this deep lake-like expansion all the fleets of Europe might be anchored."

66 (p. 50). *Cabo Branco.*—[In lat. N. 20° 46' 55", according to Admiral Roussin's observations.]—S. According to the most recent French surveys, it is thus described:—"Il forme, au S., sur l'Atlantique, l'extrémité d'une presqu'île aride et sablonneuse de 40 kil. de longeur environ, large de 4 à 5 kil., qui couvre a l'O. la baie Lévrier, partie la plus enfoncée au N. de la baie d'Arguin. Cette presqu'île se termine par un plateau dont le cap forme l'escarpement; le sommet surplomb la mer de 25 m. environ. Des éboulements de sable, que le soleil colore d'une nuance éblouissante, lui ont valu son nom. 'Le Cap Blanc est d'une access facile. Il est entouré de bons mouillages qui, au point de vue maritime, rendent cette position préférable à celle d'Arguin' (Fulcrand)."

67 (p. 53). *Eugenius the Bishop.*—[Barros adds certain reasons for this request; he says, "the Infant, whose intent in discovering these lands was chiefly to draw the barbarous nations under the yoke of Christ, and for his own glory and the praise of these Kingdoms, with increase of the royal patrimony, having ascertained the state of those people and their countries from the captives whom Antam Gonçalvez and Nuno Tristam had brought home—willed to send this news to Martin V (?), asking him, in return for the many years' labour and the great expense he and his countrymen had bestowed on this discovery, to grant in perpetuity to the Crown of these Kingdoms all the land that should be discovered over this our Ocean Sea from C. Bojador to the Indies" (Barros,*Decade I*, i, 7).]—S. Barros here apparently confuses Martin V with Eugenius IV.

[Besides this bull, Pope Nicholas V granted another, dated January 8th, 1450, conceding to King D. Affonso V all the territories which Henry had discovered (Archives of Torre do Tombo, *Maç. 32 de bullas* No. 1). On January 8th, 1454, the same Pope ratified and conceded by another bull to Affonso V, Henry, and all the Kings of Portugal their successors, all their conquests in Africa, with the islands adjacent, from Cape Bojador, and from Cape Non as far as all Guinea, with the whole of the south coast of the same. Cf. Archivo R. Maç. *7 de bull.* No. 29, and *Maç. 33*, No. 14; and Dumont, *Corp. Diplomat. Univ.*, III, p. 1,200. On March 13th, 1455, Calixtus III determined by another bull that the discovery of the lands of W. Africa, so acquired [Pg 319]by Portugal, as well as what should be acquired in future, could only be made by the Kings of Portugal; and he confirmed the bulls of Martin V and Nicholas V: cf. another bull of Sixtus IV, June 21st, 1481, and see Barros, *Decade I*, i, 7; *Arch. R. Liv. dos Mestrados*, fols. 159 and 165;*Arch. R. Maç. 6 de bull.*, No. 7, and *Maç. 12*, No. 23.]—S.

68 (p. 54). *Without his license and especial mandate.*—See Introduction to vol. ii, p. xiv.

69 (p. 54). *Curse ... of Cain.*—For "Curse of Ham." Cf. Genesis ix, 25. "Cursed be Canaan: a servant of servants shall he be unto his brethren." For this mediæval theory, used sometimes in justification of an African slave-trade, we may compare the language of Barros, quoted in note 81.

70 (p. 54). *Going out of the Ark.*—The writings of Abp. Roderic of Toledo, and of the other authors here referred to, are apparently regarded by Azurara as explanatory of the record in Genesis, ix and x. Abp. Roderic Ximenes de Rada (fl. 1212) wrote *De Rebus Hispanicis* in nine books; also an *Historia Saracenica*, and other works. Walter is doubtful. He may be Walter of Burley, the Aristotelian of the thirteenth-fourteenth century, who wrote a *Libellus de vita et moribus philosophorum*. Excluding this "Walter," our best choice perhaps lies between "Gualterus Tarvannensis" of the twelfth century; Walter of Châtillon, otherwise called Walter of Lille, author of an Alexandreis of the thirteenth century; or the chronicler Walter of Hemingburgh, or Hemingford, who is probably of the fourteenth century.

71 (p. 55). *Better to bring to ... salvation.*—Cf. the Christian hopes of the pagan Tartars in the thirteenth century.

72 (p. 55). *Land of Prester John if he could.*—See Introduction to vol. ii, p. liv. As to "Balthasar" [Barros says "he was of the Household of the Emperor Frederic III," who had married the Infanta Donna Leonor of Portugal (*Decade I*, ch. vii).]—S.

73 (p. 57). *Infant's Alfaqueque ... managing business between parties....* —The*Alfaqueque*, or *Ransomer of Captives*, must have been an interpreter as well. Later, we find "Moors" and negroes employed for this purpose.

74 (p. 57). *Who traded in that gold.*—[Azurara seems ignorant that the gold was brought from the interior by caravans, which from ancient times had carried on this trade across the great desert, especially since the Arab invasion. Under the Khalifs, this Sahara commerce extended itself to the western extremity of the continent, and even to Spain. The caravans crossed the valleys and plains of Suz, Darah and Tafilet to the south of Morocco. Cf. the *Geographia Nubiensis* of Edrisi (1619 ed.), pp. 7, 11, 12, 14; Hartmann's *Edrisi*, pp. 26, 49, 133-4. This gold came from the negro-land called Wangara, as Edrisi and Ibn-al-Wardi tell us. See *Notices et extraits des MSS. de la Bibliothèque du Roi*, fo. 11, pp. 33 and 37: so Leo Africanus and Marmol y Carvajal speak of the gold of Tiber, brought from Wangara. "Tiber" is from the Arab word Thibr = gold (cf. Walcknaer, *Recherches géographiques*, p. 14). So Cadamosto, speaking of the commerce of [Pg 320]Arguim, says, ch. x, that men brought there "gold of Tiber;" and Barros, *Decade I*, ch. vii, in describing the Rio d' Ouro, refers to the same thing:—"A quantity of gold-dust, the first obtained in these parts, whence the place was called the Rio d' Ouro, though it is only an inlet of salt water running up into the country about six leagues."]—S.

75 (p. 58). *Gete* (or Arguim).—[Barros, *Decade I*, 7, says: "Nuno Tristam on this voyage went on as far as an island which the people of the country called Adeget, and which we now call Arguim." The Arab name was "Ghir," which Azurara turns into "Gete," Barros into "Arget." The discovery and possession of this point was of great importance for the Portuguese. It helped them to obtain news of the interior, and to establish relations with the negro states on the Senegal and Gambia. The Infant began to build a fort on Arguim in 1448. Cadamosto gives a long account of the state of commercial relations which the Portuguese had established there with the dwellers in the upland; and the Portuguese pilot, author of the *Navigation to the Isle of St. Thomas* (1558), published by Ramusio, says of Arguim: "Here there is a great port and a castle of the King our Lord with a garrison and a factor. Arguim is inhabited by black-a-moors, and this is the point which divides Barbary from Negroland." Cf. Bordone's *Isolario* (1528) on the Portuguese trade with the interior. In 1638 this factory and fortress were taken by the Dutch.]—S.

The subsequent changes of this position may be briefly noticed. After passing, in 1665, from the Dutch to the English and afterwards back again, in 1678 from the Dutch to the French, in 1685 from the French to the Dutch, in 1721 once more falling into French hands, only to be recovered shortly afterwards by the Netherlanders, it became definitely and finally a French possession in 1724, and at present forms part of the great North-West African empire of the Third Republic. At the northern extremity of the Bight of Arguim, or a little beyond, near Cape Blanco, is the present boundary between the French and Spanish spheres of influence in this part of the world.

The native boats, worked by "bodies in the canoes and legs in the water," must be, Santarem remarks, what the Portuguese call "jangadas."

75A (p. 59). *An infinity of Royal Herons.*—[The Isle of Herons is one of the Arguim islands; cf. Barros, *Decade I*, ch. vii; it is marked under this name (*Ilha*, or *Banco, das Garças*) in early maps, as in Gastaldi's Venetian chart of 1564, which is founded on ancient Portuguese maps.]—S.

76 (p. 61). *Lagos ... Moorish captives.*—On the importance of Lagos in the new Portuguese maritime movement, see Introduction to vol. ii, pp. xi-xii; and note the reasons given by Azurara in ch. xviii for the change of feeling among Portuguese traders and others towards the Infant's plans.

77 (p. 63). *Lançarote ... Gil Eannes ... Stevam Affonso ... etc., ... expedition.*—This list of names includes several of the Infant's most capable and famous captains. On Lançarote see this Chronicle, chs. xviii-xxiv, xxvi, xlix, liii-v, lviii, lix; on Affonso, ch. li, lx; on John Diaz, ch. lviii; on John Bernaldez, ch. xxi; and on [Pg 321]Gil Eannes, chs. ix, xx, xxii, li, lv, lviii; also pp. x-xiii of Introduction to vol. ii, and the notices by Ferdinand Denis and others in the *Nouvelle Biographie Générale*. On the "Isle of Naar," mentioned a little later on p. 63, Santarem has the following note:—[This island is marked near to the coast of Arguim on the

map of Africa in the Portuguese Atlas (noticed before) at the Bibliothèque Royale (Nationale) de Paris.]

78 (p. 68). [In Bordone's *Isolario* (1533) all three of the islands noticed by Azurara (Naar, Garças and Tider), are indicated with the title of Isles of Herons [Ilhas das Garças]. The same is to be found in the Venetian map of Gastaldi, and in others. In the Portuguese Atlas just cited, and in another Portuguese chart made in Lisbon by Domingos Sanchez in 1618, these islands are depicted as close to the coast of Arguim, but without any name.] As to Cabo Branco [This name was, apparently, given it by Nuno Tristam.]—S. See ch. xiii (end) of this Chronicle.

79 (p. 78). *In the end.*—It is evident, from Azurara's language, that the Azanegues made a better stand in this fight at Cape Branco, and came nearer to defeating the Portuguese than on any previous occasion. It was a sign of what was to follow, for the native resistance now began to show itself, and the very next European slave-raiders (Gonçallo de Sintra and his men) were roughly handled, and most of them killed (see ch. xxvii. of this Chronicle).

80 (p. 80). *Friar ... St. Vincent de Cabo.*—This "firstfruit of the Saharan peoples, offered to the religious life," was appropriately sent to a monastery close to the "Infant's Town" at Sagres, and adjoining the promontory whereabouts centred the new European movement of African exploration.

81 (p. 81). *Sons of Adam.*—Azurara's position here is, of course, just that of the scholastics: As men, these slaves were to be pitied and well treated, nay, should be at once made free; as heathen, they were enslaveable; and being, as Barros says, outside the law of Christ Jesus, and absolutely lost as regards the more important part of their nature, the soul, were abandoned to the discretion of any Christian people who might conquer them, as far as their lower parts, or bodies, were concerned.

82 (p. 84). *As saith the text.*—Cf. Virgil, *Æneid*, i, 630 (Dido to Æneas), *Haud ignara mali miseris succurrere disco*. There is no text in the Jewish or Christian Scriptures which can be said to answer properly to Azurara's reference in this place. We may, however, cf. Judges xi, 38; Revelation i, 9.

83 (p. 87). *Tully saith.*—Cf. Cicero, *De Nat. Deorum*, i, 20, 55; *De Or.*, iii, 57, 215, 48, 159.

84 (p. 87). *Ancient sages ... others.*—Cf. Livy, v, 51, 46, 6. On the disaster of Gonçalo de Sintra, Santarem remarks:—[This event happened in 1445. The place where De Sintra perished is fourteen leagues S. of the Rio do Ouro, and in maps, both manuscript and[Pg 322]engraved, from the close of the fifteenth century, it took the name *Golfo de Gonçallo de Cintra*]. The reference in the concluding words of this chapter, *as had been commanded, etc.*, is to the passage on p. 87 of this version, towards the foot: "That he should go straight to Guinea, and for nothing whatever should fail of this:" an order which De Sintra treated with entire contempt.

85 (p. 92). *First purpose*, viz., to write the chronicle of the "Guinea Voyages," not to discuss philosophic problems. The reference here to the "wheels [or circles] of heaven or destiny" recalls the astrological passages on pp. 29, 30, 80, etc. Azurara's reference to Job is to ch. xiv, verse 5.

86 (p. 93). *Julius Cæsar ... Vegetius ... St. Augustine ...*—Azurara here, of course, indulges in some exaggeration. Cæsar's breach with the Senate did not take place because of his "overpassing the space of five years" allowed him at first (B.C. 59) for his command in Gaul. In B.C. 56 the Lex Trebonia formally gave him a second allowance, of five years more; and he was not required to disband his army and return from his province till B.C. 49, when the Civil War broke out. By "Bretanha," or "Brittany," Azurara indicates the Duchy of Bretagne, which retained a semi-independence till 1532, when it was absolutely united with the crown of France. Cæsar's campaigns against "England" are, of course, those of B.C. 55 and 54, against Germany of 55 and 53, against Spanish insurgents of 61; but he could not by any stretch be said to have made England or Germany "subject" to the Roman power in the same sense as Gaul or Spain. Had his life been prolonged twenty years, he would probably have achieved both these unfinished conquests, as well as that of Parthia.

87 (p. 93). *The enemy ... to them.*—Azurara's reference here is to Livy, Bk. XXII, cc. 42-3.

88 (pp. 93-94). *Holy Spirit ... ever be watched.*—The references in this paragraph are to Proverbs xi, 14; xxiv, 6; Tobit iv, 18; Ecclesiasticus vi, 18, 23, 32-3; xxv, 5.

89 (p. 94). *Hannibal ... for the moment.*—Cf. Livy, *3rd Decade*, Bk. XXII, cc. 4-5, 42-6. The reading of the Paris MS. (*sajaria*) is rejected, plausibly enough, by Santarem for *sagaçaria*.

90 (p. 94). *Ships of the Armada.*—I.e., the Royal Navy of Portugal; the "very great actions on the coast of Granada and Ceuta" must refer to events of 1415, 1418, and 1437. (See Introduction to vol. ii, p. viii, x.) Especially does this expression recall the naval war of 1418, when the King of Granada sent a fleet of seventy-four ships, under his nephew, Muley Said, to aid the African Moslems in recovering Ceuta from the Portuguese. Prince Henry proceeded in person to the relief of the city, and the Granada fleet, we are told, fled at the approach of the European squadron, without venturing a battle. It is possible, however, though unrecorded, that the Infant was subsequently able to engage and destroy part of the Granadine squadron. Gonçalo de Sintra, from Azurara's words, may have been with D. Henry on this occasion.

[Pg 323]On the reference to John Fernandez staying among the Azanegues "only to see the country and bring the news of it to the Infant" (close of ch. xxix, p. 95), Santarem refers to Barros' words: "Para particularmente ver as cousas daquelle sertão que habitão os Azenegues, e dellas dar razão ao Infante, *confiado na lingua delles que sabia*" (like Martin Fernandez, p. 57, c. xvi).

91 (p. 96). *The Plains thereof.*—[Comparing the account in the text with the unpublished maps already referred to, it appears that Nuno Tristam, after revisiting the isles of Arguim, followed the coast to the south, passing the following places: Ilha Branca, R. de S. João, G. de Santa Anna, Moutas, Praias, Furna, C. d'Arca, Resgate, and Palmar; the last being the point Azurara mentions as "studded with many palm trees."]—S.

92 (p. 98). *When King Affonso caused this history to be written.*—On this Santarem remarks: [This is important as showing that Azurara did not only consult written documents, but personally interviewed the discoverers, seeing that he confesses his inability to give details of this occurrence because Nuno Tristam was already dead, "When Affonso," etc. Cf. *Barros*, I, iii, 17]. Cf. Pina's "Chronicle of Affonso V," in vol. i of the *Collection of Unpublished Portuguese Historians.*

93 (pp. 98, 99). *Dinis Diaz ... convenient place.*—["Dinis Diaz" is called by Barros, and all other historians and geographers following his authority, "Dinis Fernandez."]—S.

On Azurara's statement that "the Infant provided a caravel for Dinis Diaz," Santarem adds: [Barros does not agree with Azurara in this, but says on the contrary, "que elle [Diaz] armara hum navio," etc]. The "other land to which the first (explorers) went" is apparently the Sahara coast, from Cape Bojador to the Senegal, which Azurara here admits to be quite a different country from "Guinea" proper (the land of the Blacks). This last, after the discoveries of 1445, the Portuguese recognised as beginning only with the cultivated or watered land to the south of the Sahara. The name, a very early one, whose subtle changes of meaning are very perplexing, like the "Burgundy" of the Middle Ages, was probably derived originally from the city of Jenné, in the Upper Niger Valley (see Introduction to vol. ii, pp. xlv-xlix). [Here Azurara shows that he is already beginning to recognise the geographical error of those who gave an undue extension to the term "Guinea."]—S.

On the reading at the close of this paragraph "concerning this doubt," Santarem remarks: [So it stands in the MS., as verified; but it seems to us that there must be some omission of the copyist, and we propose to restore the text thus: "Filharom quatro daquelles *que tiveram* o atrevimento," etc.].

94 (p. 100). *Aught to the contrary.*—On this passage, cf. Santarem's *Memoir on the Priority of the Portuguese Discoveries*, § III, p. 20, etc. Paris, 1840. [*Memoria sobre a prioridade dos descobrimentos dos Portuguezes*].

95 (p. 100). *Egypt ... Cape Verde.*—[This proves that our navigators were the first who gave the Cape this name. See the [Pg 324]*Memoria sobre a prioridade*].—S. On Azurara's idea that the Senegal was near Egypt, cf. Introduction to vol. ii, pp. xii, xxx, xlii, lviii, cxxii. This notion is, of course, bound up with the theory of the Western or Negro Nile, branching off from the Nile of Egypt. No mediæval geographers, and scarcely any ancient, except Ptolemy, realised the size of Africa at all adequately.

On the "rewards" given by the Infant to Diaz, Santarem well remarks: [From this and other passages it is clear that the Infant's principal object was discovery, and not the slave-raids on the inhabitants of Africa in which his navigators so often indulged]. See Introduction to vol. ii, pp. v, xxiii-vi.

Cape Verde.—The turning-point of the great north-west projection of Africa, now in French possession. It is so called, according to the general view, from the rich green appearance of the headland—"la vegetation (as the most recent French surveys describe it) qui le couvre durant l'hivernage, et que dominent deux mornes arrondis, nommés, par les marins français, Les Deux Mamelles." The peninsula of Cape Verde is one of the most remarkable projections of the African coast. Generally it has the form of a triangle, "terminé par une sorte d'éperon dirigé vers le S.E., et mesure depuis le cap terminal on point des Almadies jusqu' à Rufisque une longueur de 34 kilom. avec une largeur de 14 kilom., sous le méridien de Rufisque, pris comme base du triangle. Sa côte septentrionale, formant une ligne presque droite du N.N.E. au S.S.O. est creusée, près de l'extremité, de deux petites baies, dont la première (en venant de l'E.), la baie d'Yof, est la plus considérable; puis au delà de la pointe des Almadies, qui est le Cap Vert proprement dit, la côte court au S.E. jusqu' au Cap Manuel, roche basaltique haute de 40m., puis remonte aussitôt au N. pour, par une très légère courbe, partir droit a l'E., dessinant ainsi un éperon bien accusé qui enveloppe le Golfe de Gorée. Le corps principal de la presqu' île est bas, sablonneux et parsemé de lagunes qui s'égrènent en chapelets le long de la côte N.; la petite péninsule terminale est au contraire rocheuse, accidentée et semble un ilot marin attaché à la côte par les laisses de mer. Ses hautes falaises, d'une couleur sombre et rougeâtre, forment une muraille à pic contre laquelle la mer vient se briser, écumante." See Duarte Pacheco Pereira's *Esmeraldo*, pp. 46-49, ed. of 1892. As to the island on which Dinis Diaz and his men landed near the Cape, this may have been either (1) Goree, two kilometres from the mainland, and fronting Dakar on the S.E. of the peninsula; (2) The Madeleine islands, at the opening of a small inlet to the N.W. of Cape Manuel; (3) The Almadia islands ("Almadies"), "ilette, qui, située en avant du cap terminal, est la vrai terre la plus occidentale d'Afrique, les archipels de l'Atlantique non compris;" or (4) The isle of Yof, in the bay of Yof, on the north side of the peninsula. The Madeleine islands were once covered with vegetation, though now desert. Here the French naturalist Adanson made his famous observations on the Baobab trees, in the eighteenth century. These trees, though they have disappeared on the islands, are still numerous on the mainland near the Cape. Azurara has a good deal more to say about these islets and their baobabs in chs. lxiii, lxxii, lxxv, pp. 193, 218, 226, etc., of this version. The rounding of C. Verde opened a fresh chapter in the Portuguese circumnavigation of Africa—to S.E. and E.; see Introduction to vol. ii, pp. xii, xxx.

[Pg 325]96 (pp. 101-2). *John Fernandez... such a request.*—On this passage, and especially on Azurara's statement (middle of p. 101) that Fernandez "had already been a captive among the other Moors and in this part of the Mediterranean Sea, where he acquired a knowledge of their language," Santarem remarks: [This detail gives us another proof that Prince Henry's explorations were made systematically, and according to plans carefully worked out. In his previous captivity in Marocco, Fernandez had learnt Arabic, and probably Berber as well; he must also have gained some information about the interior of Africa. To gain more detailed knowledge, and so be able to inform the Infant better, he had now undertaken his residence among the Azanegues of the Rio do Ouro.]

See Introduction to vol. ii, pp. viii, x, xvi, on the dual nature of Henry's African schemes, land conquest and exploration going along with the maritime ventures. This was, of course, partly due to an inadequate conception of the size of the continent, which rendered even the conquest of Marocco of little use towards the circumnavigation of Africa.

"How bitter ... to hear such a request" is, of course, one of Azurara's rare touches of irony.

97 (p. 103). *Affonso Cerveira.*—[The author of the earlier account of the Portuguese conquest of Guinea, *Historia da Conquista dos Portuguezes pela costa d'Africa*, on which Azurara's present Chronicle is based. Cf. Barbosa, *Bibliotheca Lusitana*.]—S. See Introduction to vol. ii, p. cx, and note 202A.

Ergim, in ch. xxxiii, pp. 104, etc., and elsewhere, is, of course, Arguim. Santarem here refers to Barros' description in *Decade I*, i, 10. "Porque naquelle tempo para fazer algum proveito todos os hião demandar (os ilheos d'Arguim); e tinha por certo que avião elles de ir dar com elle, por ser aquella costa e os ilheos a mais povoada parte de quantas té então tinhão descoberto. E a causa de ser mais povoada, era por razão da pescaria de que aquella misera gente de Mouros Azenegues se mantinha, porque em toda aquella costa não avia lugar mais abrigado do impeto dos grandes mares que quebrão nas suas praias senão na paragem daquellas ilhas d'Arguim: onde o pescado tinha alguma acolheita, e lambujem da povoação dos Mouros, posto que as ilhas em si não são mais que huns ilheos escaldados dos ventos e rocio da agua das ondas do mar. Os quaes ilheos seis ou sete que elles são, quada hum per si tinha o nome proprio per que nesta scriptura os nomeamos, posto que ao presente todos se chamão per nome commum *os ilheos d'Arguim*; por causa de huma fortaleza que el Rei D. Affonso mandou fundar em hum delles chamado Arguim." Cf. Duarte Pacheco Pereira's *Esmeraldo*, chs. xxv-vi, pp. 43-4.*Arguim* is defined in the most recent surveys of its present French possessors as "Golfe, île, et banc de sable ... l'île est par 20° 27' N. lat., 18° 57' à 60 kilom. vers le S.E. du Cap Blanc ... Ses dimensions sont de 7 kilom. sur 4. Elle est basse, inculte, et parsemée de dunes."

98 (p. 107). *John Fernandez ... in that country.*—Santarem draws attention to Azurara's statement that the explorer, Fernandez, was personally known to him. Cf. ch. lxxvii of this Chronicle; also chs. xxix and xxxii. "That country" is of course the Azanegue or Sahara land, near the Rio do Ouro.

[Pg 326]*Setuval* (p. 106) is in Estremadura (of Portugal), twenty miles south-east of Lisbon.

99 (p. 110). *Fear to prolong my story ... though all would be profitable.*—The fondness of Azurara for these scholastic discussions and useless displays of learning is one of his worst failings; and a good deal of Cerveira's matter of fact has apparently been sacrificed to this weakness of his redactor.

100 (p. 111). *Nine negroes and a little gold-dust.*—This was the first instalment of the precious metal brought home to Portugal from the Negro-land of Guinea. The same Antam Gonçalvez had already, in 1441, brought the first gold dust from the Sahara, or Azenegue coast (see ch. xvi of this Chronicle, p. 57). As to the importance of these gold-samples in promoting the European exploring movement, see Introduction to vol. ii, pp. x-xi.

101 (p. 111). *Cape of the Ransom.*—[This name is marked upon the manuscript maps already referred to. On one great Portuguese chart of this class, on parchment, in the Bibliothèque Nationale at Paris, the reading is not Cape, but *Port* of the Ransom. The Portuguese nomenclature for the West African coast, as we see in this instance, was for a long time accepted by all the nations of Europe.]—S.

We may notice the allusion in this paragraph to the Portuguese colonisation of Madeira, in the story of Fernam Taavares (see Introduction to vol. ii, pp. xcviii-cii).

102 (p. 112). *Isle of Tider* (see note 78 to p. 68).—[Tider, marked "Tiber" in the map of West Africa before referred to. We do not meet this name in any of the many earlier charts that we have examined].—S.

103 (p. 115). *Officers who collected royal dues.*—The custom-house officers of Lisbon. We may compare with Azurara's graphic account of the return of Antam Gonçalvez in 1445, the very similar details of a much greater reception in the same port: that of Columbus on March 14th, 1493, on his home-coming from his first voyage (see the postscript of Columbus' Letter to Luis de Santangel, Chancellor of the Exchequer of Aragon, respecting the Islands found in the Indies).

104 (p. 115). *A palace of the Infant, a good way distant from the Ribeira.*—Azurara's only reference, in this Chronicle, to the Lisbon residence of the Infant Henry. This passage implies that Prince Henry was often to be found there, and must be taken with others in modification of extreme statements about his "shutting himself up at Sagres," etc. Again, at the end of this chapter we are expressly told that he was now in his dukedom of Viseu, in the province of Beira, some 50 kilometres N.E. of Coimbra, 220 kilometres N.N.E. of Lisbon.

105 (p. 115). *Profits.*—Azurara's remarks here about the change of feeling as to the Infant's plans are similar to passages in ch. xiv, p. 51, ch. xviii, pp. 60-61.

[Pg 327]106 (p. 116). *Lisbon ... profit.*—The city of Lisbon, whose name was traditionally and absurdly derived from Ulysses—"Ulyssipo," "Olisipo," and his foundation of the original settlement in the course of his voyages, was perhaps a greater city under the Moors, eighth-twelfth century, than at any time before the reign of Emmanuel the Fortunate. It was a Roman colony, but its prosperity greatly increased under the Arab rule from A.D. 714; from this port sailed Edrisi's Maghrarins, or Wanderers, on their voyage of discovery in the Western Ocean, probably in the earliest eleventh century. It was three times recovered and lost by the Christians: in 792(-812) by Alfonso the Chaste of Castille; in 851 by Ordonho I of Leon, who held it only a few months; and in 1093(-1094) by Alfonso VI of Leon, soon after his great defeat by the Almoravides at Zalacca (1086); but on each occasion it was quickly retaken—in 1094 by Seyr, General of Yusuf ibn Tashfin, the Almorvaide. In alarm at the Moslem revival, Alfonso founded the county of Portugal in 1095, giving it in charge of Count Henry of Burgundy and his natural daughter Theresa, to hold as a "march" against the Moors. In 1147 Lisbon was finally recaptured by Affonso Henriques, the first King of Portugal, in alliance with a fleet (164 ships) of English, Flemish, German and French Crusaders on their way to the Holy Land (Second Crusade). At this time it was said, perhaps with exaggeration, to contain 400,000 inhabitants; its present number is only about 240,000 (see *Cruce-signati Anglici Epistola de Expugnatione Olisiponis*, in *Portugalliæ Monumenta Historica*, vol. i, p. 392, etc). Before 1147 Guimaraens had been the capital of Portugal; and even down to the time of John I, Henry's father, Lisbon was not formally the seat of government, this being more often fixed at Coimbra. In the same reign, Lisbon also, as a commercial port, easily distanced all rivals within the kingdom, especially Oporto; and King John's erection of palaces in the city, and his successful application to the Pope for the creation of an Archiepiscopal See (thus rivalling Braga), further contributed to give point to Azurara's words in this paragraph about "the most noble town in Portugal." On the share of the commercial classes of Lisbon, Lagos, etc., in Henry's schemes, see Introduction to vol. ii, pp. x, xii.

Paulo Vergeryo is Pietro Paulo Vergerio, born at Capo d'Istria, July 23, 1370, died at Buda, 1444 (1428 according to others). He enjoyed a considerable reputation as a scholar at Padua in 1393, etc., and migrated to Hungary in 1419. See Bayle, *Dict. Crit.*IV, 430 (1741); P. Louisy, in *Nouvelle Biographie Générale*, art. (Vergerio); J. Bernardi, in *Riv. Univers.* (Florence, 1875) xxii, 405-430, in *Arch. Stor. Ital.* (1876) C., xxiii, 176-180; Brunet, *Manuel V*, 1132-3; Muratori, *Rer. Ital. Scr.* (edition of Vergerio's works) XVI, pp. 111-187, 189-215, 215-242; *Fabricius*, ed. Mansi, VI, p. 289. He has left various *Orations and Letters*, especially an *Epistola de morte Francisci Zabarekae*, and a *Historia seu Vitae Carariensium Principum ab eorum origine usque ad Jacobini mortem* (1355). See also Joachim Vadianus, *Biographia P. P. Vergerii, sen.*; and C. A. Combi, *Di Pierpaolo V. ... seniore ... memoria*, Venice, 1880.

107 (p. 116). *Gonçalo Pacheco ... Kingdom.*—Barros copies this sentence, with some omissions. The allusion to the *High Treasurer of Ceuta* (*Thesoureiro Mor das cousas de Cepta*), and his *Noble lineage, goodness, and valour*, is interesting in its proof of the detailed attention given to the new conquest, and to African affairs generally, by the Portuguese government at this time.

[Pg 328]108 (p. 117). *Cape Branco.*—On the *personnel* of this expedition we have accounts elsewhere; for Dinis Eannes de Graã and the rest, see chs. xxxvii-xlviii, and especially pp. 121, 122, 126, 130, 131, 138; for Mafaldo, especially p. 119 ("a man well acquainted with this business ... had been many times in the Moorish traffic"); also pp. 120-121, etc. Cape Branco, since its discovery by Nuno Tristam, had become the favourite rendezvous of the Portuguese expeditions on this coast. See ch. lii, p. 153 (made agreement to await one another *as usual at Cape Branco*).

On the *banners of the Order of Christ*, see Introduction to vol. ii, pp. xviii-xix; and in this Chronicle, pp. 62 (ch. xviii), 53 (ch. xv), 117 (ch. xxxvii), etc.

[Cf. a parchment atlas (unpublished), executed in Messina as late as 1567 by João Martinez, in which two Portuguese ships are painted in various points of the Eastern Ocean *with the Cross of the Order of Christ on their sails*, apparently to indicate the Portuguese dominion in those waters. This atlas passed into the Library of Heber, and afterwards into that of M. Ternaux.]—S.

109 (p. 120). *The patience with which men bear the troubles of their fellows* is another piece of irony, similar to that on p. 102; see note 96.

110 (p. 122). *Fifty-three Moorish prisoners.*—In this, as in subsequent actions, Mafaldo, rather than Gonçalo Pacheco, showed himself to be the leader of the expedition.

111 (p. 123). *Cunning ... but small in this part of the world.*—The fair inference is that, on this occasion, Mafaldo, from his previous experience, correctly estimated the danger (or absence of danger), and knew when to trust the natives. Similar trustfulness was not always equally successful, sometimes from absence of that past experience possessed by Mafaldo. See chs. xxvii, pp. 90, 91; xlviii, pp. 144-5; lxxxvi, pp. 252, etc.; xxxv, pp. 112-3. The Azanegue Moors of the Sahara on the whole showed less ability to defend themselves than the Negroes of the Sudan coast; cf. chs. xlv, pp. 137-8; lx, pp. 179-182; lxxxvi, pp. 252-6; xli, p. 130; xxxi, p. 99; contrast with pp. 126, 122, 114, 105-6, 78, 73, 36.

112 (p. 126) ... *true effects.*—Azurara certainly does not commit the error of "those historians who avoid prolixity by summarizing things that would be greatest if related in their true effects," *i. e.*, in detail. This central portion of his narrative (chs. xxxvi-lix, lxviii-lxxiv) is especially tedious, and we cannot too much regret the comparative sacrifice of the scientific interest to the anecdotal, biographical, or slave-raiding details, with which he fills so much of this Chronicle. Cf. the slender and imperfect narratives of the really important voyages of Dinis Diaz (ch. xxxi), Alvaro Fernandez (ch. lxxv), and Nuno Tristam (chs. xxx, lxxxvi), with the lengthy descriptions of the expeditions personally conducted by Gonçalo de Sintra, Gonçalo Pacheco, Lançarote, Mafaldo, and other men whose voyages resulted in scarcely any advance of exploration. In all this Azurara's narrative contrasts unfortunately with Cadamosto's, which is not only a record of exploration, but of acute original observation, a quality by no means so noticeable in the *Chronicle of Guinea*, except at rare intervals. Cf., however, chs. xxv, lxxvi-lxxvii, lxxix-lxxxiii, and see Introduction to vol. ii, pp. xxiv-xxvi, etc.

[Pg 329]

113 (p. 132). *Cape of St. Anne.*—[This passage shows the date when the name of Cape (or rather "Gulf") of St. Anne was given to that point by Alvaro Vasquez, who was on this expedition. This name was employed, like the others which we have already indicated, in the nomenclature of the hydro-geographical charts of the sixteenth and seventeenth centuries. Barros, in his corresponding chapter, not only omits this detail, but further reduces the material of chs. xxxvii, xxxviii, xxxix, xl, xli, xlii, to a few lines.]—S.

114 (p. 133). *And the Moors, like,* etc.—[From Cape Branco to the Senegal, the part of the coast of which the author treats is inhabited by various tribes composed of Moors of mixed race, who speak Arabic, are Mohammedans, and are known by the names of Trazas or Terarzah, Brakanas and others. They are in their nature very ferocious, and are the terror of the traveller. The most cruel of all are those who inhabit and extend as far as Cape Branco, called Ladessebas; and these, according to some authors, are of pure Arab race.]—S. See Introduction to vol. ii, pp. xlii-lix. Mungo Park gives a similar character of the "Moors" north of Senegal. *Travels*, chs. iii-xii.

115 (p. 136). *Came near to the coast of Guinea.*—[According to the text it appears that Alvaro Vasquez, after quitting the place to which he had given the name of Cape of St. Anne, followed his course 80 leagues towards the south, running along the coast in this direction until he arrived at the Guinea coast—that is, a little beyond Cape Verde—but Barros, who omits some of the details of this voyage, says: ... "Forão-se pela costa adiante obra de oitenta legoas, e na ida, e vinda té tornar a ilha das Garças fazer carnagem," etc.]—S.

116 (p. 136). *Where they had captured the seven Moors* [viz., at Tider; see note 78.]—S.

The reference on p. 139 to the Portuguese ships "in the Strait of Ceuta (Gibraltar) and through all the Levant Sea," may be compared with Introduction, p. viii, and notes 28, 31, etc.

117 (p. 142). *Cape Tira.*—[In the old maps we meet with no *cape* of this name, but combining this passage with what our author says in ch. xxx (How Nuno Tristam went to Tira), and with the distance of 80 leagues which they navigated after leaving the Isle of Herons, or of Arguim, it appears that the cape to which Azurara gives this name, or to which

our first navigators gave the name of Tira, was a point, or "tira," of land at the embouchure of the Senegal, at a place marked in the old maps a little beyond Palma Seca, an inscription which is to be read on many (of the ancient charts), and especially on that of João Freire of 1546, and on that of Vaz Dourado of 1571. Although on this last there appears marked a point in close proximity with the name of Tarem, which is not met with in the preceding (maps). Be this as it may, by the distances of latitude between Arguim and that point at the mouth of the Senegal, it appears that the *Cape of Tira* of which our author speaks, is the place which we indicate. Notwithstanding the unfortunate laconism of Azurara about a fact so interesting for the history of geography, we nevertheless see clearly by this passage that the exploration of the bays, inlets, and points of that part of the coast of Africa was steadily pressed on; that all these points were successively examined by our sailors; [Pg 330]and that to these same men are due the names which served for the hydro-geographical nomenclature (of W. Africa) adopted by all nations from the end of the fifteenth century to nearly the end of the seventeenth (see as to this our *Memoria sobre a prioridade dos descobrimentos Portuguezes na costa d'Africa occidental*, § ix).]—S.

118 (p. 143). *Turtles.*—[This passage shows that these mariners were navigating among the great banks and shoals of sand which exist between the isles of Arguim and the mouth of the Senegal. "And they saw an island, which is further out than all the others, but small and very sandy." Combining this account with the map which we meet in vol. i of the work of the Abbé Demanet (*Nouvelle Histoire de l'Afrique*) we perceive two islands clearly marked to the west of the last (sand-) bank, and in front of the places which, on the ancient Portuguese charts are indicated as Tarem, Palmar, and Palma Seca (as in the maps of Freire, 1546, of the Royal Library, and of Vaz Dourado).

Also in the following chapter our author says "They afterwards saw another island which was separated by an arm of the sea that ran between the two—to wit, that in which they were, and the other they had in sight."]—S.

The lake, or fiord, of Obidos, between Atouguya and Pederneira (p. 143) is in the Estremadura province of Portugal, an inlet on the coast, 47 miles N.N.W. of Lisbon.

119 (p. 146). *Arguim.*—See notes 75 and 97, pp. 58 and 103.

120 (p. 146). *Marco Polo.*—[Azurara, writing this chronicle before 1453, availed himself of a manuscript of the travels of Marco Polo, perhaps the same as the copy which the Infant Don Pedro brought from Venice. The oldest printed edition is of 1484. This book, which exercised great influence on discovery, was not only read in the beginning of the fifteenth century by our learned men, but we may notice that one of the most ancient translations which exists of the same is in Portuguese, published by Valentim Fernandez, with the journey of Nicholas the Venetian, etc., dedicated to the King Don Manuel, Lisbon, 1502, one volume, in folio gothic, a copy of which exists in the public library of Lisbon.]—S. Azurara's reference here is to Marco Polo, ch. lvii (Bk.I); ch. lxxiii (Bk. II). On Valentim Fernandez and the bibliography of the Machin story, see Introduction to vol. ii, p. lxxxiv-v. On the editions of Marco Polo, see Yule's edition, Introduction; Pauthier, *Le Livre de M. P.*

121 (p. 147). *Lançarote ... collector of royal taxes* (= Almoxarife, p. 62) *in Lagos ... judges ... alcayde ... officials of the corporation.*—Another of Azurara's references to "local," "home," or "municipal" affairs in Portugal, at this time. Cf. p. 62 of this Chronicle.

122 (p. 151). *Knight Don Pedro ... Sueiro da Costa ... Monvedro.*—On the general history alluded to by Azurara in the first paragraph of ch. li, see *Cronica de D. Alvaro de Luna*, ed. Milan, 1546, Madrid, 1784; *Histoire secrète de Connetable De Lune*, Paris, 1720; Marina, *Ensaio historico-critico*; Cardonne, *Histoire de l'Afrique et de l'Espagne...*; Hallam, *Middle Ages*, ii, 16-17. It may be summarised as follows: The reign of John II of Castille, [Pg 331]after his majority, was constantly disturbed by conspiracies and civil wars, headed by his cousins John and Henry, the Infants of Aragon, who possessed large properties in Castille, bequeathed them by their father Ferdinand. They were also assisted often by their brother the King of Aragon. The nominal object of attack was Alvaro de Luna, favourite minister of John II during thirty-five years, a man probably unscrupulous and somewhat rapacious, but of great ability and energy. At last John gave way, withdrew his favour, and the minister was tried and beheaded, meeting his fate "with the intrepidity of Strafford," to whom some have compared him.

Sueiro da Costa, Alcaide of Lagos.—Cf. notes 77, 121, etc.

The King D. Edward (Duarte) is, of course, Henry's eldest brother, King of Portugal 1433-1438 (see Introduction to vol. ii, pp. x-xi, and notes 30, 57; and pp. 3, 11, 18, 28, 39, of the text of this version; also Pina's Chronica (D. Duarte), vol. i of the *Ineditos Hist. Port.*) The allusions to Portuguese, Castilian, and Aragonese history are so intertwined in these paragraphs that some caution is necessary.

Monvedro.—Here there is a manuscript note, of later date, however, than the Chronicle itself [*Esta batalha se llama del endolar*].

123 (p. 152). *Vallaguer ... Arras.*—[The siege of Balaguer was undertaken in 1413, and in this the King, Don Fernando of Aragon, made prisoner the Count of Urgel.]—S.

Ibid., Ladislaus.—[The king of whom the author speaks here under the name of Lançaraao, is Ladislaus, King of Naples, who in the year 1404 entered Rome with his army in order to put down the rebellion of the people against the new Pope, Innocent VII. Hence our author's allusion: "When he assailed the city of Rome."]—S.

Louis of Provence.—[This was Louis II, Count of Provence. The campaign which Sueiro da Costa made with Louis appears to be that which began in 1409, which the aforesaid Prince carried on in Italy, in common with the allies commanded by Malatesta and by the famous Balthazar Cossa, legate of Bologna. This war lasted till 1411].—S.

The battle of Agincourt (the *Ajancurt* of Azurara's text) was not between the *Kings* of France and England in the strictly literal sense. The French, on October 25th, 1415, were commanded by the Dauphin, the Constable of France, and the Duke of Orleans.

Vallamont [is Valmont, 5 leagues north-west of Yvetot].—S. Really 22 kilometres.... It is on the Valmont River (Seine Inférieure), and possesses an ancient chateau, with buildings of date varying from the twelfth to the fifteenth century.

Constable of France.—[This Admiral of France, with whom served Sueiro da Costa, appears to be the Count of Foix (Foes in the text of Azurara).]

The Count of Armagnac (p. 152) [was probably Bernard VII, who, in the Civil Wars of the time of Charles VI, was at the head of the party of the House of Orleans, which fought various combats, especially in the years 1410-11.]—S.

Arras (p. 152).—[The siege of this place began in Sept. 1414.]—S.

124 (p. 152). *Lançarote ... Stevam Affonso.*—See Introduction to vol. ii, p. xii, and note 77; pp. 60-80, 83, 86 of this version.

125 (p. 152). *In that year* [viz. 1447].—S. The place is of course Lagos.

[Pg 332]

126 (p. 153). *Dinis Diaz* [see ch. xxxi].—S. See pp. 98-100 of this Chronicle. Also Introduction to vol. ii, p. xii, and notes 93, 94, 95, etc.

127 (p. 153). *Tristam ... Zarco ... Lagos.*—See Introduction to vol. ii, pp. ix, xii, xcix-cii, notes 76, 80, and pp. 192, 213, 225-9, 244-8, 60-2, 79, 83, etc., of this Chronicle.

One of Zarco's caravels was under the command of Alvaro Fernandez, the only captain on this expedition who accomplished much (see ch. lxxxvii, and Introduction to vol. ii, p. xii).

128 (p. 156). [This bird is the *Buceros nasutus* of Linnæus, the same that the French call *Calao-Tock*. Notwithstanding some exaggeration which may be noted in the description of Azurara, it is beyond doubt that the bird of which he treats here is that which the Negroes of the Senegal call *Tock*, and which the Portuguese named *Cróes*. Latham calls it *Buceros Africanus*.

Brisson made two species, Linnæus and Latham two varieties; but Buffon considered them as individuals of the same species, a fact which is otherwise witnessed to by Sonini. Buffon says that the beak, considered apart from the body, is a foot in length and of enormous size (see *Buffon*, Plate 933). The "work" of which Azurara speaks is not due only to the pores of the beak, but chiefly to a series of cuts or incisions, in the form of half-moons, which this bird has upon its beak. It was the famous naturalist Aldrovandi who first gave a picture of the enormous beak of this bird; but the oldest description of it is certainly that given by Azurara. It was not, therefore, Père Labat who first among travellers saw and carefully observed this notable bird, but Lourenço Diaz and the other Portuguese, his companions in 1447: that is, at a date almost three hundred years before Labat. On this bird the reader may also consult the Memoir of Geoffroi de Villeneuve (*Actes de la Société d'histoire naturelle de Paris*).]—S.

129 (p. 158). *Isle of Herons*.—[Since it was to these islands on the coast of Africa, that, in the first epoch of our discoveries, expeditions (by preference) usually directed their course, in conformity with the instructions of the Infant, for the reasons which (in part) Barros gives us (note 97, p. 104, note 79, p. 78 of this version). We have already indicated their position to the reader, conformably to the ancient charts, but we have nevertheless thought well, for the better illustration of the matter, to point out here their true position. In some maps, and among others on that of the famous Livio Sanuto, on the first sheet of his *Africa*, these islands are placed thus:—The Isle of Herons in the most northerly part of all the group, Tider in the most southerly of all, and the Isle of Nar (Naar) between the two.]—S.

130 (p. 159). *What we have been ordered.*—[By these expressions it is evident that the views and plans of the illustrious Infant were not concerned with making captives or slaves, or with expeditions against the natives, but only with the prosecution of the discoveries. The passage which occurs in the next chapter, as to the "great joy" of the crews, and especially of the "lower class" at meeting with the other caravels at the Isle of Herons, "in order to put in hand the matter," *i.e.*, a new incursion against the Moors, shows us the spirit which [Pg 333]animated those sailors: which spirit, perhaps, some of the captains were not able at times to hold in check and moderate.]—S.

131 (p. 164). *The Banner of the Crusade ... Gil Eannes.*—[Barros omits these details, which are so interesting for the history of those expeditions. This Gil Eannes was the same who had first passed beyond Cape Bojador. (See ch. ix of this Chronicle.)]—S. On the *Banner of the Crusade*, see Introduction to vol. ii, pp. xviii-xix.

132 (p. 165). *Alvaro de Freitas.*—[Barros says that Alvaro de Freitas was Commander of Algezur. (*Decade I*, Bk. I, ch. ii.)]—S. Cf. in this Chronicle, pp. 152, 157-8, 161, 165-6, 174, 194-5, 197.

133 (p. 167). *Fra Gil de Roma* [lived in the time of Philippe le Bel, King of France. The treatise *De Regimine Principum*, which he wrote in 1285 for the education of that Prince, was a book of the highest reputation (in its time), especially at the close of the fourteenth and fifteenth centuries. By the notice which is given us in the *Chronicle of the Count D. Pedro*, and by the quotation of Azurara, we perceive the estimation in which this book was held amongst us at the beginning of the latter century (the fifteenth).]—S. In fact, King John I (of Portugal), in his discourse at Ceuta in 1415, recalled to his fidalgos and knights the maxims and precepts which they had read in the same book, *De Regimine Principum*, and which he always kept in his own room. And if we are to believe Barbosa (*Bibliotheca Lusitana*), the Infant D. Pedro had made a Portuguese translation of the same treatise; but this learned bibliographer calls Fr. *Gil de Roma*, Fr. *Gil Correa*. This note is not a fitting place to show whether the name of *Correa*, which Barbosa gives to that author, is or is not exact. We must confine ourselves here to saying that King D. Edward (Duarte), quoting this book several times in chs. xxxi, xxxii, xxxvi, lii, lvi of his*Leal Conselheiro*, calls the author, like Azurara, Fr. *Gil de Roma*. In the library at Cambrai there exists a manuscript, No. 856, of the *De Regimine Principum*, which was finished in 1424, and consequently at an epoch subsequent to the one of which King John I made use. This is probably one of those used by King Edward and by Azurara. The first printed edition was published in 1473 (see *Dictionnaire bibliographique, La Serna Santander, etc.*) If, as we have just said, the manuscript used by King John I, by King Edward, and by Azurara, is one of the most ancient of which any notice survives, the Portuguese translation of the book of Fr. Gil de Roma by the Infant Don Pedro is also one of the most ancient versions—if we except the French translation attributed to Henry of Ghent. (On this consult the Abbé Lebœuf, *Dissertation sur l'histoire ecclésiastique et civile de Paris*, II, p. 41.) We think it well to give the reader this notice, in view of the importance of Azurara's citation in this place, which shows us the state of learning and literary culture among our people at the beginning of the fifteenth century, and at the same time the literary relations which existed between Portugal, France, and other countries at the end of the Middle Ages.]—S. See Martins, *Os Filhos de D. João I*, chs. i, iv, v, vi.

134 (p. 169). *Pero Allemain, etc.*—See p. 55 of this Chronicle, on Balthasar, an undoubted German of the "household of the Emperor."

[Pg 334]

135 (p. 173). *Directions from the Lord Infant.*—These seem to have been rather vague for purposes of exploration, and are differently given by *Gomez Pirez* (p. 173). See text of this version pp. 95, 173, etc., and next note.

136 (p. 174). *River of Nile.*—[Compare this passage with our remarks in the notes to chs. liii, xxxii, xv, and xiii, about the true plans of the illustrious Infant, author of these discoveries. These passages reveal to us, in spite of the brevity of the Chronicler, the intention and the system of the Prince in relation to these expeditions. It is clear that he desired not only to discover those countries, but above all to obtain information from the natives themselves of the interior of Africa, in order to compare it with the scientific, historical, and geographical ideas of antiquity and of the Middle Ages, with a view of prosecuting his discoveries till the East was reached. Thus, Garcia de Resende says, with good reason (*Chronicle of the King D. John II*, ch. cliv), when treating of the discovery of the Congo, made twenty-five years after the death of the Infant:—"In the year 1485, the King desiring the discovery of India and Guinea, which the Infant D. Henry, his uncle, first among all the Princes of Christendom, commenced,..."]—S. What Gomez Pirez says here implicitly contradicts Lançarote's statement, p. 172; see note 135.

137 (p. 174). *The terrestrial Paradise.*—[We call the attention of the reader to this passage, in itself very interesting, especially because the words of Alvaro de Freitas indicate beyond doubt a certain geographical idea as to the situation of the terrestrial Paradise agreeing with the cosmographical knowledge of the Middle Ages, and as to the distance at which they found themselves from those delicious parts of the world.

The sailors whom the Infant employed in these navigations and discoveries were well instructed in nautical science. They set out from Portugal furnished with "naval charts" in which the cosmographers of that time had designed not merely the hydrographical configuration of the coasts of the various countries then known, but also which is more curious, the interior of the Continents, in which they represented, by a multitude of figures, the various sovereigns, animals, birds, woodland, and other details, both real, fantastic, and hypothetical: as the curious reader may see in the Planisphere of Andrea Bianco of 1436, published in the work of Formaleone, entitled *Saggio sulla nautica antica de Veneziani*, and in the other planisphere of the famous Fra Mauro, published by Cardinal Zurla in his work, *Sulle antiche Mappe lavorate in Venezia* (1818).

The idea, then, which Alvaro de Freitas had of his distance from the terrestrial Paradise, according to his own words, shows that he considered it to be at the extremity of the earth: that idea, we repeat, proves the influence which the geography of the Middle Ages exercised upon our sailors. As a matter of fact, that idea of the position of the terrestrial Paradise dates from the time of the *Topographia Christiana* of Cosmas Indicopleustes (see Montfaucon, *Nova Collectio Patrum*, vol. ii), an idea which the journeys accomplished by land during the Middle Ages fortified and reduced to a systematic opinion. On the map of Andrea Bianco, the terrestrial Paradise is to be found marked in the most easterly part of Asia.

Alvaro de Freitas in these words of his, alluded either to the locality [Pg 335]in which Paradise was to be found on the ancient charts—and this, we think, is the more probable supposition—or he referred to the *Cosmology* of Dante, according to which Paradise was situate in the middle of the seas of the southern hemisphere (Dante, *Purgatorio*, cant. xxvi, ll. 100, 127.)]—S.

Santarem's commentary here needs a word of supplement, which we take from the *Dawn of Modern Geography*, pp. 332-3.

"The position of the Garden of Eden, the habitat of the people of Gog Magog and other monstrous races, and the existence of a literal centre for the earth-circle, were problems which exercised the patristic mind only less than the great controversy upon the 'Spherical,' 'Tabernacular,' or other shape of the world itself.

"As to the earthly Paradise, the plain word of Scripture [Genesis, ii, 8; iii, 24] compelled most Theologians to place it in the Furthest East, though a minority inclined to give a symbolic meaning to the crucial words, 'The Lord God planted a garden *eastward* in Eden ... and placed Cherubim at the East of the Garden, to keep the way of the Tree of Life.' Augustine, here as elsewhere, shows himself inclined to compromise, as well became one who attempted such a task as the re-statement of the whole Catholic Faith. His knowledge was too many-sided, and his intelligence too keen, for him not to perceive the importance of a certain liberality of temper in a creed which aspired to conquer the world, and his treatment of the question of the terrestrial Paradise is a good example of his method. For himself, he holds fast to the real existence of Eden, and the literal sense of Scripture on its position, but he allows any one who will to give the texts at issue a symbolical meaning (*De Civ. Dei*, XIII, ch. xxi; see also Eucherius, Comm. on Genesis in the *Max. Bibl. Vet. Pat.* vi, 874, and A. Graf's interesting essay on the *Legends of the terrestrial Paradise*, Turin, 1878). To the same effect, though more doubtfully, speaks St. Isidore of Seville, who in so many ways reproduces at the end of the sixth century the spirit and method of the Bishop of Hippo in the fifth. In one place the Spanish Doctor repeats the traditional language about Eden, placed in the East, blessed with perpetual summer, but shut off from the approach of man by the fiery wall which reached almost to the Heaven: yet elsewhere he seems to countenance a purely figurative sense. His scepticism is expressed in the *De Differentiis*, i, 10; his traditionalism in the *Etymologies* or *Origins*, XIV, 3 (De Asia).

"The ordinary conclusion of the more philosophic school of Churchmen is perhaps expressed by Moses Bar-Cepha, 'Bishop of Bethraman and Guardian of sacred things in Mozal' [*i.e.*, Mosul? or Nineveh], near Bagdad, about A.D. 900 [Migne's editor of Moses, in *Pat. Græc.*, cxi, pp. 482-608 (1863), places him later, about A.D. 950; but Marinelli, *Erdkunde*, 20-1, dates him about A.D. 700, doubtless with the assent of S. Günther and L. Neumann, who are responsible for the enlarged German edition of Marinelli's admirable essay. The most interesting passages of Moses' geography are in Pt. I, chs. i, ii, vii-ix, xi-xiv]. In his *Commentary on Paradise*, the ingenious prelate solves past difficulties in the spirit of Hegel himself. The terrestrial Eden had one existence under two conditions, visible and invisible, corporeal and incorporeal, sensual and intellectual. As pertaining to this world, it existed, he considers, in a land which was on, but not of, the earth that we inhabit; for it lay on higher ground, it breathed a [Pg 336]purer air, and, though many of the saints had fixed it in the East, it was really beyond our ken.

"From Augustine onwards, through the writings of Eucherius of Lyons [*Commentary on Genesis*], of St. Basil the Great, and many others, something of this tendency to compromise between the literal meaning of Scripture and the tacit opposition of geography, may be traced in this attempt to give reality to the earthly Paradise; and the same comes out in the conjecture of Severian of Gabala, adopted by Cosmas and by many of the traditionalists, that the rivers of Eden dived under the earth for a long space before reappearing in our world as Nile, Euphrates, Tigris and Pison (Severian of Gabala, v, 6; according to S., this subterranean course was to prevent men from tracking their way up to Paradise; cf. *Philostorgius*, III, 7-12.)

"Homeric and other pre-Christian fancies led many in the early Christian period still to look for Paradise in the north, among the Upper Boreans, in the south among the blameless Ethiopians, or in the west in the Isles of the Blessed, of the Hesperides, or of Fortune. Thus Capella, who was probably a pagan survival at the beginning of the most brilliant age of patristic literature, naturally enough looks for his Elysium 'where the axis of the world is ever turning' at the northern pole [*Capella*, vi, 664]; but when we find Archbishop Basil of Novgorod speculating about a Paradise in the White Sea [see Karamsin's *Russian History*, as cited by Marinelli, *Erdkunde*, p. 22, note 84; and by Cardinal Zurla, *Vantaggi derivati alla Geografia*, etc., p. 44] we have a better illustration of the undying vigour of the oldest and most poetic of physical myths, under almost any changes of politics and religion."

138 (p. 176). *Or else upon their feathers for the rest of the time ... other fish.*—[This bird is the *Phœnicopterus*.]—S.

Ibid: Other birds, etc.—[See note 128 to p. 156, on the *Buceros Africanus*.]—S.

Ibid: Other fish.—[This is the *Pristis*.]—S.

139 (p. 176). *Quite alive.*—[This fish appears to be the *Remora*.]—S.

140 (p. 176). *The two palm trees, etc.*—[These palm trees exist on some old MS. maps. We may compare this passage with what the author says in ch. xxxi, and with the notes on pp. 96, 177; also Introduction, p. iv. Barros (*Decade I*, ch. xiii) says "Lancerote reached the two palm trees which Dinis Fernandez, when he went there, marked out as a feature worthy of notice ... where the natives of the land say the Azanegue Moors are divided from the idolatrous Negroes." And, in fact, the course of this stream forms a remarkable boundary between the Moors, or Berbers, who inhabit the northern bank, and the Negro Jaloffs who dwell on the southern bank (see *Durand*, vol. ii, p. 60, and *Rennell*, Appendix, p. 80).]—S.

141 (p. 177). *This green land.*—[On the manuscript map of João Freire of 1546, appears marked at the entrance of the river Senegal, the "arvoredo" of which Azurara speaks.]—S.

142 (p. 177). *Azanegue prisoners.*—[Compare this important passage with what Azurara says in other places, pp. 41, 45-6, 48-9, 55; and [Pg 337]Introduction to vol. ii, pp. iv, xxvi, lviii, lix, about the Infant and the information which he collected from the natives, and which he compared with the geographical charts he was constantly studying.]—S.

143 (p. 178). *Entereth into it so.*—[This same confusion which the Portuguese mariners made between the Senegal and the Nile is one more proof of the influence which the geographical system of the ancients exercised over them. According to Pliny, the Niger was an arm of the Nile. The river Senegal traverses in its course nearly 350 leagues from its source in the country of Fouta (Jallon) to the Atlantic (see Durand, *Voyage au Sénégal*, p. 343, and Demanet, *Nouvelle histoire d'Afrique*, vol. i, p. 62, iv, xii, xxii-xxv, xxxiii, xlii-xliii, xlvii-xlix, lviii.)]—S. Also see Introduction to vol. ii, p. lviii, etc.

144 (p. 180). *Mediterranean Sea, etc.*—[This passage shows that Azurara only had notice at that time of the ivory commerce which was carried on through the ports of the Levant situated on the Mediterranean, and that he had no knowledge that a like commerce was carried on through the ports of the empire of Marocco, situated on the west coast of Africa. "I learnt," says he, "that in the eastern part of the Mediterranean Sea," etc. ... and these words of his are important, as showing that a man, otherwise well informed in matters of commerce and navigation, was not aware that the ivory trade was carried on by the western coast; which gives us one more proof of the priority of the Portuguese in the discovery of Guinea. Our author, then, knew the truth: for until that epoch the trade in ivory was carried on by the Arabs by way of Egypt, the Arabs going to the coast of Zanzibar to seek for the same, since there the better quality was to be found (see Masudi, *Notices et Extraits des MSS. de la Bibliothèque du Roi*, i, p. 15; *Ibn-al-Wardi, ibid*, ii, p. 40; *El Bakoui, ibid*, pp. 394, 401). The Arab caravans also brought ivory from places in the neighbourhood of the Niger. These caravans followed the routes of the ancient Itineraries (see *Ibn-al-Wardi, Notices et Extraits des MSS.*, ii, pp. 35-7, and Edrisi (Jaubert), vol. i, pp. 10-26, 105-120, 197-293). But the principal centre of this commerce with the interior of Africa was in the northern part, then already known under the name of Barbary, and in the countries which form to-day the kingdoms of Fez and Marocco. The expressions of Azurara about the size of the elephant are evidently exaggerated, because the species indigenous to Africa is only the second in size in the (animal) family of the Proboscidians, or "trunked" Pachyderms. The African elephant is smaller than the Asiatic elephant, although the tusks of the latter are smaller than those of the former. The details given in this part of our Chronicle are, in our opinion, so important for the information they give about the state of knowledge among our first discoverers, the influences of ancient tradition, and the mediæval spirit which dominated them, that it seems opportune to indicate here to the reader what we consider most worthy of study and of reflection, in order that we may be able to estimate the state of instruction in Portugal relative to those matters in the beginning of the fifteenth century, seeing that up to now no (writing) work has yet appeared upon the subject from any one of our nation. Among other passages of this Chronicle we noted, on p. 156, note 128, the extraordinary exaggeration with which our seamen described the beak of the *Buceros Africanus*, of which they said "the mouth and maw of these birds is so great that the leg of [Pg 338]a man, however large it were, could go into it as far as the knee." We have also seen another marvellous description of the beak of the *Phœnicopterus*, and finally the one which was inspired by the account given them of the elephant by the Negroes—an exaggeration which reminds one of the description given by a Byzantine writer of the eleventh century, Michael Attaliotes, when he saw an elephant for

the first time in Constantinople (see the extract from the Greek MSS. of the Royal Library at Paris [Bibliothèque Nationale], on p. 499 of the work of M. Berger de Xivrey: *Recits de l'antiquité sur quelques points de la fable, du merveilleux et de l'histoire naturelle*). In these exaggerated and marvellous accounts, therefore, of birds and animals which were unknown as late as then, we find a proof of the influence of the teratological traditions of antiquity and of the Middle Ages, in consequence of the studies which men had previously made of the figures they saw depicted in the planispheres and Mappemondes of their time; and also we may see in this a result of the reading of Pliny, and above all of the *Treatise on Marvels*, attributed to Aristotle, "the philosopher," as Azurara calls him (see p. 12, note 19), whose authority was so great among the Portuguese of the fifteenth century that even the "Proctors of the People" (in the *Cortes* of 1481), quoted his work on "Politics" (see our *Memoir on the Cortes*, ii, p. 186). We see, then, that our seamen of that period were impregnated with these traditions, and were diligent readers of works which during the Middle Ages were given the title of *Mirabilia*, the reading of which enchanted (in that age) not only men of education, but even students, and often the people, to whom ecclesiastics read in public those marvellous relations, as we see, among other examples from the case of Giraldus Cambrensis, who thrice read to the people in Oxford his description of Ireland; and still more in the celebrated statutes made in 1380 by Bishop Wykeham for the college which he founded in the same city, in which he determined that the chronicles of various realms should be read to the students and the marvels of the world (*Mirabilia Mundi*); see *Sprengel*, p. 221, and Wharton,*History of English Poetry*, i, p. 92. In the period at which the statutes we mention were given to (New) College in Oxford, the relations between Portugal and England were knit more closely than in preceding centuries. The Court of the King, D. John I, adopted most of the English usages, and the literary communication between the two peoples was more extensive than in earlier time. The citation of the romances of chivalry made by the King to his knights, the adoption of the French language (which was then that of the Court of England), the devices and mottoes of which the Infants made use, prove the existence of that influence. Besides this, divers passages of King D. Duarte's *Leal Conselheiro* show that the Infants of the House of Aviz (often) discussed various literary matters with the King, their father, and other literary persons, and that they even debated about the rules and regulations for properly translating classical works. We have also noticed that King D. John I, in the discourse which he made to the fidalgos who remained at Ceuta in 1415, cited the *De Regimine Principum* of Fr. Gil de Roma, bidding them recall to memory how they had often read the same in his Privy Chamber. So then, at that epoch of discoveries, in which the greatest enthusiasm prevailed for the prosecution of enterprises of such moment, the reading of the *Marvels of the World*, and of the *Travels of Marco Polo*, which the Infant D. Pedro brought from Venice, formed beyond doubt [Pg 339]the delight of all those famous men, courtiers of the Infant D. Henry, of his illustrious father, and of his brothers—courtiers, moreover, who received their education in the royal or princely palaces. The passages, then, which we read in this Chronicle, and which we indicate to the reader, in spite of their brevity, and of the defects which the critical study of our own time enables us to note—these passages, we say, are of the highest importance when they are studied in harmony with other contemporary documents. The great men of the fifteenth century, formed in the school of the Infant Don Henry, were unquestionably possessed of great erudition for those times—an erudition and knowledge which at first eludes observation, through being muffled up in the rudeness of a language without polish, and which was more energetic in action than explicit and agreeable in writing, but it is nevertheless clear that they knew all that was known in their age.

It was this notable school, therefore, which prepared the great body of geographical learning which we note appearing in the famous congress of Portuguese and Spanish geographers at Badajoz in 1524 and 1525: at which, in the discussion which took place on the demarcation of the Moluccas and on the size of the world, Aristotle was quoted along with Strabo, Eratosthenes, Macrobius, St. Ambrose, Pliny, Theodosius, Marinus of Tyre, Alfergani, and Pierre d'Ailly, etc.]—S.

Long as this note is, a word must be added to it:—

Santarem here covers a large part of the field of mediæval geography, but his treatment in this place is hardly so clear or exhaustive as one might expect from the author of the *Essai sur Cosmographie*, or the compiler of the leading *Atlas* of mediæval maps. As to the immediate subject, the phrase *Mediterranean [Sea]* was first used in the sense of a proper name by St. Isidore of Seville, *c.* A.D. 600 (*Origins* or *Etymologies*, Book xiii); though its adjectival use, like the parallel expressions "Our [sea]," "the Roman [sea]," "the Inner [sea]," was of course much earlier. As late as Solinus (*c.* A.D. 230) this last is clearly the only shade of meaning. As to the commerce of North Africa, we must refer to the Introduction to vol. ii, pp. xxii-xxvi, xlv-lvi, lxiv. As to the mediæval *Mirabilia*, it is strange that Santarem gives no adequate reference to the great sources of these collections: Pliny's *Natural History*, and above all Solinus' *Collectanea*, principally compiled from Pliny, Mela, and Varro, and itself reproduced (wholly or partially) in well-nigh every mediæval work of similar character, translated into the pictorial language of Mappemondes, such as that of *Hereford*, of *Ebstorp*, or of the *Psalter* (Brit. Mus. *Add. MSS.* 28,681). On these, see *Dawn of Modern Geography*, pp. 243-273, 327-391. Santarem's remarks hardly give a sufficient idea of the systematic domination exercised over much of mediæval thought, not only in geography, natural history and ethnology, but in other departments also by the pseudo-science represented in these *Mirabilia*.

145 (p. 183). *Paulus Orosius.*—[Here we must note the omission of the name of Diodorus Siculus among the authors cited by Azurara, especially as he is, among all the ancient historians, the one who has left us the most important and circumstantial account of the Nile. The first Latin version of Diodorus by Poggio only appeared in 1472, nineteen years after Azurara had finished this chronicle. The works [Pg 340] of Orosius were held in high estimation among the learned of the Middle Ages. This writer was born at Braga in Lusitania, agreeably to the opinion of some authors. (See *Fr. Leam de St. Thomas, bened. lusit. I*, ii, p. 308; and Baronius, an. 414.) His work, *Historiarum adversus Paganos*, which begins with the creation of the world and comes down to the year 316 of Jesus Christ, was printed for the first time in 1471, that is, eighteen years after Azurara had finished his Chronicle, but during the Middle Ages copies of this work were so multiplied that even in England the book was to be found in the hands of the Anglo-Saxon people (see Wright, *Essay on the State of Literature and Learning under the Anglo-Saxons*, p. 39), a detail which affords one proof the more of the literary relations between the Spanish peninsula, and the peoples and nations of the North in the first centuries of the Middle Ages.]—S. See *Dawn of Modern Geography*, pp. 353-5.

146 (p. 184). *Mossylon Emporion (Mossille Nemporyo).*—[Azurara alters the name. The passage to which the Chronicler refers is the following:—*Et Ægyptum superiorem fluviumque Nilum, qui de litore incipientis maris Rubri videtur emergere in loco qui dicitur Musilon Emporium*, not *Mossile Nemporyo*. (Orosius, Bk. I, vi.)]—S. On this *Emporion*, see Bunbury's *Ancient Geography*, vol ii, pp. 692; *Solinus*, ch. lvi.

147 (p. 184). *Josepho Rabano.*—[This is the celebrated author of the history of the Jews, Flavius Josephus, whose work was first composed in Syriac and afterwards in Greek. It was so much esteemed by the Emperor Titus that he ordered it to be put into the public library. The first Latin translation which was printed, according to some bibliographers, was in 1470, seventeen years after this Chronicle was finished.]—S.

148 (p. 184). *Meroë.*—[On this African island the reader can consult *Ptolemy*, iv, 8; *Herodotus*, ii, 29; *Strabo*, Bks. XVII-XVIII; and, above all, *Diodorus Siculus*, i, 23, etc. The Master Peter quoted by Azurara is the famous Petrus Aliacus, or de Aliaco (d'Ailly), in his book *Imago Mundi*, finished in 1410: a book which had a great vogue in the fifteenth and even in the sixteenth century.]—S. Cf. also Pliny, *H. N.*, ii, 73; v, 9; Cailliaud, *L'isle de Meroe*.

149 (p. 184). *Gondojre.*—[According to our belief the reading should be Gondolfo. This writer had travelled in Palestine, and his life is (to be found) written in *Anglia Sacra*, tom. ij].—S. The Master Peter mentioned just before is rather a doubtful case. He is possibly the writer of the eleventh-century treatise "Contra Simoniam," etc., or the "Magister Scholarum" of the thirteenth, usually called the "Master of Stommeln."

150 (p. 185). *Crocodiles.*—Here we have an original MS. note.—[This is an animal, as Pliny relateth, which breedeth in the Nile, and whose custom and nature is to live by day on land and by night in the water; in the water to feed on the fish upon which it liveth and maintaineth itself, and on the land to sleep and refresh itself. But when it cometh out in the

morning to the bank, if it findeth a boy or a man [Pg 341]it quickly killeth him, and it is said that it swalloweth them whole. And it is a very evil and very dangerous beast.]

Compare other original notes of MS. written in the same character on pp. 7, 8, 13, etc. On the Nile and its crocodiles and other wonders, as conceived by mediæval writers, we may also compare *Solinus*, ch. xxxii.

On Azurara's reference to *Cæsarea* (Cherchel) immediately preceding, Santarem remarks as follows:—[This is Julia Cæsarea, now Cherchel, as is proved by various Roman inscriptions discovered there lately, and communicated to the Institute of France (Royal Academy of Inscriptions) by M. Hase. This city was one of the busiest of the ancient Regency of Argel.]

151 (p. 188). *Dog Star (Canicolla)*.—Here we have an original MS. note.—[This star, as saith the interpreter of Ovid, giveth its name to the Dog Days, which are those days which begin on July 5th and finish on September 5th. And this name came from a bitch which guarded the body of Icarus, when he was slain by the reapers, as Master John of England relateth. And he relateth that because that bitch guarded faithfully the body of its lord, it was numbered among the signs; and because it was a little bitch, the Dog Days took this name of theirs in this form, "Canicullus" for "Cam," or "Canicolla" for "Cadella." And because that bitch of Icarus was poisoned with the stench of its master, who lay dead and already stank, therefore did that star become also a poisonous one; and therefore does the sun still poison when it passeth through that sign, and so do the rays of the sun then poison the meats on earth. Wherefore those thirty-two days which the sun taketh in passing through that sign, are held by physicians to be days hurtful to the health of the body.] [*John of England is John Duns Scotus, Franciscan friar, called Doctor Subtilis, one of the chief philosophers of the Middle Ages, and Professor in Oxford (see Wadding, Vita J. Duns Scoti, doctoris subtilis, published in 1644*).]—S.

152 (p. 188). *Ellice and Cenosura*.—Here we have another manuscript note.—[These are the two poles, to wit, Arctic and Antarctic. And the interpreter of Ovid saith that each one of these two signs are called *Arcom*, and that *Arcom* is a Greek word, and signifieth what in Latin is meant by *Ursi*, and in the Portuguese language by *Ursas*; and that, besides, by each of these signs we call the North.]

153 (p. 189). *So directly passeth the sun, etc.*—[See Strabo, Bk. XVII, who refers to the wells without shade during the summer solstice.]—S.

[153a] (pp. 188-9). *Bishop Achoreus*.—[Azurara refers here to Achoreus, the Egyptian high priest of whom Lucan speaks in the *Pharsalia*, Canto x. The passage to which Azurara refers begins with the following verse:—Vana fides veterum, Nilo, quod crescat in arva. Comparing this chapter of Azurara with the episode of Canto x of the *Pharsalia*, we see clearly that it was from Lucan he derived the whole of his description of the Nile.]—S.

154 (p. 191). *The marvels of the Nile*.—[So great was the influence of the systematic geography of the ancients upon the imagination of [Pg 342]the Portuguese of the fifteenth century, that, on arriving at the Senegal, and seeing that the water was sweet very near to the mouth, and very clear, in the same manner as the Nile (*Nulli fluminum dulcior gustus est*, said Seneca), and observing the same phenomena, they did not doubt for a moment that they had discovered the Nile of the Negroes. In these two chapters we see something of the vast erudition of Azurara, and at the same time something of the historical and cosmographical knowledge of our first discoverers. Moreover, we must call the attention of the reader to a very important detail, namely, that while Azurara shows himself imbued with the reading of the ancient authors on these matters, in the same way as our mariners, the latter, if we study the spirit of their words, show that they had some knowledge of the system of the Arab geographers in this respect. These latter applied the same terms (as our first Portuguese explorers) to the two rivers, distinguishing the Nile of Egypt and the Nile of the Negroes. This opinion of the Niger being an arm of the Nile was even maintained in our own day by Jackson, in his work entitled, *An Account of the Empire of Marocco and the District of Suze*. In vol. xiv of the *Annales des Voyages*, by Malte-Brun, 1811, and in vol. xvii of the same work, p. 350, we meet with a curious analysis of this work of Jackson's on the identity of the two rivers.]—S.

What Azurara says here about the Nile, etc., is largely borrowed from Solinus,*Collectanea*, xxxii; Pliny, *Natural History*, v, 51-59; viii, 89-97; *Pomponius Mela*, iii, viii, 9.

We may also (for mediæval ideas on the Nile, etc.) cf. Dicuil, *De Mensura Orbis Terrae*, vi, 4, 7, etc.; ix, 6 (on Mount Atlas); St. Basil, *Hexaemeron*, iii, 6; Vibius Sequester; Procopius, *De Bell. Goth.*, ii, 14, 15; iv, 29; St. Isidore, *Origins*, xiv, 5; Ven. Bede, *De Natur. Rer.*; and above all, Edrisi (Jaubert), i, 11-13, 17-19, 27-33, 35, 37, 297, 301-5, 312, 315, 320-325, ii, 137; Masudi, *Meadows of Gold*, ch. xiv (see Introduction to vol. ii, pp. xliv-l, and *Dawn of Modern Geography*, pp. 267-8, 323-6, 367, 462-3, 348, 363, 365.)

155 (p. 191). *Fish or some other natural product of the sea.*—[This important passage is one proof the more of the priority of our discoveries on the west coast of Africa.]—S. Not, of course, an absolute proof, though it strengthens the plausibility of the Portuguese claim.

156 (p. 193). *Arms of the Infant.*—[This island, as well as the other of which mention is made above, where these sailors encountered the Arms of the Infant carved upon the trees, are very clearly marked, as between Cape Verde and the Cape of Masts, on a curious map of Africa in the unpublished *Atlas* of Vaz Dourado, executed in 1571 (see *Mémoire sur la navigation aux côtes occidentales d'Afrique*, by Admiral Roussin, p. 61—*Des îles de la Madeleine*).]—S.

157 (p. 193). *This tree*, etc.—[This is the baobab, a tree noted for its enormous size, and which is to be met with on the Senegal, on the Gambia, and even on the Congo, at which point Captain Tucklay (Tuckey) mentions it among the trees to be found on the banks of the Zaire. This tree had been described by Adanson (*Histoire Naturelle du Sénégal*, Paris, 1757, pp. 54 and 104), and from this circumstance Bernardo Jussieu gave it the name of Adansonia. Its [Pg 343]trunk is sometimes more than 90 ft. in circumference (see the work cited above). Our mariners, and Azurara himself, however, described it 310 years before the French naturalist who gave it the botanical name by which it is now known.]—S.

158 (p. 194). *Rio d'Ouro.*—[Some French writers, who have lately treated of the famous Catalan Atlas in the Royal Library of Paris, to which they assign the date of 1375, assert that the Catalans reached the Rio d'Ouro before the Portuguese, because on this map is marked a galliot, with a legend referring to Jayme Ferrer, who sailed to a river of that name (in 1346).

Without discussing this point here, let us say, nevertheless, that as to this voyage of the Catalans, whose arrival at the said river is not attested by any document, the reader should consult the map of M. Walckenaer, published in the scientific journal, *Annales des Voyages*, tom. 7, p. 246 (A.D. 1809), in which that learned geographer says, with good reason, that the said legend and project of Jayme Ferrer's voyage (as stated) does not at all prove that geographical knowledge in 1346 extended beyond Cape Bojador, or even beyond Cape Non (see also our *Memoir on the priority of our discoveries*, and the *Atlas* which accompanies the said memoir).]—S. Cf. Introduction to vol. ii, pp. lxiii-lxiv.

159 (p. 194). *To the Kingdom.*—[By this passage, and similar ones in chs. x, xi, and xvi, it is proved that the commercial relations of the Portuguese with the west coast of Africa beyond Bojador were established before the middle of the fifteenth century. The imports then consisted of gold-dust, slaves, and skins of sea-calves.]—S. Cf. Introduction to vol. ii, pp. x-xiii, lxi-lxxi.

160 (p. 198). *Tider.*—[An island hard by Arguim (or forming one of the Arguim group). We must now add to what we said before, that this island, as well as those of the Herons (Ilha das Garças), and of Naar, is very clearly marked on the unpublished map of Vaz Dourado, but without the names given in this Chronicle. That cosmographer (Dourado) included them all under the denomination of *Isles of Herons*.]—S.

161 (p. 199). *Isle of Cerina.*—[Comparing our text with the excellent map of Vaz Dourado, we find on the latter this island marked as nearest to the continent, and also nearest to the mouth of the St. John River. Dourado marks Arguim to the north, and to the south of *P. dos Reys* marks four islands, which are those of Herons, of Naar, of Tider, and this one of which Azurara speaks. On the map of D'Anville, which is to be found in the work of P. Labat, *Nouvelle relation de l'Afrique*, tom. I, a map which includes the part of the coast from Cape Branco to the River of St. John, we read over an island very near Tider the word "Grine," which appears to be the Cerina of Azurara.]—S.

162 (p. 204). *Arrived at the end*, etc.—[On the position of this stream, see the map of d'Anville, published in the work of P. Labat, *Nouvelle relation de l'Afrique*, tom. I; and

the *Mémoire sur la navigation aux côtes occidentales d'Afrique*, by Admiral Roussin, at p. 44, where he speaks of the *Baie du Lévrier*, which is 8 leagues [Pg 344]in extent from N. to S., and 6 leagues across. This bay, in which our sailors entered, is to the north of the Cape of St. Anne.]—S.

163 (p. 212). *This Prince.*—[Compare this passage with what we said in note 92, ch. xxx, as to the authority of this chronicle.]—S.

164 (p. 214). *Point of Santa Anna.*—[It is situate to the south of the Rio de S. João, on the chart of João Freire of 1546.]—S.

165 (p. 218). *Islands.*—[We think that these islands are the ones marked on certain charts, principally French, with the name of "Ilhas da Madalena."]—S].

166 (p. 220). *Buffaloes.*—[It was, in fact, the African buffalo that our seamen saw there.]—S.

167 (p. 224). *Hermes.*—(Ἑρμᾶς). Azurara refers here to the book of this author entitled*The Shepherd*, composed in the pontificate of St. Clement sometime before the persecution of Domitian which began in the year 95. Origen, Eusebius, St. Jerome, St. Clement of Alexandria, and Tertullian mentioned this work. By this passage we see that Azurara, in citing it, did not admit the view of Gelasius, who classed it among the apocryphal books.]—S.

168 (p. 225). *As he could.*—[Compare this passage with what we have said in previous notes about the Infant's plans.]—S.

169 (p. 225). *Nile.*—[The Senegal, or Nile of the Negroes.]—S.

170 (p. 226). *An island.*—[It must be the Island of Gorea (Goree), situate in 14° 39' 55" N. lat. On this island see Demanet, *Nouvelle histoire de l'Afrique*, tom. 1, pp. 87-97, passim. *Notices statistiques sur les colonies françaises* (troisième partie, pp. 187-189), a work published by the Ministry of Marine in 1839.]—S.

171 (p. 228). *Cape of the Masts.*—[This cape appears marked with this name in nearly all the ancient MS. maps of the sixteenth century. It is clear then that the name of this cape was first given to that point by Alvaro Fernandez. Barros (*Decade I*, liv. 1, fol. 26, ed. 1628) says of this voyage: "He passed to the place they now call the Cabo dos Mastos: a name he then gave it on account of some bare palm trees that at first sight looked like masts set up."]—S.

172 (p. 229). *A hind.*—[This description leaves not the smallest doubt that the animal which our seamen saw there, and of which the author treats, is the antelope, and probably "the other beasts" were herds of the same kind. On the history of the antelopes the reader should consult Buffon and Cuvier.]—S.

173 (p. 230). *Dwellings (Essacanas).*—[This word is not to be found either in the*Elucidario* or in Portuguese dictionaries; it is met with, however, in the heptaglot of Castell, and in Golius, but there the meaning of this Arabic word is given as being "a place where a person dwells." Even if this be admitted for the explanation of the [Pg 345]text, the latter still remains obscure; however, it seems to us that the author meant to say, that all those observations were made in the "(Essacanas) dwellings ... that exist on certain sandbanks, according," etc. The mariners drew their charts, and marked the coasts, banks, etc., on the very spots themselves.]—S.

174 (p. 230). *Charts.*—[This passage shows in the clearest manner that the first hydrographical maps of the west coast of Africa, beyond Bojador, were made by the Portuguese under the orders of the Infant D. Henrique, and that these maps were adopted and copied by the cosmographers of the whole of Europe (see *Memoria sobre a prioridade dos descobrimentos dos Portuguezes*, etc., §§ ix, x, and xi).]—S.

175 (p. 230). *Oadem.*—[We judge this to be the place called by Cadamosto Hoden (Guaden), and of which he says: "On the right of Cape Branco inland there is an inhabited place named Hoden, which is distant from the coast a matter of six days' journey by camel;" but he says the contrary of what we read in the text, for he adds: "The which is not a place of dwelling, but the Arabs foregather there, and it serves as a calling-place for the caravans that come from Timbuctoo and other Negro parts to this our Barbary from here." This spot, with the very name given by Cadamosto, is marked agreeably to this account on the chart of

152

the Itineraries of the caravans which M. Walckenaer added to his work, *Recherches géographiques sur l'intérieur de l'Afrique.*]—S.

176 (p. 231). *Carts.*—[*Alquitões*, an Arabic term not met with either in our dictionaries or in the *Elucidario*, but found in the heptaglot dictionary of Castell, in the word "Alquidene," "waggons for the transport of women and men," and in Golius. We do not find this word in the war regulations of the Kings D. John I and D. Affonso V (Souza,*Prov. da hist. gen.*, iii). Azurara thus employed in this place an Arabic term which had fallen out of use in Portuguese in the fifteenth century.]—S.

177 (p. 231). *Few.*—[See the description in the travels of Clapperton.]—S.

178 (p. 231). *Confetti.*—[See the *Itinèraire de Tripoli de Barbarie à la ville de Tomboctu*, by the Cheyk Hagg-Kassem, published by M. Walckenaer in his *Recherches sur l'intérieur de l'Afrique*, p. 425; the account agrees with that in the text.]—S.

179 (p. 231). *Bestiality.*—[This same description and expression is to be found in *Leo Africanus.*]—S. The last may be read in the Hakluyt Soc. ed., vol. i, pp. 130-3, 153-4, 158-161, 218.

180 (p. 232). *Fernandez.*—[As to João Fernandez, see ch. xxix, and the note on the stay of this traveller at the Rio do Ouro in 1445, and also ch. xxxii.]—S.

181 (p. 232). *Went with them.*—[Though this account of João Fernandez is very important, because anterior by almost a century to [Pg 346]the description of the well-known Leo Africanus, yet the most important part of it is wanting: namely, the route he followed, and the places he visited during the seven months he spent with the caravans. Despite the omission of these details, however, his description which this chapter contains, and its exactness, is confirmed by the later writings of Leo Africanus, Marmol, and other travellers, to whom we refer the reader.]—S.]

182 (p. 232). *All of sand.*—Here is another note of the original MS.: [Of this land speaketh Moses in the 15th chapter of Exodus, and Josephus and Master Pero (*Peter*), who commented on it, where they write of the troubles of the people of Israel for want of water, and of how they found a well of pure water; where he relateth how Moses, by God's command, threw in the piece of wood and made it sweet. And this took place before they arrived at the place where God sent them the manna.] See note 148 (to p. 183).

183 (p. 232). *Tagazza (Tagaoz).*—[This land is the Tagaza of Cadamosto (ch. xii, p. 21), and Tagazza of Jackson, on the way from Akka to Timbuctoo.]—S. See Leo Africanus, Hakluyt Soc. ed., 117, 798, 800, 816, 829; Pacheco Pereira, *Esmeraldo*, 43; Dr. Barth,*Reise*, iv, 616.

184 (p. 233). *Palms.*—[See Denham and Clapperton.]—S.

185 (p. 233). *Water.*—[See the Itineraries already cited and published in M. Walckenaer's *Recherches*, etc., and also the *Description of Africa*, by Leo Africanus.]—S.

186 (p. 233). *Write.*—[This detail is very curious, because it indicates that in the fifteenth century, when João Fernandez journeyed with the caravans, some of those tribes which we suppose to be Berbers had not yet adopted the Arabic characters. It is to be deplored that Azurara is not more explicit in this place, seeing that Arabic authors mention books written in this language. Oudney tells of various inscriptions, written in unknown characters, which he saw in the country of the Touariks. Very few of this tribe speak Arabic, which he was surprised at, because of the frequent communication between them and nations that only speak that tongue.—*Vide* Clapperton's Travels, and Leo Africanus in Ramusio, etc.]—S. See the Hakluyt Soc. Leo Africanus, pp. 133, 165-7.

187 (p. 233). *Berbers.*—[According to Burckhardt, *Trav.*, pp. 64 and 207, these are the Berbers. Our author includes here the Lybians. Compare with Leo Africanus in Ramusio.]—S. See the Hakluyt Soc. Leo Africanus, pp. 129, 133, 199, 202-5, 218.

188 (p. 233). *These last.*—[It appears from this passage that the Touariks are treated of, and their conflicts with the Negro Fullahs, or of the Foullan.]—S. On the Tuâreg, see Leo (Hakluyt Soc. ed.), pp. 127, 151, 198, 216, 798-9, 815-6; also Dubois, *Tombouctou la mystérieuse*, and Hourst, *Sur le Niger*.

189 (p. 233). *To sell.*—[It was this trade in Negro slaves which the Christian merchants carried on with North Africa that led to the [Pg 347]singular claim of Zuniga and other Spanish writers, that the Castilians—and in particular the Andalusians—trafficked in the

Negroes of Guinea before the Portuguese; and by a confusion, either ignorant or intended, they tried to dispute with us the priority of our discovery of Guinea, and our exclusive commerce with this part of Africa which we were the first to find. See our *Memoria*, already cited, § xvii.]—S.

190 (p. 234). *Not certain.*—[This passage shows that Azurara did not believe in the existence of the great empire of Melli very rich in gold mines, though in the preceding century it had been visited by the celebrated Arab traveller Ibn-Batuta.]—S. On Melli, cf. Leo Africanus (Hakluyt Soc. ed.), pp. 125, 128, 133-4, 201, 823, 841.

191 (p. 234). *On the heavens.*—[Leo Africanus says that amongst the Arabs and other African peoples many persons are to be met with who, without ever having opened a single book, discourse fairly well on astrology.]—S. See Leo Africanus, (Hakluyt Soc. ed.), pp. 177, 460, 600.

192 (p. 234). *Hussos francos.*—Meaning unknown. The word is not found in Portuguese dictionaries.

193 (p. 235). *Fifty leagues.*—[This figure does not seem to be exaggerated. *Vide*Rennell's "Memoir on the rate of travelling as performed by camels," in the*Philosophical Transactions*, vol. lxxxi, p. 144. The author refers to certain camels of the desert and the country of the Touariks (Tuâreg), which by their extreme speed travel in one day a distance that takes an ordinary camel ten. But these do not journey with the ordinary caravans, but are used only for warlike enterprises.]—S.

194 (p. 236). *Resin [Anime].*—See Garcia de Orta's *Simples e Drogas*, ed. Conde de Ficalho, vol. ii, pp. 43, 44.

195 (p. 236). *Six hundred leagues.*—[We think this should read 200 and not 600 as in the text, which seems to be a mistake, because the known portion of the west coast of Africa to Cape Bojador has not an extension agreeing with the numeral letters in the text.]—S.

196 (p. 237). *Already heard.*—[On this important passage, see our *Memoria sobre a prioridade*, etc., §§ ix, x, xviii.]—S.

197 (p. 238). *Maciot.*—[Compare this with what is said in the book: *Histoire de la première descouverte et conqueste des Canaries faite dès l'an 1402 par messire Jean de Bethencourt, ensuite du temps même par F. Pierre Bontier, et Jean Le Verrier, prestre domestique dudit Sieur de Bethencourt*, etc., published in Paris in 1630. It is clear that Azurara had collected information of this expedition of Bethencourt from ancient accounts. This chronicle was finished in the library of King Affonso V in 1453, and Cadamosto sailed in the service of Portugal two years later (1455), so that his account of the Canaries is posterior to that of Azurara.]—S.

[Pg 348]

198 (p. 242). *Bad man.*—Another MS. note. ["Marco Polo saith that in the realm of Grand Tartary there are other like men, who when they receive their guests, thinking to give them pleasure, let them have their women, in the belief that as they do this for them in this world, so the gods will do likewise for themselves in the other. And this they hold because they are idolaters and have no law, but live only in those first idolatries."]

199 (p. 245). *Discover.*—[This passage shows that the Infant had in view the discovery of Guinea from the commencement of the expeditions he fitted out. In this, Azurara differs somewhat from Cadamosto's account.]—S.

200 (p. 246). *Machico.*—[Compare with Barros, *Decade I*, i, ff. 6, 7 and 8, ed. Lisbon, 1628. The silence preserved by Azurara about Robert Machim and Anne d'Arfet seems to show that this romance had not been invented in his day.]—S.

201 (p. 247). 1445 ... *Gonçalo Velho.*—[In the unpublished chart of Gabriel de Valsequa, made in Majorca in 1439, the following note is written in the middle of the Azores islands: "The which islands were found by Diego de Sevill, pilot of the King of Portugal, in the year 1432" (according to the better reading). We transcribe this note because of the date and the name of the discoverer, seeing that the date agrees with what Padre Freire says in his *Life of Prince Henry* (pp. 319, 320), *i.e.*, that it was in 1432 that the island of Santa Maria (Azores) was discovered by Gonçalo Velho, and not by Diego de Senill, as Valsequa says. De Murr, in his dissertation on the globe of Martin de Behaim, also declares that the Azores were found in 1432. Nevertheless, a great confusion as to the true date of the discovery of the Azores exists among the authorities; and if maps anterior to 1432 are compared with

what Padre Freire says (p. 323) as to the discovery of the Island of St. Michael, that the existence of this island "accorded (as the Infant said) with his ancient maps," the discovery of the Azores would appear to have been effected before 1432. In fact, in the Parma map of the fourteenth century, these islands are marked; while the Catalan Map of the Paris National Library shows the following islands in the archipelago of the Azores named in Italian:— Insula de Corvi marini (Island of Corvo); Le Conigi; San Zorzo (St. Jorge); Li Colombi; Insula de Brasil; Insule de Sante (Maria?).

In the unpublished map of the Pinelli Library, the date of which has been fixed as between 1380 and 1400, the said islands are marked with the following names:—Caprana; I. de Brasil; Li Colombi; I. de la Ventura; Sã Zorzi; Li Combi; I. di Corvi marini.

In the Valsequa Chart of 1439 these islands indicated by the cosmographer are marked to the number of eight, three being small ones. The names are:—Ilha de Sperta; Guatrilla; Ylla de l'Inferno; Ylla de Frydols; Ylla de Osels (Uccello); Ylla de ...; Ylla de Corp-Marinos; Conigi.

It is noteworthy that the names of these islands, in the map of the Majorcan cosmographer, which is the most modern, are all altered, while in the Catalan map made by his compatriots, sixty-four years earlier, the following names given by the Portuguese discoverers are found: Ilha de Corvo, de S. Jorge, and de Santa Maria, just as in the[Pg 349]Italian maps of the fourteenth century.]—S. The seven islands mentioned rather confusedly by Azurara at end of ch. lxxxiii (p. 248, top) are the Azores.

[201a] (p. 248). *Reasonings.*—Azurara here omits a document of extreme interest, which was given in full by Affonso Cerveira—another instance of the superiority of our unhappily-lost original to the court historian's copy.

202 (p. 252). *Algarve.*—[The Kings of Castille complained of these invasions, and there were many disputes between Portugal and Castille as to the lordship of these islands. Las Casas, in his *Historia de India*, an unpublished MS., treats at length of this subject, especially in ch. viii. Compare with what Azurara says in this chapter, Barros, *Decade I*, i, cap. 12, fol. 23, ed. 1628.]—S.

[202a] (p. 252). *Enregistered.*—Viz., by Affonso Cerveira, in the original chronicle.

203 (p. 254). *Tristam.*—[This river kept the name of Rio de Nuno, or Rio de Nuno Tristão, as appears from nearly all the old maps, in memory of this catastrophe.]—S.

[203a] (p. 255). *Twenty-one.*—Again not counting Nuno Tristam himself.

204 (p. 257.). *Sines.*—Sines, on the extreme S.W. coast of the Estremadura province of Portugal, was the birthplace of Vasco da Gama, discoverer of the sea-route to India, and one of the world's great navigators. It lies 147 miles S.S.E. of Setubal.

205 (p. 258). *Cape of Masts.*—[*Vide* note to p. 227 of this version.]

206 (p. 260). A *river.*—[This river is marked in the map of Juan de La Cosa (1500) with the name of Rio de Lagos, in that of João Freire (1546) and in others with that of Rio do Lago; and though Dourado marks a river to the south of the Cabo dos Matos, he gives it no name.]—S.

207 (p. 261). *Beyond C. Verde.*—[The great inlet which they had reached, and which is situate 110 leagues south of Cape Verde, is beyond Sierra Leone, and is marked in the maps of Juan de la Cosa (1500), Freire (1546), and Vaz Dourado, with the cape of Santa Anna to the south.

On this voyage, then, counting from the Rio de Lagos, our mariners passed the following spots marked on the above-mentioned ancient maps:—R. Gambia; R. de Santa Clara; R. das Ostras; R. de S. Pedro; Casamansa; Cabo Roxo; R. de S. Domingos; R. Grande; Biguba; Besegi; Amallo; R. de Nuno; Palmar; Cabo da Verga.

We have also R. de Pichel (maps of La Cosa and Dourado; R. da Praia in Freire); R. de Marvam (in Freire [1546]; Rio do Ouro in Dourado); R. do Hospital (in La Cosa [1500]; R. das Soffras in Freire [1546], and called by Dourado R. dos Pes [1571]); R. da Tamara (La Cosa); R. da Maia (Freire), and de Tornala in Dourado; R. de Caza (de Case in La Cosa and Freire); Serra Leoa (Sierra Leone).]—S.

[Pg 350]208 (p. 264). *River ... caravels.*—[Undoubtedly the Rio Grande. Cf. Walckenaer,*Histoire générale des Voyages*, vol. i, p. 79, note: where he corrects the mistake of Clarke in his *Progress of Maritime Discovery* (1803), p. 221.]—S.

209 (p. 265). *Cape of ... Ransom.*—[On old maps this cape is marked to the south of Arguim, and it appears under the same name in that of Juan de La Cosa, while in João Freire it is called *Porto do Resgate.*]—S.

210 (p. 267). *Expenses with ... Moors.*—[This passage shows that trading relations with Africa were already beginning to assume a more regular character.]—S.

211 (p. 268). *Porto da Caldeira.*—[A name not met with in the oldest maps (*e.g.*, Benincasa of 1467), which is one of those most nearly contemporaneous with our discoveries, and contains many names given by our explorers; the same remark applies to those of La Cosa (1500) and Freire (1546), etc. It seems, then, that our seamen gave this name to a port within the *Rio do Ouro*, as the text would indicate. The caravel of Gomez Pirez reaching the mouth of this river, cast anchor; afterwards the captain decided to go to the end of the river, that is, six leagues up; and arriving there he entered a port on which our men had previously bestowed the name of *Porto da Caldeira.*]—S.

212 (p. 268). *Well content.*—[To our mind this important passage shows that before the discovery of the Rio do Ouro by the Portuguese, Europeans did not trade there. The very declaration of the Arabs seems to us to contradict the opinion held by some that the Catalans knew this river in 1346, and that Jacques Ferrer made his way to this point (see p. 194, note 158, and note 74). In fact, it is clear that the Arabs of that part were well aware that to get caravans to that place meant a journey of many days across the desert, and also that, even were this journey undertaken, they would perhaps find a difficulty in persuading others to change the roads used from remote antiquity, and come and traffic at a point of which they know little, and give it a preference to the recognised *entrepôts* of ancient caravan commerce.]—S.

213 (p. 274). *Land ... level.*—[The low land marked on ancient maps to the north of the Rio do Ouro.]—S.

214 (p. 275). *Rocks.*—[We saw before how Gomez Pires, on reaching the Rio do Ouro, cast anchor at the mouth of the river, and afterwards made his way up the stream to a port at its furthest part, which our mariners had named the Porto da Caldeira, where he stayed twenty-one days in order to establish commercial relations with the Arabs of the African hinterland. But, as these negociations came to nothing, he set sail and moved four leagues from there towards the other bank of the river, and came upon an island in the river (the "ilot de roches très élevé" of the maps of Admiral Roussin); and after they had made eleven leagues in all, they met with the Arabs, who took refuge in "some very big rocks that were there." These rocks are the seven mountains marked in maps by our mariners of that time, and they are depicted in the Mappemonde of Fra Mauro (1460), and copied from [Pg 351]these very Portuguese nautical charts—the "lofty mountains" of the globe of Martin de Behaim, of Nuremburg.]—S.

215 (p. 277). *Meça.*—[A city in the province of Sus and empire of Morocco. *Leo Africanus*, Book II, says it was built by the ancient Africans.]—S.

216 (p. 278). *Guineas.*—[This passage shows that even then traffic in the Guinea negroes was carried on through the ports on this side of Cape Não. The Infant then knew, before he undertook the business, that this was one of the commercial *entrepôts* between Marocco and the Negro States, just as is since 1810 the small kingdom (founded by Hescham) of the independent Moors to the south of Marocco, of the commerce between Marocco and Timbuctoo.]—S.

217 (p. 278). *Eighteen Moors.*—[This detail shows the great influence possessed by João Fernandez over the Moors, doubtless owing to his speaking Arabic and having travelled with them. M. Eyriès, in the biographical article he wrote on this intrepid traveller (*Biographie universelle*) says, with justice, that he was the first European to penetrate into the interior of Africa, and that the details of his story present a great analogy with those of the account given by Mungo Park.]—S.

218 (p. 280). *Denmark, Sweden and Norway.*—[King Christopher then reigned in these three Kingdoms. He was grandson of the Emperor Robert, and nephew of Eric XII, who had abdicated in 1441. He died on January 6th, 1448, and the three crowns were separated.]—S. They were united in 1397 by the Union of Calmar.

219 (p. 286). *Lost men ... Returned to the Kingdom.*—[This detail, which is not to be found in ch. xv of the *First Decade* of Barros, where he treats of this expedition, is of the greatest importance, because it explains the event related in the letter of Antoniotto Usus di Mare, *i.e.*, Antonio da Nole, dated December 12th, 1455, and found in the archives of Genoa in 1802 by Gräberg (*Annali di geografia e di statistica*, vol. ii, p. 285), in which that traveller tells how he met in those parts with a man of his own country, whom he took to be a member of the expedition of Vivaldi, which had set out one hundred and seventy years before, and of which nothing had been heard since its departure, according to Italian writers. Now it cannot be admitted that a descendant of the Genoese expeditioners of Thedisio Doria and Vivaldi would have kept his white colour if his ancestor had remained among the negroes, nor could he know the language. Therefore, Antoniotto can have seen no other white man in those parts except one of the mariners of the Portuguese caravel of Affonso and Vallarte of which Azurara treats in the text: especially as neither the different Portuguese captains, nor Cadamosto, found in any part of the African coast beyond Bojador a single vestige or tradition of other Europeans having gone there before their discovery by the Portuguese. Of the expedition of Vivaldi no news arrived after its departure in the thirteenth century. In the time of Antoniotto there remained a tradition only that it had set out intending to pass through the Straits of Gibraltar and make an unaccustomed voyage to the West. Antoniotto was a man of good education, [Pg 352]and we see that he knew the authors who treated of this event; but having imbibed these traditions, and knowing of the existence of a Christian who had remained in these parts, he came to the conclusion—of course in ignorance of the fact mentioned by Azurara—that this man might be a descendant of the members of Vivaldi's expedition, "ex illis galeis credo Vivaldœ qui se amiserit sunt anni 170." If this important passage of Azurara's chronicle be confronted with the letter of Antoniotto, and both with the account of Cadamosto's second voyage, there remains not the least doubt that the man mentioned by Antoniotto was one of the three belonging to the caravel of Fernando Affonso and Vallarte, who had remained there in 1447, that is, eight years before Antoniotto visited the same parts, and that he was not a descendant of the men of Vivaldi's caravel, whose destiny had then for nearly two centuries been unknown. The passage also seems to refute the conjecture of the publisher of the said letter, and the induction of Baldelli in his *Millone*, vol. i, p. 153, etc., about the Medicean Portulano and the two maps of Africa therein, which we have analysed in our "Memoir on the priority of the Portuguese in the Discovery of the West Coast of Africa beyond Cape Bojador," where we show that these maps, far from disproving our priority, rather confirm it.]—S.

220 (p. 286). *The Cabo dos Ruyvos.*—[Otherwise the *Angra dos Ruivos* of ancient maps (see note 53). On the great abundance of fish in these parts, see the curious and erudite work of M. Berthelot (*De la pêche sur la côte occidentale d'Afrique*. Paris, 1840).]—S.

221 (p. 288). *Path of Salvation.*—[Some modern writers, founding themselves on the accounts of Cadamosto, have tried to make out that the Portuguese were the first among modern nations to introduce the slave trade from the beginning of their discoveries on the coast of Africa. It does not fall within the limits of this note to show how erroneous such assertions are; but we will nevertheless say that the celebrated Las Casas, in his *Historia de las Indias*, MSS., ch. xix, says that Jean de Bethencourt brought many captives from the Canaries whom he sold in Spain, Portugal, and France.]—S.

222 (p. 289). *Toil in arms.*—[Barros could not supply the want of a continuation of the text of Azurara (*Dec. I*, Bk. I, cap. i, fol. 32). This great historian confesses that everything he relates of the prosecution of these discoveries is taken from some memoranda he found in the Torre and in Treasury Books of King Affonso V. To show how deplorable it is that Azurara did not complete this Chronicle, at least as far as the death of the Infant, and include the discoveries made from this year of 1448 to 1460, it suffices to say that from this year henceforward all is confusion in the dates and events relative to this prosecution both in Barros and in Goes (*Chronica do principe D. João*, ch. viii, which is devoted to these discoveries).

Barros limits himself to citing, in the year 1449, the licence given by the king to D. Henry to people the seven islands of the Azores. From this year he leaps to the year 1457, in which he only speaks of the king's donation to the Infant D. Fernando, and only in the year

1460 does he relate that at this time Antonio de Nolli, a Genoese by nation and a noble man, "who owing to some troubles in his own country had come to this kingdom" in company with Bartholemew de [Pg 353]Nolli, his brother, and Raphael de Nolli, his nephew, obtained a licence from the Infant to go and discover the Cape Verde Islands; and that some servants of the Infant D. Fernando went on the same discovery at the same time by Prince Henry's order.

So he (Barros) leaves us in ignorance of the regular progress of our discoveries on the west coast of Africa from 1448, the year in which Azurara finished this Chronicle, until 1460, in which the Infant died. Damião de Goes, who pretended to relate more exactly and circumstantially these events, leaves us in the same confusion in ch. viii of the*Chronicle of the Prince D. John*, where he treats of Prince Henry's discoveries; and, besides, he makes a great mistake regarding the portion of coast discovered to the year 1458 (see ch. xvi, pp. 39 and 40 of the work cited), an error which is refuted by what Azurara says in ch. lxxviii of this present Chronicle.]—S.

Santarem is mistaken in assuming (see note 219, to p. 286) that "Antonio da Nole" and Antoniotto Uso di Mare are one and the same.

223 (p. 289). *Albert the Great.*—[Albertus Magnus, Bishop of Ratisbon, one of the most learned men of the Middle Ages. His works were published at Lyons in twenty-one folio volumes. See the art., *Albert le Grand*, in vol. xix of the *Histoire littéraire de la France*, p. 362, etc.]—S.

In addition to works already mentioned, see the *Occidente* for March 11th, 1894 (especially Brito Rebello's article on Lagos, the Villa do Iffante, etc.); Pinheiro Chagas,*Historia de Portugal*; L. de Mendonça on Portuguese ships of the fifteenth century, in*Memorias da Commissão Portugueza* (Columbus Centenary); *Historia da Universidade da Coimbra* (Braga), vol. i, pp. 135-140.

APPENDIX.

ADDENDA TO INTRODUCTION TO VOL. I.

Dr. Sousa Viterbo, writing on Azurara in the *Revista Portugueza Colonial e Maritima*(October 20th, 1898), supplies the following fresh facts relating to the life of the Chronicler, gleaned by him from the *Chartulary* of the Convent of the Order of St. Bernard at Almoster, near Santarem. On December 27th, 1465, Azurara was appointed Procurator of that famous convent by the Abbess, and in this capacity his name appears in various documents, *e.g.*, of January 21st, 1471, and February 22nd, 1472. The post was an important, and doubtless also a lucrative, one. He had a residence in Santarem, and no doubt lived there for a portion of each year during the last eight years of his life. On December 1st, 1473, we find him in Lisbon on convent business, and on April 2nd, 1474, his servant, one Gonçalo Pires, was named Procurator in his stead. It seems, therefore, that the Chronicler died between the last two dates.

[Pg 354]

Azurara, though he was forbidden to marry owing to his position as a Knight of the Order of Christ, nevertheless had a son and two daughters by one Inez Gonçalves, as appears from certain Royal letters of legitimation. Their names were:—

(1) Caterina da Silveira—of the household of the Countess of Loulé—legitimated by letters of June 22nd, 1482 (*v.* Torre do Tombo Liv° 2 D. João II, f. 138).

(2) Gonçalo Gomez de Azurara—Squire of the household of King John II—legitimated by letters of April 14th, 1483 (*v.* Torre do Tombo, Liv° I, Legitim. de Leitura Nova, f. 243).

(3) Filipa Gomez—legitimated on the same day as her brother, Gonçalo Gomez (same reference as No. 2).

The foregoing information was kindly supplied by General Brito Rebello, who had discovered these letters during his researches in the Torre.

* * * * *

As to the date when the *Chronicle of Guinea* was written, *vide* vol. ii of the standard work of Dr. Gama Barros, entitled *Historia da Administração Publica em Portugal nos Seculos XII a XV*, note 14, pp. 396-9, where the question is fully discussed.

As to the history of the MS. of the same *Chronicle*, *vide* the *Boletim de Bibliographia Portugueza*, vol. i, p. 41, etc. Art. by Senhor Ernesto do Canto.

In support of the reliability of the events recorded in the same *Chronicle*, it should be remembered that Affonso de Cerveira, from whose notes the book was compiled, was factor at Benim, and was thus enabled to obtain information at first hand.

Made in United States
Troutdale, OR
06/15/2024